MALVERN J. GROSS, Jr., C.P.A., is a partner of Price Waterhouse & Co. and for many years has had extensive experience with the accounting and financial problems of nonprofit organizations. A Certified Public Accountant in New York, Michigan, North Carolina, and Louisiana, Mr. Gross has served as Adjunct Professor of Accounting at Lehigh University. He has played a prominent advisory role on matters affecting nonprofit organizations in various government and professional groups. Mr. Gross is the author of many articles on accounting problems of nonprofit organizations and is a contributor to a book on church management and one on accounting applications of computers.

FINANCIAL AND ACCOUNTING GUIDE
FOR
NONPROFIT ORGANIZATIONS

MALVERN J. GROSS, JR., C.P.A.
PARTNER, PRICE WATERHOUSE & CO.

SECOND EDITION

THE RONALD PRESS COMPANY · NEW YORK

Library of Congress Catalog Card Number: 74–19862
PRINTED IN THE UNITED STATES OF AMERICA

To my late friend and teacher
Roy B. Cowin

Preface

A major objective of this book is to help the nonprofit organization better communicate its financial activities and financial condition to its members and to the public. The book is intended to aid the directors of such organizations in fully understanding the periodic financial report and thus to assist them in making informed decisions. For the treasurer and chief executive of the eleemosynary institution, and for the professional accountant, it offers a wide range of practical guidance.

In this Second Edition the reader will find a comprehensive discussion of the recently issued AICPA guides for accountants who examine the financial statements of hospitals, colleges and universities, and voluntary health and welfare organizations. These guides, which contribute greatly to the establishment of generally accepted accounting and reporting principles in the nonprofit sector, are analyzed with appropriate interpretive comment. In addition the reader will find detailed discussions of the particular accounting and reporting problems of a number of nonprofit entities for which no definitive guides exist. These include museums, private foundations, libraries, religious organizations, associations and professional societies, and clubs. Where the author feels that accounting principles have not been clearly defined, he has indicated alternative accounting and reporting methods and ranked them according to degree of acceptability in a series of tables at the end of the book.

Throughout, innovative suggestions are offered based on the author's direct experience with the problems of many organizations. It is recommended, for example, that all legally unrestricted funds be reported as a single fund rather than, arbitrarily, as a series of separate funds. This avoids the common problem in separate reporting that the unknowledgeable reader tends to become confused and does not grasp the total financial picture. A distinction is made between keeping track of such separate board-designated funds internally, for bookkeeping purposes, and reporting on them separately in the statement. In view of the wide applicability of the new AICPA Guide for Voluntary Health and Welfare Organizations, the author takes satisfaction in observing that the basic form of financial statement recommended, the columnar format, is very similar to that proposed in the First Edition of this book.

The book continues to provide detailed help on tax form preparation, presents systematically the compliance requirements for each state, and offers several chapters of procedural advice for the smaller organization. This includes setting up and keeping the books, maintaining proper internal controls, developing and presenting a meaningful budget, and dealing with the mechanics of pooled investments.

Grateful acknowledgment is due to many people for their assistance in the preparation of this book. While responsibility for the opinions and conclusions expressed is solely the author's, sincere thanks are due for the generous help of his associates, particularly J. H. Anderson, M. F. Baumann, A. C. Henry, J. R. Jordan, G. S. Kannry, E. J. Lynott, J. J. McAndrew, G. J. McLenithan, W. S. Sobon, and G. C. Watt. Special appreciation is expressed to Miss O. Paluszkiewicz for her help in typing the manuscript.

Finally, appreciation is expressed to the author's father, M. J. Gross, for his invaluable guidance in the preparation of the First Edition, and to the author's family whose understanding and forbearance again greatly facilitated the preparation of the manuscript.

MALVERN J. GROSS, JR.

Washington, D. C.
September, 1974

Contents

PART IV · CONTROLLING THE NONPROFIT ORGANIZATION

PART V · TAX AND COMPLIANCE REPORTING REQUIREMENTS

PART VI · SETTING UP AND KEEPING THE BOOKS

APPENDIXES

FINANCIAL AND ACCOUNTING GUIDE
FOR
NONPROFIT ORGANIZATIONS

1

Responsibilities of Treasurers and Chief Executive Officers

Nonprofit organizations are among the most influential and powerful institutions in our free society. These organizations range in size from small, local organizations to large national and international ones. Their scope covers almost every activity imaginable—health and welfare, research, education, religious, social organizations and professional associations. They include foundations, membership societies, churches, hospitals, colleges, and political organizations. It is estimated that there are more than 450,000 nonprofit organizations in the United States and they own property representing from 10 to 33 per cent of the tax roll in many large cities.

Typically, these organizations are controlled by boards of directors composed of leading citizens who volunteer their time. Where the organization is large enough, or complex enough in operation to require it, the board may delegate limited or broad operating responsibility to a part time or full time paid executive, who may be given any one of many alternative titles—executive secretary, administrator, manager, etc. Regardless of size, the board will usually appoint one of its own part-time volunteer members as treasurer, and, in most cases, he is second in importance only to the chairman of the board simply because its programs revolve around finances. While he is not always responsible for raising funds, he is charged with stewardship of these funds and with the responsibility of anticipating problems and difficulties before they occur.

The treasurer is usually a businessman who is extremely active in both his own and in community affairs, and so has only a limited amount of time to devote to the organization. Where there is a paid chief executive, many of the operating duties and responsibilities of the treasurer can be delegated to this executive and, in large organizations, through this executive to a chief accountant or business manager. However, in small organizations there may be no chief executive to delegate to, and in the following pages this will be assumed to be the case, both because small nonprofit organizations predominate, and because it simplifies the presentation. It will further be assumed that he is not an accountant and doesn't want to become one, but at the same time recognizes that he does need to understand something about the principles of nonprofit accounting and, more important, financial reporting.

The treasurer has significant responsibilities, including the following:

1. Keeping financial records
2. Preparing accurate and meaningful financial statements
3. Budgeting and anticipating financial problems
4. Safeguarding and managing the organization's financial assets
5. Complying with federal and state reporting requirements

While this list certainly is not all inclusive, most of the financial problems the treasurer will face are associated with these five major areas.

KEEPING FINANCIAL RECORDS

The treasurer is charged with seeing that the organization's financial records are recorded in an appropriate manner. If the organization is very small, he will keep the records himself, probably in a very simple and straightforward manner. If the organization is somewhat larger, he will possibly have a part-time employee—perhaps a secretary—who, amongst other duties will keep simple records. If the organization is still larger, there may be a full-time bookkeeper, or perhaps even a full-time accounting staff reporting to the chief executive and responsible for keeping the records of the organization. Regardless of size, the ultimate responsibility for seeing that adequate and complete financial records are kept is clearly that of the treasurer. This means that to some extent he must know what is involved in elementary bookkeeping and accounting, although this does not mean that he needs to be a bookkeeper or a CPA. Bookkeeping and accounting are largely a matter of common sense and with the guidance provided in this book he should have no difficulty in understanding basic procedures and requirements.

The important thing to emphasize is that the treasurer is responsible for seeing that reliable records are kept. He may delegate to others the detailed procedures to be followed, but it is up to him to see that the procedures are being followed and that the records are reasonably accurate. This is emphasized because frequently in larger organizations the treasurer feels somewhat at a disadvantage because he is a volunteer with relatively few hours to spend and is not an experienced accountant. The bookkeeping staff on the other hand is full-time and presumably competent. There is a natural reluctance for the treasurer to ask questions and to look at the detailed records to satisfy himself that sound bookkeeping procedures are being followed. Yet the responsibility is his, and he must question and probe to ensure that the record-keeping function is being competently performed.

PREPARING ACCURATE AND MEANINGFUL
FINANCIAL STATEMENTS

One of his most important responsibilities is to see that complete and straightforward financial reports are prepared for the board and membership that clearly tell what has happened during the period. To be meaningful, these statements should have the following characteristics:

1. They should be easily comprehensible so that any person taking the time to study them will understand the financial picture. This characteristic is the one most frequently absent.

2. They should be concise so that the person studying them will not get lost in detail.

3. They should be all-inclusive in scope and should embrace all activities of the organization. If there are two or three funds, the statements should clearly show the relationship between the funds without a lot of confusing detail involving transfers and appropriations.

4. They should have a focal point for comparison so that the person reading them will have some basis for arriving at a conclusion. In most instances this will be a comparison with a budget, or figures from the corresponding period of the previous year.

5. They should be prepared on a timely basis. The longer the delay after the end of the period, the longer the period before corrective action can be taken.

These statements must represent straightforward and candid reporting—that is, the statements must show exactly what has happened. This means that income should not be arbitrarily buried in some subsidiary fund or activity in such a way that the reader is not likely to be aware that it has been received. It means that if the organization has a number of "funds" the total income and expenses of all funds should be shown in the financial statements in such a manner that no one has to wonder whether he is seeing all of the activities for the period. In short, the statements have to communicate accurately what has happened. If the statement format is confusing to the reader, and he doesn't understand what it is trying to communicate, then it is not accomplishing its principal objective.

It will be noted that the characteristics listed above would apply equally to the statements of almost any type of organization or business. Unfortunately, financial statements for nonprofit organizations frequently fail to meet these characteristics. There are a number of reasons for this. Probably the most important is that the treasurer is doing his job on a part-time basis and does not have the time to develop a new format or set of statements. It is easier to continue with what has been done in the past. Also there is a marked reluctance on the part of the non-accountant to make changes in statement format because he lacks confidence in his abilities to tinker with the "mysteries" of accounting. Furthermore, just about the time that the treasurer is really becoming conversant with the statements and could start to make meaningful changes, his term may expire.

"Grandmother Test"

Since the purpose of any set of financial statements is to communicate to the reader, a good test of whether they accomplish this objective is the "grandmother test." Can these statements be clearly understood by any interested "grandmother" of average intelligence who is willing to take some time to study them? When she finishes studying them, will she have a good understanding of the overall financial activities for the year? If she doesn't, then the statements are not serving their purpose and should be revised and simplified until they do meet this test.

Many readers may protest, saying that financial statements are normally read and understood only by the board of trustees or relatively few individuals. They may also point out that you cannot expect an average grandmother to understand the "mysteries" of accounting. To these protests, it can only be pointed out that a financial statement is a form of communication, and if this communication cannot be prepared in simple enough English so that the uninitiated reader will understand it, then it has failed in its principal purpose. Every time a financial statement is prepared its effectiveness should be measured against this "grandmother test."

There are illustrations of all types of financial statements throughout this book, as well as suggestions on how to simplify financial statements to make them more readable. If these suggestions are followed, the statements should meet this test.

BUDGETING AND ANTICIPATING FINANCIAL PROBLEMS

Another major responsibility of the treasurer is to anticipate the financial problems of the organization so that the board or membership can take steps to solve these problems on a timely basis. A carefully prepared budget is the principal tool that should be used. Budgets can take many different forms, from the very simple to the fairly complex, and all have as their primary objective the avoidance of the "unexpected." Budgets and budgeting techniques are discussed in some detail in Chapter 17.

But there is more to budgeting than merely anticipating the activities of the coming year. Budgeting in a very real sense represents planning ahead for several years in an effort to foresee social and economic trends and their influence on the organization's program. This means that the treasurer must be a forecaster of the future as well as a planner. In many organizations this is done in a very informal, almost intuitive manner. In others, this function is more formalized.

SAFEGUARDING AND MANAGING FINANCIAL ASSETS

Unless the organization is very small there will be a number of assets requiring safeguarding and, again, it is the responsibility of the treasurer to be sure that there are both adequate physical controls and internal controls over these assets.

Physical controls involve making sure that the assets are protected against unauthorized use or theft, and seeing that adequate insurance is provided. Internal controls involve division of duties and record-keeping functions that will ensure control over these assets and adequate reporting of deviations from authorized procedures. Another function of internal control is to provide controls that will help remove undue temptation from the employees of the organization. Chapters 20 and 22 offer guidance on these matters.

Another responsibility of the treasurer is to see that the organization's excess cash is properly invested to insure maximum financial return. One of the accounting techniques often followed by nonprofit organizations is to combine cash from several funds and to make investments on a pooled basis. Chapter 22 discusses the technique of pooling of investments and discusses some of the physical safeguards that should be established.

COMPLYING WITH FEDERAL AND STATE REPORTING REQUIREMENTS

The treasurer and chief executive officer are also charged with complying with the various federal and state reporting requirements. Most tax-exempt organizations, other than churches, are required to file annual information returns with the Internal Revenue Service, and some are even required to pay federal taxes. In addition, certain organizations must register and file information returns with certain of the state governments even though they are not resident in the state. All of these requirements taken together pose a serious problem for the treasurer since he is usually not familiar with either the laws involved or the reporting forms used. Chapters 23, 24, and 25 discuss these requirements in some detail.

SUMMARY

Few positions have more opportunity to influence institutions that affect society than that of the volunteer treasurer of a nonprofit organization. In the past many treasurers have struggled to perform their duties but have become mired in detail or lost in the intricacies of the apparently different accounting and financial principles applicable to nonprofit organizations. One of the principal objectives of this book is to help the treasurers and chief executive officers of such organizations discharge their responsibilities in an effective manner with the least expenditure of time.

PART I

KEY FINANCIAL CONCEPTS

2

Accounting Distinctions Between Nonprofit and Commercial Organizations

Many businessmen, as well as many accountants, approach nonprofit accounting with a certain amount of trepidation because of a lack of familiarity with such accounting. There is no real reason for this uneasiness because, except for a few troublesome areas, nonprofit accounting follows many of the same principles followed by commercial enterprises. This chapter explores the principal differences and pinpoints the few troublesome areas.

STEWARDSHIP VERSUS PROFITABILITY

One of the principal differences between nonprofit and commercial organizations is that they have different reasons for their existence. In oversimplified terms, it might be said that the ultimate objective of a commercial organization is to realize net profit for its stockholders through the performance of some service wanted by other people, whereas the ultimate objective of a nonprofit organization is to meet some socially desirable need of the community or its members.

So long as the nonprofit organization has sufficient resources to carry out its objectives, there is no real need or justification for "making a profit" or having an excess of income over expense. While a prudent board may want to have a "profit" in order to provide for a rainy day in the future, the principal objective of the board is to fulfill the functions for which the organization was founded. A surplus or profit is only incidental.

Instead of profit, many nonprofit organizations are concerned with the size of their cash balance. They can continue to exist only so long as they have sufficient cash to provide for their program. Thus the financial statements of nonprofit organizations often emphasize the cash position. Commercial organizations are, of course, also very much concerned with cash but if they are profitable they will probably be able to finance their cash needs through loans or from investors. Their principal concern is profitability and this means that commercial accounting emphasizes the matching of revenues and costs.

Nonprofit organizations have an accountability for funds that they have received. This accountability may be for certain specific funds that have been given for use in a specific project, or it may be a general accountability to use all resources effectively toward the objectives of the organization. Thus the emphasis is on accountability and stewardship. To the extent that the organization has received gifts restricted for a specific purpose, it will probably segregate those assets and report separately on their receipt and disposition. This separate reporting of restricted assets is called fund accounting. As a result, the financial statements of nonprofit organizations can often be voluminous and complex because each restricted fund grouping may have its own set of financial statements which summarize all of its activities. While there has been much discussion and criticism about meaningful disclosure and comparability with commercial organizations, their financial statements are relatively easy to understand because there is only one set of statements, and the terminology and format are usually familiar. Also, accounting principles are much more clearly defined.

PRINCIPAL AREAS OF ACCOUNTING DIFFERENCES

There are five areas where the accounting principles followed by nonprofit organizations often differ from the accounting principles followed by commercial organizations. While the accounting significance of these five areas should not be minimized, it is also important to note that once the reader has understood the significance of each he will have a good understanding of the major accounting principles followed by nonprofit organizations. The principal remaining difficulty will then be designing a set of financial statements that is straightforward and easy to understand. The five areas are as follows.

Cash Versus Accrual Accounting

In commercial organizations the records are almost always recorded on an accrual basis. The accrual basis simply means keeping your records so that in addition to recording transactions resulting from the receipt and disbursement of cash, you also record the amounts you owe others, and others owe you. In nonprofit organizations the cash basis of accounting is frequently used instead. Cash basis accounting means reflecting only transactions where cash has been involved. No attempt is made to record unpaid bills owed by you or amounts due you. Most small nonprofit organizations use the cash basis, although more and more of the medium and larger organizations are now using the accrual basis.

The accrual basis usually gives a more accurate picture of an organization's financial condition than a cash basis. Why, then, is the cash basis frequently used by nonprofit organizations? Principally because it is simpler to keep records on a cash basis than on an accrual basis. Everyone has had experience keeping his own checkbook. This is cash basis accounting. A non-accountant can learn to keep a checkbook but is not likely to comprehend readily how to keep a double-entry set of books on the accrual basis. Furthermore, the cash basis is often used when the nature of the organization's activities is such that there are no material amounts owed to others, or vice versa, and so there is little meaningful difference between the cash and accrual basis.

Sometimes nonprofit organizations follow a modified form of cash basis where certain items are recorded on an accrual basis and certain items on a cash basis. Other organizations keep their records on a cash basis but at the end of the year convert them to the accrual basis by recording obligations and receivables. The important thing is that the records kept are appropriate to the nature of the organization and its needs. Chapter 3 discusses cash and accrual accounting.

Fund Accounting

In commercial enterprises the use of separate "funds" or fund accounting is not used. Fund accounting is an accounting concept which is not familiar to most businessmen and can cause real difficulty. In fund accounting, assets are segregated into categories according to the restrictions that donors place on their use. All completely unrestricted assets are in one fund, all endowment funds in another, all building funds in a third, and so forth. Typically in reporting, an organization using fund accounting presents separate financial statements for each "fund." Fund accounting is widely used by nonprofit organizations because it provides stewardship reporting. While this concept of separate funds in itself is not particularly difficult, it does cause difficulty in presenting financial statements that are straightforward enough to be understood by most readers, i.e., to pass the "grandmother test." Chapter 4 is devoted to a discussion of fund accounting.

Treatment of Fixed Assets

In commercial enterprises, fixed assets are almost always recorded as assets on the balance sheet, and are depreciated over their expected useful lives. In nonprofit accounting, fixed assets may or may not be recorded.

The handling of fixed assets, and depreciation, probably causes more difficulty and confusion than any other type of transaction because everyone seems to have a different idea about how fixed assets should be handled, and there is no single generally accepted principle or practice to follow. Some organizations "write off" or expense the asset when purchased; others record fixed assets purchased at cost and depreciate them over their estimated useful life in the same manner as commercial enterprises. Still others "write off" their fixed asset purchases, and then turn around and capitalize them on the balance sheet. Some depreciate; some do not. All of this presents the treasurer with the need for some practical suggestions as to when each approach is appropriate. Fixed asset accounting and depreciation are discussed in Chapters 6 and 7 respectively.

Transfers and Appropriations

In nonprofit organizations transfers are frequently made between "funds." Unless carefully disclosed, such transfers tend to confuse the reader. Some organizations make "appropriations" for specific future projects (i.e., set aside a part of the fund balance for a designated purpose). Often these appropriations are shown, incorrectly, as an expense in arriving at the excess of income over expenses. This also tends to confuse. Transfers and appropriations are not accounting terms used by commercial enterprises. Each is discussed in Chapter 5.

Contributions, Pledges, and Noncash Contributions

In commercial or business enterprises there is no such thing as a "pledge." If the business is legally owed money it is recorded as an account receivable. A pledge to a nonprofit organization may or may not be legally enforceable. Some nonprofit organizations record pledges because they know from experience that they will collect them. Others do not because they feel they have no legally enforceable claim. A related problem is where and how to report both restricted and unrestricted contributions in the financial statements. Contributions and pledges are discussed in Chapter 9.

Noncash contributions include donations of securities, equipment, supplies and services. Commercial enterprises seldom are recipients of such "income." When and at what values it is appropriate to record such noncash contributions is discussed in Chapter 9.

CONCLUSION

The five areas discussed above are the principal differences in accounting found between nonprofit and commercial organizations. While each of these can cause real problems for the casual reader if the statements are not carefully prepared, it is significant to note again that there are only these five areas, and often only one or two will be present in any given organization. It has been noted that part of the reason for these differences stems from the different objectives in nonprofit and commercial organizations.

In the one, accountability for program activities and stewardship is the objective. In the other the objective is a proper matching of revenues and costs with the resultant measurement of profitability. The treasurer familiar with commercial financial statements should have no difficulty preparing nonprofit financial statements once he understands the nature of each of these five areas of accounting differences. And if he keeps the objectives of financial statements in mind' he should be able to prepare financial statements that meet the "grandmother test" for clarity and effectiveness in communicating with the reader.

3

Cash Versus Accrual Basis
Accounting

In the previous chapter it was noted that although more and more of the medium and larger nonprofit organizations are now keeping their records on an accrual basis, most smaller organizations still keep their records on the cash basis of accounting. The purpose of this chapter is to illustrate both bases of accounting, and to discuss the advantages and disadvantages of each.

CASH AND ACCRUAL STATEMENTS ILLUSTRATED

Perhaps the easiest way to fully appreciate the differences is to look at the financial statements of a nonprofit organization prepared on both the cash and accrual basis. The Johanna M. Stanneck Foundation is a "private" foundation with assets of about $200,000. The income from these assets plus any current contributions to the foundation are used for medical scholarships to needy students. Figure 3–1 shows the two basic financial statements that, in one form or another, are used by nearly every profit and nonprofit organization, namely, a Statement of Income and Expenses for a given period, and a Balance Sheet at the end of the period. Figure 3–1 shows these statements on both the cash basis and the accrual basis, side by side for ease of comparison. In actual practice, of course, an organization would report on one or the other basis, and not both bases, as here.

As can be seen most easily from the Balance Sheet, there are a number of transactions not involving cash that are reflected only on the accrual basis statements. These transactions are:

19

THE JOHANNA M. STANNECK FOUNDATION

STATEMENT OF INCOME, EXPENSES AND SCHOLARSHIP GRANTS*
For the Year Ended December 31, 1974

	Cash Basis	Accrual Basis
Income:		
Dividends and interest income	$ 8,953	$ 9,650
Gain on sale of investments	12,759	12,759
Contributions	5,500	7,500
Total	27,212	29,909
Administrative expenses:		
Investment advisory service fees	2,000	2,200
Bookkeeping and accounting expenses	2,350	2,500
Federal excise tax	350	798
Other expenses	1,654	2,105
Total ·...........................	6,354	7,603
Income available for scholarships	20,858	22,306
Less: Scholarship grants	(17,600)	(21,800)
Excess of income over expenses and		
scholarship grants	$ 3,258	$ 506

*On a cash basis the title should be "Statement of Receipts, Expenditures and Scholarships Paid" to emphasize the "cash" aspect of the statement. There would also have to be a note to the financial statement disclosing the amount of scholarships granted but not paid at the end of the year.

Fig. 3–1. Cash basis and accrual basis statements side by side to highlight the differences in these two bases of accounting.

1. Uncollected dividends and accrued interest income at December 31, 1974 of $3,550 is recorded as an asset on the Balance Sheet. Since there were also uncollected dividends and accrued interest income at December 31, 1973, the effect on the accrual basis income as compared to the cash basis income is only the increase (or decrease) in the accrual at the end of the year. In this example, since the cash basis income from this source is shown as $8,953 and the accrual basis as $9,650, the increase during the year must have been the difference, or $697, and the amounts not accrued at December 31, 1973, must have been $2,853.

2. An uncollected pledge at December 31, 1974, of $2,000 is recorded as an asset on the Balance Sheet; and because there were no uncollected pledges at the end of the previous year, this whole amount shows up as increased income on an accrual basis.

3. Unpaid expenses of $950 at the end of the year are recorded as a liability on the accrual basis Balance Sheet, but on the accrual basis expense statements are partially offset by similar items unpaid ($149) at the end of the previous year.

THE JOHANNA M. STANNECK FOUNDATION

BALANCE SHEET*
December 31, 1974

	Cash Basis	Accrual Basis
Assets:		
Cash	$ 13,616	$ 13,616
Marketable securities at cost		
(market value $235,100)	186,519	186,519
Dividends and interest receivable	–	3,550
Pledge receivable	–	2,000
Total assets	$200,135	$205,685
Liabilities:		
Accrued expenses payable	–	$ 950
Federal excise tax payable	–	798
Scholarships payable—1975	–	12,150
Scholarships payable—1976	–	2,000
Total liabilities	–	15,898
Fund balance	200,135	189,787
Total liabilities and fund balance	$200,135	$205,685

*On a cash basis the title should be "Statement of Assets and Liabilities Resulting from Cash Transactions."

Fig. 3–1.   Continued.

4. The 4 per cent federal excise tax not yet paid on 1974 net investment income is recorded as a liability and as an expense on the accrual basis. The $350 tax shown on the cash basis expenditure statement is the tax actually paid in 1974 on 1973 net investment income. (See Chapter 23 for a discussion of taxes as they affect private foundations.)

5. Unpaid scholarships granted during the year are recorded as an obligation. Most of these scholarships will be paid within the following year but one scholarship has been granted that extends into 1976. As in the case of the other items discussed above, it is necessary to know the amount of this obligation at the prior year end and to take the difference into account in order to relate accrual basis scholarship expenses to cash basis expenditures.

As a result of these noncash transactions, there are significant differences in the amounts between the cash and accrual basis. On the cash basis, expenditures for scholarships are shown of $17,600 compared to $21,800 on the accrual basis; excess of income of $3,258 compared to $506; and a fund balance of $200,135 compared to $189,787. Which set of figures is more appropriate?

In theory, the accrual basis figures are. What then are the advantages of the cash basis, and why would someone use the cash basis?

Advantages of Cash Basis

The principal advantage of cash basis accounting (as previously stated in Chapter 2) is its simplicity, and the ease with which non-accountants can understand and keep records on this basis. The only time a transaction is recorded under this basis of accounting is when cash has been received or expended. A simple checkbook is often all that is needed to keep the records of the organization. When financial statements are required, the treasurer just summarizes the transactions from the checkbook stubs. This sounds almost too easy, but a checkbook can be an adequate substitute for formal bookkeeping records, provided a complete description is recorded on the checkbook stubs.* The chances are that someone with no bookkeeping training could keep the records of the Johanna M. Stanneck Foundation on a cash basis, using only a checkbook, files of paid bills, files on each scholarship, etc. This would probably not be true with an accrual basis set of books.

Many larger organizations, including many with bookkeeping staffs, also use the cash basis of accounting primarily because of its simpler nature. Often the difference between financial results on a cash and on an accrual basis are not materially different, and the accrual basis provides a degree of sophistication not needed. For example, in the illustration above, what real significance is there between the two sets of figures? Will the users of the financial statements do anything differently if it has accrual basis figures? If not, the extra costs to obtain accrual basis statements have to be considered.

Another reason organizations often keep their records on a cash basis is that they are following the age-old adage of not counting their chickens before they are hatched. They feel uneasy about considering a pledge receivable as income until the cash is in the bank. These organizations frequently pay their bills promptly, and at the end of the period have very little in the way of unpaid obligations. With respect to unrecorded in-

* Chapter 26 discusses cash basis bookkeeping and illustrates how this checkbook approach can be used.

come, they also point out that because they consistently follow this method of accounting from year to year, the net effect on income in any one year is not material. Last year's unrecorded income is collected this year and tends to offset this year's unrecorded income. The advocates of a cash basis say, therefore, that they are being conservative by using this approach.

Advantages of Accrual Basis

With all of these advantages of the cash basis of accounting, what are the advantages of the accrual basis? Very simple—in many instances the cash basis just does not present accurately the financial affairs of the organization. The accrual basis of accounting becomes the more appropriate basis when the organization has substantial unpaid bills or uncollected income at the end of each period and these amounts vary from period to period. If the cash basis were used, the organization would have great difficulty in knowing where it actually stood. These unpaid bills or uncollected income could materially distort the financial statements.

In the illustration above, there probably is not a great deal of difference between the two bases. But assume for the moment that toward the end of 1974 the foundation had made a grant of $100,000 to a medical school to be paid in 1975. Clearly, not recording this large transaction would distort the financial statements.

Nonprofit organizations are becoming more conscious of the need to prepare and use budgets as a control technique.* It is very difficult for an organization to effectively use a budget without being on an accrual basis. A cash basis organization has difficulty because payment may lag for a long time after incurring the obligation. For this reason organizations that must carefully budget their activities will find accrual basis accounting essential.

COMBINATION CASH ACCOUNTING AND ACCRUAL STATEMENTS

One very practical way to avoid the complexities of accrual basis accounting, and still have meaningful financial statements on an annual or semi-annual basis, is to keep the books on a cash

---

* Budgets are discussed in detail in Chapter 17.

basis but make the necessary adjustments on work sheets to record the accruals for statement purposes. These "adjustments" could be put together on worksheets without the need to formally record the adjustments in the bookkeeping records.°

It is even possible that monthly or quarterly financial statements could be prepared on the cash basis, with the accrual basis adjustments being made only at the end of the year. In this way, it is possible to have the simplicity of cash basis accounting throughout the year, while at the end of the year converting the records through worksheets to accrual basis accounting.

Figure 3–2 gives an example of the type of worksheet that can be used. This shows how the Johnstown Orphanage converted a cash basis statement to an accrual basis statement at the end of the year. Cash basis figures are shown in column 1, ad-

---

JOHNSTOWN ORPHANAGE

WORKSHEET SHOWING CONVERSION OF CASH TO ACCRUAL BASIS
For the Year Ended December 31, 1974

	Cash Basis (Col. 1)	Adjustments: Add (Deduct) (Col. 2)	Accrual Basis (Col. 3)
Income:			
Investment income	$225,000	$ 5,000	$230,000
Fees from city	290,000	25,000	315,000
Total	515,000		545,000
Expenses:			
Salaries and wages	430,000	(5,000)	425,000
Food and provisions	50,000	2,000	52,000
Fuel	15,000	1,000	16,000
Maintenance	40,000	1,000	41,000
Children's allowances	10,000	–	10,000
Other	15,000	–	15,000
Total	560,000		559,000
Excess of expenses over income	$ 45,000		$ 14,000

Fig. 3–2. An example of a worksheet which converts a cash basis statement to an accrual basis statement.

° A simplified accrual bookkeeping system is discussed in Chapter 27 in which the records are kept on a cash basis except at the end of the period when accrual entries are recorded in the books.

justments in column 2, and the resulting accrual basis amounts in column 3. The financial statement to the board would only show column 3.

Adjustments were made to the cash statement in column 2 as follows:

Investment income—$20,000 of dividends and interest that were received during the current year applicable to last year were deducted. At the same time at the end of the year there were dividends and interest receivable of $25,000 which were added. Therefore, on an accrual basis, a net adjustment of $5,000 was added.

Fees from the city—This year the city changed its method of paying fees for children sent to the orphanage by the courts. In prior years the city paid $15 a day for each child assigned at the beginning of the month. This year because of a tight budget the city got behind and now pays in the following month. At the end of the year the city owed $25,000, which was added to income.

Expenses—All the unpaid bills at the end of the year were added up and compared to the amount of unpaid bills as of last year (which were subsequently paid in the current year). Here is a summary of these expenses.

	Add unpaid at end of this year	Less paid in current year applicable to last year	Net add (deduct)
Salaries	$15,000	$20,000	$(5,000)
Food	12,000	10,000	2,000
Fuel	3,000	2,000	1,000
Maintenance	5,000	4,000	1,000
Children's allowance	—	—	—
Other	1,000	1,000	—

As can be seen, it is not difficult to adjust a cash basis statement to an accrual basis in a small organization. The bookkeeper just has to go about it in a systematic manner, being very careful not to forget to remove similar items received, or paid, in the current year which are applicable to the prior year.

Actually, in this illustration there is relatively little difference between the cash and accrual basis except for the $25,000 owed by the city due to their change in the timing of payments. Possibly the only adjustment that need be made in this instance is the recording of this $25,000. The problem is that until this worksheet has been prepared there is no way to be sure that the other adjustments aren't material. Accordingly, it is recommended that a worksheet similar to this one always be prepared to insure that all material adjustments are made.

MODIFIED CASH BASIS

Some nonprofit organizations use a "modified cash basis" system of accounting. On this basis of accounting, certain transactions will be recorded on an accrual basis and other transactions on a cash basis. Usually, on a modified cash basis all unpaid bills will be recorded on an accrual basis but uncollected income on a cash basis. However, there are many different variations.

Sometimes only certain types of unpaid bills are recorded. Payroll taxes that have been withheld from employee salaries but which have not yet been paid to the government are a good example of the type of transaction, not involving cash, which might be recorded. Clearly, these taxes are just as much of an obligation as the salaries.

On a modified cash basis it is not necessary for the organization to have a complex set of books to record all obligations and receivables. In small- and medium-sized nonprofit organizations it is quite sufficient to keep the records on the cash basis and then at the end of the month tally up the unpaid bills and the uncollected receivables and either record these formally in the books through journal entries or record them through a worksheet in the manner described above.*

Under the cash basis, one of the practical ways some smaller organizations use to record all accrued expenses is to hold the disbursement record "open" for the first four or five days of each month. This allows the bookkeeper to pay last month's bills as they arrive about the first of the month and record them in the prior month's records. While the organization actually pays such amounts in the first few days of the new period, it considers the payment as having been made on the last day of the prior period.

---

* Chapters 27 and 28 discuss the bookkeeping procedures to formally record accrual basis adjustments in the accounts.

This means that the organization does not show accounts payable but instead a reduced cash balance. This is frequently a useful practice for reporting internally to the board because it gives reasonable assurance that all expenditures incurred are recorded in the proper period. Of course, in financial statements prepared for external use, such payments subsequent to the end of the period should be shown as accounts payable instead of a decrease in cash.

When Accrual Basis Reporting Should Be Used

There are many advantages of cash basis accounting and reporting, but the accrual basis is ordinarily necessary for fair presentation of the financial statements. Unless the organization does not have any material amounts of unpaid bills or uncollected income at the beginning or end of the period, accrual basis reporting is required to present an accurate picture of the results of operations and of the financial position of the organization.

Accrual basis reporting is also required if an organization is trying to measure the cost of a product or service. It is impossible to know what a particular activity cost during the year if unpaid bills have not been included as an expense in the statement. The same is true where services are provided for a fee but some fees have not been billed and collected during the period. If a board or its membership is trying to draw conclusions from the statements as to the cost or profitability of a particular service, accrual basis statements are essential. The same is true when an organization is on a tight budget and budget comparisons are made with actual income and expense to see how effectively management has kept to the budget. Without including unpaid bills or uncollected income, such a comparison to budget can be very misleading and useless.*

Generally accepted accounting principles for both commercial and nonprofit organizations include the use of accrual basis accounting. Organizations that have their books audited by certified public accountants have to either keep their records on the accrual basis, or make the appropriate adjustments at the end of

* Budgets are discussed in Chapter 17.

the year to convert to this basis in order for the CPA to report that the financial statements are prepared in accordance with generally accepted accounting principles. Otherwise the opinion of the CPA will have to be appropriately qualified.*

LEGAL REQUIREMENTS

For some organizations soliciting funds from the public, there are legal requirements with respect to using the accrual basis of accounting. In New York, for example, most nonprofit organizations, other than schools and churches, are required to report to the state on an accrual basis if they have contributions and other revenue of more than $50,000 annually. However, even in New York the requirement is not that the records be kept on an accrual basis, but only that the organization file reports prepared on an accrual basis. This means the organization could still keep cash basis records throughout the year, provided it adjusted them to accrual basis for report purposes. Chapters 23, 24, and 25 discuss the legal reporting requirements for nonprofit organizations. If an organization is required to file reports with one or more state agencies, it should examine the instructions accompanying the report very carefully to see what the reporting requirements are.

CONCLUSION

There are two bases for keeping records—the cash basis and the accrual basis. The vast majority of small nonprofit organizations use the cash basis of accounting, and this is probably an acceptable and appropriate basis. The chief reason for using the cash basis is its simplicity. Where there are no significant differences between the cash and accrual basis, clearly, the cash basis should be used. Where there are material differences, however, the records should either be kept on an accrual basis, or cash basis statements should be modified to reflect the major unrecorded amounts.

Appendix A–1 provides a table that summarizes the circumstances when accrual basis reporting is appropriate.

* Independent audits and auditors' opinions are discussed in Chapter 21.

4

Fund Accounting

Fund accounting is peculiar to nonprofit organizations.* Most readers of commercial financial statements are not familiar with this type of accounting or its form of reporting. As a result, fund accounting more than any other single concept of nonprofit accounting tends to confuse the reader. The purpose of this chapter is to clarify the concept of fund accounting, and discuss its advantages and disadvantages. Chapter 12 discusses the presentation of fund-accounting financial statements that will pass the "grandmother test" for clarity.

FUND ACCOUNTING DEFINED

Fund accounting is a system of accounting in which separate records are kept for assets donated to an organization which are restricted by donors or outside parties to certain specified purposes or use. Assets which carry similar restrictions are usually commingled in a single "fund" and accounted for together rather than separately. The financial statements usually also follow this separate accountability and often separate statements are prepared for each fund.

* Readers are cautioned against trying to apply the principles and terminology used in governmental accounting to nonprofit accounting. While both types of accounting follow fund accounting concepts, their application and terminology are different. It is, of course, in large measure because of these differences that this book has been written. Readers interested in governmental accounting will find a number of well written texts available.

There is really nothing difficult about fund accounting other than mechanics. It is an accountability or stewardship concept, used principally by nonprofit and governmental organizations that are legally responsible for seeing that certain funds or assets are used only for specified purposes. This need for separate accountability arises whenever a nonprofit organization receives restricted contributions.

For example:

The Johnstown PTA receives a special contribution of $5,000 which the donor specifies is to be used only in connection with an educational program on drug abuse.

The Springtown Methodist Church decides that they need an addition to the Church and a building fund drive is established to raise $100,000. Contributors are told the money will be used only for this building addition.

The Boy Scout Council of Johnstown receives a $250,000 gift from a wealthy businessman (an ex-Boy Scout) to be used as an endowment fund.

In each instance, there is a restriction on the contribution and once the organization accepts a restricted gift, it has an obligation to follow the donor's instructions.* In fund accounting, restricted contributions are treated as separate "funds," and separate statements are often prepared for each grouping of similar-type funds. In preparing its financial statements, the organization separates the funds which carry restrictions from those funds that are unrestricted.

In addition, some organizations, as a matter of convenience and by board action, establish one or more additional funds in order to segregate certain amounts which the board intends to use for specified purposes in the future. An example of a board-created fund would be a "Board Designated Endowment Fund." The important thing to note about these funds is that they carry no legal restrictions and only represent an internal designation for the convenience of the organization. By contrast, donor-

---

* One of the responsibilities of the treasurer is to be sure that controls are established to ensure that restricted funds are expended only for the purpose intended. Usually this control is established through the use of fund accounting. Every new treasurer in an organization should review the disbursement procedures to be sure that restricted funds cannot be inadvertently spent in violation of the restriction.

restricted funds do carry legal restrictions, and the approval of the original donor or the court is usually required to divert these contributions to other purposes.

CATEGORIES OF FUNDS

An organization that receives many restricted contributions, each having a separate restriction, is faced with the practical problem of having to keep track of and report on many separate funds. While it is possible to keep separate records on almost an unlimited number of restricted funds, these separate funds are usually classified by the type of donor restriction. For example, in a college building fund drive, one donor may specify that he wants his gift used for a new chemistry building; another may specify a dormitory. Both represent restricted contributions to a category of funds generally referred to as "Building Funds." For reporting purposes, both gifts would be shown under this broad classification, and detailed records would be kept on both contributions to insure that they are used only for the purposes specified.

There are five categories or groupings of funds which nonprofit organizations generally use. The description or title indicates the type of restriction on the funds. The following are the five groupings and titles most commonly encountered.

General Fund

Several titles are given to the fund that carries out the general activities of the organization. It may be known as the "Operating Fund," "General Fund," "Current Fund," "Current General Fund" or "Unrestricted Fund." This fund contains no restricted assets, and the Board can use the fund as it chooses to carry out the purposes for which the organization was founded.

All unrestricted contributions,* gifts, and income should be recorded in this fund. Except for transactions involving one of the other four categories of funds, all transactions of the organization are included in this fund. If the organization never receives restricted gifts or contributions, then this fund could show

* Chapter 9 discusses contributions and the appropriate form of reporting.

all activity. In that case the organization would not be using fund accounting as it is commonly thought of.

Restricted Fund

Various titles are given to the fund that accounts for monies given to an organization to be spent for certain specified purposes. It may be known as "Funds for Specified Purposes," "Donor Restricted Funds," "Current Restricted Funds," or "Restricted Funds." For example, the $5,000 given to the Johnstown PTA for education on drug abuse would be added to such a fund. Often the funds are relatively small in amount and are used in the year received. Generally the aggregate of all these restricted funds are summarized for financial statement purposes and are not individually reported in detail.

Most restricted funds are given for a particular purpose which the organization normally carries out as a part of its activities. At other times the contribution may be for a purpose that is not normally part of its regular activities or perhaps will not be expended for some time. An example might be a building fund contribution. For this reason some organizations separate these two types of gifts, and actually show two separate funds on their financial statements: "Current Restricted Funds" and "Other Restricted Funds." The word "current" refers to activities normally carried out each year. Neither of these funds should contain any "board designated" funds. There is an extended discussion in Chapter 9 on reporting current restricted contributions.

Endowment Fund

This title is given to the fund that contains assets donated to the organization with the stipulation by the donor that only the income earned can be used. Generally the income itself is not restricted and can be used to carry out the organization's principal activities. Occasionally gifts are received which have restrictions on the uses to be made of the income. It is also possible to receive gifts that are restricted for a period of years, after which time the principal can be used as desired by the board. Another possibility is a gift, the income from which is paid to the donor during his life, but which becomes completely unrestricted on his death. Obviously, it is very important to keep track of these restrictions and to properly reflect them in the financial statements.

It is also possible that some donors, while not formally placing restrictions, will orally express the "desire" that the gift be put in the endowment fund. However, if the decision is left to the board, such amounts are unrestricted and should be added to the general fund. If desired, they may be subsequently transferred to the "Board Designated Endowment Fund" (see below). Legally unrestricted gifts should not be added to the endowment fund. All amounts in the endowment fund should bear legal restrictions that the board cannot normally alter.

Board-Designated Endowment Fund

Any of several titles may be given to funds that arise as the result of board action through a transfer of otherwise unrestricted funds. It may be known as "Board-Designated Endowment Funds," "Funds Functioning as Endowment," or "Quasi-Endowment." There is a significant distinction between "board-designated" endowment funds and "donor-designated" endowment funds. In the case of donor-created endowments, the board generally has no access to the principal of these funds. On the other hand, monies set aside by action of the board as "endowment" can obviously be used if the board wishes to reverse its previous action.

In the past it has been common for board-designated endowments and donor-contributed endowments to be commingled in one fund. This is still the prevailing practice for colleges and universities. However, the accounting profession has recently indicated that this is not acceptable for certain categories of nonprofit organizations * and the author believes that in due course this prohibition will apply to all nonprofit organizations.

The author does not recommend the use of board-designated funds. The artificial separation of certain unrestricted funds from the balance of the unrestricted funds is bound to cause confusion for the unknowledgeable reader. As discussed elsewhere in this book, one of the most important reporting principles is to keep the reporting and accounting simple enough so

* Voluntary health and welfare organizations and hospitals. See Chapters 13 and 15.

that the reader has a good chance of understanding what has happened. The use of a separate board-designated fund will not help the reader and it has no legal significance. Its use should be avoided where possible.

Fixed Asset Fund

Several titles may be given to the fund in which the cost of fixed assets (land, buildings, furniture and fixtures, equipment, etc.) is recorded. Such a fund will probably also include those restricted contributions given to the building fund. It may be referred to as the "Fixed Asset Fund," "Land, Building, and Equipment Fund," or "Plant Fund." The principal reason this fund is often used is that the board wants to remove these assets from the "general" fund. In this way the general or current fund then represents principally the current activity of the organization and funds available for current program use. Fixed assets, such as buildings, are not really available in the sense that they can be, or would be, converted to cash and expended. Therefore, many boards believe that fixed assets should be placed in a separate fund. This is largely a board decision, and there is no reason why such a separate fund must be established.* If a separate fund is not set up, then any building fund contributions would be included as part of the "Funds for Specified Purposes." There is an extended discussion about accounting for fixed assets in Chapter 6.

The use of a separate plant fund, while acceptable, is not recommended. A separate plant fund creates considerable confusion for the reader without really offering any advantage. Fixed assets are a necessary part of the resources that are available to the board for carrying out the purposes for which the organization was formed. Fixed assets are usually unrestricted assets, and the board has control over them and is usually free to dispose of them as it deems appropriate. Separating these assets from the other unrestricted assets of the organization is an artificial distinction since they remain unrestricted assets. By separating them, considerable bookkeeping and reporting prob-

---

* The AICPA Hospital Audit Guide provides that fixed assets should be reported in the "unrestricted" fund and not as a separate fund. See Chapter 15. The 1973 AICPA Audit Guides for Colleges and Universities and Voluntary Health and Welfare Organizations both provide for the use of a separate fixed asset fund. See Chapters 13 and 14.

lems arise with the increased likelihood that the reader will not understand the statements.

This is particularly true if the organization records depreciation on its fixed assets in the current operating fund. As is explained in more detail in Chapter 7, charging depreciation in the current operating fund and then transferring this depreciation to the plant fund is very confusing. Few readers will understand this transfer. For this reason, a separate plant fund should not be used if assets are depreciated.

NEED TO LIMIT NUMBER OF FUNDS

Occasionally a donor will give such a large sum of money, often for endowment purposes, that the board will want to include a separate fund with the name of the donor in the financial statements, rather than including this separate fund with all other similar funds. Examples would be the "Robert Mills Scholarship Fund" or the "Josie Henderson Memorial Fund." The principal reason for this separate reporting is to give the donor public recognition for his substantial gift.

The objective is fine, but it does create some presentation problems since an organization could find itself with a substantial number of funds in the financial statements. When this happens, there is a risk that the reader will become confused. Unless there are only one or two "name" funds, they should all be summarized and included under one of the major categories of funds discussed. At the same time public recognition can be given by preparing a supporting schedule showing the details of each name fund. If this schedule is skillfully prepared it will not detract significantly from the clarity of the main statement. An example of such reporting is shown in Chapter 12 (Figure 12–8). It is important that the purpose of each name fund be clearly indicated when the financial statements include a supporting schedule of "name" funds.

A TYPICAL "FUND" FINANCIAL STATEMENT

Figure 4–1 shows a simplified Statement of Income, Expenses and Changes in Fund Balances of a church having four separate funds—a general fund, a board-designated endowment fund, a fund for specified purposes, and an endowment fund. This pres-

ST. JAMES' CHURCH
GENERAL FUND
STATEMENT OF INCOME, EXPENSES AND CHANGES IN FUND BALANCE
For the Year Ended August 31, 1974

Income:

Contributions and gifts	$210,000	
Nursery school income	11,000	
Investment income from endowment funds	59,000	
Investment income, other	3,000	
Other income	7,000	
Total income		$290,000

Expenses:

Clergy	89,000	
Education	41,000	
Music	20,000	
Youth	23,000	
Nursery school	12,000	
Administration	24,000	
Operating	40,000	
Diocesan	3,000	
Other	5,000	
Total expenses		257,000
Excess of income over expenses		33,000
Fund balance, beginning of year		7,000
Less transfer to Board-Designated Endowment Fund		(25,000)
Fund balance, end of year		$ 15,000

Fig. 4–1. A typical set of income statements where each fund is reported in a separate statement.

entation is typical of a small organization using fund accounting. The format makes separate accountability of each fund quite evident. It also shows the main problem associated with fund accounting, namely, the difficulty in getting an overall picture of the church's affairs without a careful review of the statements.

The principal advantage of fund accounting is that the activities of each fund are reported on separately. There is no question of accountability since the reader can see exactly what has taken place. This is the stewardship aspect.

The principal disadvantage of fund accounting is that it is difficult to really understand the total activities of the church without a careful review of all the statements and perhaps a little bit of pencil pushing. For example, what was the total excess of in-

ST. JAMES' CHURCH

BOARD-DESIGNATED ENDOWMENT FUND
STATEMENT OF CHANGES IN FUND BALANCE
For the Year Ended August 31, 1974

Fund balance beginning of year	$	50,000
Add transfer from General Fund		25,000
Fund balance end of year	$	75,000

FUNDS FOR SPECIFIED PURPOSES
STATEMENT OF CONTRIBUTIONS, EXPENSES
AND CHANGES IN FUND BALANCE*
For the Year Ended August 31, 1974

Contributions		$	24,000
Expenses:			
Flowers for altar	$ 3,000		
Minister's special fund	5,000		
Black Affairs Council	5,000		
Poverty projects	5,000		
Other	5,000		
Total expenses			23,000
Excess of contributions over expenses			1,000
Fund balance, beginning of year			10,000
Fund balance, end of year		$	11,000

ENDOWMENT FUND
STATEMENT OF INCOME AND
CHANGES IN FUND BALANCE*
For the Year Ended August 31, 1974

Income:		
Contributions and gifts	$	25,000
Gain on sale of investments		46,000
Total		71,000
Fund balance, beginning of year		1,037,000
Fund balance, end of year		$1,108,000

*The title used in actual practice would probably be just "Statement of Changes in Fund Balance." See Chapter 12 for a discussion of this type of statement.

Fig. 4–1. Continued.

come over expenses for all funds? To answer this question it is necessary to add three figures and to be careful to pick out the right figures ($33,000 + $1,000 + $71,000 = $105,000).

This statement presentation is simpler than that used by some organizations. Some organizations incorrectly record unrestricted investment income in the endowment fund and then transfer this income to the general fund below the caption "Excess of income over expenses." In this illustration, $59,000 would have been shown in the endowment fund and would then have been shown in the general fund as a transfer to the general fund in the same section of the statement as the transfer to board-designated funds. This would have been incorrect. Unrestricted endowment income is by definition unrestricted and all such income should be reported in the general fund. If this income had been handled as a transfer the excess of income in the general fund would appear to have been a *deficit* of $26,000. Few readers would realize from this incorrect presentation that the general fund actually had an excess of income of $33,000.

There is no choice as to whether fund accounting is used or not. If monies are given to the organization which are clearly restricted by the donor, they must be recorded as a separate "fund." The only option is how these activities are reported in the financial statements. At the same time it should be noted that fund accounting is required only when there are binding restrictions on the use of the funds. An action by the board transferring certain of the general fund assets to a separate board-designated fund is artificial since this action is not binding. In this illustration the statements would have been considerably simpler if the board-designated fund hadn't been separated from the general fund. This would have eliminated one statement and the interfund transfer of $25,000 to the board-designated fund.

There is another way to simplify fund accounting statements and that is to show all funds on a single statement in columnar format. In this format each fund is shown in a separate column side by side. The St. James' statements have been recast in this columnar format and are shown in Chapter 12 (Figure 12–1).

Interfund Borrowing

As was previously noted, one of the problems with having a number of separate "funds" is that there is sometimes difficulty in keeping all the transactions completely separate. For example,

in the St. James' Church illustration, the general fund often runs
out of cash over the summer months when parishioners are on
vacation and the board authorizes a cash loan from the other
board-designated endowment funds. In theory there is no difficulty in keeping track of these borrowings, but it does create one
more area where the reader can become confused if he is not
careful or knowledgeable. Figure 4–2 shows the balance sheet
for the four funds used by St. James' Church. Notice the number
of interfund transactions.

ST. JAMES' CHURCH

BALANCE SHEET
August 31, 1974

Assets		Liabilities and Fund Balance	

GENERAL FUND

Cash	$ 50,000	Accounts payable	$ 17,000
Pledges and receivables....	13,000	Due to other funds	31,000
			48,000
		Fund balance..........	15,000
	$ 63,000		$ 63,000

BOARD-DESIGNATED ENDOWMENT FUND

Due from General Fund ..	$ 25,000	Fund balance..........	$ 75,000
Investments	50,000		
	$ 75,000		$ 75,000

FUNDS FOR SPECIFIED PURPOSES

Cash.................	$ 13,000	Accounts payable	$ 3,000
Due from General Fund ..	1,000	Fund balance..........	11,000
	$ 14,000		$ 14,000

ENDOWMENT FUND

Cash.................	$ 3,000	Fund balance..........	$1,108,000
Due from General Fund...	5,000		
Investments	1,100,000		
	$1,108,000		$1,108,000

**Fig. 4–2. A typical Balance Sheet where each fund is reported
separately.**

Note that the general fund has borrowed $31,000 — $25,000 from the board-designated endowment fund, $1,000 from the funds for specified purposes, and $5,000 from the endowment fund. While this is perfectly clear to the person knowledgeable about fund accounting, or to the careful reader, some readers are neither knowledgeable nor careful.

One word of caution with respect to interfund borrowings. A fund should not borrow from another fund unless it is clear that the borrowing fund will have the financial resources to repay. It is not appropriate to finance a deficit operation through interfund borrowing.

Furthermore, if the general fund is constantly borrowing from a board-designated fund, this suggests that part or all of the board-designated fund should be transferred back to the general fund. The artificial separation of unrestricted funds causes confusion, and if, on top of this, the general fund must constantly borrow then the separation serves no purpose.

It should also be observed that, before funds are borrowed from legally restricted funds, advice should be sought from legal counsel as to whether such borrowings are permissible. It would appear entirely inappropriate for an organization to raise funds for a building addition and then "lend" such amounts to help finance general operations of the organization.

The St. James' Church statements presented above were fairly simple statements. There were only four funds. There also could have been a fixed asset fund, and the endowment fund might have been reported as several separate funds—one for each major donor. As the number of funds increases, there will be more transfers between funds and the complexity increases. Fund accounting and reporting can become very difficult, not so much because the concepts are difficult but because of the confusion to the reader created by so many funds. It is not enough to merely report the activities of the organization; it is equally important that the statements be effective in communicating what has actually happened. If this is not accomplished, the statements have not served their purpose and the treasurer has failed in one of his most important responsibilities. Chapter 12 discusses alternative presentations to help simplify the financial statements.

CONCLUSION

Fund accounting is simply a common sense answer to the problem of recording and reporting funds given to an organization for a restricted purpose. There is nothing particularly difficult about the concepts involved. However, once the board by its own action transfers unrestricted funds into board-designated funds, the complexity increases significantly. If, in addition, there are many individual restricted funds, the reporting problems are magnified considerably and there is considerable risk that the reader of the financial statements will not fully understand what has actually happened during the period. For this reason great care must be taken in preparing the financial statements where fund accounting is involved. Appendix A–2 provides a table that summarizes some of the alternatives discussed in this chapter and the degree of acceptability of each.

5

Inter-Fund Transfers and Appropriations

As pointed out in the last chapter the use of fund accounting, while often necessary, creates a certain amount of confusion and adds to the problem of meeting the "grandmother test." In this chapter two other problem areas will be explored. One relates to fund accounting—the use of "transfers" between funds—and the other relates to the use of "appropriations." Both add to the complexity of financial statements. Transfers between funds are frequently unavoidable; appropriations, on the other hand, serve very little purpose and should be avoided.

TRANSFERS BETWEEN FUNDS

Nonprofit organizations following fund accounting procedures have a number of different funds, some restricted and some unrestricted. The board has the right to transfer assets between unrestricted funds and there are occasions when this is appropriate. For example, if the board has established a board-designated endowment fund, it may from time to time transfer funds from the general fund to this fund. Or, alternatively, it may find at some time that it needs some of the funds previously transferred and will, in turn, transfer some of these funds back to the general fund.

Transfers can very easily cause confusion for the reader. If a transfer is not properly shown, the reader may not understand what has happened. Special care must be taken in preparing financial statements to ensure that "transfers" will be understood.

Presentation of Transfers

There are several principles that should be followed in presentation of "transfers" in the financial statements. The first and most important is that a transfer should be shown in the Statement of Changes in Fund Balances or if that statement is not used, in the Statement of Income, Expenses and Changes in Fund Balance after the caption "Fund balance, beginning of year." It should not be shown as an expense. Only transactions which result in income or expense to the organization are shown in the income or expense section of a financial statement, and a transfer is purely an internal action not involving either. For this reason great care must be taken to avoid a presentation that suggests that the transfer is either an income or an expense item.

Columnar Statement. The use of a columnar statement is the most effective manner in which to present a transfer between funds with a minimum risk of misunderstanding. In a columnar statement, the activity of each fund is shown in a separate column, side by side.*

The reason why this is a desirable format is that the reader can then easily see both sides of the transfer: the funds going out of one fund and the funds going into the other fund.

Figure 5–1 shows an example of this columnar presentation. The Board of the Corvallis YMCA decided to transfer $40,000 from its general fund to a board-designated endowment fund. Notice how this was handled in a columnar format, in a Statement of Income, Expenses and Changes in Fund Balances. † The transfer was shown after the caption "Fund balance, beginning of year." In this way there is no inference that the transfer had

* Chapter 12 discusses the use of columnar-format statements and their advantages and disadvantages. The reader may want to refer to this discussion since no attempt will be made to discuss this format in this chapter although it will be used throughout.

† Chapter 12 discusses the Statement of Income, Expenses and Changes in Fund Balances. The reader may want to refer to this discussion since this statement will be used throughout this chapter.

CORVALLIS Y.M.C.A.

STATEMENT OF INCOME, EXPENSES, AND CHANGES IN FUND BALANCES
For the Year Ending December 31, 1974

	General Fund	Funds for Specified Purposes	Board-Designated Endowment Fund	Combined All Funds
			(in thousands)	
Income				
Membership	$255			$255
Community fund	50			50
Program activities	372			372
Contributions and other income	45	$17		62
Investment income	13			13
Gain on sale of investments. .	15			15
Total income	750	17		767
Expenses				
Program	326			326
General administration	265			265
Property repairs and maintenance	50			50
Depreciation	35			35
Other	14	7		21
Total expenses	690	7		697
Excess of income over expenses	60	10		70
Fund balance, beginning of year	415	10	$200	625
Transfer between funds	(40)		40	
Fund balance, end of year	$435	$20	$240	$695

Fig. 5-1. Reporting a transfer in a columnar format Statement of Income, Expenses, and Changes in Fund Balances.

anything to do with either income or expenses of the general fund for the year. Rather, only a portion of the fund balance, accumulated over many years, was transferred to another board-controlled fund.

Transfers in Statement of Changes in Fund Balances. Some organizations do not present a combined Statement of Income, Expenses and Changes in Fund Balances. They will either have two separate statements—a Statement of Income and Expense and a

Statement of Changes in Fund Balances—or, they will have only a Statement of Income and Expense. If two separate statements are presented, the transfer should be shown in the Statement of Changes in Fund Balances. It should not be shown in the Statement of Income and Expense since a transfer represents an adjustment of the fund balance rather than an item of income or expense. Figure 5–2 shows an example of the Corvallis YMCA statements where both statements are used.

Transfers in Statement of Income and Expense.   The third possibility is that the organization will not show the changes in fund balance either in the income statement or as a separate statement. This might occur where the only change between the beginning and ending fund balance is the excess of income for the year. In that instance it is necessary to report the transfer in the Statement of Income and Expense. Figure 5–3 shows the transfer after the caption "Excess of income over expenses."

Transfer of Income or Deficit.   The boards of some organizations use "transfers" as a device to reduce or increase the general fund balance to a predetermined amount. Where this transfer into or out of the general fund is reported directly on the Statement of Income and Expenses (rather than on a Statement of Changes in Fund Balances), the casual reader is likely to be misled. This is often what the board has in mind.

Figures 5–4 and 5–5 show two examples of this type of transfer, and at the same time provide perfect examples of why fund accounting is so hard for most readers to understand when separate statements are presented for each fund.

In each of the examples the casual reader is likely to look at only the last figure in the statement: the $500 excess of income over expenses and transfers. These are the wrong figures to focus on. What should be observed is a $15,000 excess of income in the first example and the $8,000 deficit in the second.

Transfers are made at the "discretion" of the board, and if this type of transfer is made the board can "window dress" the statements to suit its objectives. In the first illustration it appears that the board may be somewhat embarrassed by the surplus and has disposed of it by transferring it into another fund.

CORVALLIS Y.M.C.A.

STATEMENT OF INCOME AND EXPENSE
For the Year Ending December 31, 1974

	General Fund	Funds for Specified Purposes	Board-Designated Endowment Fund	Combined All Funds
		(in thousands)		
Income:				
Membership	$255			$255
Community fund	50			50
Program activities	372			372
Contributions and other income	45	$17		62
Investment income	13			13
Gain on sale of investments	15			15
Total income	750	17	—	767
Expenses:				
Program	326			326
General administration	265			265
Property repairs and maintenance	50			50
Depreciation	35			35
Other	14	7		21
Total expenses	690	7	—	697
Excess of income over expenses	$ 60	$10	—	$ 70

STATEMENT OF CHANGES IN FUND BALANCES
For the Year Ending December 31, 1974

	General Fund	Funds for Specified Purposes	Board-Designated Endowment Fund	Combined All Funds
		(in thousands)		
Fund balance, beginning of the year	$415	$10	$200	$625
Excess of income over expense...............	60	10		70
Transfer between funds	(40)		40	
Fund balance, end of the year	$435	$20	$240	$695

Fig. 5–2. Reporting a transfer when a separate Statement of Changes in Fund Balances is presented.

CORVALLIS Y.M.C.A.

STATEMENT OF INCOME, EXPENSE AND TRANSFER
For the Year Ending December 31, 1974

	General Fund	Funds for Specified Purposes	Board-Designated Endowment Fund	Combined All Funds
		(in thousands)		
Income				
Membership	$255			$255
Community fund	50			50
Program activities	372			372
Contributions and other				
income................	45	$17		62
Investment income	13			13
Gain on sale of investments..	15			15
Total income	750	17		767
Expenses				
Program	326			326
General administration	265			265
Property repairs and				
maintenance	50			50
Depreciation	35			35
Other	14	7		21
Total expenses	690	7		697
Excess of income over				
expenses	60	10		70
Transfer between funds	(40)		$40	
Excess of income after				
transfer	$ 20	$10	$40	$ 70

Fig. 5–3. A transfer reported in a Statement of Income and Expense. This presentation would not be acceptable if a separate Statement of Changes in Fund Balances is also presented.

Perhaps the motivation is fund raising. It is hard to convince a contributor that his money is needed if there is a big surplus. While the careful reader will see that there is a big surplus, the casual reader, or the reader who does not understand that transfers are made at the discretion of the board, may think the net income for the year was only $500. In the second illustration, it could appear that the board allowed expenses to get out of hand and has tried to cover up the deficit. Again, only the careful

THE JOHNSTOWN MUSEUM

STATEMENT OF GENERAL FUND INCOME, EXPENSES AND TRANSFERS
For the Year Ending December 31, 1974

Income		$152,000
Less—Expenses....................................		(142,000)
Excess of income over expenses.....................		10,000
Less—Transfers to:		
Building fund	$ 4,500	
Board-designated endowment fund	10,000	14,500
Excess of income over expenses and transfers		$ 500

Fig. 5–4. An example of a transfer which reduces the general fund income. The casual reader is likely to confuse this transfer with an expense, and may wrongly conclude the excess of income is $500.

reader will understand that the transfer is merely a bookkeeping device.

This is not to say that the board may not have a good motive for making these transfers. But, in the author's opinion, assets should be transferred out of the general fund only when there is a legal reason why the funds are not available for the general uses of the organization. If a surplus builds up in the general fund, these assets can still be invested by the board in securities in the same manner as with endowment funds. There is no real

THE SMITHVILLE MUSEUM

STATEMENT OF GENERAL FUND INCOME, EXPENSES AND TRANSFERS
For the Year Ending December 31, 1974

Income	$102,000
Less—Expenses	(110,000)
Excess of expenses over income................................	(8,000)
Add—Transfer from Board-designated endowment fund	8,500
Excess of income and transfers over expenses	$ 500

Fig. 5–5. A transfer which covers a general fund deficit for the year. The casual reader is likely to confuse this transfer with income, and may wrongly conclude the excess of income as $500.

reason why this excess need be placed in a separate "board-designated" fund and as noted in Chapter 4 the author does not recommend the use of a separate board-designated fund. Some boards look upon the general fund as a sort of "working capital" fund which should contain only enough cash and current assets to provide for the day-to-day operations of the organization. This approach, however, serves very little real purpose, and tends to confuse the reader.

If, nevertheless, separate board-designated funds are used, transfers should not be made to keep the general fund balance at "zero" or at some minimum amount. Transfers from the general fund to these board-designated funds should be made only when it is obvious that there are surplus funds in the general fund that are not likely to be needed in the foreseeable future. Likewise, transfers should not be made to the general fund from board-designated funds just to cover a particular year's deficit as long as there is a surplus remaining from prior years. Transfers should be made to the general fund only at the time when the general fund has gotten so small that it needs the cash from other funds for operations.

Also, if the board makes frequent transfers it should minimize much of the confusion by presenting a Statement of Changes in Fund Balances, and, as noted above, including all transfers in this statement. The author's preference is that such a statement be combined with the Statement of Income and Expenses to avoid a third statement, but it is equally acceptable to use a completely separate statement.

Other Transfers

Occasionally there are other transfers between funds. In some instances expenditures for "current" activities are made from the general fund but are later paid for by a transfer from another fund. This is often handled as a transfer. This is extensively discussed in Chapter 9.

Another type of transfer involves depreciation expense which is shown in the general fund, but is then transferred from the general fund to the plant fund. Chapter 7 shows several illustrations of this type of transfer.

APPROPRIATIONS

An "appropriation" is an authorization to expend funds in the future for a specific purpose. An appropriation is not an expenditure nor does it represent an obligation that has already been incurred. It is only an internal authorization indicating how the board intends to spend part of the fund balance. Once funds have been "appropriated," they are usually set up in a separate account, but as part of the fund balance or net worth of the organization. They are not shown as a liability. All that happens when the board makes an appropriation is that part of the fund balance is set aside for a particular purpose. Since appropriations are made by the board, it can subsequently reverse its action and restore these funds to the general use of the organization.

It should be emphasized that an appropriation is an authorization for a future expenditure and is not an expenditure that has already been incurred. In many ways an appropriation is very similar to a "transfer between funds" and often the two terms are incorrectly used. If moneys are going from one fund to another fund, a "transfer" is involved. If amounts are being set aside within a single fund, an appropriation is involved. Figure 5–6 shows a simplified example of the presentation of an appropriation where a separate Statement of Changes in Fund Balance is not used.

Appropriation accounting is both confusing and subject to abuse. It is confusing because very few understand exactly what an appropriation is. Most do not realize that an appropriation does not represent an expenditure but only an internal "authorization" for a future expenditure. Appropriation accounting is also confusing because the presentation in the financial statements is often not made in a straightforward manner. So when a casual reader sees the term "appropriation" on a financial statement he is probably not really sure what it is. Since the appropriation has been deducted from net income, the average reader assumes the money has been spent or an obligation incurred.

Appropriation accounting is subject to abuse because it is a device frequently used to give the appearance of an expenditure of funds out of the net income for the year. This, obviously,

THE BETHLEHEM SERVICES ORGANIZATION

STATEMENT OF INCOME, EXPENSES AND APPROPRIATION
Year Ending December 31, 1974
(in thousands)

Income	$100
Less—Expenses................................	80
Excess of income over expenses.................	20
Less—Appropriation for Project A	(15)
Excess of income over expenses and appropriation ...	$ 5

BALANCE SHEET
December 31, 1974

Cash..		$100
Other assets		100
Total assets		$200
Accounts payable		$100
Fund balance		
Appropriated—Project A	$15	
Unappropriated	85	100
		$200

Fig. 5—6.   Handling an appropriation in the financial statements, when a separate Statement of Changes in Fund Balances is not used.

reduces the net income reported to the membership. As discussed with regard to transfers, it is understandable that a board, interested in raising funds from its membership, finds it difficult to go "hat-in-hand" if the income statement shows a large net income for the preceding year. One way that boards occasionally try to overcome this, is to "appropriate" a substantial amount of this income for some future project. Often, and incorrectly, the appropriation appears on the financial statement as another item of expense. This leaves the false impression that the money has truly been expended.

This is not to suggest that the board may not have a specific and very real project in mind when it makes an appropriation. There are many organizations that have sizable projects that only take place every few years. Often the board wants to provide for the funds over a period of time. The key point is that financial statements should represent transactions that have taken place in the past and not transactions that may or may not take place in the future.

Occasionally an organization with a number of funds will decide to transfer the net income to several other funds. Instead of using the word "transfer," the treasurer will use the word "appropriation." This confuses the reader since he doesn't really understand what an appropriation is. So if a transfer is being made between funds, use the word "transfer."

Appropriation Accounting Not Recommended

Appropriation accounting is not recommended. It creates more confusion than clarification. It fails the "grandmother test." When an organization wants to put aside or reserve amounts to provide for some future need, no bookkeeping entry is required. If the board wants to do anything, perhaps it should put the desired amount in a savings account or earmark part of the investment securities. This action does not result in a bookkeeping entry or a presentation problem.

Essential Rules

Notwithstanding the reservations about the use of appropriations, there are some organizations that have used and will continue to use appropriation accounting. For these relatively few organizations, the following rules must * be followed to provide a straightforward and meaningful presentation of what has happened:

1. Appropriations should be only for specific projects or undertakings. There should be no appropriations for general, undetermined contingencies, or for any indefinite future losses. The unexpended balance of a department's budget should not be carried over to future periods in the guise of an appropriation.

---

* All three AICPA Audit Guides indicate that appropriation may not be charged to expense, and that appropriations are only a form of segregation of fund balance. See Chapters 13, 14, and 15.

2. All new appropriations and all remaining appropriations from prior years should be specifically authorized by the board *each* year. This function should not be delegated. All prior-year appropriations should be carefully reviewed to be certain they are still necessary. If all or part of a prior-year appropriation is no longer applicable, it should be reversed.

3. An appropriation is really only a form of transfer. The appropriation must not be included as part of expenses. An example of an *improper* presentation would be:

STATEMENT OF INCOME, EXPENSES, AND APPROPRIATION

Income		$100
Expenses:		
Total expenses	$80	
Appropriation for Project A	15	
Total expenses		95
Excess of income over expenses and		
appropriation		$ 5

It is too easy for the reader to think that the $15 appropriation is a real expense for the period rather than an authorization to spend $15 in the future.

4. Appropriations should be reported in a separate Statement of Changes in Fund Balance, in the following manner:

STATEMENT OF CHANGES IN FUND BALANCE

Appropriated:	
Balance, beginning of year	–
Add—appropriated for Project A	$ 15
Balance, end of year	15
Unappropriated:	
Balance beginning of year	$ 80
Excess of income over expenses for	
the year	20
Less—Appropriated for Project A	(15)
Balance, end of year	$ 85
Total appropriated and unappropriated	
fund balance	$100

---

5. If, contrary to the above recommendation, a separate Statement of Changes in Fund Balance is not presented, then the appropriation must be shown after the excess of income over expense caption in the Statement of Income and Expense, as follows:

STATEMENT OF INCOME, EXPENSES, AND APPROPRIATION

Income	$100
Expenses	(80)
Excess of income over expenses	20
Less—Appropriated for Project A	(15)
Excess of income over expenses and	
appropriation	$ 5

6. When the expense is incurred in a subsequent period out of the funds previously appropriated, such expense must be included in the Statement of Income and Expenses for that year. It is not appropriate to charge such expense directly against the "appropriation." To do so has the effect of burying the expense and the reader has a right to know what has been incurred. This means then that in addition to including the expense in the year's Statement of Income and Expense the appropriation must be reversed in the same manner as it was set up. Figure 5–7 shows an example of how to report the $15 appropriation for Project A, and the subsequent year's expense of $13.

7. If a separate Statement of Changes in Fund Balance is not presented, the reversal of the appropriation in 1975 would be made in the same manner as the appropriation was originally set up (see item 5 above) and using the wording in Figure 5–7.

8. The appropriation on the Balance Sheet must appear in the Net Worth or Fund Balance section, not in the liability section (see Figure 5–7).

There is one final alternative and that is to make no reference to appropriations on any of the statements. The board can go ahead and make appropriations but handle them strictly in the footnotes to the financial statements. If this approach is followed, the footnotes to the Balance Sheet would disclose the amount appropriated. For example such a footnote might read:

"Of the total fund balance of $100, $15 has been appropriated by the Board for future use in Project A."

This fully discloses the appropriation but eliminates all of the confusion on the statements. This is the approach which is easiest to understand and therefore the one recommended if appropriations are made.

THE BETHLEHEM SERVICES ORGANIZATION

STATEMENT OF INCOME AND EXPENSES

(in thousands)

	Year Ending December 31,	
	1974	1975
Income	$100	$100
Expenses:		
Other than Project A	80	80
Project A	–	13
Total expenses	80	93
Excess of income over expenses....................	$ 20	$ 7

STATEMENT OF CHANGES IN FUND BALANCE

	Year Ending December 31,	
	1974	1975
Appropriated:		
Balance, beginning of year	–	$ 15
Add—Appropriation for Project A	$ 15	–
Less—Appropriation no longer needed	–	(15)
Balance, end of year	15	–
Unappropriated:		
Balance, beginning of year	80	85
Excess of income over expenses for the year..........	20	7
Less—Appropriated for Project A	(15)	–
Add—Appropriation no longer needed	–	15
Balance, end of year	85	107
Fund balance	$100	$107

BALANCE SHEET

	December 31,	
	1974	1975
Assets	$200	$207
Liabilities.....................................	$100	$100
Fund balance:		
Appropriated*: for Project A	15	–
Unappropriated	85	107
Total liabilities and fund balance	$200	$207

*Sometimes the word "allocated" will be used instead of "appropriations."

Fig. 5–7.   An example of the recommended manner in which to report an appropriation, and the subsequent year's reversal when the actual expenditure is made.

CONCLUSION

Confusing and complicated? Absolutely, and this is one of the major reasons why appropriation accounting should be avoided. As already repeatedly stated, it serves little legitimate purpose, and usually confuses the reader, often including the board members themselves. If a board is truly concerned about setting aside a "reserve" or appropriation for some future year, all that it needs to do is to decide that it will not spend that amount. Furthermore, there is no reason why the monies represented by the appropriation can't be invested or put in a separate savings account. This is not to minimize the practical problem of actually setting this money aside and not spending it. This is always difficult. But appropriation accounting is not the answer.

Appendix A–3 provides a table of alternatives among fund transfer and appropriation practices.

6

Fixed Assets—Some Accounting Problems

Fixed assets and their depreciation present difficult accounting and reporting problems for nonprofit organizations. Some organizations record fixed assets, some do not. Some record depreciation, some do not. There is no area of nonprofit accounting in which, until recently, opinion was so divided. This chapter summarizes current accounting thinking, presents alternatives for recording fixed assets, and offers several recommendations as to when each is appropriate. The next chapter discusses the related problem of depreciation.

NATURE OF THE PROBLEM

Fixed assets present a problem because many nonprofit organizations handle their affairs on a cash basis. When these organizations need to purchase a new building or equipment they turn to their membership to raise cash for these purchases in a building or equipment fund drive. Having raised the money and purchased the building, there is relatively little significance in having the fixed asset on the organization's Balance Sheet except as a historical record of what it cost.

This is in contrast to a commercial enterprise which is dependent upon recovering the cost of the fixed asset through the sale of goods or services to outsiders. In a commercial business it is entirely appropriate to record the asset on the Balance Sheet and to depreciate (i.e., to systematically allocate) the cost of the asset over its estimated useful life. Depreciation is an expense which is charged against income for the period. If income from the sale of goods or services is not large enough to recover all the expenses, including depreciation charges, then the commercial enterprise is considered to have had a loss. If such losses occur over an extended period of time the enterprise will, of course, go bankrupt.

So one of the principal reasons why fixed assets give so much trouble is that the nature of nonprofit organizations is such that there usually is no compelling need to record the asset and then to depreciate it over a period of time. The element of matching income and costs often doesn't exist.

Another factor is that nonprofit organizations frequently have as their principal asset buildings acquired many years ago. Because of inflation and growth in real estate values, these buildings and land are frequently worth several times their cost. To many it seems incongruous to depreciate a building which is known to be worth more than its original cost.

Another factor is that, if fixed assets were originally purchased out of a special building or equipment fund drive, it is difficult to justify recording them on the books and then depreciating them since this depreciation represents a charge against current income. Effectively it appears that they have been charged twice; once when the funds were originally raised and once when the assets are written off through the depreciation charge. Some believe it is unethical to raise funds for fixed assets and subsequently to seek to recover the costs of such assets from the users of the facility or from future donors. Of course, the building or asset can be recorded and not depreciated but this goes against the grain of accounting for fixed assets as used by commercial enterprises. The result of all this is that there are many approaches followed, and much confusion.

ALTERNATIVES FOR HANDLING FIXED ASSETS

There are three basic alternative approaches for recording fixed assets.* These are:

1. Immediate write-off method, where assets are written off as purchased, in the Statement of Income and Expenses.
2. Capitalization method, where the full cost of the asset is capitalized and recorded on the Balance Sheet. This is now the generally accepted accounting principle.
3. Write-off, then capitalize method, where the asset is written off in the Statement of Income and Expenses but then capitalized on the Balance Sheet.†

Each of these three approaches is discussed in detail in the following sections. Each can be used for both accrual basis and cash basis organizations.

Immediate Write-Off Method

The "immediate write-off" approach is the simplest and the most frequently used. The organization treats all fixed asset purchases as any other category of expense, and does not capitalize the purchase as assets. The purchase is included as another expense in the Statement of Income and Expenses.

A good example would be the Rathskeller Youth Center **
which raised $25,000 for building alterations in 1973. In 1974,

---

* Part III of this book discusses the various published accounting guides for nonprofit organizations. Several of these guides prescribe the fixed asset and depreciation procedures which are acceptable for certain categories of organizations. The reader should refer to this discussion to determine if any of these standards apply to an organization he is interested in.

† This method of handling fixed assets was originally recommended in the 1964 edition of *Standards of Accounting and Financial Reporting for Voluntary Health and Welfare Organizations* (see Chapter 13) and was widely followed between then and 1974. However, with the issuance of the 1973 AICPA Audit Guide which states that such organizations are required to capitalize fixed assets and follow depreciation accounting, this method can no longer be considered generally accepted. The 1974 revised edition of *Standards of Accounting and Financial Reporting for Voluntary Health and Welfare Organizations* has deleted all reference to the "write-off, then capitalize" method. It will probably be several years before this approach completely disappears, and for this reason the author has included a discussion of it in this chapter.

** The Rathskeller Youth Center is located in a small town and provides a place where teenagers can congregate. The center occupies a small building

the Center purchased furniture and fixtures for $5,000. In this illustration the Center is on an accrual basis of accounting, but the principles would be the same if it were on a cash basis.

The Rathskeller Youth Center's Statement of Income and Expenses and Balance Sheet for these two years are shown in Figure 6–1.

Advantages. The principal advantage is simplicity. Since, in the first year, a building fund drive was conducted to raise income for the building alteration, this statement shows clearly the expenditure for this purpose. The amount shown as excess of income over expenses represents the actual amount which remains after all bills are paid and pledges collected. While this is not the cash balance of the Center, it has much the same significance as though it were. With this presentation there is no confusion as to the amount available for the board to spend. This approach recognizes that while the Center has equity in a building, the building is not likely to be converted into cash except at a time the Center is dissolved. The building is essential to the continued operation of the Center and therefore has no value in terms of cash requirements of the Center's day-to-day program.

Disadvantages. The principal disadvantage is that the historical cost of the asset is not reflected on the Balance Sheet and therefore the fund balance does not truly represent the "net worth" of the organization. In addition, the Balance Sheet doesn't show the asset "accountability." Also the pride that the members have in owning the building is not reflected in the financial statement. This can be upsetting to many people, particularly those who have made large contributions toward the building. Another disadvantage, although not applicable in this case, is that by writing off the asset all at one time, no allocation of cost is made against future years' revenue-producing projects. This will be discussed in Chapter 7.

Another related problem is that by writing off fixed assets as purchased, there can be considerable fluctuation in such expendi-

---

near the high school that a wealthy businessman donated for this purpose. Operating expenses are covered principally from donations from the general public, although there is a small membership fee that each teenager pays to belong.

RATHSKELLER YOUTH CENTER
STATEMENT OF INCOME AND EXPENSES

	Year Ending December 31,	
	1973	1974
Income:		
Membership fees	$ 4,000	$ 5,000
Contributions:		
General	37,900	39,600
Building Fund	25,000	–
Total income	66,900	44,600
Expenses:		
Salaries	11,000	10,000
Building maintenance	5,000	5,200
Coffee and food	12,800	12,600
Music and entertainment	2,000	2,400
Other	8,000	5,900
Building alterations	25,000	–
Furniture and equipment	–	5,000
Total expenses	63,800	41,100
Excess of income over expenses....................	$ 3,100	$ 3,500

BALANCE SHEET

	December 31,	
	1973	1974
Assets:		
Cash	$ 2,000	$ 4,000
Pledges receivable	6,500	6,700
Total assets	$ 8,500	$10,700
Liabilities:		
Accrued salaries	$ 3,000	$ 2,000
Accounts payable	400	100
Total liabilities	3,400	2,100
Fund balance:		
Beginning of year	2,000	5,100
Excess of income over expenses	3,100	3,500
End of year...................................	5,100	8,600
Total liabilities and fund balance	$ 8,500	$10,700

Fig. 6–1.   An example of the statements of an organization that follows the immediate write-off method of handling fixed assets.

tures between years. In this instance, observe that the furniture and equipment purchases of $5,000 in 1974 were not matched by similar purchases in 1973.

A further disadvantage is that this method is not "generally accepted" and a CPA would be required to qualify his opinion on these statements. See page 359 for a discussion of the significance of qualified opinions.

Capitalization Method

The second approach is for the organization to capitalize all of its fixed asset purchases. Figure 6–2 shows the Statement of Income and Expenses and Balance Sheet under this capitalization approach. Organizations that want an unqualified opinion on their financial statements from CPAs will, in most instances, have to follow this method.

Under this capitalization approach, depreciation could be taken, or, alternatively, the fixed assets written down from time to time as their value decreases. This subject is covered in Chapter 7.

Advantages. The principal advantage is that the fixed assets purchased are now reflected on the Balance Sheet. This makes it possible for the reader to see the amount of assets the board was responsible for. In this instance it will be noted that prior to 1973 the center had acquired land and building of $90,000 and furniture and fixtures of $20,000. The fund balance now reflects the cost of these significant assets.

Many businessmen feel more comfortable seeing financial transactions recorded on this capitalization method since commercial businesses also capitalize their fixed assets.

Disadvantages. The reader may find this income statement more difficult to understand. The biggest risk is that he will confuse the large excess of income over expenses with the amount of "cash" available to the board for use. He may be left with the impression that in 1973 the center has excess income of $28,000, and therefore does not need his contribution. This is a real risk.

RATHSKELLER YOUTH CENTER

STATEMENT OF INCOME AND EXPENSES

| | Year Ending December 31, | |
	1973	1974
Income:		
Membership fees	$ 4,000	$ 5,000
Contributions:		
General	37,900	39,600
Building Fund	25,000	–
Total income	66,900	44,600
Expenses:		
Salaries	11,000	10,000
Building maintenance	5,000	5,200
Coffee and food	12,800	12,600
Music and entertainment	2,000	2,400
Other	8,000	5,900
Total expenses	38,800	36,100
Excess of income over expenses	$28,100	$ 8,500

BALANCE SHEET

| | December 31, | |
	1973	1974
Assets:		
Cash	$ 2,000	$ 4,000
Pledges receivable	6,500	6,700
Land and original building	90,000	90,000
Building alterations	25,000	25,000
Furniture and equipment	20,000	25,000
Total assets	$143,500	$150,700
Liabilities:		
Accrued salaries	$ 3,000	$ 2,000
Accounts payable	400	100
Total liabilities	3,400	2,100
Fund balance:		
Beginning of year	112,000	140,100
Excess of income over expenses	28,100	8,500
End of year	140,100	148,600
Total liabilities and fund balance	$143,500	$150,700

Fig. 6–2.   An example of the statements of an organization that follows the capitalization method of handling fixed assets.

Write-Off, Then Capitalize Method

An organization can combine these two approaches and write off purchases of fixed assets on its Statement of Income and Expenses and then turn around and capitalize or record the assets on its Balance Sheet.*

The theory is that a nonprofit organization should charge off all purchases as incurred. This allows the organization to show the expenditure for the fixed assets, which reduces the amount of the excess of income over expenses. This eliminates the disadvantage of the capitalization method discussed above. In this case, the building alterations have been paid for from contributions which are reflected in the Statement of Income and Expenses and the organization does not look to recover the building cost through charges to income over a period of years through depreciation. At the same time the asset is recorded on the Balance Sheet to reflect its cost and more fairly show the net worth of the organization. From time to time these assets are removed from the Balance Sheet as the assets decline in value by directly reducing the carrying value on the Balance Sheet. Figure 6–3 shows the financial statements of Rathskeller Youth Center on this method.† Obviously the part that is most confusing in this approach is the adding back or capitalizing the fixed assets in the Fund Balance section of the Balance Sheet.

Advantages. Most of the advantages of both the immediate write-off and the capitalization methods are present in this hybrid approach. The reader sees the expenditure for the fixed assets in the Statement of Income and Expenses, and the excess of income over expenses has been reduced by this purchase, offset by any contributions that may have been received for such asset purchases in the current year. Accordingly, the reader is not misled into thinking there is a large excess of income which can be expended. At the same time, by capitalizing the asset in the Balance Sheet, the accountability for the assets is not lost.

---

* See the footnote at the bottom of page 59 which discusses the changing attitude toward the acceptability of this approach.

† This direct write-down is illustrated on page 81.

RATHSKELLER YOUTH CENTER
STATEMENT OF INCOME AND EXPENSES

	Year Ending December 31,	
	1973	1974
Income:		
Membership fees	$ 4,000	$ 5,000
Contributions:		
General	37,900	39,600
Building Fund	25,000	–
Total income	66,900	44,600
Expenses:		
Salaries	11,000	10,000
Building maintenance	5,000	5,200
Coffee and food	12,800	12,600
Music and entertainment	2,000	2,400
Other	8,000	5,900
Building alterations	25,000	–
Furniture and equipment	–	5,000
Total expenses	63,800	41,100
Excess of income over expenses	$ 3,100	$ 3,500

BALANCE SHEET

	December 31,	
	1973	1974
Assets:		
Cash	$ 2,000	$ 4,000
Pledges receivable	6,500	6,700
Land and building	90,000	90,000
Building alterations	25,000	25,000
Furniture and equipment	20,000	25,000
Total assets	$143,500	$150,700
Liabilities:		
Accrued salaries	$ 3,000	$ 2,000
Accounts payable	400	100
Total liabilities	3,400	2,100
Fund balance:		
Beginning of year	112,000	140,100
Excess of income over expenses	3,100	3,500
Building and equipment capitalized	25,000	5,000
End of year	140,100	148,600
Total liabilities and fund balance	$143,500	$150,700

Fig. 6–3.   An example of the statements of an organization that follows the write-off, then capitalize, method of handling fixed assets.

Disadvantages. The capitalizing of the asset directly in the fund balance is very confusing to most, and there is a high degree of risk that the reader won't understand it. It appears to mix apples and oranges in that it is saying purchases of fixed assets should be handled on more or less a cash basis in the Statement of Income and Expenses but on an accrual basis in the Balance Sheet. This seems illogical. Also, this method does not follow generally accepted accounting principles.*

Another related disadvantage is that under this method there is no way to provide depreciation charges in the Statement of Income and Expenses since the asset has already been written off. As more fully discussed in the next chapter, it is frequently appropriate to provide depreciation charges in order to try to match income and costs. While this may not be appropriate in the case of the "Center," it will be for many other types of nonprofit organizations. Accordingly, this method should not be used by organizations where depreciation is appropriate. Another related disadvantage is that if asset purchases fluctuate from year to year, they can have a significant effect on the excess of income over expenses. This would not be so if the assets were capitalized and depreciated. Only the depreciation charge would then appear in the Statement of Income and Expenses.

RESTRICTED BUILDING FUND

No distinction has been made in the illustrations in this chapter between restricted and unrestricted contributions for the building fund. These contributions have been treated as though they were unrestricted for ease in illustrating the three basic ways in which to handle fixed assets. If, however, these amounts were "restricted" then they would normally be reported in a separate restricted fund, or in a building or a fixed-asset fund as discussed in Chapter 4.

---

* If an organization following this method were to have its statements audited by a CPA, the CPA would be required to qualify his opinion since this method is not generally accepted. See page 359 for a discussion of the significance of qualified opinions.

Immediate Write-Off

If a separate building or fixed-asset fund were used, the principles outlined in this chapter would still apply. In the first approach (immediate write-off) restricted building fund contributions would be added to the building fund when received. As expenditures were made, they would be shown as expenses of that fund. The amount remaining in the fund at any time would be the unexpended restricted gifts. Expenditures for fixed assets not covered by restricted gifts, such as the $5,000 for furniture and fixtures in 1974, would still be shown in the general fund.

Capitalization

If the second approach were followed (capitalization), the organization would probably have a separate fixed-asset fund in which fixed assets would be recorded and in which all restricted building fund contributions would be reported when received. The actual purchase of a fixed asset would be reflected in a fixed-asset-fund Balance Sheet in a manner similar to that shown in Figure 6–2. The major difficulty with having a separate fixed-asset fund is that if fixed assets are purchased from unrestricted funds they must be transferred to the fixed-asset fund to keep all fixed assets together in one fund.

The author does not recommend the use of a separate fixed-asset fund, for the reasons discussed in Chapter 4. Instead, fixed assets should be included in the general or current fund. If the organization does follow this recommendation and includes its fixed assets in the general fund, it will still record restricted contributions in a restricted building fund. However, at the time that fixed assets are purchased from these restricted funds, a transfer would be made from the restricted fund to the general fund of the cost of the assets purchased. This transfer would be reported in the manner outlined in Chapter 5. Figure 6–4 shows an example of this reporting for the Rathskeller Youth Center, assuming that the $25,000 had been restricted contributions.

Two minor points should be noted. First, note that the interfund transfer is shown in the fund balance section of the Balance Sheet. As is discussed in Chapter 5, transfers should not

RATHSKELLER YOUTH CENTER

STATEMENT OF INCOME AND EXPENSES
For the Years Ending December 31, 1973 and 1974

| | 1973 | | 1974 | |
	General Fund	Building Fund	General Fund	Building Fund
Income:				
Membership fees	$ 4,000		$ 5,000	
Contributions	37,900	$25,000	39,600	
Total income	41,900	25,000	44,600	
Expenses:				
Salaries	11,000		10,000	
Building maintenance	5,000		5,200	
Coffee and food	12,800		12,600	
Music and entertainment . .	2,000		2,400	
Other	8,000		5,900	
Total expenses	38,800		36,100	
Excess of income over				
expenses	$ 3,100	$25,000	$ 8,500	

BALANCE SHEET

| | December 31, 1973 | | December 31, 1974 | |
	General Fund	Building Fund	General Fund	Building Fund
Assets:				
Cash	$ 2,000		$ 4,000	
Pledges receivable	6,500		6,700	
Land and original building .	90,000		90,000	
Building alterations	25,000		25,000	
Furniture and equipment . .	20,000		25,000	
Total assets	$143,500		$150,700	
Liabilities:				
Accrued salaries	$ 3,000		$ 2,000	
Accounts payable	400		100	
Total liabilities	3,400		2,100	
Fund balance:				
Beginning of year	112,000		140,100	
Excess of income over				
expenses.	3,100	$25,000	8,500	
Interfund transfer	25,000	(25,000)	–	
End of year	140,100	–	148,600	
Total liabilities and				
fund balance	$143,500		$150,700	

Fig. 6–4. An example of the statements of an organization that records contributions in a separate Building Fund but carries all fixed assets in the General Fund.

be shown in the Statement of Income and Expenses as either an income or an expense item. While it is acceptable to show a transfer after the caption "Excess of income over expenses" this is not recommended because it may still lead the reader into thinking the transfer is an item of income or expense. Transfers should be shown in the fund balance section of the Balance Sheet or in a Statement of Changes in Fund Balances.

The other minor matter that should be noted is that in the illustration used throughout this chapter it has been assumed that the amount of building funds received during the year was exactly expended in the same year. This is seldom the case. In Figure 6–4 there are no amounts shown in the 1974 column. In all probability in actual practice some contributions would have been received in 1974 and some expenditures would have been incurred.

Write-Off, then Capitalize

If the third approach to handling fixed assets were followed (write-off, then capitalize), the procedures outlined would still apply. Restricted contributions received would be reported in either a building fund or a fixed asset fund. If a separate fixed-asset-fund Balance Sheet were used in which all fixed assets were then capitalized, the capitalization procedures outlined on page 62 would also apply to that fund. If, instead, the organization followed the practice, as recommended, of reporting all fixed assets in the general fund, the same reporting procedures would be followed except that instead of capitalizing the assets in a separate fixed asset fund and then transferring these assets to the general fund, they would be capitalized directly in the general fund. Since the asset is already written off in the fixed asset fund there is no need to "transfer" the assets, as such, to the general fund. The assets can be recorded directly in the general fund.

RECOMMENDATIONS

As discussed in the first chapter, the most important principle to be considered in keeping records and preparing financial statements is that they be successful in communicating to the reader what has happened during the year. If the statements are too complicated, they fail in communicating to the reader and their usefulness is limited. The organization should adopt methods of accounting and reporting appropriate to its activities, and to the user of its statements.

The first approach, i.e., immediate write-off, would appear appropriate for a small- or possibly medium-sized organization with relatively unsophisticated readers or for organizations on the cash basis. This is particularly so if the primary concern is raising enough cash each year to cover expenses, whether the organization is on the cash or accrual basis. The bookkeeping complexities of the capitalization method just do not seem warranted particularly because the financial statements prepared on this basis often leave the reader with the wrong impression of results of operations.

On the other hand, if the organization is larger, or is already on the accrual basis, there may be good reason to use the second approach, i.e., capitalization. If the organization merely writes off, or expenses, all fixed assets as purchased the reader could lose track of what assets the organization had and part of the stewardship is potentially lost. Also, a larger organization is less likely to keep its fixed assets for an indefinite period of time. It is more likely to outgrow its building, sell it, and buy a new one. It may also have other types of fixed assets which will be replaced from time to time, such as office equipment and vehicles. Another type of organization that should use this approach is the organization that has a reason to match revenues and costs. This would be the case where the organization sold a product or service, the income from which had to recover all of its costs. A direct write-off approach would distort the result of operations for these organizations. Instead, assets should be capitalized and the costs recovered through depreciation charges. This is the only method which can be considered as a "generally accepted accounting principle" and for this reason is the method which must be followed by organizations wanting an unqualified opinion from their CPAs.

However, even when fixed assets are recorded and not written off, it still will be appropriate to write off small equipment purchases to avoid the paper work of keeping track of them. Many organizations "expense" amounts under $100; others have higher limits of $500 or $1,000 depending on their size.

The third approach, i.e., write-off, then capitalize, is not recommended. This approach appears to depart too much from generally accepted accounting principles and very few understand it. It will often confuse more than it will help. Furthermore, this method effectively precludes an organization from depreciating its assets through its income statement. This means that organizations that must depreciate their assets in order to show total costs of a service or product cannot use this method. Also organizations that have widely fluctuating amounts of fixed asset additions each year will find this method will cause greater fluctuation in "excess of income over expenses" than would occur if it capitalized and then depreciated its assets.

See Appendix A–4 for a table of alternatives summarizing the author's recommendations and acceptable practice under present usage.

7

Fixed Assets—Depreciation

Depreciation is a problem related to fixed assets that can be difficult for nonprofit organizations to handle. If the organization follows the immediate write-off method of handling fixed assets, there are no assets on the balance sheet to depreciate. But many organizations do record fixed assets and are faced with a very basic question of whether to depreciate these assets or not. This has been a very controversial question until recently but now depreciation accounting is becoming more generally accepted.

ARGUMENTS FOR AND AGAINST TAKING DEPRECIATION

There are a number of reasons advanced for not taking depreciation. Probably the most relevant is that depreciation is a concept associated with commercial enterprises trying to match income and cost to determine profit. Nonprofit organizations are usually not concerned with a direct matching of income and cost. Therefore depreciation serves little purpose.

Another reason often suggested is that nonprofit organizations frequently raise the funds they need for major fixed-asset additions through special fund drives. When it comes time for the replacement of these assets, additional funds will be raised. There is no need to recover the costs of assets from income in the form of a depreciation charge.

Another consideration advanced is that, with inflation, the value of fixed assets often increases as fast, or faster than the deterioration through passage of time. Depreciation is often thought of, incorrectly,* as a method of trying to measure loss in value, and, therefore, many ask why depreciate an asset that is worth twice what was paid for it 25 years ago.

Another practical argument is that depreciation is difficult to show in the financial statements, particularly when fund accounting is followed. If depreciation serves no real purpose, why confuse the reader with bookkeeping entries that don't involve cash?

There are several arguments for taking depreciation. Most nonprofit organizations provide services that are measured in terms of costs. Depreciation is a cost. By not including this cost the reader is misled into thinking the actual costs were less than, in reality, they were. The board of an organization is charged with the responsibility of effectively using all of the resources available to it to carry out the program of the organization. By excluding a significant amount from the costs of the program, the board gives the reader the impression that the program has been carried out more efficiently than it has. The board fails to "charge itself" with full accountability for all the resources available to carry out the program.

Most nonprofit organizations, even those that do raise funds for major fixed asset additions through special fund-raising drives, must replace certain assets out of the recurring income of the organization. If no depreciation is taken and these assets are written off as purchased, the excess of income over expenses of the organization will fluctuate from year to year depending on the pattern of purchases. On the other hand, if depreciation charges are made the pattern of charges will be consistent from year to year and not dependent on the actual timing of purchases.

* Depreciation was defined by the Committee on Terminology of the American Institute of Certified Public Accountants as follows: "Depreciation accounting is a system of accounting which aims to distribute the cost or other basic value of tangible capital assets, less salvage (if any), over the estimated useful life of the unit (which may be a group of assets) in a systematic and rational manner. It is a process of allocation, not of valuation. Depreciation for the year is the portion of the total charge under such a system that is allocated to the year. Although the allocation may properly take into account occurrences during the year, it is not intended to be a measurement of the effect of all such occurrences." Copyright 1961 by the American Institute of Certified Public Accountants, Inc.

Another argument is that nonprofit organizations should follow the accrual accounting principles generally accepted for commercial enterprises. Depreciating of assets is required for such organizations. By excluding depreciation from the accounts, nonprofit organizations make it more difficult for businessmen to understand the financial statements.

WHEN DEPRECIATION SHOULD BE RECORDED

Depreciation accounting is now required for hospitals and voluntary health and welfare organizations although not by colleges and universities. As is discussed in Chapter 16, the author believes that depreciation accounting is applicable to most nonprofit organizations, particularly in the following situations:

1. A nonprofit organization with assets that must be replaced periodically from recurring or ordinary income should record depreciation. An example is a country club where member's dues and charges are intended to cover all costs including the cost of fixed assets used in the operation. If depreciation were not charged, the country club would have to write off assets at the time of replacement. This would mean that in some years the amounts written off would be disproportionately high and the excess of income over expenses would be distorted.

2. A nonprofit organization that sells products or provides services to outsiders, which are also available from commercial enterprises, should record depreciation for those assets involved with this revenue producing function. Once the organization engages in the sale of goods or services, it has an interest in matching income and costs in a manner similar to commercial enterprises. If no depreciation is taken, there is an appearance of profit which may not be appropriate.

   Furthermore, nonprofit organizations are subject to federal income taxes on "unrelated business income." Depreciation is a cost that should be recorded to reduce the profits subject to tax. Depreciation should be charged even if there is no profit because there may be profits in the future. It is always difficult to change accounting principles at a later date and start taking depreciation if the activity starts becoming profitable. Chapter 23 discusses the problems of unrelated business income under the Tax Reform Act of 1969.

3. A nonprofit organization that sells products or services to government agencies, Blue Cross, or other organizations where a "reimbursement" formula is involved, or potentially involved, should charge depreciation. The reasons for taking depreciation are much the same as those noted in the preceeding paragraph. If no depreciation is taken on the books it is always difficult to justify using a depreciation factor in a rate making or reimbursement situation. On the other hand, if depreciation has consistently been recorded on the books over a period of time, it will be difficult for the governmental or other agency to argue against using a depreciation factor in the rate or reimbursement base.

If the organization does not now sell a service to a governmental agency, it may in the future. It is conspicuous to start taking depreciation only when a product or service is first charged to an agency. Many organizations have found, much to their surprise, that at some point they have undertaken a project involving government reimbursement. A good example is a professional engineering society that undertakes to do research under a government grant on a cost reimbursement basis.

As can be seen, depreciation is appropriate for most organizations that follow the practice of recording fixed assets on their Balance Sheet.* Since depreciation is a concept that is used by commercial organizations, it should cause relatively little confusion in financial statements.

PRESENTATION IN THE FINANCIAL STATEMENTS

The presentation of depreciation in the financial statements is straightforward and similar to that used by commercial enterprises. Figure 7–1 shows depreciation in the financial statements of the Corvallis YMCA. † The Corvallis YMCA has both its own building and substantial amounts of equipment. While it receives some support from the public, most of its income is received from program fees. Accordingly the organization follows the practice of capitalizing all fixed assets and depreciating them. The building is depreciated over a fifty-year life, and all

---

* Depreciation is not applicable, however, to those organizations following the write-off, then capitalize method discussed in Chapter 6 because the asset has already been written off at the time it was purchased. See page 80.

† The Corvallis YMCA financial statements were presented in greater detail on page 44.

equipment over a five-year life. Depreciation has been included in the Statement of Income and Expenses, calculated as follows:

	1973	1974
Building (50 years)		
Cost: $450,000 — 2%/year	$ 9,000	$ 9,000
Equipment (5 years)		
Cost: $120,000 — 20%/year	24,000	
Cost: $130,000 — 20%/year		26,000
Total	$33,000	$35,000

The captions and presentation are familiar ones, and should cause no problem in a single fund organization. In this instance the YMCA has several funds but presents all of its financial statements in a columnar format.

Considerable difficulty does arise, however, if the organization has a separate plant fund and wishes to provide the depreciation charge in the general fund. The problem is a mechanical one of transferring the accumulated depreciation created by the depreciation charge from the general fund to the plant fund since the accumulated depreciation should be in the plant fund where the assets are recorded.

Here is an example how this transfer * can be made where there are separate plant funds:

MORRISTOWN HISTORICAL SOCIETY
STATEMENT OF INCOME, EXPENSES AND TRANSFERS

	General Fund	Plant Fund	Total All Funds
Income	$100,000	$8,000	$108,000
Expenses:			
Other than depreciation	(90,000)		(90,000)
Depreciation	(5,000)		(5,000)
Excess of income over expenses...........	5,000	8,000	13,000
Transfer of depreciation to plant fund	5,000	(5,000)	—
Excess of income over expenses after			
transfer...........................	$ 10,000	$3,000	$ 13,000

* If a Statement of Changes in Fund Balances is used, this transfer would be shown on that statement rather than on the Statement of Income and Expenses as illustrated here. See Chapter 5.

CORVALLIS Y.M.C.A.

STATEMENT OF INCOME AND EXPENSES
(Condensed)

	Year Ending December 31,	
	1973	1974
Income (in total)	$721,000	$767,000
Expenses:		
Other than depreciation	676,000	662,000
Depreciation	33,000	35,000
Total expenses	709,000	697,000
Excess of income over expenses	$ 12,000	$ 70,000

BALANCE SHEET
(Condensed)

	December 31,	
	1973	1974
Current assets (in total)	$ 68,000	$ 78,000
Investments in marketable securities at cost (market value $135,000 in 1973 and $183,000 in 1974)	132,000	176,000
Fixed assets:		
Land	50,000	50,000
Building	450,000	450,000
Equipment	120,000	130,000
Total	620,000	630,000
Less—Accumulated depreciation	(106,000)	(141,000)
Net fixed assets	514,000	489,000
Total assets	$714,000	$743,000
Liabilities (in total)	$ 89,000	$ 48,000
Fund balance (in total)	625,000	695,000
	$714,000	$743,000

Fig. 7–1. An example of the financial statements of an organization that records depreciation.

Things would be simpler if the depreciation charge were included directly in the plant fund and not shown as a transfer. The principal reason why this is usually not done is that the organization wants to show depreciation in the general fund to match income and costs. Here is how the statement would look if the depreciation were included directly in the plant fund:

MORRISTOWN HISTORICAL SOCIETY
STATEMENT OF INCOME AND EXPENSES

	General Fund	Plant Fund	Total All Funds
Income	$100,000	$8,000	$108,000
Expenses:			
Other than depreciation.	(90,000)		(90,000)
Depreciation		(5,000)	(5,000)
Excess of income over expenses	$ 10,000	$3,000	$ 13,000

This simplifies the presentation. Furthermore, in a columnar approach the reader's attention is probably going to focus primarily on the "total all funds" column, and the figures are exactly the same for both presentations in this column.

The real confusion occurs when instead of preparing the statements in a columnar approach, separate statements are prepared for each of the funds, as was illustrated on pages 36 and 37. It is difficult for the reader to fully understand transfers between funds. This is particularly true with depreciation because the concept of transferring depreciation back and forth is a difficult one to comprehend.

Because of these problems of presentation, it is recommended that whenever depreciation expense is going to be shown in the general fund, all fixed assets should also be included in this same fund. This means there would be no separate plant fund and thus there would be no need to transfer depreciation between funds. This greatly simplifies the financial statement presentation. This approach is the one recommended by the hospital Audit Guide * and is illustrated on page 253.

DIRECT WRITE-OFF OF FIXED ASSETS CAPITALIZED

Some organizations capitalize fixed-asset purchases but do not write off such assets through regular depreciation charges in the Statement of Income and Expense. Instead they continue to

---

* In 1972 the Committee on Health Care Institutions of The American Institute of Certified Public Accountants issued an Audit Guide recommending auditing and accounting standards to be followed by independent auditors in making examinations of hospitals. This Guide is discussed in Chapter 15.

carry these assets in the Balance Sheet at their original cost. Where this approach is followed, it may still be necessary to periodically write-down the carrying value of these assets so that the Balance Sheet is not overstated.

There are two approaches for handling this write-down in value. The first is to directly reduce both the asset carrying value and the fund balance by the amount of the write-down. Under this approach the write-down does not appear at all in the Statement of Income and Expense. The write-down would appear in a Statement of Changes in Fund Balance.* This is the approach followed in the 1973 AICPA Audit Guide for Colleges and Universities.

The other approach is to show the write-down in the Statement of Income and Expense, appropriately labeled. Here is how this latter approach would appear.

MORRISTOWN HISTORICAL SOCIETY
STATEMENT OF INCOME AND EXPENSES

Income		$100,000
Expenses:		
Operating expenses	$90,000	
Write-down of worn-out office equipment and automobile	3,500	93,500
Excess of income over expenses...................		$ 6,500

This second approach is the one preferred by the author because the reader is clearly shown all expenses in one statement. If the write-down were made directly to the fund balance, the reader is not as likely to know the total expense of the organization. At the same time, if this second approach is followed, the organization should rethink its policy of not providing depreciation. The advantage of regular depreciation charges is just that— it is regular, and no one year is charged with a disproportionately high amount of expense.

---

* If a Statement of Changes in Fund Balance is not used, the write-down could appear directly on the Balance Sheet itself, in the fund balance section (see Figure 7–2).

DEPRECIATION ON THE WRITE-OFF, THEN
CAPITALIZE METHOD

If the organization follows the "write-off, then capitalize" method, discussed in Chapter 6, fixed assets are written off in the Statement of Income and Expense when purchased and then capitalized on the Balance Sheet. In this case it is not appropriate to make a charge for depreciation on the income statement since the asset was written off when purchased. But the Balance Sheet amount should be reduced from time to time to reflect any decrease in value of the fixed assets. What must be done is to record the reduction of the fixed-asset amount directly on the Balance Sheet. Figure 7–2 shows the Balance Sheet of the Rathskeller Youth Center where a direct reduction in asset values is made. The figures used are the same figures used in Chapter 6 (Figure 6–3). Since the Statement of Income is not affected by this direct write-down, the statement shown in Figure 6–3 is still applicable.

It should be observed that the "write-off" has been reflected as a direct adjustment of the fund balance because the write-off cannot be reflected on the Statement of Income and Expense since the asset was previously expensed when purchased. If the organization presents a Statement of Changes in Fund Balances, this write-off would appear on that statement. All of this is confusing to many, and it is partly because of the depreciation problem that the write-off, then capitalize method for recording fixed assets is not recommended.

FUNDING DEPRECIATION

Some organizations in addition to depreciating their fixed assets also set aside cash to be used for subsequent replacement of their fixed assets. This is referred to as "funding" the depreciation. All that is involved in this funding is the physical segregation of cash, often in a separate savings account. If the organization does not have a separate plant fund, the only bookkeeping entry would be to record the movement of cash from one

RATHSKELLER YOUTH CENTER

BALANCE SHEET

	December 31, 1973	December 31, 1974
Assets:		
Cash	$ 2,000	$ 4,000
Pledges receivable	6,500	6,700
Land and building............................	90,000	90,000
Building alterations...........................	25,000	25,000
Furniture and equipment	10,000	13,000
Total assets	$133,500	$138,700
Liabilities:		
Accrued salaries	$ 3,000	$ 2,000
Accounts payable	400	100
Total liabilities	3,400	2,100
Fund balance:		
Beginning of year	112,000	130,100
Excess of income over expenses	3,100	3,500
Building and equipment capitalized	25,000	5,000
Write-off of worn-out equipment	(10,000)	(2,000)
End of year.................................	130,100	136,600
Total liabilities and fund balance	$133,500	$138,700

Fig. 7–2. An example of a Balance Sheet for an organization that periodically writes off fixed assets in the Balance Sheet as a direct reduction of the fund balance.

bank account to the other. The Balance Sheet would probably show this segregation, as follows:

BALANCE SHEET
(In Part)

Assets:	
Cash	$15,000
Savings account (for replacement of equipment).	10,000
Receivables	10,000
Equipment (net of accumulated depreciation	
of $10,000)	40,000
Total assets	$75,000

At the time the equipment is replaced, the amount of cash in the savings account applicable to this equipment would be used toward the cost of replacement equipment.* All that has been done is to segregate the cash as a matter of convenience. The only advantage of this "funding" is that cash has been physically set aside, and will be less likely to be used on other things. This technique is primarily a form of discipline.

Separate Plant Fund

Sometimes depreciation will be charged in the plant fund *and* a transfer of cash made from the general fund to the plant fund to fund the depreciation. When this is done, the effect is to transfer part of the net worth of the general fund to the plant fund. This can be very confusing, particularly if separate statements are presented for the general fund and the plant fund. If, on the other hand, the statements are shown in columnar form, the reader can see what has happened. The following condensed income statement shows depreciation in the plant fund and the transfer of an equal amount of the fund balance (in the form of cash) from the general fund to the plant fund:

MORRISTOWN HISTORICAL SOCIETY

STATEMENT OF INCOME, EXPENSES, AND CHANGES IN FUND BALANCES

	General Fund	Plant Fund	Total All Funds
Income	$100,000	$ 8,000	$108,000
Expenses:			
Other than depreciation	(90,000)		(90,000)
Depreciation		(5,000)	(5,000)
Excess of income over expenses	10,000	3,000	13,000
Fund balance, beginning of year	50,000	100,000	150,000
Transfer to plant fund	(5,000)	5,000	—
Fund balance, end of year	$ 55,000	$108,000	$163,000

Another possibility is that the organization will record depreciation in the general fund and then transfer this depreciation to the plant fund in the manner illustrated on page 76, *and* also

---

* It should be noted, however, that because of inflation or technological advances the setting aside of funds equal to depreciation on an historical cost basis will probably not cover the cost of replacement.

"fund" the depreciation in the manner illustrated above. If this were done, the combination would look like this:

MORRISTOWN HISTORICAL SOCIETY

STATEMENT OF INCOME, EXPENSES, AND CHANGES IN FUND BALANCES

	General Fund	Plant Fund	Total All Funds
Income	$100,000	$ 8,000	$108,000
Expenses:			
Other than depreciation	(90,000)		(90,000)
Depreciation	(5,000)		(5,000)
Excess of income over expenses	5,000	8,000	13,000
Fund balance, beginning of year	50,000	100,000	150,000
Transfer of depreciation expense to			
plant fund	5,000	(5,000)	—
Transfer of assets to plant fund	(5,000)	5,000	—
Fund balance, end of year	$ 55,000	$108,000	$163,000

The effect of these transfers is a wash as far as "excess of income after transfers" is concerned. However, often the board will not transfer an amount equal to the depreciation. There is no reason why both transfers can't be netted for statement presentation. If, as in this instance, they net out to zero, no transfer need be shown at all. The entries would still be made on the books but to show both transfers in the statement would be confusing to most readers.

The use of "funding" techniques for depreciation is acceptable under present usage but the author feels the complexities, particularly when a separate plant fund is involved, outweigh the advantages. Therefore this approach is not recommended.

TRANSFERS OF REPLACEMENT FUNDS TO THE PLANT FUND

Some organizations do *not* provide depreciation at all in the income statement but, instead, transfer an amount (usually cash) from the general fund to the plant fund as a "replacement fund" to build up cash for future acquisitions. As in the preceding example, this transfer is not an expense but represents a transfer of part of the fund balance of the general fund to the separate plant fund. Here is an example.

MORRISTOWN HISTORICAL SOCIETY

STATEMENT OF INCOME, EXPENSES, AND CHANGES IN FUND BALANCES

	General Fund	Plant Fund	Total All Funds
Income	$100,000	$ 8,000	$108,000
Less expenses (excludes depreciation)	(90,000)		(90,000)
Excess of income over expenses............	10,000	8,000	18,000
Fund balance, beginning of year	50,000	100,000	150,000
Transfer to plant fund replacement fund	(5,000)	5,000	–
Fund balance, end of year	$ 55,000	$113,000	$168,000

The amount transferred to the plant fund builds up over the years and represents a fund from which future purchases or replacement of present buildings and equipment can be made. The amount of this transfer can vary from year to year. The board will often establish a policy to transfer amounts exactly equal to a charge for depreciation although no depreciation has been charged against income. The effect on the "general fund" *balance* in such circumstances is exactly the same as though depreciation had been taken. The difference is that the reported excess of income over expenses includes no charge for depreciation.

The use of a replacement fund, while acceptable, is not recommended. If the board deems it prudent to set aside funds for future replacement, this suggests it should be depreciating its assets. While replacement cost may be greater than the original cost being depreciated, depreciation should still be taken and charged against income each year. To the extent that the board wants to set aside additional funds for replacement plant use it may do so, but such amounts should not be confused with depreciation.

It should also be noted that the use of a separate plant fund is not recommended. If this recommendation is followed, then the practice of setting up a replacement fund becomes academic since such a fund would remain part of the general fund balance.

CONCLUSION

Once the question of capitalizing or writing off fixed assets when purchased has been resolved, the question of whether to depreciate the assets recorded on the Balance Sheet is also largely resolved. If the asset has been written off, no depreciation is appropriate. If fixed assets have been recorded and the organization wants to follow "generally accepted accounting principles," depreciation accounting is required for most nonprofit organizations. Even where depreciation accounting is not mandatory, it is clearly applicable where the organization must look to replacing its assets periodically from current income, the organization sells goods or services to the public, or cost reimbursement from a government agency or organization is involved. This means depreciation should be recorded by most nonprofit organizations that capitalize fixed assets.

Appendix A–5 provides a table that summarizes the alternatives and the acceptability of each.

8

Investment Income,
Gains and Losses,
and Endowment Funds

In the last few years increasing attention has been given to investments and rate of return on endowment funds, particularly in view of inflation and rising costs. Traditionally, organizations with endowments tended to invest largely in fixed income bonds, or preferred stocks. When common stocks were acquired only the bluest of blue chips were considered. Recently, more and more nonprofit organizations are reversing this dependence on fixed income issues and are investing sizable portions of their portfolios in common stock of less quality but with greater potential for growth. This is resulting in substantially less current income from interest and dividends. These organizations feel this will be more than offset over a period of years by capital gains resulting from both inflation and real growth. However, this new emphasis has created accounting and reporting problems. The purpose of this chapter is to discuss the accounting principles that are generally followed by nonprofit organizations in recording their investments in endowment and other restricted and unrestricted funds. The accounting implications of the new emphasis on capital gains is also covered.

ACCOUNTING PRINCIPLES

In discussing the accounting principles followed for investment income, it is important to distinguish between the two types of income which arise from investment. The first is interest and dividends, and this is what is usually referred to as investment income. The second is the capital gain (or loss) arising at the time investments are sold. Traditionally, gains or losses have not been thought of as "income" but rather as part of principal. In the discussion that follows the accounting principles applicable to each of these two types of income will be discussed.

Investment Income on Unrestricted Funds

All dividends and interest income on unrestricted funds, including board-designated funds, should be recorded in a general fund Statement of Income and Expenses or in a combined Statement of Income, Expenses, and Changes in Fund Balances. It is not appropriate to record such income directly in a separate Statement of Changes in Fund Balances; it must be shown in a Statement of Income and Expenses so the reader will be fully aware of its receipt.

Unrestricted Investment Income on Endowment Funds

Unrestricted investment income on endowment funds should be reported directly in the general fund, in the same manner as other unrestricted investment income. It is not appropriate to report such unrestricted investment income in the endowment fund and then to transfer it to the general fund. The reason for this is that only donor-restricted funds are reported in the endowment fund. If the terms of the donor's endowment gift are that the income is automatically unrestricted income, then this income is never restricted income. This presentation applies even where a columnar statement presentation is used in which all funds are shown side by side.

Some argue that with a columnar statement format it is acceptable to report the income first in the endowment fund column and then to transfer it to the general fund, perhaps showing the transfer in the income section rather than below the caption "excess of income over expenses." Their argument is that in this way it is easier for the reader to see the total endowment income in relation to the size of the endowment fund, and thus the reader can form a judgment on management's investment skill. While this argument has merit, there is too much chance of the reader being confused when a transfer is shown. The reader can still be shown, in the general fund, the amount of investment income arising from endowment funds, as distinct from other sources, by showing this income as a separate line item in the income statement. (See Figure 4–1.)

Restricted Investment Income

The income from certain endowment funds, and usually from all other restricted funds, is restricted for use of a specified purpose. This income should be reported directly in the appropriate restricted fund. For example, the investment income from some endowment funds is to be used for specified purposes. In this situation the investment income should be reported directly in the fund for specified purposes and not reported first in the endowment fund and then transferred. In some instances it will be appropriate to add such income back to the endowment fund. For example, some donors will specify that the investment income is to be added to endowment principal for a period of years, after which time the income and, perhaps, the accumulated income and principal will become unrestricted. It is important to keep track of all these restrictions and to handle each according to the terms provided.

Gains or Losses on Endowment Funds

Traditionally, gains or losses on endowment investments have not been considered income but adjustments of the principal of the fund. Thus, gains or losses on endowment funds are usually added back to the principal of that fund and all of the restrictions associated with the principal are considered applicable to these gains. Presumably the theory for this treatment is that, with inflation, capital gains largely reflect a price-level adjustment of the original principal.* In addition many lawyers have felt that, historically, this treatment was required by law.

As a result, capital gains or losses on endowment funds are usually not reported in the general or current fund. Instead they are reported in the endowment fund, either in a Statement of Income and Expenses, or, more often, in a separate Statement of Changes in Fund Balances. The author's preference is to reflect such gains in a combined Statement of Income, Expenses, and Changes in Fund Balances with the gains shown as part of income. An example of this type of presentation is shown in Figure 12–1.

It is argued by many that capital gains are not income and should not be shown as income, and therefore must be shown in the Changes in Fund Balance section of the statements. This approach, while acceptable under present usage,† is not recommended. As is discussed more fully on page 94, in many ways gains on investments are income in the same sense that interest and dividends are income, except where by law or donor restriction they are required to be added to principal. As such the reader has a right to know the amount of such gains. When gains are included in the Changes in Fund Balance section of the statement, the effect is often to bury them. The reader has a right to know what the total excess of income over expenses including gains was. He should not have to look at two or more statements, or, where only a Statement of Changes in Fund Balances is used, to have to interpret the meaning of the various items causing the fund balance to change.

Some organizations do not keep track of the gains or losses by individual "name" fund within the endowment fund, but place all such gains (or losses) in a separate fund within the endowment fund with the title "Gains or Losses on Investments." This fund is accumulated over a period of years in the endowment fund and effectively is kept in perpetuity.

---

* It should be noted that in the case of bonds and other fixed income securities inflation is usually ignored. If inflation were considered, a portion of the fixed income would have to be retained as an addition to principal. This approach, while logical, is not followed, and would not be considered an acceptable approach at this time.

† Except for voluntary health and welfare organizations. See Figure 13–1.

As is discussed later on in this chapter, there is now some question whether gains on endowment funds are legally restricted or not. As is noted, a number of states now permit nonprofit organizations to include realized and in some instances unrealized gains as part of income from restricted funds. Where it is determined that gains are legally unrestricted, then all such gains should be reported in the same manner as the income from that fund. In the case of endowments where the income is unrestricted, the gains would then also be unrestricted, and they should be reported directly in the general fund.

Gains or Losses on Unrestricted Funds

Gains or losses on board-designated endowment funds are not restricted except as the board might designate. Where restrictions have been placed on funds voluntarily by the board, it is essential that the absence of externally imposed restrictions be clearly indicated and gains or losses on such unrestricted funds should always be recorded directly in the general fund.

Unrealized Gains and Losses

So far our discussion on gains or losses has been focused on realized gains or losses. Gains and losses are realized in an accounting sense only when the investments involved have actually been sold. What about unrealized gains and losses—increases or decreases in market value of investments over their original cost?

Prior to 1973, investments could only be carried at cost.* Under this method realized gains are not recognized until such time as the investment is sold and the gain "realized"; at the same time, under certain circumstances unrealized losses were recognized. In 1973 two Audit Guides † were issued which indicated these organizations could carry their investments at market. While the Guides are addressed to only two specific types of or-

---

* The 1967 *AICPA Guide for Audits of Voluntary Health and Welfare Organizations* did indicate that there may be valid reasons for recording investments at market but it gave no examples. Very few such organizations carried their investments at market.

† Voluntary Health and Welfare Organizations and Colleges and Universities (see Chapters 13 and 14).

ganizations, effectively all types of nonprofit organizations can now follow this practice (other than hospitals; see page 260). Therefore, nonprofit organizations have the option of carrying their investments at market or at cost, and therefore of recognizing gains (and losses) on a continuing basis.

Investments Carried at Cost. Where an organization carries its investments at cost and not at market, gains can be recorded only when they are realized. The theory behind this is that until such time as an investment is actually sold there can be no complete assurance that the market value of the investment won't decline to or even below the original cost. Therefore no gain is recorded until such time as the investment is sold and the gain is realized by conversion to cash.

On the other hand, if the market value of an investment is less than cost, consideration must be given to writing down the carrying values to the market value. Needless to say, there is a great deal of reluctance to write-down investments as the market prices decline. Yet many organizations, even those with substantial bond positions, have recently discovered that market values go down as well as up, and sometimes the value can decline substantially.

The question is frequently asked whether marketable securities must be written down if it is believed that the decline is merely "temporary." This is difficult to answer. Certainly, market values fluctuate both up and down. It is not the intent of this principle to require a write-down every time market values go below the cost of an investment. The general principle is that if an investment's carrying value is permanently "impaired" either a provision for loss should be set up or the investment written down. To answer the question of what constitutes "permanent" impairment, it is necessary to look at the nature of the individual securities. If they are being held temporarily or if, based on past buying and selling experience, the probability is that many of the individual stocks or bonds will be sold within the next year or two, then a provision for decline in market value should be set up. This is optional, on the other hand, if the investments are bonds which, based on past experience, can reasonably be expected to be held until maturity, or if the decline in stocks appears truly temporary.

For example, in the case of stocks, if the loss is caused by a general downward movement in the stock market, as distinct from a downward movement in the price of the particular stock held, there may be less reason to be concerned. A key factor is whether it can be reasonably expected that the organization will sustain a loss.

Where it appears necessary to write down part of the carrying value of the investments, the provision for decline should appear in the Statement of Income, Expenses, and Changes in Fund Balance in the same place in the statement as realized gains or losses are presented (see below). Perhaps a caption should be used such as "Provision for decline in market value of investments." The provision set up in this manner should be disclosed in the Balance Sheet and netted against the carrying value of the investments.

In subsequent periods actual losses when realized would be charged to the provision. When it is apparent that the remaining portion of the provision is no longer required, it should be reversed in exactly the same manner as set up, i.e., as a credit in the Statement of Income, Expense, and Changes in Fund Balances with a caption "Add reserve for decline in market value no longer needed."

One final observation. There is a tendency to resist setting up a provision when market prices go down since this publicly acknowledges a loss. This is particularly so when one believes the decline is temporary. The alternative is to bury one's head in the sand and to pretend there is no loss. This often has an even more unfortunate result—inaction with respect to investment decisions. If a loss has already been recognized there will be no reason not to sell at the appropriate time.

Investments Carried at Market. Where an organization carries its investments at market, it records the increase or decrease in unrealized gains or losses for the period in the Statement of Income, Expenses, and Changes in Fund Balances in the same manner and in the same place in the statement as it records realized gains or losses. It is important to recognize that it is not permissible to report realized gains (or losses) in one place in the statement and then to report the unrealized portion in an entirely separate place in the statement. Once the organization elects to carry investments at market it is acknowledging that there is no effective distinction between realized and unrealized gains. This is shown below.

Presentation of Gains or Losses in the Financial Statements

The presentation of gains in the Statement of Income, Expenses, and Changes in Fund Balances is fairly straightforward. Gains or losses can be shown in the income section of the statement (as illustrated above), or toward the bottom of the statement to separate investment income including gains from operating income. Sometimes investment income excluding gains or losses is shown in the income section but gains or losses are shown toward the bottom of the statement but before the caption "Excess of income over expenses." This splitting of investment income and gains is acceptable but not recommended by the author. As is discussed in the next section, organizations are increasingly looking to the total return, which includes gains.

Presentation Where Investments Carried at Market. Where investments are carried at market, the increase or decrease in market value would be shown as illustrated below:

STATEMENT OF INCOME, EXPENSES, AND CHANGES IN FUND BALANCE

Income:
Contributions	$ 55,000	
Program activities	115,000	
Interest and dividends	50,000	
Net increase (decrease) in carrying value of investments	(20,000)	
Total income		$200,000
Expenses (in total)		(165,000)
Excess of income over expenses		35,000
Fund balance, beginning of year		100,000
Fund balance, end of year		$135,000

BALANCE SHEET
(In Part)

Cash	$ 60,000
Investments at market (cost $275,000)	350,000
Other assets	60,000
Total assets	$470,000

Observe in presenting unrealized gains or losses in the Statement of Income, Expenses, and Changes in Fund Balances, there appears little purpose in reporting *realized* gains or losses separately from *unrealized* gains or losses. In fact, to report the two separately can result in an awkward presentation.

For example, assume an organization sells for $130 an investment that was purchased in a prior year at a cost of $100, but which had a market value at the beginning of the year of $150. From an economic standpoint, the organization had a loss during the year of $20 (carrying value of $150 vs. sales price of $130). Yet, from the standpoint of reporting realized gains, there is a gain of $30 (cost of $100 vs. sales price of $130). If the realized gain were separately reported, the presentation would be:

Realized gain	$ 30
Less gain previously recognized	(50)
Net loss	$ (20)

This presentation is likely to confuse most readers. Since there appears to be no real significance to reporting these two portions separately, the following presentation would appear more appropriate:

Net increase (decrease) in carrying value of investments	$ (20)

FIXED RATE OF RETURN CONCEPT

As was noted above, one of the traditional principles followed by nonprofit organizations having endowment funds is that realized gains are added to the principal of the endowment fund, and are not recognized as "income." Only dividends and interest are considered income. This creates a dilemma. If an organization's $1 million endowment fund is invested in 5 per cent bonds, income would be $50,000 a year. If, instead, it were invested in common stocks, paying 2 per cent in dividends but which could be expected to double in value every ten years, annual income would be $20,000. Obviously over the ten-year period (if the doubling assumption is correct) the organization will realize far more from the common stocks than from the bonds:

	Common Stocks		Bonds
Interest/dividends over 10 years	$ 200,000		$500,000
Increase in value over 10 years	$1,000,000	or	—
	$1,200,000		$500,000
Average per year	$ 120,000		$ 50,000

Under traditional accounting practices if the organization wants maximum current income, the "bonds" in this illustration are the correct choice of investment. But from an economic standpoint, it is the wrong choice. Should the accounting treatment influence an economic or investment decision?

Interfund Transfer of Realized Gains

A number of universities have adopted an accounting approach to this problem which involves a transfer to the general fund of a portion of the previously realized and unrealized gains from the endowment and board-designated endowment fund. The amount thus transferred is then used for current operations. Typically the board determines the amount of the transfer by first deciding what rate of return it could achieve if it emphasized interest and dividends rather than capital growth. This rate of return is often selected as the "spending rate." This "spending rate" is then compared to the actual dividends and interest income. The deficiency is the amount transferred.

For example, using the illustration above, if the board felt confident that over a period of time its common stock investments would realize a 5 per cent return after considering inflation, the amount of dividends plus "transfer" should equal 5 per cent of the $1 million, or $50,000. Figure 8–1 shows how this transfer

	Current Operating Fund	Endowment Fund
Income:		
Program income	$100,000	
Dividend income	20,000	
Realized gains.		$ 50,000
Total income.	120,000	50,000
Expenses.	(140,000)	
Excess (deficit) of income over expenses	(20,000)	50,000
Fund balance, beginning of year	50,000	1,000,000
	30,000	1,050,000
Transfer of a portion of realized gains		
from endowment fund.	30,000	(30,000)
Fund balance, end of year	$ 60,000	$1,020,000

Fig. 8–1. An example of how the transfer from the endowment fund to the current operating fund should be presented under the total return approach.

would be presented in both the current operating fund and the endowment fund.

Transfer Must Not Be Reported in the Income Section. Note that in Figure 8–1 the transfer from the endowment fund is presented in the changes in fund balance section, below the caption "Excess of income over expenses." Some organizations have—incorrectly —presented the transfer in the income section. This incorrect presentation is shown in Figure 8–2, and is not acceptable under generally accepted accounting principles.*

Many readers have difficulty understanding why accountants will not permit this transfer to be shown as income since the amounts transferred will be used for current purposes just as though they were dividends and interest. What troubles many accountants is that inclusion of the transfer in the income section (Figure 8–2) allows the board to arbitrarily determine what its excess of income over expenses will be. If the board were to consistently transfer all of the legally available realized gains rather than only an arbitrarily determined portion, most accountants would not be troubled by reflecting such amounts as income.

* See pages 186 and 234.

	Current Operating Fund	Endowment Fund
Income:		
Program income	$100,000	
Dividend income	20,000	
Realized gains.		$　50,000
Transfer of portion of realized gains		
from endowment fund.	30,000	(30,000)
Total income.	150,000	20,000
Expenses.	(140,000)	
Excess of income over expenses	10,000	20,000
Fund balance, beginning of year	50,000	1,000,000
Fund balance, end of year	$　60,000	$1,020,000

Fig. 8–2. **An example of an unacceptable presentation in which the transfer from the endowment fund is reported in the income section of the current operating fund.**

It is when the board decides to transfer only a portion that it appears to the accountant that there may be an attempt at income manipulation. This is not to suggest that the method which the board uses in determining its "spending rate" is not rational, but it is still arbitrary. For this reason, when the board decides to transfer part—but not all—of such gains, the presentation of this transfer should be shown outside of the income section in the fund balance section, as shown in Figure 8–1.

It should be emphasized, however, that accountants are not trying to tell the board how to handle their investments or how much of their resources should be utilized for current operations. This is outside the accountant's purview or interest. However, it is within his sphere to indicate how the board's action—in this case the transfer of funds—should be presented in the financial statements so as not to mislead the reader. Looking at Figure 8–1 no one can misinterpret the results of the year's activities in the current operating fund—a deficit of $20,000. However, if the reader were looking at Figure 8–2 it would be an unusual reader who would not think that the current operating fund had an excess of $10,000.

Fixed Return from an Independent Investment Fund

Because of the popularity of the total return approach, several independent investment management funds have been established which provide the nonprofit organization a flat "spending rate" amount each year. These are set up in much the same way as mutual funds. Probably the best known of these independent investment funds is *The Common Fund* in which a number of colleges have invested. If the institution elects, The Common Fund will return annually 5 per cent of the market value of the institution's share of the Fund rather than actual dividends, interest, and realized gains.

Accounting for Fixed Annual Payment. The accounting for this 5 per cent return must be handled in exactly the same manner as it would be if the organization were making its own investments in its own separate endowment fund. It is not acceptable to record the full 5 per cent payment as dividend income. This means that it is necessary for the organization to know how much its share was of the actual dividends and realized gains of the outside investment fund. Its share of the actual dividends is recorded as general fund income and its share of the actual total realized gains is recorded as gains in the endowment fund, without regard to the 5 per cent cash payment received from the investment fund. The carrying value of the organization's share of this investment fund is thus increased or decreased to the investment fund's cost basis just as though there were no separate investment fund.

The excess of the 5 per cent cash payment over the dividends and interest earned represents a return of a portion of the organization's investment in this outside fund. If the organization wishes to utilize this excess for general purposes, it should account for this excess as a transfer from the endowment fund to the current operating fund, as in Figure 8–1. In short, the accounting for the dividends and interest and realized gains is completely independent of the 5 per cent cash payment. It is dependent on the underlying actual results of the investment fund.

Here is an example. Assume that the organization described above makes a $1 million cash investment in an outside investment fund, which constitutes 10 per cent of the total independent investment fund's assets. Here is the activity for the first year:

	Outside Investment Fund	Our Organization's Share (10%)
Balance beginning	$10,000,000	$1,000,000
Dividend income	200,000	20,000
Realized gains	500,000	50,000
Less 5% payments	(500,000)	(50,000)
Balance ending	$10,200,000	$1,020,000
Unrealized appreciation	$ 500,000	$ 50,000

The appropriate reporting for our organization, assuming it carries its investments at cost, would be the same as contained in Figure 8–1.

Accounting Where Investments Are Carried at Market. If the organization followed the practice of recording its investments at market, then $50,000 would be recorded in the endowment fund as realized gains and in addition $50,000 would also be recorded as unrealized appreciation. The $30,000 transfer would again be handled as in Figure 8–1.

Inflation Index To Protect Principal

It should be noted that the discussion so far has not touched on the budgeting considerations that an organization's board may consider in establishing the amounts to be transferred from the endowment fund to the current operating fund. The most common approach is the "spending rate" approach (described above) in which the board decides on the amount to be spent in total and then, after deducting actual dividends and interest, transfers the balance. It is referred to as the spending rate because often it is arrived at—in part at least—by determining what income could be achieved if emphasis were placed on current income rather than on growth.

Inflation Protection Approach. The author believes this spending rate approach is backward. The more appropriate approach is for the board to first establish the rate to which the endowment fund must be increased to protect it from inflation. Transfers to the general fund should then be made only to the extent that gains exceed the amount which has to be added to principal to protect it from inflation.

There is a significant difference between the spending rate approach and this inflation protection approach. The spending rate approach may or may not protect the principal against inflation, depending on the assumptions used in arriving at the spending rate. Yet the first concern of the board should be to protect the principal against inflation. Only if there are gains in excess of this requirement should transfers be made to the current operating fund.

Figure 8–3 shows an example of how an inflation index could be used to determine the amount to be transferred. Assuming inflation of 5 per cent a year, again our original principal of $1 million, 2 per cent dividends, and realized gains of $50,000, $40,000, and $120,000 in each of three years, the amount which would be transferred in each of three years would be calculated as shown in Figure 8–3.

	1973	1974	1975
Principal at beginning of year, adjusted for inflation	$1,000,000	$1,050,000	$1,102,500
Add inflation factor of, say, 5%.	50,000	52,500	55,125
Principal end of year as adjusted for inflation	$1,050,000	$1,102,500	$1,157,625
Dividends	$ 20,000	$ 20,000	$ 20,000
Realized gains	50,000	40,000	120,000
Total	70,000	60,000	140,000
Less amount retained as an adjustment for inflation	(50,000)	(52,500)	(55,125)
Balance, for current operations	$ 20,000	$ 7,500	$ 84,875

Fig. 8–3. An example showing how the amount of the transfer would be calculated under the total return approach using an inflation protection approach.

In this illustration a constant inflation rate of 5 per cent has been assumed. In actual practice, the rate would vary and the board would, of course, peg its rate to the appropriate index presumably published by the government.

The advantage of this approach is that all income is transferred except for the portion which must be retained as an inflation adjustment to protect the value of the endowment fund. This means that the full impact of the board's investment decisions will be felt, whether conservative or speculative.

Income does fluctuate because of the timing of realized capital gains. Notice that in Figure 8–3 only $7,500 of income is available in 1974. Possibly one refinement is to provide that the amount of the transfer should be averaged over a three-year period. This would have the effect of dampening large changes due to the timing of the realized gains.

Market Value Approach. Some nonprofit organizations carry their endowment fund investments at market value and this same inflation index approach can be followed by these organizations. Carrying investment at market, of course, eliminates the fluctuation due to the timing of realized gains. At the same time, it should be noted that a general stock market decline at the end

	1973	1974	1975
Dividends	$ 20,000	$ 20,000	$ 20,000
Realized gains	50,000	40,000	120,000
Unrealized gains—			
increase (decrease)	50,000	80,000	(20,000)
Total	120,000	140,000	120,000
Less amount retained as an adjustment for inflation			
(see Figure 8–3)	(50,000)	(52,500)	(55,125)
Balance, for current operations	$ 70,000	$ 87,500	$ 64,875

Fig. 8–4. An example showing how the amount of the transfer would be calculated using an inflation protection approach and recognizing unrealized gains in the calculation.

of any one year could also result in a loss rather than income. Again, a three-year moving average might become appropriate.

Most nonprofit organizations carry their investments at cost, but there is no reason why a board couldn't adopt the market value approach solely for the purpose of determining the amount of realized gains to be transferred. If this were done, the calculation shown in Figure 8–3 would also be made but instead of using only the amount of realized gains, unrealized gains or losses would also be added or deducted. Figure 8–4 shows how this would be handled.

Presentation in the Financial Statement. Under present accounting rules, the board can follow either of the approaches discussed above for determining the amount of realized gains or losses to transfer, but the transfer must not be reported as income. This means that the amounts reported as income in the current operating fund calculated as shown in Figure 8–3 or 8–4 would be the amounts of actual dividends and the balance would have to be reported as a transfer. In some years it is possible that such divi-

	Current Operating Fund		
	1973	1974	1975
Income:			
Program income	$ 100,000	$ 100,000	$ 100,000
Dividend income	20,000	20,000	20,000
Total	120,000	120,000	120,000
Expenses.	(140,000)	(140,000)	(140,000)
Excess of expense over income	(20,000)	(20,000)	(20,000)
Transfer of portion of realized gains from endowment funds			64,875
Transfer of portion of current operating fund to endowment fund to protect principal from inflation.		(12,500)	
Excess (deficit) of income and transfer over expenses	$ (20,000)	$ (32,500)	$ 44,875

Fig. 8–5. An illustration showing the presentation in the current operating fund of transfers which have been calculated using an inflation protection approach.

dends would exceed the amount available. When this happens a transfer must be made back to the endowment fund.* Figure 8–5 shows this presentation for the organization which calculates the amount of the transfer on the basis of *realized* gains only (as calculated in Figure 8–3).

May Realized Gains Be Legally Transferred?

Implicit in the above discussion is the assumption that at least part of the realized gains on funds donated to an organization for endowment purposes can, in fact, be transferred to the general operating fund of the organization. Is this a valid assumption?

Changing Attitude on Income Transfer. Over the years there has been a tendency to assume that the law requires endowment funds and the realized gains on the sales of endowment fund investments to be kept sacrosanct. There now appears to be some authoritative support for the view that the realized gains on endowment funds may also be transferred to the general fund. In 1969, in a widely publicized report to the Ford Foundation entitled "The Law and the Lore of Endowment Funds," W. L. Cary and C. B. Bright concluded:

> If the managers of endowment funds wish to seek long-term appreciation in their investments, the need of their institutions for current yield should not dissuade them. We find no authoritative support in the law for the widely held view that the realized gains of endowment funds can never be spent. Prudence would call for the retention of sufficient gains to maintain purchasing power in the face of inflation and to guard against potential losses, but subject to the standards which prudence dictates, the expenditure of gains should lie within the discretion of the institution's directors.

Latitude Under State Law. Subsequent to Cary and Bright's report, a number of states† have adopted legislation which spe-

---

* Some organizations might object to transferring to the endowment fund some of their dividend income. One modification might be to not make such transfers back to the endowment fund but instead to reduce future years' transfers to the current operating fund by the amount of such deficiencies. If this modification were followed, the 1975 transfer in Figure 8–4 would be $52,375 ($64,875 less $12,500).

† To date, the following states have passed legislation: California, Colorado, Connecticut, Illinois, Kansas, Maine, Maryland, Minnesota, New Hampshire, New Jersey, New York, Pennsylvania, Rhode Island, Tennesssee, Vermont, Virginia, and Washington. In addition, legislation has been introduced in a number of other states. The provisions of each state's legislation vary and the reader should consult legal counsel for the specific provisions applicable to his organization.

cifically permits most nonprofit organizations to include capital gains in usable income. In fact, the model uniform law provides that not only realized gains may be considered usable income but also *unrealized* gains.

Endowment Fund Distinction.   There is another important factor to consider. Many institutions, particularly colleges and universities, combine two types of endowment funds—board-designated endowment funds and true donor-restricted endowments. There is a great deal of difference between the two. In the first the restriction is internally and voluntarily created whereas in the other the restriction is donor-fixed.

There would appear to be no question that the board may transfer not only the realized gains but also the principal of board-designated endowments. After all, the board's designation was voluntary and it could therefore reverse its designation and transfer such funds to the general fund. Board-designated endowment funds usually constitute a substantial portion of the endowment funds of most large educational institutions.

9

Contributions, Pledges and Noncash Contributions

So far we have not discussed the problems of recording and reporting the principal resource most nonprofit organizations depend upon—contributions. At first it might appear that this is a fairly straightforward subject that would not involve significant difficulty. In fact the opposite is true. An organization can receive contributions with a wide range of restrictions attached. These must be properly recorded in the right fund and reported in such a way that the reader is fully aware of their receipt and restrictions. Some contributions are made in the form of pledges which will be paid off over a period of time. Accounting questions arise as to when such amounts should be recorded. Also there are a variety of noncash contributions that an organization can receive, ranging from marketable securities, buildings, and equipment, to contributed services. All of these present accounting and reporting problems to the organization.

UNRESTRICTED CONTRIBUTIONS

It was noted in Chapter 4 that all unrestricted contributions should be reported in the general fund. This principle is fairly well accepted and followed by most nonprofit organizations. What is not uniformly followed is the method of reporting such unrestricted contributions. Some organizations have followed the practice of adding unrestricted contributions directly to the fund balance either in a separate Statement of Changes in Fund Balances or in the fund balance section where a combined Statement of Income, Expenses, and Changes in Fund Balances is used. Others report some or all of their contributions directly in a board-designated endowment fund, and worse still, some report unrestricted contributions directly in the endowment fund as though such amounts were restricted. The result of all these practices is to make it difficult for the reader to recognize the amount and nature of contributions received. Often this is done in an attempt to convince the reader that the organization badly needs his contribution.

All unrestricted contributions should be reported in a Statement of Income and Expenses, or if a combined Statement of Income, Expenses, and Changes in Fund Balances is used, such unrestricted contributions should be shown before arriving at the "excess of income over expenses" caption. It is not acceptable to report unrestricted contributions in a separate statement of Changes in Fund Balances or to report such gifts directly in a board-designated endowment fund.

RESTRICTED CONTRIBUTIONS

Restricted contributions are often divided into two categories —contributions for "current" purposes and contributions for "noncurrent" purposes. The accounting and reporting practices are somewhat different for each type.

Noncurrent Restricted Contributions

Noncurrent restricted contributions are those that are given for a specific purpose other than to meet the current expenses of the organization. Examples of noncurrent contributions would be gifts to an endowment fund, or to a building fund. The distinction is that such gifts will not be used in the current operations of the organization to pay for services that it regularly carries out. The restrictions on the use of these gifts are always designated by the donor, and not by the board. Board-designated gifts are unrestricted gifts.

Noncurrent restricted contributions should be reported directly in the restricted fund designated by the donor. If a Statement of Income and Expenses is presented for the restricted fund, the income should be reported in that statement. Alternatively, if only a Statement of Changes in Fund Balances is presented, the gift would be shown in that statement. The author prefers the use of a combined statement with the title Statement of Income, Expenses, and Changes in Fund Balances. An example of this type of presentation is shown in Figure 9–1.

Another presentation would occur where a columnar approach is used. In this approach the activity of all funds is shown in a single statement with each fund being shown in a separate column. An example is shown in Chapter 12 (Figure 12–1) along with a discussion of the advantages and disadvantages of this type of presentation.

Restricted Contributions for "Current" Purposes

Restricted contributions for current purposes are contributions that can be used to meet the current expenses of the organization, although restricted to use for some specific purpose. Restricted contributions for current purposes are not as easily handled and cause difficult reporting problems. The difficulty arises because the contribution is for a "current" purpose activity which is normally a function of the general or unrestricted fund. If the contribution and the expenditure is reported in a current restricted fund statement, the reader has difficulty seeing all of the current activities of the organization since they are then reported in two places, in the general fund, and in the current restricted fund.

An illustration will show the reporting problems. The Johnstown Museum received a contribution of $50,000 to be used for salary costs of staff involved in a travelling exhibition which visits schools and brings museum activities to the children in the greater Johnstown area. In the first year only $40,000 of this $50,000 was expended for this purpose. The reporting problem relates principally with where to show the receipt and the related expenditure since this activity is an important function of the museum which should be clearly disclosed to the reader. Some of the reporting possibilities follow.

Reporting in the Current Restricted Fund. The first approach is to report both the receipt and the expenditure in only the restricted fund. This approach is the obvious one. Using the separate statement approach illustrated in Chapter 4, Figure 9–1 shows the Statement of Income, Expenses, and Changes in Fund Balances in condensed form for both the general fund and the restricted fund.

The major difficulty with this presentation is that salary costs are shown on two statements. The reader, looking only at the general fund statement, will not be aware of the significant amount of other "current" activities of the museum. If he is a

---

THE JOHNSTOWN MUSEUM

GENERAL FUND
STATEMENT OF INCOME, EXPENSES, AND
CHANGES IN FUND BALANCES
For the Year Ending June 30, 1974

Income:

Contributions	$ 20,000	
Other income	300,000	
		$320,000

Expenses:

Salaries	170,000	
All other	145,000	
		315,000
Excess of income over expenses		5,000
Fund balance, beginning of the year		100,000
Fund balance, end of the year		$105,000

CURRENT RESTRICTED FUND
STATEMENT OF CONTRIBUTIONS, EXPENSES,
AND CHANGES IN FUND BALANCES
For the Year Ending June 30, 1974

Contributions for travelling exhibition	$ 50,000
Less salaries for travelling exhibition	(40,000)
Excess of contributions over expenses	10,000
Fund balance, beginning of the year	20,000
Fund balance, end of the year	$ 30,000

Fig. 9–1. An example of statements showing current restricted contributions and expenses reported in a separate current restricted fund.

careful reader and looks at all statements, he will see the $40,000 expense on the restricted fund statement but, even then, he may not realize exactly how that expenditure relates to the $170,000 of salaries shown on the general fund statement.

At the same time this is clearly an accurate presentation of what has happened and is shown in typical fund accounting style. Accordingly, this presentation is an acceptable one, although it is not recommended.

Reporting as a Transfer to General Fund.   The second approach is to report the receipt in the restricted fund but then transfer the portion expended to the general fund. This overcomes the major disadvantage of the first approach since all salaries including the salaries for the travelling exhibition, are reported in the general fund. The transfer from the restricted fund is exactly the amount actually expended. The transfer is shown, as discussed in Chapter 5, after the caption "excess of income over expenses." Figure 9–2 shows how this approach would look.

As can be easily seen, this presentation is awkward. The transfer from the restricted fund has been handled, properly, as a transfer, and as a result it appears that the General Fund has a deficit of $35,000 during the year. Likewise, it appears that the restricted fund has an excess of $50,000. On the other hand, full salary costs are shown and the reader will see the total current activities of the museum. While this presentation is technically accurate (and thus acceptable) it is certainly not a recommended approach.

Reporting as a Transfer in the Income Section.   This next approach is to report the receipt in the restricted fund and then transfer the expended portion to the general fund but show the transfer in the income section of the general fund. This is the approach followed by many organizations * that present separate statements for each fund. Figure 9–3 shows how this presentation would appear.

In this presentation the general fund shows fairly clearly the expenditures during the period and the sources of revenue which

---

* This is the approach provided in the AICPA Audit Guides for colleges and universities and hospitals. See Chapters 14 and 15.

THE JOHNSTOWN MUSEUM

GENERAL FUND
STATEMENT OF INCOME, EXPENSES, AND
CHANGES IN FUND BALANCES
For the Year Ending June 30, 1974

Income:

Contributions	$ 20,000	
Other income	300,000	
Total		$320,000

Expenses:

Salaries	210,000	
All other	145,000	
Total		355,000
Excess of expenses over income		(35,000)
Fund balance, beginning of the year		100,000
Add transfer from restricted funds to offset salaries		
included above		40,000
Fund balance, end of the year		$105,000

CURRENT RESTRICTED FUND
STATEMENT OF CONTRIBUTIONS, TRANSFERS,
AND CHANGES IN FUND BALANCES
For the Year Ending June 30, 1974

Contribution for travelling exhibition	$ 50,000
Less: Transfer to general fund to offset salaries for travelling	
exhibition	(40,000)
Excess of contributions over transfer	10,000
Fund balance, beginning of the year	20,000
Fund balance, end of the year	$ 30,000

Fig. 9–2. An example of statements showing current restricted contributions transferred to the General Fund to the extent expended.

were used. The confusion which can result from showing a "transfer" has been eliminated, as well as the large excess of expenses over revenue shown in the preceding approach.

At the same time, note the change in title of the restricted fund statement; it is no longer a Statement of Contributions, Expenses and Changes in Fund Balances. It is only a Statement of Changes in Fund Balances. In this approach, the restricted contribution of $50,000 is added directly to the fund balance

THE JOHNSTOWN MUSEUM

GENERAL FUND
STATEMENT OF INCOME, EXPENSES, AND
CHANGES IN FUND BALANCES
For the Year Ending June 30, 1974

Income:

Unrestricted contributions	$ 20,000	
Current restricted contributions expended		
during period	40,000	
Other income	300,000	
Total		$360,000

Expenses:

Salaries	210,000	
All other	145,000	
Total		$355,000
Excess of income over expenses....................		5,000
Fund balance, beginning of the year		100,000
Fund balance, end of the year		$105,000

CURRENT RESTRICTED FUND
STATEMENT OF CHANGES IN FUND BALANCES
For the Year Ended June 30, 1974

Fund balance, beginning of the year	$ 20,000
Add: restricted contribution	50,000
Less: Expenditures for restricted purposes reported in	
general fund	(40,000)
Fund balance, end of the year	30,000

Fig. 9–3. An example of statements showing current restricted contributions transferred to the General Fund to the extent expended and reported in the income section of that fund.

without implying that it is income. The restricted fund becomes a sort of suspense or deferred-income account into which all restricted income is placed until it is transferred to the general fund to offset current expenses. If this statement were labeled "Contributions, Transfers, and Changes in Fund Balances," as in the previous example, it would appear to the reader that the contribution was being reported twice, once when it was reflected in the restricted fund and then again when it was included in the general fund.

The main disadvantage of this approach is that the reader will probably not realize that the total restricted contributions were $50,000 and not the $40,000 shown in the general fund. At the same time there is a risk that the reader will try to add this $50,000 to the $360,000 shown as total revenue in the general fund and, erroneously, conclude that total revenues and contributions were $410,000. It takes a skilled and careful reader to fully understand what has taken place.

This approach is generally accepted and followed by many nonprofit organizations. If separate statements are presented for each fund, this approach is the one that should be followed.

Reporting Only in the General Fund. Another approach is to report all current restricted contributions directly in the general fund, footnoting the amount of unexpended restricted contributions. This approach takes the very practical position that all "current" restricted contributions should be reported directly in the general fund in full when received since they will be expended quite promptly. This is probably the simplest approach and therefore the one most easily understood by the reader. There is no "current" restricted fund as such, although there can still be other restricted funds (endowment fund, funds for building projects, etc.). Figure 9–4 shows how the statement would look.

This approach offers the practical advantage of simplicity. Note that here, for the first time, the reader sees in the general fund the total current restricted contributions received ($50,000), whereas in the previous illustration he saw only the amount which was expended during the period ($40,000). Those that argue against this approach point out that the reader may not understand the parenthetical note and may think the museum had $15,000 excess which could have been used for any purpose. This is a valid argument, and if the amount of unexpended current restricted contributions is normally large in relation to the general fund balance or to the excess of income over expenses, then this approach is not appropriate. However, if current restricted contributions are normally used entirely within the year received or if the unexpended balances are not large, this approach is a very practical one recommended by the author.

THE JOHNSTOWN MUSEUM

STATEMENT OF INCOME, EXPENSES, AND
CHANGES IN FUND BALANCES
For the Year Ending June 30, 1974

Income:

Contributions, including $50,000 of restricted current contributions..........................	$ 70,000	
Other income	300,000	
Total		$370,000
Expenses:		
Salaries	210,000	
All other	145,000	
Total		355,000
Excess of income over expenses (includes $10,000 of unexpended current restricted contributions)		15,000
Fund balance, beginning of the year		120,000
Fund balance, end of the year (includes $30,000 of unexpended current restricted contributions)		$135,000

Fig. 9–4. An example of a General Fund Statement of Income in which all restricted and unrestricted contributions are reported in full when received.

Reporting in Columnar Statements. Another approach is to report the contribution and expenditure in the restricted fund but use a columnar statement format in which all funds are reported side by side.* As will be discussed more fully in Chapter 12, the use of a single statement in columnar format offers many advantages. This type of presentation can assist the reader in seeing the total picture of the organization, while at the same time preserving the traditional fund-accounting concepts. Figure 9–5 shows a columnar statement for the museum. It is assumed that the museum has no other funds; if there were, they would also be shown in this statement.

In this presentation the reader sees both the contribution in total and the amount expended. He also sees the total salary ex-

---

* This is the approach recommended in the AICPA Audit Guide for voluntary health and welfare organizations. See Chapter 13.

THE JOHNSTOWN MUSEUM

STATEMENT OF INCOME, EXPENSES, AND CHANGES IN FUND BALANCES
For the Year Ending June 30, 1974

	General Fund	Current Restricted Fund	Combined All Funds
Income:			
Contributions	$ 20,000	$50,000	$ 70,000
Other income	300,000		300,000
Total	320,000	50,000	370,000
Expenses:			
Salaries	170,000	40,000	210,000
All other	145,000		145,000
Total	315,000	40,000	355,000
Excess of income over expenses..........	5,000	10,000	15,000
Fund balance, beginning of year	100,000	20,000	120,000
Fund balance, end of year	$105,000	$30,000	$135,000

Fig. 9–5. An example of a columnar statement presentation in which restricted income and expenses are shown in a restricted fund column.

pense for the period, and not just the $170,000 expended from the general fund.

Those who argue against this type of presentation are concerned with the inference that the income and fund balance amounts shown in the "combined all funds" column can be expended for any purpose. They are concerned that the reader will not pay close enough attention to the column headings or footnotes. This is a valid concern but the advantage of clarity and the combined presentation of *all* activities in this statement outweighs these arguments.

Summary

In summary, there are a number of possible approaches to handling current restricted contributions. If such amounts are small in amount and the amounts unexpended at the end of the year are not material, the approach illustrated in Figure 9–4 should be followed where all current restricted contributions are included in the general fund directly. If the amounts are material, the columnar approach illustrated in Figure 9–5 is recommended. If the columnar approach is not followed, then the approach illustrated in Figure 9–3 should be followed, where all current restricted contributions are added directly to the restricted fund balance and then transferred to the general fund, as income is expended.

PLEDGES

A pledge is a promise to contribute a certain sum to an organization. Typically, fund-raising organizations solicit pledges because a donor either does not want or is not able to make a contribution in cash in the amount desired by the organization. As with consumer purchases, the "installment plan" is a way of life. Organizations find donors are more generous when the individual amounts being contributed are small and spread out over a period of time.

A pledge may or may not be legally enforceable. The point is moot because few organizations would think of trying legally to enforce a pledge. The unfavorable publicity that would result would only hurt future fund raising. The question, then, is: "Should a pledge be recorded as income at the time the pledge is received?" The answer to this question depends basically on whether the amount of uncollected pledges is material to either the Balance Sheet or the Statement of Income and Expense. The fact that the pledge is not legally enforceable is not germane to the question. The only relevant question is will it be collected. If the answer is "yes" and if it is material, then it should be recorded.

For many organizations pledges are a significant portion of their income. The timing of the collection of pledges is only in part under the control of the organization. Yet over the years most organizations find they can predict with reasonable accuracy the collectible portion of pledges, even when a sizable percentage will not be collected. Accordingly, pledges should be recorded if they are material in amount, and an allowance established for the portion that it is estimated will not be collected.

Allowance for Uncollectible Pledges

The key question is how large the allowance for uncollectible pledges should be. Most of the time the organization has past experience to help answer this question. If over the years 10 per cent of pledges are not collected, then unless the economic climate changes, 10 per cent is probably the right figure to use. Care must be taken, however, because while an organization's past experience may have been good, times do change as many organizations discovered to their sorrow in 1970 and 1971. Another factor that has to be considered is the purpose for which the pledges will be used. Some people will hesitate to default on a pledge for a worthwhile current year's project but may be less conscientious about a pledge for a building fund or a long-term project.

One thing to be kept in mind in setting up an allowance is that if a pledger defaults on an installment once, he is likely to do so again. If he defaults and hears nothing from the organization he assumes his contribution is not really needed, and it will be easier for him to skip the next payment. So once a donor becomes delinquent on even a single installment, a 100 per cent allowance for the total pledge is probably required, and not just for the delinquent portion. In addition, the organization should review the amount of allowance needed for other non-delinquent pledges; once there are signs of any delinquency the overall collection assumptions may be in doubt. If so, the organization should be conservative and set up additional allowances.

Recognition as Income

A related problem occasionally arises as to when a pledge should be recognized as "income." Consider for example the situation where an organization receives a pledge of $1,500 to be paid $500 this year, $500 next year, and $500 the following year. Should the $1,500 be recorded as income at the time the pledge is received, or should only the amount that will be received in the current year ($500) be recorded? The answer depends on the donor's intention.

Future Years' Support. If the donor has agreed to give $500 a year for 3 years beginning this year to meet the normal and recurring expenses of the organization, then only the $500 should be recorded in the current year as income. The entire pledge ($1,500) should, however, be recorded as an asset. In that case there will be deferred pledge income of $1,000 in the Balance Sheet, as follows:

BALANCE SHEET

Assets:
Cash. . . . . $ 600
Pledges   1,000
      Total assets $1,600
Liabilities:
Accounts payable . . . . $ 200
Deferred pledge   1,000
      Total   1,200
Fund balance   900
      Total liabilities and
         fund balance $2,100

As can be seen, $1,000 has been deferred. Each year $500 would be transferred from deferred income and recorded as current income.

Some organizations, on the other hand, follow the practice of not recording pledges for future years' support. They feel that this type of long-term pledge for current operations should not be recorded because such pledges are harder to collect and the delinquency factor is much greater. Further, they point out that recording a pledge and deferred income may inflate the Balance Sheet. These arguments have validity, and organizations should consider very carefully recording pledges for future support, particularly for periods beyond the following one or two years.

Current Year Support.   It is also possible that it is the intention of the donor to have the full $1,500 recorded as income in the current year to meet the costs of a specific program. Sometimes donors are unwilling, perhaps for tax reasons, to pay their entire pledge in the first year. In that instance it would be appropriate to record the entire $1,500 as the current year's contributions and to record the pledge as a long-term pledge receivable.

On the other hand, if a very large and unusual pledge is received to be paid off over a long period of time (say, three to five years) the organization should consider carefully the advisability of recording this pledge in the current year. In that circumstance the potential risk of not collecting this large amount has to be carefully considered. If this amount were not collected the current year's statements could be seriously misleading.

Building Fund Pledges. If the pledge of $1,500 is made toward a building or capital fund, then the full $1,500 is normally recorded as income of the building fund at the time the pledge is received.

THE TIMING OF RECORDING BEQUESTS

Often an organization is informed that it is a beneficiary under a decedent's will long before the estate is probated and distribution made. When should such a bequest be recorded—at the time the organization first learns of the bequest or at the time of receipt?

Bequests should be recorded as income at the time the organization can first be certain that it will be a beneficiary *and* the amount of the bequest is known. Thus, if an organization is informed that it will receive a bequest of a specific amount, say $10,000, it should record as income this $10,000. If instead the organization is informed that it will receive 10 per cent of the estate and because real estate or other nonliquid assets are involved the amount this 10 per cent represents is not determinable, then nothing would be recorded although footnote disclosure would be necessary.

CONTRIBUTED SERVICES

Many organizations depend almost entirely on volunteers to carry out their program functions. The question frequently asked is whether such organizations should place a value on these contributed services and record them as "contributions" in their financial statements. The answer is definitely "yes" if the following conditions exist. First, there must be reasonably good control over the employment of such services; second, there must be an objective basis on which to value these services; and third, the services must be an essential part of the organization's activities. In practice, the only organizations that do record such amounts are those where the omission of such amounts would materially distort the organization's financial statements.

When a person volunteers his services to an organization, he usually does not agree to do everything the organization wants at the time the organization wants it. He reserves the right, as it were, to pick and choose. If someone tells him to do an unpleasant task, he has the option of balking and saying "no" far more readily than a paid employee. He may tend to socialize more while "on the job." All of this is recognized by nonprofit organizations and is taken into account in planning jobs to be done with volunteer help. As a result, the organization normally does not have the same degree of control over the person as over a paid employee.

The second problem and a very practical one is measurement of the value to be placed on such contributed services. Unless the organization has a paid employee performing the same type of work, it is hard to measure the real value of the contributed service. While this can be overcome, often the paperwork and headaches involved in getting adequate support for such amounts are just more trouble than they are worth.

Services That Should Not Be Recorded

There are several categories of contributed services that are not recorded as revenue. First, volunteer fund raising efforts are usually not recorded, because fund raising as such is not directly fulfilling the objectives of the organization. Furthermore the organization usually does not have control over these workers and it is almost impossible to place an objective value on their services.

Another category of services not normally recorded is that associated with supplementary services that would not normally have been provided by the organization. For example, a church often arranges for home visits to the sick or aged by members of the church. These visits provide a benefit but of a nature that might not be provided by paid staff. A hospital coffee shop staffed with volunteers would be another example. The contributed services have to be of a type that the organization would otherwise hire someone to perform.

OTHER NONCASH CONTRIBUTIONS

Frequently an organization will receive contributions which are not in the form of cash. Typical examples are stocks and bonds, supplies, equipment, a building, etc. These contributions should normally be recorded if they are significant in amount. The values recorded should be the fair market value at the date received. Marketable stocks and bonds present no serious valuation problem and should be recorded at their market value on the date of receipt or, if sold shortly thereafter, at the amount of proceeds actually received. Supplies and equipment should be recorded at the amount which the organization would normally pay for similar items. This means that if they normally get a discount on supplies and equipment because of their nonprofit status, this lower price should be used. The valuation of a donated building or nonmarketable securities is more difficult and it is usually necessary to get an outside appraisal to determine its value. The financial statement in Figure 11–5 in Chapter 11 shows an illustration of donated materials being reflected as income.

One word of caution for "private foundations." The Tax Reform Act of 1969 provides that the donors' tax basis on all appreciated property be carried over to the foundation. This means that the foundation must determine the donors' basis and there may be an excise tax on these contributions at a future date. This problem is discussed in Chapter 23.

Appendix A–7 summarizes the alternative treatments for handling contributions as discussed in this chapter. The degree of acceptability of each treatment is indicated.

PART II

FINANCIAL STATEMENT PRESENTATION

10

Cash Basis Financial
Statements

Most small, and some medium-size, nonprofit organizations keep their records on a cash basis of accounting.* As was discussed in some detail in Chapter 3, for many organizations the cash basis is the best one. Probably the most important reason for this is the simplicity of record keeping. Another reason is that cash basis financial statements are the easiest type of statements to prepare and understand since the accounting principles are so straightforward.

SIMPLE CASH BASIS STATEMENT

Figure 10–1 shows the financial statement of a typical small church that keeps its records on the cash basis. It also follows the principle of writing off all fixed assets as purchased so there are no fixed assets to be reflected in a Balance Sheet.

Characteristics

This statement shows not only cash receipts and disbursements but also the cash balance of the church. Since there are no receivables or payables in cash basis accounting, the only asset reflected is cash. This being so, this presentation shows the reader

---

* Note, however, that "generally accepted accounting principles" require accrual basis statements. Organizations that want an unqualified opinion from their CPA must prepare their financial statements on an accrual basis.

123

ALL SAINTS CHURCH

STATEMENT OF CASH RECEIPTS, DISBURSEMENTS,
AND CASH BALANCE
For the 12 Months Ending December 31, 1974

	Actual	Budget
Receipts:		
Plate collections	$ 4,851	$ 5,000
Envelopes and pledges..................	30,516	32,200
Special gifts..........................	5,038	4,000
Nursery school fees....................	5,800	6,000
Total	46,205	47,200
Disbursements:		
Clergy	14,325	15,000
Music	8,610	8,400
Education	6,850	7,000
Church office	5,890	6,200
Building maintenance	4,205	4,300
Missions	2,000	2,000
Other	3,318	1,600
Total	45,198	44,500
Excess of cash receipts over disbursements	1,007	$ 2,700
Cash balance, January 1, 1974..............	4,300	
Cash balance, December 31, 1974	$ 5,307	

Fig. 10–1. An example of a simple cash basis statement that combines both the activity for the year and the ending cash balance.

everything he would want to know about the cash transactions for the twelve months.

The words "receipts" and "disbursements" have been used, rather than the words "income" and "expenses." Traditionally "receipts" and "disbursements" are used in cash basis statements since both words signify an event that has taken place (i.e., cash has been received or disbursed). The words "income" and "expense" usually refer to accrual basis statements. Also, note that the words "net income" have not been used since this usually refers to profit-oriented (i.e., business) entities.

Budget Comparison

One of the first principles to be remembered in preparing financial statements—whether cash basis or accrual basis—is that the reader should be given a point of reference to help him judge the results. This can be a comparison with last year's statement or it can be a comparison with the budget for the current year. The important thing is that the reader's attention is directed to deviations from either past experience or anticipated results. In Figure 10–1 a comparison with the budget gives the reader a point of reference. By looking carefully he can see where receipts and disbursements have deviated from what was expected. In this illustration, the reader will note that "envelopes" and "plate collections" have not met expectations. Most expenditures (except "other" disbursements) have been close to the budget.

SIMPLE STATEMENT WITH LAST YEAR'S FIGURES AND BUDGET

While the statement in Figure 10–1 has a comparison with the budget, some organizations also add last year's figures. An even more elaborate statement would contain a column showing the amount of deviation of actual receipts and disbursements from the budget. Figure 10–2 shows the same statement but with these additional columns to help the reader quickly pin-point problem areas.

Quickly look down the column labeled "Actual better (worse) than budget." See how rapidly the three significant items that have deviated from the budget can be spotted. This is the advantage of the deviation column.

Comparison with Last Year's Actual Figures

The 1973 comparison column gives additional information to help the reader interpret the current year's statement. For example, note that in 1974 every category of receipts is up from 1973, as is every category of disbursements. The thoughtful reader has to ask if the board wasn't overly optimistic in budgeting receipts of almost $7,000 more than the prior year. Perhaps on that basis the less-than-budget envelope and pledge receipts for 1974 do not look as bad. At the same time, the reader will observe that the board went ahead and spent more than was budgeted. This comparison with both last year's actual and budget helps the reader to obtain insight into the financial statement.

ALL SAINTS CHURCH

STATEMENT OF CASH RECEIPTS, DISBURSEMENTS,
AND CASH BALANCE
(SHOWING A COMPARISON WITH LAST YEAR AND BUDGET)
For the 12 Months Ending December 31, 1974

	Actual 1973	Actual 1974	1974 Budget	Actual Better (Worse) Than Budget
Receipts:				
Plate collections	$ 4,631	$ 4,851	$ 5,000	($ 149)
Envelope and pledges	28,722	30,516	32,200	(1,684)
Special gifts..............	1,650	5,038	4,000	1,038
Nursery school fees.......	5,650	5,800	6,000	(200)
Total	40,653	46,205	47,200	(995)
Disbursements:				
Clergy	13,400	14,325	15,000	675
Music	7,900	8,610	8,400	(210)
Education	5,651	6,850	7,000	150
Church office	4,317	5,890	6,200	310
Building maintenance	3,105	4,205	4,300	95
Missions	1,500	2,000	2,000	—
Other.................	3,168	3,318	1,600	(1,718)
Total	39,041	45,198	44,500	(698)
Excess of cash receipts over disbursements	1,612	1,007	$ 2,700	($1,693)
Cash balance, January 1	2,688	4,300		
Cash balance, December 31 ..	$ 4,300	$ 5,307		

**Fig. 10–2. An example of a simple cash basis statement that
shows last year's actual figures and this year's budget to give the
reader a basis for drawing a conclusion.**

At the same time, including last year's actual figures may be
more distracting than helpful for some readers. In preparing financial statements, careful consideration must be given to the
needs, and limitations of the reader. Careful thought must be
given to the degree of sophistication which is appropriate. Accordingly, statements for the board might contain this full
four-column presentation while the statements for the church
membership could contain only the two-column presentation in
Figure 10–1. Or, perhaps the appropriate information for the
membership may be the two "actual" columns.

COMBINED CASH BASIS INCOME
STATEMENT AND BALANCE SHEET

In Chapter 2 it was noted that cash basis accounting reflects only transactions involving cash. This means that a cash basis Balance Sheet does not show accounts receivable or accounts payable since no cash has been involved. However, there are assets and liabilities that do result from cash transactions and these assets and liabilities should be reflected on the Balance Sheet. There are three types of transactions that are frequently reflected in a cash basis Balance Sheet: those involving securities or investments, fixed assets, and loans payable.

Securities or investments can arise either from an outright purchase for cash, or as a result of a donation. If they result from a donation, they should be treated as "cash" income and be recorded as an asset. Fair market value at the date of receipt should be used for valuation purposes.

The purchase of fixed assets for cash may or may not be reflected on the Balance Sheet depending on the principles being followed for fixed asset accounting. Chapter 6 discussed the problems of accounting for fixed assets.

Occasionally a cash basis organization will borrow money from a bank or from an individual. A good example is a church that has a drop in contributions over the summer months and needs a short-term loan to tide it over until fall pledge collections pick up. These loans are "cash" transactions and should be reflected on the Balance Sheet.

Figure 10–3 shows an example of a statement showing assets resulting from cash transactions. The Friends of Evelyn College is a small nonprofit organization whose function is to raise funds amongst alumnae for the ultimate benefit of their alma mater.

Characteristics

Note the second part of the title—"Net assets resulting from cash transactions." Another title sometimes used is "Fund balance resulting from cash transactions." Normally the use of the words "balance sheet" are avoided since these words imply the accrual basis.

THE FRIENDS OF EVELYN COLLEGE, INC.

STATEMENT OF INCOME COLLECTED, EXPENSES DISBURSED,
AND NET ASSETS RESULTING FROM CASH TRANSACTIONS
For the Year Ended December 31, 1974

Income collected:

Contributions received	$146,797	
Interest income...............................	2,150	
Total		$148,947

Expenses disbursed:

Grants to Evelyn College........................	125,000	
Audit fee.....................................	573	
Other expenses	832	
Total		126,405
Excess of income collected over expenses disbursed......		22,542
Net assets, January 1, 1974		20,604
Net assets, December 31, 1974		$ 43,146

Net assets comprised:

Cash	$ 943	
U.S. treasury bills, at cost which approximates market ..	47,211	
Marketable securities at contributed value (market		
value $6,958)...............................	4,992	
		$ 53,146
Less: Loan payable to bank		(10,000)
		$ 43,146

**Fig. 10–3. An example of a simple cash basis financial state-
ment which combines in a single statement both income and expenses
for the year and the assets and liabilities at the end of the year.**

This format provides a description of the assets held at the
end of year right on the Statement of Income Collected and Expenses Disbursed. This makes it possible for the reader to obtain
a total picture of the organization by looking at only one statement. This simplicity is a real advantage.

This organization has used the words "income collected" and
"expenses disbursed" whereas in Figures 10–1 and 10–2 the words
"receipts" and "disbursements" were used. It was previously
noted that the words "income" and "expense" generally refer to
accrual basis accounting and should be avoided in cash basis
statements. Here, however, the use of the words "collected" and
"disbursed" clearly indicate that cash transactions are involved
and therefore there is no reason not to use these titles.

The term "net income" is more familiar to most than the phrase used in this illustration, "Excess of income collected over expenses disbursed" or the phrase used in Figures 10–1 and 10–2, "Excess of cash receipts over disbursements." As was previously noted, the words "income" and "expense" usually refer to accrual basis transactions. Still, many like to use the words "net income" in cash basis statements because they feel the reader understands this term better than one of the other expressions. If the organization wants to use the words "net income," it should then add the words "on a cash basis" so there can be no confusion.

Note that the market value is shown parenthetically on both the U. S. treasury bills and the marketable securities. As is discussed in Chapter 8, marketable securities are normally carried at cost. However, it is important to show the market value on the statements so that the reader can see how much unrealized appreciation (or depreciation) there is.

SEPARATE STATEMENT OF RECEIPTS AND EXPENSES AND STATEMENT OF NET ASSETS

It is not always possible to combine a Statement of Assets with the Statement of Receipts and Disbursements. This is particularly true where the Statement of Receipts and Disbursements is long and complicated or where the assets and liabilities are voluminous. Figure 10–4 shows the first two years' operation of a private swim club that purchased land and built a pool, borrowing part of the monies needed. Two statements are used although the cash balance is also shown on the Statement of Cash Receipts and Disbursements.

Cash Basis Emphasized

All cash transactions have been included in this Statement of Cash Receipts, Disbursements, and Cash Balance, but all transactions not involving income or expenses as such have been segregated to aid the reader. If these transactions had not been segregated it would have been more difficult for the reader to see what the on-going pattern of income and expenses would be.

Notice that in this presentation the statement comes down to the cash balance at the end of the year. The purpose of this is

CROMWELL HILLS SWIM CLUB

STATEMENT OF CASH RECEIPTS, DISBURSEMENTS, AND CASH BALANCE
RESULTING FROM CASH TRANSACTIONS
For the Years Ended December 31, 1973 and 1974

	1973	1974
Income collected:		
Membership dues	$25,000	$25,000
Interest income	125	300
Total	25,125	25,300
Expenses disbursed:		
Salaries of manager	2,000	2,200
Salaries of life guards	12,000	13,000
Payroll taxes	820	730
Pool supplies	2,000	2,200
Mortgage interest	1,200	2,300
Lawn furniture	800	—
Other miscellaneous	1,380	670
Total	20,200	21,100
Excess of income collected over expenses disbursed	4,925	4,200
Other cash transactions-receipts (disbursements):		
Mortgage principal repayments	(3,800)	(5,700)
Member's capital contributions	50,000	—
Bank loan received	40,000	—
Land acquisition	(25,000)	—
Pool construction cost	(62,500)	—
Net other cash transactions	(1,300)	(5,700)
Excess of cash receipts over (under) disbursements for the year	3,625	(1,500)
Cash balance, beginning of the year	—	3,625
Cash balance end of the year	$ 3,625	$ 2,125

Fig. 10–4. Cash basis statements where cash balance is shown in the Statement of Cash Receipts and Disbursements, and a separate Statement of Net Assets is also presented.

to accent the most important asset. The statement could have stopped at the "excess of cash receipts over disbursements" caption, but by showing the cash balance the importance of cash is emphasized. This is important for organizations with constant cash problems.

CROMWELL HILLS SWIM CLUB

STATEMENT OF NET ASSETS RESULTING FROM CASH TRANSACTIONS
December 31, 1973 and 1974

	1973	1974
Net Assets		
Cash	$ 3,625	$ 2,125
Fixed assets, at cost:		
Land	25,000	25,000
Pool	62,500	62,500
Total assets	91,125	89,625
Less—Bank Loan	(36,200)	(30,500)
Net assets	$54,925	$59,125
Represented by		
Capital contributions	$50,000	$50,000
Excess of income collected over expenses disbursed:		
Beginning of the year	—	4,925
For the year	4,925	4,200
End of the year	4,925	9,125
	$54,925	$59,125

Fig. 10–4. Continued.

Mortgage Repayments

The mortgage principal repayment is shown as an "other cash" transaction. This allows the reader to see the cash position at the end of the year. On an accrual basis neither the loan proceeds nor the mortgage principal repayment would be shown.

Certain Assets Not Capitalized

Notice that the lawn furniture has not been considered a fixed asset. This is because lawn furniture will be replaced every year or two and therefore there is little point in setting it up as a fixed asset. Cash basis organizations normally do not depreciate assets, and if these assets were recorded they probably would have to be depreciated since they have such a short life.

STATEMENT OF INCOME
WITH CERTAIN CASH TRANSACTIONS OMITTED

There is still another way to show the Cromwell Hills Swim Club statements. In this presentation certain cash transactions which affect the Balance Sheet are not shown in the Statement of Receipts. In 1973 these are the loan of $40,000, repayment of $3,800, and the purchases of land and pool of $87,500. Figure 10–5 shows how statements presented on this basis would look.

Characteristics

As noted above, the Statement of Income Collected, Expenses Disbursed, and Capital Contributed does not contain all cash transactions. Those transactions affecting only the Statement of Assets are not reflected. As a result the last line on the Statement of Income is no longer the cash balance, but "excess of income collected and capital contributed over expenses disbursed." This means that the emphasis on the cash balance is gone, and this creates a risk that the reader may misinterpret the meaning of this "excess" line. Most will readily recognize that the $54,925 in 1973 is not the cash balance at the end of the year, but some may think the club had a "cash" surplus in 1974 of $4,200. Many will fail to realize that there was a mortgage principal repayment of $5,700 and that the actual cash balance decreased $1,500 during the year.

In this presentation, the Statement of Assets could have been added at the bottom of the Statement of Income in a manner similar to that of Figure 10–3. Figure 10–6 shows how this would look in condensed form. This is a better approach because the reader does not have to make the transition from one statement to another, or to understand the title at the top of the second statement.

MODIFIED CASH BASIS STATEMENTS

In Chapter 2 it was noted that cash basis organizations often reflect certain noncash transactions in their financial statements. This may be a large receivable from a brokerage house for securities that have been sold at the end of the year, or it may be a large bill owed to someone which would materially distort the statements if omitted. In each case these transactions are reflected in the statements to avoid material distortions.

CROMWELL HILLS SWIM CLUB

STATEMENT OF INCOME COLLECTED, EXPENSES DISBURSED, AND CAPITAL CONTRIBUTED
For the Years Ended December 31

	1973	1974
Income collected:		
Membership dues	$25,000	$25,000
Interest income	125	300
Total	25,125	25,300
Expenses disbursed:		
Salaries of manager	2,000	2,200
Salaries of life guards	12,000	13,000
Payroll taxes	820	730
Pool supplies	2,000	2,200
Mortgage interest	1,200	2,300
Lawn furniture	800	—
Other miscellaneous	1,380	670
Total	20,200	21,100
Excess of income collected over expenses disbursed	4,925	4,200
Capital contributed	50,000	—
Excess of income collected and capital contributed over expenses disbursed	$54,925	$ 4,200

STATEMENT OF NET ASSETS RESULTING FROM CASH TRANSACTIONS

December 31	1973	1974
Cash	$ 3,625	$ 2,125
Fixed assets, at cost:		
Land	25,000	25,000
Pool	62,500	62,500
Total assets	91,125	89,625
Less—Bank loan	(36,200)	(30,500)
Net assets	$54,925	$59,125

Fig. 10–5. An example of cash basis statements where certain cash transactions are not reflected in the Statement of Income Collected, Expenses Disbursed, and Capital Contributed.

There is absolutely nothing wrong with an organization including such noncash transactions in the statements. The important thing is that the statements be meaningful. Care should be taken, however, to label noncash transactions in the statement so the reader knows they have been included.

CROMWELL HILLS SWIM CLUB

CONDENSED STATEMENT OF INCOME COLLECTED, EXPENSES
DISBURSED, CAPITAL CONTRIBUTED, AND NET ASSETS
For the Years Ended December 31, 1973 and 1974

	1973	1974
Income collected	$25,125	$25,300
Expenses disbursed	(20,200)	(21,100)
Excess of income collected over expenses disbursed	4,925	4,200
Capital contributed	50,000	—
Excess of income collected and capital contributed over expenses disbursed	54,925	4,200
Net assets, beginning of the year	—	54,925
Net assets, end of the year	$54,925	$59,125
Net assets comprised:		
Cash	$ 3,625	$ 2,125
Land (at cost)	25,000	25,000
Pool (at cost)	62,500	62,500
Total assets	91,125	89,625
Less—Bank loan	(36,200)	(30,500)
Net assets....................................	$54,925	$59,125

Fig. 10–6.   An example of a cash basis statement in which the Statement of Income is combined with a Statement of Net Assets.

CONCLUSION

More nonprofit organizations use cash basis than accrual basis accounting. Except where fixed assets and loans are involved, cash basis statements are very simple to prepare and understand. And even with the complication of fixed assets and loans, it is possible to present meaningful statements that most readers will understand. In developing the appropriate financial statement presentation the treasurer should consider carefully what he is trying to emphasize. If the cash position of the organization is the crucial item, then the statement should come down to the cash balance at the end of the period. If cash is not a problem, the last line should either be the caption "excess of income over expenses on the cash basis" or "net assets at the end of the year." This is largely a matter of judgment, knowing the readers of the statements and their level of sophistication.

11

Accrual Basis Financial Statements

In the previous chapter several cash basis statements were illustrated. One of the reasons cash basis accounting is followed is the simplicity of record keeping. Unfortunately for many organizations cash basis accounting is just not appropriate. They have too many unpaid bills at the end of the year or too much uncollected revenue. The only meaningful basis of accounting for these organizations is the accrual basis.*

Accrual basis accounting is more complicated, but this does not mean that the financial statements prepared on an accrual basis need be complicated or hard to understand. The key, however, is careful planning. This is the laying out of the financial-statement format so that the statements tell the organization's story as simply and effectively as possible. Easy-to-understand financial statements do not just happen; they must be carefully prepared with the reader in mind.

In this chapter three sets of accrual basis financial statements are discussed. Each has been prepared with the reader in mind. Many of the accounting principles discussed in previous chapters are also illustrated in these statements.

* "Generally accepted accounting principles" require accrual basis statements. Organizations that want an unqualified opinion on their financial statements by their CPA must prepare them on an accrual basis.

SIMPLE ACCRUAL BASIS STATEMENTS

Camp Squa Pan is a typical medium-size boys' camp sponsored by a local YMCA but operated as a separate entity. It was started in the late 1940's with a contribution of $50,000 from the local YMCA, and over the years has broken even financially. Figures 11–1 and 11–2 show the financial statements on an accrual basis.

CAMP SQUA PAN, INC.

STATEMENT OF INCOME, EXPENSES, AND CHANGES
IN FUND BALANCE
For the Years Ended December 31, 1973 and 1974

	1973	1974
Income:		
Campers' fees	$203,760	$214,400
Interest	212	412
Total income	203,972	214,812
Expenses:		
Salaries	89,606	93,401
Food	36,978	40,615
Repair and maintenance	25,741	29,415
Horse care and feed	3,983	4,010
Insurance	6,656	6,656
Advertising and promotion	2,563	2,201
Depreciation	12,570	13,601
Other miscellaneous	21,141	26,415
Total expenses	199,238	216,314
Excess of income over (under) expenses	4,734	(1,502)
Fund balance, beginning of the year	55,516	60,250
Fund balance, end of the year	$ 60,250	$ 58,748

Fig. 11–1. An example of a simple accrual basis Statement of Income, Expenses, and Changes in Fund Balance.

Income

The principal transaction reflected in these statements, which would have been handled differently on a cash basis, is the receipt in the current year of camp deposits for the following year. In 1973 the camp notices were sent out in October and many deposits had been received by December 31. In 1974, however,

CAMP SQUA PAN, INC.

BALANCE SHEET
December 31, 1973 and 1974

ASSETS

	1973	1974
Current assets:		
Cash	$ 13,107	$ 9,997
U.S. treasury bills at cost which approximates		
market	10,812	—
Accounts receivable.	1,632	853
Prepaid insurance	2,702	1,804
Total current assets	28,253	12,654
Fixed assets, at cost:		
Land	13,161	13,161
Buildings.	76,773	76,773
Furniture and fixtures.	22,198	23,615
Automobiles	13,456	14,175
Canoes and other equipment	12,025	12,675
	137,613	140,399
Less: Accumulated depreciation.	(71,242)	(76,629)
Net fixed assets	66,371	63,770
Total assets	$ 94,624	$ 76,424

LIABILITIES AND FUND BALANCE

Current liabilities:		
Accounts payable and accrued expenses	$ 4,279	$ 3,416
Camp deposits	18,275	1,610
Total current liabilities	22,554	5,026
Deferred compensation payable.	11,820	12,650
Fund balance:		
Original YMCA contribution	50,000	50,000
Accumulated excess of income over expenses	10,250	8,748
Total fund balance	60,250	58,748
Total liabilities and fund balance	$ 94,624	$ 76,424

Fig. 11–2. An example of a simple accrual basis Balance Sheet.

the notices didn't get out until almost Christmas and very few deposits had been received. If Camp Squa Pan had been on a cash basis, the income for 1974 would have been substantially less, since the $18,275 of deposits received in 1973 for 1974 camp fees would have been 1973 income. Offsetting this would have been the $1,610 of deposits received in 1974 for 1975 camp fees. Here is what 1974 income would have looked like on a cash basis:

1974 accrual basis income	$214,400
Less 1974 deposits received in 1973	(18,275)
Plus 1975 deposits received in 1974	1,610
1974 cash basis income	$197,735

As can be seen, there is a $16,665 difference between the cash and accrual basis. This difference is material when measured against the excess of expenses over income in 1974 of $1,502. On a cash basis this excess would have been $18,167 and the cash basis statements would have been misleading.

Depreciation

Depreciation is recorded by Camp Squa Pan. As is more fully discussed in Chapter 7, nonprofit organizations that capitalize their fixed assets should also depreciate them. In this case the camp director felt the building and equipment would deteriorate with time and he knew there was little likelihood that the YMCA would make another major contribution for new buildings or equipment. Accordingly, he concluded that it was appropriate to depreciate the fixed assets and to include depreciation as an expense so that he would be forced to set camp fees high enough to recover these depreciation costs.*

Fund Balance

The camp uses the term "fund balance" on their Balance Sheet. This is a term which is similar in meaning to "stockholders' equity," "net worth," "capital," or "net assets." Since nonprofit organizations do not normally have stockholders as such, the term "stockholders' equity" is not appropriate. However, the terms "net worth," "net assets," or even "capital" are all terms that are used to represent the aggregate net value of the organization. In this case, Camp Squa Pan has kept the composi-

---

* There are a number of accounting policies which each organization must determine. The handling of fixed assets and depreciation are good examples. Since there are a number of acceptable alternatives, each organization should disclose the accounting policies it has adopted in its notes to the financial statements so that all readers will be fully aware of them.

tion of the fund balance segregated on the Balance Sheet between the original YMCA contribution and the accumulated excess of income over expenses of the camp. Many organizations keep amounts separated in this way on their financial statements, although this is a matter of preference more than anything else. From a practical standpoint, the historical source of the funds is of little significance for a nonprofit organization except where there are restrictions which relate to these balances. In the example here, there is no reason why a single line could not have been shown with the title "fund balance" and the amount $58,748.

A minor point to note is that the camp has set up a deferred compensation liability for its caretaker who lives at the camp year round. This will be paid to him sometime in the future, probably when he retires. The point to note is that if the organization has a commitment for this type of expense, it should be recorded currently on an accrual basis.

ACCRUAL BASIS STATEMENTS— FUND-RAISING ORGANIZATION

The Richmond Hill Area United Fund Drive is a typical community fund-raising organization. It raises contributions on behalf of about twenty agencies serving the Richmond Hill area. Its annual drive takes place in late September. A substantial portion of the contributions are raised through pledges to be paid from payroll deductions over the period October through May. After the annual drive is completed and the board knows how much has been received or pledged, it makes allocations to the various agencies that will receive funds. As the cash is received it is turned over to these agencies. The records are kept on an accrual basis and pledges are recorded. The fiscal year ends on July 31. Figures 11–3 and 11–4 show the comparative financial statements for the six-month periods ending January 31, 1973 and 1974.

Pledges

The Statement of Income, Allocations, and Fund Balance clearly shows both the total pledges and the amount that is estimated will not be collected. Many organizations are reluc-

UNITED FUND DRIVE OF RICHMOND HILL, INC.

STATEMENT OF INCOME, ALLOCATIONS AND FUND BALANCE

	6 Months Ending January 31,	
	1973	1974
Income available for allocation:		
Pledges	$597,342	$726,661
Interest income	90	765
Less—Provision for uncollectible pledges	(31,161)	(39,192)
	566,271	688,234
Less—Administrative expenses	(25,344)	(27,612)
Income available for allocation	540,927	660,622
Allocations to agencies:		
American Red Cross	42,759	50,000
Richmond Hill Area Urban League	17,640	28,025
Big Brothers	—	13,971
Boy Scouts of America	70,220	72,385
Camp Fire Girls	40,531	40,905
Black Affairs Council	13,816	15,000
Child Guidance Clinic	6,010	—
Day Care Center	—	15,000
Family and Children's Service	107,026	116,760
Girl Scouts	40,422	56,000
Goodwill Industries.	30,650	32,700
Legal Aid Society	11,719	10,700
Salvation Army	36,757	40,967
Summer Youth Program	—	10,000
Visiting Nurse Association	4,010	6,689
Hebrew Community Center	25,783	28,038
Y.M. and Y.W.C.A.	42,392	43,075
Richmond Hill Hospital.	68,127	65,069
	557,862	645,284
Excess of income over (under) allocations	(16,935)	15,338
Fund balance, August 1	24,237	9,502
Fund balance, January 31	$ 7,302	$ 24,840

Fig. 11–3. An example of an accrual basis Statement of Income and Allocations for a typical united fund drive.

tant to record pledges until received. Yet experience shows that a fairly consistent pattern of collection will usually exist for most organizations. There is no reason why pledges, less the anticipated uncollectible portion, should not be recorded. In this case, if pledges were not recorded, the financial statements would have little meaning.

UNITED FUND DRIVE OF RICHMOND HILL, INC.

BALANCE SHEET

	January 31,	
	1973	1974
ASSETS		
Cash	$ 38,727	$ 59,805
Pledges receivable, less allowance for uncollectible		
pledges of $31,161 in 1973 and $39,192 in 1974	168,516	229,517
Total assets.	$207,243	$289,322
LIABILITIES AND FUND BALANCE		
Allocated to agencies	$557,862	$645,284
Less: Payments to date	(361,536)	(389,517)
Net unpaid	196,326	255,767
Payroll taxes and accounts payable	3,615	8,715
Total liabilities	199,941	264,482
Fund balance	7,302	24,840
Total liabilities and fund balance	$207,243	$289,322

Fig. 11–4. An example of an accrual basis Balance Sheet for a typical united fund drive.

Fiscal Period

Obviously the organization's fiscal year-end should not fall in the middle of the period when both collections and payment of the allocations are in process. This is what would happen if December 31 were the year-end. In this case the year-end is July 31 since all pledges are normally paid by May 31. At July 31 the organization will have collected and paid to agencies all of the previous year's fund drive pledges. For newly formed organizations the year-end date must be elected on a timely basis for federal tax reporting purposes. Page 388 discusses this requirement.

Income Statement Format

There is considerable detail on the Statement of Income, Allocations, and Fund Balance, but it all concerns the principal function of the drive, allocations to agencies. While there are some administrative expenses, no details have been shown because to do so would distract from the main purpose of the statement. Presumably the board would receive a supporting schedule accounting for these expenses.

Notice the caption "Income available for allocation." It is important in fund raising statements that the amount which is actually available for the purposes for which the organization exists be clearly shown. An alternative presentation would be:[*]

	1974
Income	$688,234
Expenses:	
Allocations to agencies (in detail)	645,284
Administrative expenses (in detail)	27,612
Total	672,896
Excess of income over expenses	$ 15,338

There is certainly nothing wrong with this format except that it is too easy to get lost in the details of the administrative expenses and miss the central point, that $645,284 was distributed to agencies out of an available amount of $660,622 ($688,234 less $27,612). The administrative expenses are a real cost of raising the income and should be shown as a deduction from the gross income raised.

Balance Sheet Format

Notice that, to make it easier for the reader, on the Balance Sheet the gross amount allocated to agencies has been shown and then payments-to-date have been deducted to arrive at the net amount still payable. It would certainly be correct to show only one figure, the remaining $255,767, but then it would be more difficult for the lay reader to understand exactly what that figure represented. He might mistakenly conclude this was the total amount allocated.

[*] The Second Edition of *Standards of Accounting and Financial Reporting for Voluntary Health and Welfare Organizations* illustrates a presentation similar to this one, although followng the terminology of the AICPA Audit Guide for Voluntary Health and Welfare Organizations (i.e., Revenue, Support, Program Services, Supporting Services). See Chapter 13 and pages 206–209.

Notice that the estimated uncollectible amount of pledges is shown on the Balance Sheet. This gives the reader some idea as to the percentage that is expected to be collected.

ACCRUAL BASIS STATEMENTS— INTERNATIONAL ORGANIZATION

There are many large nonprofit organizations, some of which have international operations. This does not mean, however, that the financial statements are necessarily complex or involved. The financial statements of Children Overseas Inc. are a good example. Children Overseas Inc. is a large organization serving poor and destitute children in eleven countries. Its funds are raised principally by encouraging contributions toward the support of particular children. Most of the contributions are in cash, but in addition the contributors can also send gift parcels. Figures 11–5, 11–6 and 11–7 show the financial statements of this large, international organization.

One of the first things that may strike the reader is that the figures are shown only in thousands of dollars. There is no point in carrying figures out to the last dollar. Round off to the significant figure. The extra digits only make the reader work harder and incorrectly suggests that there is significance in the detail. Where there is concern that the absence of the extra digits reduces the impact of the numbers, another alternative is to use zeros to replace amounts rounded (i.e., $8,206,000). In this way readability is retained along with the usual impact of the amounts.

Income Statement Format

The Consolidated Statement of Income, Expenses, and Changes in Fund Balance (Figure 11–5) shows some detailed sources of income, but only total expenses. A separate supporting statement (Figure 11–6) shows the details of the expenses by country for the interested reader. It would have been possible to include much of this "by country" detail on the Statement of Income, but this could very well have confused the reader by

CHILDREN OVERSEAS INC.

CONSOLIDATED STATEMENT OF INCOME, EXPENSES, AND CHANGES IN FUND BALANCE

(in thousands)

	For the Year Ended June 30	
	1972	1973
Income:		
Pledges for children	$ 9,210	$ 9,073
Gifts for special purposes	1,372	1,514
Contributions, endowment gifts, and		
bequests	450	661
Government refunds	155	82
Investment and miscellaneous income	44	74
Provision for unrealized loss on		
investments	(44)	—
Reduction in provision for unrealized		
loss on investments no longer needed	—	92
Total income	11,187	11,496
Expenses (Figure 11-6):		
Aid and services to children	8,649	8,206
Supporting operations	2,081	2,353
Promotion and advertising	454	583
Total expenses	11,184	11,142
Excess of income over expenses	3	354
Fund balance (deficit), beginning of year	(514)	(511)
Fund balance (deficit), end of year	$ (511)	$ (157)

Fig. 11–5. An example of a comparative Statement of Income, Expenses, and Changes in Fund Balance for a large international nonprofit organization.

having too much detail. The supporting schedule has been carefully prepared to help the reader see how it ties into the income statement ($8,206; $2,353; $583 and $11,142). This makes it easy for the reader to quickly orient himself when looking at this supporting schedule. If the organization had wanted to give even more detail in this supporting schedule, it could have used a wide sheet of paper and listed the details by type of expenses down the side and by country across the page. It would have taken a wide sheet, but here (in part) is the way it would have looked:

	Total	Bolivia	Brazil	Colombia
Aid and services to children:		(in thousands)		
Monthly cash grants	$4,317	$ 68	$200	$ 542
Purchased goods	636	8	49	107
Gifts for special purposes	1,461	15	40	143
Health services	650	29	38	158
Special services and projects	305	17	25	50
Social workers	472	14	37	65
Shipping and warehousing ..	145	6	6	18
Translation costs	220	8	24	33
Total	$8,206	$165	$419	$1,116

The key thing to remember is that if details are going to be given they should have totals that tie in to the main schedule so the reader knows exactly what the details represent. For example, in this partial schedule, the $8,206 ties in to the Statement of Income.

CHILDREN OVERSEAS INC.

ANALYSIS OF EXPENSES BY COUNTRY
(in thousands)

	Year Ended June 30, 1973				
Country	Aid and Services to Children	Supporting Operations	Promotion and Advertising	Total	1972 Total
United States	—	$1,287	$425	$ 1,712	$ 1,767
Canada	—	192	70	262	122
Australia	—	74	88	162	7
Bolivia	$ 165	59	—	224	107
Brazil	419	59	—	478	392
Colombia	1,116	85	—	1,201	1,223
Ecuador	841	65	—	906	907
Greece	957	100	—	1,057	1,214
Hong Kong	851	80	—	931	1,226
Indonesia	67	38	—	105	43
Korea..............	1,308	98	—	1,406	1,438
Peru	588	85	—	673	592
Philippines	1,165	61	—	1,226	1,257
Vietnam............	729	70	—	799	889
1973 Total	$8,206	$2,353	$583	$11,142	
1972 Total	$8,649	$2,081	$454		$11,184

Fig. 11–6. An example of a supplementary statement showing details of expenses. This statement would provide details not shown on the Statement of Income and Expenses.

CHILDREN OVERSEAS INC.

CONSOLIDATED BALANCE SHEET
(in thousands)

	June 30	
	1972	1973
ASSETS		
Cash	$ 563	$ 704
Investments, at cost less provision for unrealized loss of $137,000 in 1972 and $45,000 in 1973, which approximates market	1,066	1,331
Accounts receivable:		
Estimated unpaid pledges and gifts due from foster parents.	155	135
Foreign government refunds	24	18
U.S. government refunds	3	3
Other receivables	—	22
Prepaid expenses	73	35
Land, building, and equipment, net of allowance for depreciation of $85 in 1972 and $105 in 1973	60	65
Total assets	$ 1,944	$ 2,313
LIABILITIES AND FUND BALANCE		
Liabilities:		
Advance payments for children	$ 1,963	$ 1,992
Accounts payable and accrued payroll taxes	84	48
Estimated statutory severance pay liability	92	101
Unremitted gifts for special purposes	316	329
Total liabilities	2,455	2,470
Fund balance (deficit)	(511)	(157)
Total liabilities and fund balance	$ 1,944	$ 2,313

Fig. 11–7. An example of Balance Sheet for a large international nonprofit organization.

Provision for Unrealized Losses

In Chapter 8 it was noted that nonprofit organizations should consider setting up a provision for a decline in value in investments where the market is less than cost. These statements present an example of how to set up such a provision and how to reverse it when it is no longer needed. In 1973 the market value went back up and part of the reserve was no longer needed. Note that it has been reversed in exactly the same manner as it was set up.*

As was discussed in Chapter 8, many consider investment income and gains on investments to be similar in nature and both reportable in the same section of the statement. In Figure 11–5, investment income and the provision for unrealized loss are reported in the same section.

CONCLUSION

The illustrations in this chapter show many of the features of accrual basis financial statements for nonprofit organizations. There are many possible format variations, but readability is the key consideration that must be considered when preparing financial statements. What does the organization want to tell its reader? Once it is determined what information to include, it should be possible to design a statement format that will communicate this information to both sophisticated and unsophisticated readers.

---

* Of course, in this example it could be argued that the provision should not have been set up since part of it was not ultimately needed. However, in this instance because of a fund deficit the board felt it prudent to provide a provision since there appeared to be a possibility that part of the investments would have to be sold.

12

Fund Accounting Financial Statements

One of the characteristics of nonprofit organizations is that they have a stewardship responsibility to their members and to the public for the funds they receive. This stewardship frequently results in a type of accounting referred to as "fund accounting." The principles of fund accounting were discussed in Chapter 4.

Fund accounting offers many advantages if the financial statements are carefully prepared. It can provide a form of presentation that clearly shows the reader what financial activity has taken place within the restrictions placed on each of the individual funds. Unfortunately, all too often instead of clarifying the financial situation, fund accounting confuses the reader because the statements are not put together with the reader in mind. They may be technically accurate statements but they fail in their principal objective, communication.

On pages 36 and 37 the fund accounting statements of St. James' Church were presented. Refer back to these statements, and observe that there are four separate income statements, one for each fund. Note there is a transfer between funds and that to determine the overall excess of income of the church the reader really has to have a pencil to add up several numbers. Observe also that there may be some hesitation in knowing which numbers to add together.

This presentation is typical of fund accounting and no technical fault can be found with these statements. However, the reader may have some difficulty in ascertaining the overall financial picture of the church. The important question is, therefore, not whether the statements are technically accurate, but whether the reader will understand them. If the reader gives up after only a quick review then the statements have failed to accomplish their objective. This is the problem of fund accounting statements—they can be so complex that the reader gets lost or doesn't understand the terminology of the statements. The objective of this chapter is to show how to present fund accounting statements that will have the maximum chance of being understood by the lay reader.

COLUMNAR FORMAT PRESENTATION

One of the things that can be done to simplify fund accounting is to present the activities of all funds on a single statement in columnar format. In this type of presentation the activity of each fund is shown in a separate column, side by side. In this manner it is possible to see all the funds at one time. Figures 12–1 and 12–2 show the St. James' statements recast in this columnar format.

Characteristics and Advantages

Once the reader has oriented himself to this format it is possible for him to see at a glance the total activity of the church.

It is significant that the church received net income of $105,000 for the year, and not the $33,000 which is the first impression that the reader gets when he looks at only the separate general fund statement in Chapter 4. In this presentation he also sees the total income of the other funds, and by being given a total he doesn't have to work to get the overall results of operations. While the $71,000 of endowment income may not be available for general purposes, it represents a real asset to the church that will generate unrestricted income in the future. The reader should be fully aware of this amount.

Some accountants will argue against showing a "total all funds" column. They point out that this implies that all of the

ST. JAMES' CHURCH

STATEMENT OF INCOME, EXPENSES, AND CHANGES IN FUND BALANCES
For the Year Ending August 31, 1974

| | Unrestricted | | Restricted | | |
	General Fund	Board-Designated Endowment Fund	Funds for Specified Purposes	Endowment Fund	Total All Funds
Income:					
Contributions and gifts ..	$210,000		$24,000	$ 25,000	$ 259,000
Investment income	62,000				62,000
Gain on sale of investments.				46,000	46,000
Nursery school	11,000				11,000
Other income	7,000				7,000
Total income	290,000		24,000	71,000	385,000
Expenses:					
Clergy	89,000				89,000
Education	41,000				41,000
Music	20,000				20,000
Youth	23,000				23,000
Nursery School	12,000				12,000
Administration	24,000				24,000
Operating	40,000				40,000
Diocesan	3,000				3,000
Specified projects			23,000		23,000
Other	5,000				5,000
Total expenses	257,000		23,000		280,000
Excess of income over expenses	33,000		1,000	71,000	105,000
Fund balance, beginning of the year.	7,000	$50,000	10,000	1,037,000	1,104,000
Interfund transfers	(25,000)	25,000			
Fund balance, end of the year	$ 15,000	$75,000	$11,000	$1,108,000	$1,209,000

Fig. 12–1.   An example of a columnar Statement of Income, Expenses, and Changes in Fund Balances.

funds can be used for any purpose, whereas in reality there are restrictions. In this example, two thirds of the excess of income of $105,000 is endowment-fund gifts and gains which cannot be used.° They feel that to add the two together is mixing apples

---

° With respect to the $48,000 of gains on endowment fund investments, there now appears to be some question whether such amounts are legally restricted. See pages 103 to 104.

ST. JAMES' CHURCH

BALANCE SHEET
August 31, 1974

	Unrestricted		Restricted		
	General Fund	Board-Designated Endowment Fund	Funds for Specified Purposes	Endowment Fund	Total All Funds
Cash	$50,000		$13,000	$ 3,000	$ 66,000
Accounts receivable . . .	13,000				13,000
Investments		$50,000		1,100,000	1,150,000
Interfund receivable (payable)	(31,000)	25,000	1,000	5,000	—
Total assets	32,000	75,000	14,000	1,108,000	1,229,000
Less: Accounts payable	(17,000)		(3,000)		(20,000)
Fund balance	$15,000	$75,000	$11,000	$1,108,000	$1,209,000

Fig. 12–2.   An example of a columnar Balance Sheet.

and oranges. This is true to a point, but as long as the column headings across the page are reasonably descriptive as to the type of restrictions involved, no one can be seriously misled by this columnar approach.* Furthermore, the reader is more likely to be misled if he doesn't understand the significance of the separate statement presentation, and perhaps comes away thinking the church's excess of income was only $33,000.

Transfer and Fund Balance Section

Notice the ease in handling the transfer from the general fund to the board-designated endowment fund. While any transfer can cause confusion, the confusion is minimized when both sides of the transaction are shown in a single statement as they have been here. Notice that the transfer has been shown in the fund balance section. As is discussed in Chapter 5, this helps to remove any suggestion that the transfer is an expense or is coming from income.

---

* If there is any question about the reader understanding the restrictions, a detailed description should be included in the notes to the financial statement, appropriately cross-referenced to the column heading.

When several funds are shown in a columnar format, often one or more of the funds will have very little activity and a number of the captions will not be applicable. This is particularly so in this instance with the board-designated endowment fund. Yet the blank spaces should not detract from the statement, and the very absence of figures in this column is informative because it tells the reader that, in fact, there has been no activity.

Another related problem is trying to fit some types of expenses into major categories so as not to have too many categories. In this instance all of the expenditures in the "funds for specified purposes" were shown on a single line, and no detail is given. This may not be satisfactory, in which case additional categories of expenses could be shown. Or, alternatively, a supporting schedule could be prepared showing the details of the $23,000. But even if a supporting schedule is prepared the figures should still be shown "in total" in the columnar statement. Otherwise the reader will not be able to see the total picture. There is a risk of confusion in having the same figures in two statements but this can be minimized by putting a caption on the separate supporting statement along the lines "Included in total on Statement of Income, Expenses, and Changes in Fund Balances." See Figure 12–8.

Statement Omitting Changes in Fund Balances

It will be noted that in Figure 12–1 the statement is labeled Statement of Income, Expenses, and Changes in Fund Balances. Many organizations prefer to omit reference to "changes in fund balance" and present only a Statement of Income and Expenses and a Balance Sheet. When this is done, interfund transfers are shown on the Statement of Income and Expense after the caption "Excess of income over expenses," and the change in fund balance for the year is shown in the fund balance section of the Balance Sheet. Figure 12–3 shows in condensed form the St. James' statements with only a Statement of Income and Expenses and a Balance Sheet, which shows the change in fund balance directly in the fund balance section.

This presentation has the advantage of emphasizing the excess of income over expenses (and transfers). The unsophisticated reader is more likely to remember the last figure in a set of state-

ST. JAMES' CHURCH

STATEMENT OF INCOME, EXPENSES, AND TRANSFERS
For the Year Ending August 31, 1974
(condensed)

	General Fund	Board-Designated Endowment Fund	Funds for Specified Purposes	Endowment Fund	Total All Funds
Income (in total)	$290,000		$24,000	$ 73,000	$ 387,000
Expenses (in total)	257,000		23,000	2,000	282,000
Excess of income over expenses	33,000		1,000	71,000	105,000
Interfund transfers	(25,000)	$25,000			—
Excess of income over expenses and transfer	$ 8,000	$25,000	$ 1,000	$ 71,000	$ 105,000

BALANCE SHEET
August 31, 1974
(condensed)

	General Fund	Board-Designated Endowment Fund	Funds for Specified Purposes	Endowment Fund	Total All Funds
Total assets	$ 32,000	$75,000	$14,000	$1,108,000	$1,229,000
Accounts payable	17,000		3,000		20,000
Fund balance, beginning of the year.	7,000	50,000	10,000	1,037,000	1,104,000
Excess of income over expense and transfer . .	8,000	25,000	1,000	71,000	105,000
Fund balance, end of the year.	15,000	75,000	11,000	1,108,000	1,209,000
Total liabilities and fund balance	$ 32,000	$75,000	$14,000	$1,108,000	$1,229,000

Fig. 12–3.   An example of accrual basis statements in which the changes in fund balance are shown in the Balance Sheet.

ments than one in the middle, no matter how well labeled. In Figure 12–1 the excess of income over expenses of $105,000 for all funds is clearly shown, but several lines from the bottom of the page. In Figure 12–3 the $105,000 is shown twice, including the last line. If an organization wants to emphasize this excess line, then this presentation has some advantage.

One of the major disadvantages of this presentation is that the transfer between funds has been shown on this statement. As discussed in Chapter 5 transfers should be reported apart from the Statement of Income and Expenses whenever possible to avoid any inference that the transfer is an expense or an income item. Another possibility is to show the interfund transfer directly on the Balance Sheet. If this were done, the Income Statement in Figure 12–3 would have ended at the line "excess of income over expenses." The interfund transfer of $25,000 would have then been shown in the Balance Sheet in a new line labeled "interfund transfer" immediately after the "excess of income over expenses" line.

This presentation is, of course, somewhat awkward. This can be overcome by using a separate Statement of Changes in Fund Balances. Figure 12–4 shows a Statement of Changes in Fund Balances in which the only changes shown within that statement are the excess of income over expenses and the transfer between funds.

STATEMENT OF CHANGES IN FUND BALANCES

Many organizations show all activity for the year for each fund other than the general fund in a Statement of Changes in Fund Balances. In Figure 12–4 the only activity shown was the excess of income over expenses and the interfund transfer. Instead, many organizations use this statement as a means by which to show all activity of the restricted funds in lieu of using a Statement of Income and Expenses (Figures 12–1 and 12–3). Where an organization uses a Statement of Changes in Fund Balances to show all activity of restricted funds, there will usually be a Statement of Changes in Fund Balances for the general fund also. This statement, however, will show only the excess of income and any interfund transfers in the same manner as presented in Figure 12–4.

Some organizations use a single columnar statement format to show the Changes in Fund Balances for all funds on one statement. Figure 12–5 shows such a single columnar format for St. James' Church. Also shown in Figure 12–5 is the Statement of Income and Expenses of the general fund. This Statement of

ST. JAMES' CHURCH

STATEMENT OF CHANGES IN FUND BALANCES
For the Year Ending August 31, 1974

	General Fund	Board-Designated Endowment Fund	Funds for Specified Purposes	Endowment Fund	Total All Funds
Fund balance, beginning of the year.	$ 7,000	$50,000	$10,000	$1,037,000	$1,104,000
Excess of income over expenses	33,000		1,000	71,000	105,000
Transfers between funds.	(25,000)	25,000			—
Fund balance, end of the year	$15,000	$75,000	$11,000	$1,108,000	$1,209,000

Fig. 12–4. An example of a separate Statement of Changes in Fund Balances in columnar format.

Income, Balance Sheet and the Statement of Changes in Fund Balances would constitute the set of financial statements for St. James' Church.

The difficulty with this separate Statement of Changes in Fund Balances is that the reader may not know how to interpret it. For example, the general fund is included in this statement even though there is a separate Statement of General Fund Income and Expense. Many readers will not comprehend the relationship of this column with the Statement of Income and Expenses and they may be confused. Also, while all of the changes in the other funds have been carefully labeled as to what each item represents, nowhere is the reader told what the relationship of the activity in this statement is to the activity in the Statement of General Fund Income and Expense. Few will recognize that the fund balance of all funds has increased $105,-000 during the year.

Those who favor this separate Statement of Changes in Fund Balances argue that one of the major advantages of this form of statement is that the reader is not likely to confuse unrestricted general fund income with restricted fund income. They feel that

ST. JAMES' CHURCH
STATEMENT OF GENERAL FUND INCOME AND EXPENSES
For the Year Ending August 31, 1974
(condensed)

Income:

Contributions	$210,000
Nursery school income	11,000
Investment income	62,000
Other income	7,000
Total income	$290,000
Expenses (in total)	257,000
Excess of income over expenses.....................	$ 33,000

STATEMENT OF CHANGES IN FUND BALANCES
For the Year Ending August 31, 1974

	General Fund	Board-Designated Endowment Fund	Funds for Specified Purposes	Endowment Fund	Total All Funds
Fund balance, beginning of the year	$ 7,000	$50,000	$10,000	$1,037,000	$1,104,000
Excess of income over expenses	33,000				33,000
Restricted contributions			24,000	25,000	49,000
Gain on sale of investments.........				48,000	48,000
Investment advisory fee				(2,000)	(2,000)
Expended for restricted purpose............			(23,000)		(23,000)
Interfund transfers.....	(25,000)	25,000			—
Fund balance, end of ... the year............	$15,000	$75,000	$11,000	$1,108,000	$1,209,000

Fig. 12–5. An example of columnar statements illustrating the use of a separate Statement of Changes in Fund Balances in which all activity for funds other than the general fund is reported.

in a statement labeled Statement of Income, Expense, and Changes in Fund Balances (Figure 12–1) the reader may conclude that $105,000 is available for any purpose, which is certainly not correct. The format in Figure 12–5 is somewhat neutral in terms of identifying certain of the additions to the funds as "income." Many believe that this is desirable and that, for example, gains on sale of investments in the endowment fund are not income and should not be shown as income.[*] They feel the same way about restricted contributions for specified purposes. The organization does not have an unrestricted right to these funds and, in theory, would have to return them if they were not spent for the purposes designated. Accordingly, they say, these funds are held in trust until expended, and should not be shown in a manner that suggests they are income as such.

Recommendation

There is some merit to all of these arguments. The author, however, does not recommend the use of this separate Statement of Changes in Fund Balances. Instead, the combined Statement of Income, Expenses, and Changes in Fund Balances illustrated in Figure 12–1 is recommended. The major reason for this recommendation is that most readers will not fully understand the significance of the separate statement presentation and will not comprehend the overall financial picture of the organization. It is certainly accurate to say that restricted funds are not available for general purposes but the board would not have accepted such funds if it did not believe that they would contribute to the objectives of the organization. Accordingly, it is important that the reader see all of the activities, and not just those that result from unrestricted income and expense. The board can guard against misinterpretation by carefully labeling each column heading and, if appropriate, describing the restrictions in footnotes.

Some organizations present individual Statements of Changes in Fund Balance for each of their funds. The presentation on page 36 for St. James' Church is very similar to the form individual statements would take. They would, however, follow the same format presentation as the columnar format (Figure 12–5) and start out with the "fund balance at the beginning of the year." This gets the reader away from the income and expense concept.

If an organization insists on using a separate Statement of Changes in Fund Balances, it is recommended that all funds be

[*] Gains on investments are discussed in Chapter 8.

THE ROY B. COWIN SCHOOL

STATEMENT OF INCOME, EXPENSES, AND
CHANGES IN FUND BALANCES
For the Year Ending June 30, 1974

	General Fund	Board-Designated Endowment Funds	Endowment Funds	Funds for Specified Purposes	Total All Funds
Income:					
Tuition and fees	$724,701				$ 724,701
Contributions and legacies.	41,216		$ 122,504	$ 27,515	191,235
Investment income . . .	92,793		1,640	16,556	110,989
Gain on sales of investments	33,660		229,334	33,486	296,480
Total	892,370		353,478	77,557	1,323,405
Expenses:					
Instruction	461,313			21,500	482,813
Administration	166,360				166,360
Maintenance	112,044				112,044
Depreciation	43,525				43,525
Scholarship	3,000			9,200	12,200
Library	8,587			18,156	26,743
Other	21,516			5,500	27,016
Total	816,345			54,356	870,701
Excess of income over expenses for the year .	76,025		353,478	23,201	452,704
Fund balance, beginning of the year	845,200	$258,925	1,888,247	257,594	3,249,966
Interfund transfers	(35,000)	42,119	(7,119)		—
Fund balance, end of the year	$886,225	$301,044	$2,234,606	$280,795	$3,702,670

Fig. 12–6. An example of a columnar Statement of Income, Expenses and Changes in Fund Balances in which activity for all funds is reported.

shown in a columnar format as in Figure 12–5. Otherwise the reader is even less likely to see the overall financial activity for the year.

A COMPLICATED SET OF FUND FINANCIAL STATEMENTS

The St. James' Church statements are relatively straightforward and not particularly complicated. In many organizations,

THE ROY B. COWIN SCHOOL
BALANCE SHEET
June 30, 1974

	General Fund	Board-Designated Endowment Funds	Endowment Funds	Funds for Specified Purposes	Total All Funds
ASSETS					
Current assets:					
Cash	$ 174,860	$ 2,315	$ 15,615	$ 20,515	$ 213,305
Marketable securities, at cost (market value $3,250,000) ..		256,610	2,231,080	255,310	2,743,000
Tuition receivable	7,500				7,500
Other receivables	2,345				2,345
Inventories of books and supplies	14,200				14,200
Total current assets	198,905	258,925	2,246,695	275,825	2,980,350
Fixed assets at cost:					
Land	100,000				100,000
Buildings...........	1,749,250				1,749,250
Vehicles	25,500				25,500
Total	1,874,750				1,874,750
Less: Accumulated Depreciation	(1,056,200)				(1,056,200)
Net fixed assets	818,550				818,550
Total assets	$1,017,455	$258,925	$2,246,695	$275,825	$3,798,900
LIABILITIES AND NET WORTH					
Accounts payable	$ 47,845				$ 47,845
Withholding taxes	6,300				6,300
Tuition paid in advance .	42,085				42,085
Interfund payable (receivable)	35,000	$ (42,119)	$ 12,089	$ (4,970)	—
Total liabilities	131,230	(42,119)	12,089	(4,970)	96,230
Fund balances	886,225	301,044	2,234,606	280,795	3,702,670
Total liabilities and fund balances	$1,017,455	$258,925	$2,246,695	$275,825	$3,798,900

Fig. 12–7.   An example of a columnar Balance Sheet.

this simplicity does not exist. The thing that most frequently complicates the statements is showing a number of "name" funds. These are frequently endowment funds, but may also include funds for specified purposes and possibly board-designated en-

THE ROY B. COWIN

STATEMENT OF CHANGES IN INDIVIDUAL ENDOWMENT FUNDS AND

For the Year Ending

(All income and expenses have been shown in total on the Statement of Income,

	Contributions and Legacies	Investment Income		Capital Gains (Losses)	
		Reported Directly in General Fund	Other	Reported Directly in General Fund	Left in Fund
Endowment funds:					
Principal and income restricted:					
The Malmar Fund					($ 3,015)
Clyde Henderson Fund			$ 1,150		8,165
Evelyn I. Marnoch Fund			490		(2,156)
			1,640		2,994
*Principal only restricted:					
The Roy B. Cowin Memorial Fund.		$73,859			213,369
The Lillian V. Fromhagen Fund .		2,392			6,911
Donna Comstock Fund	$ 16,153	1,670			3,661
Josephine Zagajewski Fund	100,000	2,250			
The Peter Baker Fund	6,351	688			1,580
	122,504	80,859			225,521
*Restrictions lapsed in 1973:					
The Alfred P. Koch Fund		283			819
Total endowment funds	$122,504	$81,142	$ 1,640		$229,334
*Board-designated endowment:					
Elmer C. Bratt Fund		$11,651		$33,660	
*Funds for specified purposes:					
Scholarship Fund	$ 3,000		$ 6,683		$ 19,307
Library Fund	18,615		603		1,756
Faculty pensions	4,150		3,742		10,811
Malmar Repair Fund	700		5,078		312
100th Anniversary Fund	1,050		450		1,300
Total funds for specified purposes	$ 27,515		$16,556		$ 33,486

*Funds have been "pooled" for investment purposes. See Chapter 22 for a discussion of pooled investments.

Fig. 12–8. An example of a supplementary statement illustrating fairly complex fund

dowment funds. The characteristic of "name" funds is that the donor's name is associated with the fund. As was discussed in Chapter 4, the use of "name" funds, if carried to an extreme, can cause confusion because it adds detail. The real risk is that the reader will not see the forest for the trees.

There are two principal financial statements that most readers want to see. Most important is a Statement of Income and Expense and, of lesser importance, the Balance Sheet. If all transactions have been skillfully summarized on these two statements, it is then possible to provide a third schedule that shows the appropriate detail of the information on the two primary state-

SCHOOL

FUNDS FOR SPECIFIED PURPOSES
June 30, 1974
Expenses and Changes in Fund Balances)

Disbursed for Specified Purpose	Other Interfund Transfers Add (Deduct)	Net Change in Fund	Fund Balance Beginning of Year	Fund Balance End of Year
		($ 3,015)	$ 110,700	$ 107,685
		9,315	25,601	34,916
		(1,666)	10,871	9,205
		4,634	147,172	151,806
		213,369	1,641,300	1,854,669
		6,911	53,165	60,076
		19,814	28,160	47,974
		100,000		100,000
		7,931	12,150	20,081
		348,025	1,734,775	2,082,800
	($ 7,119)	(6,300)	6,300	–
	($ 7,119)	$346,359	$1,888,247	$2,234,606
	$42,119	$ 42,119	$ 258,925	$ 301,044
($ 9,200)		$ 19,790	$ 148,516	$ 168,306
(18,156)		2,818	13,511	16,329
(21,500)		(2,797)	83,167	80,370
(5,500)		590	2,400	2,990
		2,800	10,000	12,800
($54,356)		$ 23,201	$ 257,594	$ 280,795

how changes in individual name funds can be presented for a accounting structure.

ments. The key to successful presentation in this third schedule is showing totals on this schedule which tie back into the Statement of Income and Expenses.

The Roy B. Cowin School financial statements are a good example of how substantial detail can be provided on "name" funds without detracting from the reader's overall understanding of the results of operations. While these statements relate to a private secondary school, the form would essentially be the same for almost any type of organization. Figures 12–6, 12–7 and 12–8 show these statements.

Overall Impression of Complexity

The reader's first impression of these statements may be that they "look" complicated and will be hard to understand. This is particularly so with respect to Figure 12–8 which shows changes in the individual "name" funds. Before studying this statement, however, take a few minutes to study the first two statements (Figures 12–6 and 12–7) to get an overall impression of what has happened during the year. Look first at the "total all funds" column on the Statement of Income and Expenses and the description of the items of income and expense. The reader should focus on the total picture before he looks at some of the detail by individual funds. The same thing should be done with the Balance Sheet. Look first at the total, and only then at the detail by funds.

The statement of activity by individual "name" funds is more difficult. The stewardship concept has been introduced in considerable detail on this statement. Apart from the many individual "name" funds, this statement also shows these funds segregated by the type of restriction associated with each fund. Some funds contain restrictions only with respect to the original principal; others restrict both the income and the principal. While this statement is complicated, there is a great deal of information on the statement that the reader should be able to understand if he takes some time to study it. On the other hand if the reader isn't interested in this detail, he still has the overall Statement of Income and Expense which clearly summarizes all income and expenses. This is a key point—everything is summarized in total, and the reader is required to look at detail only to the extent he wishes to do so.

One final observation about the overall impression these statements make. If these same statements had been presented in a separate statement format, including separate statements for each "name" fund, the resulting set of statements would most certainly have discouraged and probably confused all but a few readers. There would be just too much detail; few readers would be able to get any meaningful understanding of the overall financial picture of this school. So while the supplementary summary on individual "name" funds may seem complex, the alternative would be far less comprehensible.

Statement of Income and Expenses

On the Statement of Income, Expenses, and Changes in Fund Balances the number of columns have been limited to the four fund groupings that have distinctive significance. While there are varying degrees of restrictions associated with the endowment funds, no attempt is made to indicate these on the face of the statement because this represents a detail that can best be left to a supporting statement. It is important that the reader not get lost in detail on the summary statement.

Transfers. There are two transfers between funds in this statement. The first is a transfer from the endowment fund of a term endowment on which the restrictions have lapsed. This transfer of $7,119 * went directly to the general fund since this amount became unrestricted. The second transfer is a transfer from the general fund to the board-designated endowment fund, in the amount of $42,119. In the general fund column, only the net amount of $35,000 is shown.

It should be noted that there are no contributions or gains shown directly in the board-designated endowment fund. All unrestricted contributions or gains are shown in the general fund. The board can then transfer any portion of such income to the board-designated endowment fund but it should not show such income directly in that fund. Unrestricted income must be reported initially in the general fund.

---

* This $7,119 was a term endowment, the restrictions on which lapsed in 1974. Since the restrictions had lapsed, this fund became an unrestricted fund and the principal and accumulated gains were transferred to the general fund. Some argue that the $7,119 of lapsed term endowment should be shown as general fund income rather than as a transfer. Their argument is that this amount is now available for unrestricted purposes and thus is unrestricted income. Usually, such persons also take exception to the use of an "income" statement in connection with the endowment fund preferring instead a Statement of Changes in Fund Balance. Thus they argue that the original receipt of the term endowment has not been previously reflected in income. However, if statements are being presented in a columnar format, as here, the receipt of the original term endowment was included as part of income for the endowment fund, and thus part of total all funds income. Accordingly, it would be wrong to again include the same item in income, albeit, general fund income.

Unrestricted Investment Income. It will be noted that unrestricted endowment fund investment income of $92,793 has been shown directly in the general fund. It would not have been appropriate for the board to have left this amount in the endowment fund since the endowment fund should contain only restricted funds. To assist the reader in seeing how much income each separate fund earned, this unrestricted income is also shown in the Statement of Changes in Individual Funds in the column "reported directly in general fund." Inclusion of this column in the statement is optional.

Gains and Losses. Endowment fund gains aggregating $229,-334 have been shown in the endowment fund column. While there is some legal question whether endowment fund gains are restricted and must be added to endowment principal,* it is generally accepted that they are. On the other hand, board-designated endowment fund gains should be reported in the general fund. These gains, as with investment income, represent unrestricted income and should be reported as such. There is no reason why the board can't transfer all or part of these gains back to the board-designated endowment fund, but this should be handled as a transfer. †

Comparison with Last Year's Figures. An additional column may be added to either the Balance Sheet or the Statement of Income and Expenses to show last year's actual figures so the reader has a point of reference. This comparison is usually to the total all funds column, although sometimes a comparison is made only to the general fund. If the comparison column is to the total all funds column then this additional column should be next to the current year's total column to make it easier for the reader. If the comparison is only to the general fund it should be set up as shown on page 165.

Instead of a comparison to last year's figures, the comparison could have been to this year's budget.

---

* See page 103.

† Where a columnar format statement is used, as here, it is permissible to report board-designated endowment fund gains or losses and investment income directly in the board-designated endowment fund column.

	General Fund		Board-Designated Endowment Funds	Endowment Funds	Funds for Specified Purposes	Total All Funds
	Last Year	This Year				
Income:						
Tuition and fees	$689,188	$724,701				$ 724,701
Contributions	23,444	41,216		$ 22,504	$27,515	91,235
Legacies ...				100,000		100,000
Investment income	83,598	92,793		1,640	16,556	110,989
Gain on sale of investment	11,345	33,660		229,334	33,486	296,480
Total ..	$807,575	$892,370		$353,478	$77,557	$1,323,405

Balance Sheet

Fixed assets have not been set up as a separate fund. Instead, they have been included as a part of the general fund. This greatly simplifies the problem of depreciation since depreciation can then be handled in exactly the same manner as it would be handled by a commercial enterprise. The presentation problems in handling depreciation if a separate plant fund is used are discussed more fully in Chapter 7.

One of the principal reasons why many prefer to see fixed assets in a separate fund is that the general fund balance then represents the current assets of the organization. In our illustration the fund balance of $886,225 is mostly represented by fixed assets. If the plant fund assets had been shown separately, the general fund balance would have been only $67,675. But this lower figure has limited significance because there are other unrestricted current assets that are available for general purposes if the board chooses to use them. These other unrestricted current assets are, of course, the $301,044 of "board-designated" endowment funds. Many, including the author, recommend that *all* unrestricted funds, including both fixed assets and board-designated funds, be combined into the general fund. In this instance, the fund balance would then be $1,187,269.

One effective way of showing this "unrestricted" total while still keeping the present format is to split the fund balance figures on the balance sheet into two amounts, restricted and unrestricted. Here is how this would look.

	General Fund	Board-Designated Endowment	Endowment Funds	Funds for Specified Purposes	Total All Funds
Fund balances:					
Restricted			$2,234,606	$280,795	$2,515,401
Unrestricted ...	$886,225	$301,044			1,187,269
	$886,225	$301,044	$2,234,606	$280,795	$3,702,670

Some will argue that the fixed asset amounts should not be included in the "unrestricted" figure since the organization could not exist without school buildings. This may be so, but there is no reason why the school has to use its present buildings. They could be sold and new ones built on less expensive land or in a better location. These are all decisions that the board is free to make and, being free to make them, the assets are unrestricted.

Balance Sheet Format. In the St. James' Church statements (Figure 12–2) the Balance Sheet was set up to show total assets less liabilities equaling the fund balance:

Total assets	$1,229,000
Less Liabilities	(20,000)
Fund balance	$1,209,000

In the Roy B. Cowin statements (Figure 12–7) the more conventional Balance Sheet approach was followed showing total assets equaling the sum of the liabilities and fund balance:

Total assets	$3,798,900
Liabilities	$ 96,230
Fund balance	3,702,670
Total liabilities and fund balance	$3,798,900

Either approach is acceptable. The first is more appropriate for organizations with relatively few categories of liabilities, and therefore for smaller organizations.

Statement of Changes in Individual Funds

Notice the line at the top of Figure 12–8: "All income and expenses have been shown in total on the Statement of Income, Expenses, and Changes in Fund Balance." This or a similar statement helps the reader to recognize that he doesn't have to add the income and expense shown on this statement to the amounts shown on the Statement of Income, Expenses, and Changes in Fund Balance (Figure 12–6) in order to get total income and expense. While technically there is no requirement that this type of caption be shown, it helps the reader understand the nature of this statement. Most of the totals shown on this statement can be tied in directly to the Statement of Income, Expenses, and Changes in Fund Balances.

Restricted Income From Endowments. Income on endowment funds that are restricted to a specified purpose should be transferred to the funds for specified purposes and reported directly in that fund. Normally the endowment fund would not directly disburse restricted income except to another fund. Note that in the Malmar endowment fund no investment income has been shown. Actually $4,970 of income was received but it was reported directly in the funds for restricted purposes in a separate fund maintained for this income (Malmar Repair Fund). This $4,970 plus $108 of income earned on this restricted fund balance is the $5,078 reported as investment income.

Alternatively, some organizations prefer to leave restricted income which can be used currently for restricted purposes in the endowment fund, appropriately labeled. Often this income is shown by adding an additional column in the following manner:

	Fund Balance End of Year	
	Principal	Income
The Malmar Fund	$107,685	$2,990

The Balance Sheet under this approach should then clearly indicate that the endowment fund includes restricted income which can be spent currently for restricted purpose. This can be indicated on the Balance Sheet in the fund balances section by breaking out the fund balance into several categories:

	General Fund	Board-Designated Endowment	Endowment Funds	Funds for Specified Purposes	Total All Funds
Fund balances:					
Unrestricted ...	$886,225	$301,044			$1,187,269
Restricted income			$ 2,990	$277,805	280,795
Restricted endowment			2,234,606		2,234,606
	$886,225	$301,044	$2,237,596	$277,805	$3,702,670

THE ROY B. COWIN

ANALYSIS OF EXPENSES AND COMPARISON

For the Year Ending

	Actual Last Year	Budget This Year	Actual This Year	Instruction
Salaries and payroll				
taxes	$581,615	$615,000	$618,686	$425,851
Retirement benefits	23,151	33,000	33,833	21,463
Major medical	3,656	4,500	4,578	3,155
Books and instructional				
materials	34,616	42,000	41,374	29,488
Concerts and other				
music	3,518	6,900	8,356	2,856
Stationery and supplies . . .	41,717	40,000	33,596	
Insurance	5,751	6,000	5,951	
Bad debts	3,748	5,000	6,116	
Depreciation.	39,516	43,000	43,525	
Contracted repairs and				
maintenance	14,819	9,600	15,054	
Utilities and fuel	19,151	20,000	19,268	
Other	36,118	35,000	40,364	
Total	$807,376	$860,000	$870,701	$482,813
Budget		$860,000		$480,000
Actual last year	$807,376			$451,254

Fig. 12–9. An example of an analysis of expenses by both
to both budget and

It is usually less confusing to the reader, however, to transfer this restricted income from the endowment fund to the funds for specified purposes. In this way all restricted funds are in one place where the reader can clearly and quickly see what amounts are available for restricted purposes.

There are two other endowment funds with restrictions on the income. In both instances the income has been left in the endowment fund. Presumably the donor specified that the income was to be accumulated for a period of time before it could be spent. There is no disclosure of the terms of the fund on the statement, but if they were significant a footnote could be added to tell the reader. However, unless the terms of the restriction are significant, footnote details should be avoided.

SCHOOL

WITH BUDGET AND LAST YEAR'S ACTUAL
June 30, 1974

Administration	Maintenance	Depreciation	Scholarship	Library	Other
$119,701	$ 59,247			$13,887	
8,105	3,650			615	
658	410			355	
				11,886	
					$ 5,500
19,181	14,415				
					5,951
					6,116
		$43,525			
	15,054				
	19,268				
18,715			$12,200		9,449
$166,360	$112,044	$43,525	$12,200	$26,743	$27,016
$165,000	$100,000	$43,000	$12,000	$25,000	$35,000
$143,222	$104,774	$39,516	$10,000	$24,611	$33,999

**function and types of expense, along with a comparison
last year's actual.**

There is no reason why board-designated endowment funds couldn't also have "names" associated with them. Here all of the board-designated funds are shown as the Elmer C. Bratt Fund. The board could also have had several other "name" funds, all part of the total board-designated fund.

While it is not obvious from this statement, most of the investments are "pooled" together and individual funds have a percentage or share interest in the total investment portfolio. Since all of the individual funds are "pooled" together, each gets its proportionate share of income and gains or losses on the sale of investments. Chapter 22 discusses the mechanics of "pooling" investments.

Other Supporting Statements

There are other supporting statements that could be included with the three statements we have just discussed. For example, many readers might want to see a great deal more of the details of the expense categories than are shown in total on the Statement of Income and Expense, and perhaps also a comparison with the budget or last year's actual figures. Figure 12–9 shows an example of this type of supporting schedule. Again, as with all supporting or supplementary statements the format must be so designed that the reader clearly sees how the figures tie into the main statement. It is for this reason that several expense categories which need no analysis as such (depreciation and scholarship) are also included on this supporting statement. In this way the totals will agree with the primary statement.

The reader who wants to see detail gets a great deal of information when he looks at this type of analysis. There is a comparison with both budget for the year and with last year's actual expenses, by type of expense and function. It must be remembered that the more detail provided, the greater the risk that the reader will get lost in the detail. Financial statements are not necessarily improved by providing details or additional supporting schedules. In fact, often they detract from the overall effectiveness.

SUMMARY OR CONDENSED STATEMENTS

Frequently for fund-raising purposes or for the general information of the membership, the board will want to distribute summary or condensed financial statements. Often the board will prefer not to show a large excess of income since this might discourage fund raising. In the case of the Roy B. Cowin School, the board might want to show only the general fund activities, which as will be recalled, had an excess of income of $76,025. Yet actually the school had a total "all fund" excess of $452,704.

The board may prefer issuing statements for only the general fund. This is not recommended. At some point the credibility

---

THE ROY B. COWIN SCHOOL

CONDENSED SUMMARY OF INCOME AND EXPENSES
For the Year Ending June 30, 1974
(in thousands)

Income:

Tuition and fees	$725	
Contributions and legacies	191	
Investment income	111	
Gain on sale of investments	296	
Total income		$1,323

Expenses:

Instruction	483	
Administration	166	
Maintenance	112	
Depreciation	43	
Scholarship	12	
Library	27	
Other	27	
Total expenses		870
Excess of income over expenses		$ 453
Excess restricted by donor	377	
Unrestricted	76	
Total		$ 453

Fig. 12–10. An example of a condensed Summary of Income and Expense for all funds, suitable for inclusion in an annual report or fund raising literature.

THE ROY B. COWIN SCHOOL

SUMMARY OF UNRESTRICTED INCOME AND EXPENSES
(Note)
For the Year Ending June 30, 1974
(in thousands)

Income:

Tuition and fees	$725	
Contributions and legacies	41	
Investment income	93	
Gain on sale of investments	33	
Total income		$892

Expenses:

Instruction	461	
Administration	166	
Maintenance	112	
Depreciation	43	
Scholarship	3	
Library	9	
Other.	22	
Total expenses		816
Excess of unrestricted income over expenses		$ 76

Note: In addition to the above unrestricted income and expenses, the School received restricted contributions and legacies of $150,000, of which $122,000 was added to the endowment fund and $28,000 to the funds for specified purposes. In addition, the School realized gains on sales of investments of $263,000 and received investment income of $18,000. Of these amounts, $231,000 was added to the endowment fund and $50,000 to the funds for restricted purposes. The School also expended an aggregate of $54,000 from funds for specified purposes.

Fig. 12–11. An example of a Condensed Statement of Unrestricted Income and Expense which provides footnote disclosure of the amount of restricted income and expenditures.

of the board and its statements may come into question if some of the readers feel information is being withheld.

There are two acceptable approaches open to the board. The first would be to present a condensed statement showing income and expense for all funds but clearly indicating the amount of the excess of income that was donor restricted. Figure 12–10 shows this presentation. The second approach is to present a statement showing the income and expense of all funds over which the board has control (i.e., the general fund and the board-designated endowment funds), and then showing in a footnote the activity in the other funds. Figure 12–11 shows this second presentation.

The reader can convert this second condensed statement into an all-inclusive statement if he wishes. The important thing is that the board cannot be accused of hiding the large gains in the endowment fund from the reader. This is particularly important since legal questions are now starting to be raised about the availability of capital gains for general purposes.

It would be entirely inappropriate, however, to eliminate the board-designated endowment fund activities from the condensed statement of unrestricted income. Board-designated funds have all of the characteristics of general funds since the board can act at any time to convert board-designated funds back into general funds. These funds must be considered part of general unrestricted funds any time when condensed financial statements are presented.

CONCLUSION

This chapter has presented a number of illustrations to help the reader more readily understand the complexities of presenting fund accounting financial statements. The use of the columnar approach has been discussed because it offers many advantages over presenting separate statements for each fund, the approach followed by many organizations. It has been indicated that it is extremely important that these statements be all-inclusive so that the reader can get a broad overall picture of the activities of the organization before he gets down into the detail. Several illustrations were given showing how typical detail can be presented with a minimum risk of confusing the reader. Finally, condensed or summary financial statements were discussed and the importance of disclosing all income, either in the body of the statement or in footnote was emphasized. Failure to do so creates a credibility gap which can only hurt the organization.

Appendix A–8 provides a summary table of alternative statement presentations together with the author's recommendations on each.

PART III

ACCOUNTING AND REPORTING GUIDELINES

13

Voluntary Health and Welfare Organizations

In 1973 the American Institute of Certified Public Accountants issued a revised * "Audit Guide" prepared by its Committee on Voluntary Health and Welfare Organizations. This Audit Guide was prepared to assist the independent auditor in his examination of voluntary health and welfare organizations. Included in this revised Audit Guide is a discussion of accounting and reporting principles which should be followed by this type of organization. This chapter summarizes the accounting and reporting principles discussed in this Guide.

Neither the Accounting Principles Board or its predecessor, the Accounting Procedures Committee of the American Institute of Certified Public Accountants, issued any pronouncement on what may be considered "generally accepted" accounting principles for nonprofit organizations. To date, the successor to the Accounting Principles Board, the Financial Accounting Standards Board, likewise has not issued any pronouncements.†

---

* The original Audit Guide was issued in 1967.

† Until June 30, 1973, authoritative pronouncements of accounting principles were normally issued only by the Accounting Principles Board of the American Institute of Certified Public Accountants (AICPA). Subsequent to this date the new Financial Accounting Standards Board (FASB) assumed responsibility for issuing authoritative pronouncements of the accounting principles (now referred to as "standards"). The Accounting Principles Board of the AICPA did not issue

The revised Audit Guide for voluntary health and welfare organizations does not represent the establishment of accounting principles. The Guide * was published for the guidance of members of the Institute in examining and reporting on the financial statements of this type of organization and, of course, represents the views of the members of that Committee. While this guide is not an authoritative pronouncement of the AICPA, the contents have obviously been carefully considered by this Committee and must be given substantial weight. Where an organization deviates from the principles outlined in an Audit Guide, the burden is on the CPA to justify such deviation as being in accordance with generally accepted accounting principles if an unqualified opinion is to be given by the CPA on the financial statements.

Applicable to Many Categories of Organizations

"Voluntary health and welfare organizations" are those nonprofit organizations which "derive their revenue primarily from voluntary contributions from the general public to be used for general or specific purposes connected with health, welfare, or community services."† From this definition it can be seen that many nonprofit organizations fall into this classification—community funds, YMCA's, national organizations dealing with medical research, etc.

Many organizations fit the second part of this definition, but receive a substantial portion of their revenues from sources other than public contributions. For example, an opera company would not be a voluntary health and welfare organization because its

---

any opinion on accounting principles for nonprofit organizations, but it did authorize the issuance of the three Audit Guides discussed in this and succeeding chapters. Until such time as the FASB issues its opinion on accounting principles for nonprofit organizations, each independent auditor must weigh the principles followed by current usage to determine if they represent principles generally accepted by similar organizations. The independent auditor must bear the burden, however, of justifying departures from these approved Audit Guides. Once the principles of accounting have been established by the FASB, all members of the AICPA thereafter will be required to disclose in their opinions any material departure therefrom.

* Hereafter in this chapter the word "Guide" refers to *Audits of Voluntary Health and Welfare Organizations,* Copyright © 1974 by the American Institute of Certified Public Accountants, Inc.

† Page v, *Audits of Voluntary Health and Welfare Organizations, ibid.*

primary source of income is box office receipts, although it exists for the common good.

This Guide has significance, however, to many organizations that do not fall into this definition. This Guide and the college and hospital Guides (Chapters 14 and 15) discuss almost all accounting and reporting problems nonprofit organizations have, and represent a substantial and authoritative body of opinion as to the appropriate accounting and reporting treatment for transactions that are common to most organizations. If a problem is discussed in this or one of the other two Guides it would be difficult for the CPA to take a contrary position even where the organization is not one contemplated by the three Guides. This is discussed further in Chapter 16.

In the pages that follow, the reader will observe that most of the principles followed are similar to those used by other categories of nonprofit organizations, and most were discussed in the first part of this book which dealt with accounting principles. The reader should refer to this earlier discussion for any detail of how the principles outlined are actually applied. The purpose of this and the succeeding chapters is merely to outline the practices and principles discussed in these specific Guides.

FUND ACCOUNTING

Classification of Funds

The Guide lists the funds commonly used, and the types of transactions normally associated with each fund. The fund groupings listed by the Guide and the type of transactions recorded in each are discussed below.

Current Unrestricted Fund. This fund "accounts for all resources over which the governing Board has discretionary control to use in carrying on the operations of the organization . . . except for unrestricted amounts invested in land, buildings and equipment that *may* be accounted for in a separate fund." * These are all of the completely unrestricted assets of the organization, in-

---

* Page 2, *Audits of Voluntary Health and Welfare Organizations*, AICPA, 1974.

cluding board-designated endowment funds or other resources allocated by the board for some specific purpose.

Prior to the issuance of this Guide many voluntary health and welfare organizations set up separate board-designated funds which were reported on separately from the other unrestricted activities of the organization. This Guide specifically provides that all such unrestricted income, expenses, assets, and liabilities must be reported in a single fund so that the reader can quickly see the total amount the Board has at its disposal. This is a major and significant change. It means that for these organizations there are no longer any separate board-designated funds. It means that the prior practice followed by many organizations of "designating" certain gifts as endowment (and then reporting these gifts directly in the endowment fund) is no longer permissible.

This does not prevent the Board from "designating" certain portions of the "current unrestricted fund" *balance* for specific purposes, but such designations must be reported only in the fund balance section of the Balance Sheet. See the discussion below on "Appropriations."

Current Restricted Fund. These are the amounts which have been given to the organization for a specific "operating" or "current" purpose. Excluded from this classification would be amounts given for endowment purposes or for building funds. Typically these current restricted gifts are for purposes which the organization normally carries on, as distinct from some purpose not directly related to the organization's objectives.

Current restricted funds would, of course, include only amounts given to the organization by outside persons. They would not include amounts which the board had "designated" for some future board-restricted purposes.

Land, Building, and Equipment Fund. This is used to record the organization's net investment in its fixed assets. Also included in this fund are donor-restricted contributions which have been given for the purpose of purchasing fixed assets.

While the Guide provides for this separate land, building, and equipment fund, it does not prohibit the organization from combining this fund (excluding unexpended donor-restricted building fund gifts) with the current unrestricted fund. Many organizations in the past have preferred to use a separate fixed asset fund, principally so that the current unrestricted fund would exclude long-term assets such as fixed assets and board-designated endowment or other funds. This meant that the current unrestricted fund was then a form of "current working capital" fund. Under this new Guide, however, the use of separate board-designated endowment or other funds is no longer permitted. As a result many organizations have concluded that there is no practical reason for segregating fixed assets in a separate fund and have combined their fixed asset fund and their current unrestricted fund. When this is done the title of the current unrestricted fund would become "unrestricted fund."

The major reason why this Guide still permits the use of a separate fixed asset fund is principally historic usage. That is, most nonprofit organizations have traditionally carried their fixed assets in a separate fund and the authors of the Guide concluded that the continued use of this separate fund would not distort the financial picture provided the plant fund is reported with all other funds in a single columnar-format statement. (See Figure 13–1, page 193.) The author would have preferred, however, that the plant fund were combined with the current unrestricted fund in the same manner as recommended in the earlier issued Audit Guide for hospitals, discussed in Chapter 15 (see Figure 15–1, page 250).

Endowment Fund.   This fund is to be used for all assets donated to the organization with the stipulation by the donor that only the income earned can be used. Generally the income itself is not restricted and can be used to carry out the organization's principal activities, although occasionally gifts are received which have restrictions on the uses to be made of the income. It is also possible to receive gifts that are restricted for a period of years, after which time the principal can be used as desired by the Board. Another possibility is an endowment gift under which the income earned on the principal of the gift is paid to the donor during his life but becomes completely unrestricted at his death.

It is important to note that this endowment fund is to be used only for gifts that have been restricted by the donor. Occasionally a donor, while not formally placing restrictions on a gift, will orally express the "desire" that the gift be put in the endowment fund. However, if the decision is left to the board, such amounts are unrestricted, and should be added to the current unrestricted fund. Legally unrestricted gifts cannot be added to the endowment fund. All amounts in the endowment fund must bear legal restrictions that the board cannot normally alter.

Custodian Fund. These are funds "established to account for assets received by an organization to be held or disbursed only on instructions of the person or organizaton from whom they were received." * Since these funds are not normally the property of the organization they are not reflected in the Statement of Support, Revenues and Expenses, and Changes in Fund Balances.

ACCOUNTING PRINCIPLES

Summarized in the following paragraphs are the accounting principles (or practices) that are prescribed by the Audit Guide for voluntary health and welfare organizations.

Accrual Basis

The Guide concludes that the accrual basis of accounting is normally necessary for financial statements prepared in accordance with generally accepted accounting principles. While cash basis statements are not prohibited, the auditor cannot issue an unqualified opinion† on cash basis financial statements unless these financial statements do not differ materially from the statements prepared on the accrual basis. The same caution is made with respect to modified accrual basis statements.**

Unrestricted Gifts

All unrestricted gifts and donations are recorded as revenue or "support" of the current unrestricted fund. As noted above,

---

* Page 3, *Audits of Voluntary Health and Welfare Organizations,* AICPA, 1974.
† See page 359 for a discussion of the significance of an unqualified opinion.
** Modified accrual basis statements are discussed in Chapter 3.

in the past some organizations have internally restricted certain donations but such self-imposed restrictions in no way change the characteristics of the gift and must be reported in this current unrestricted fund.

Restricted Gifts

Normally there would be only three types of restricted gifts: gifts for a "current" purpose (reported in the current restricted fund); gifts for building fund purposes (reported in the land, building, and equipment fund); and gifts for endowment (reported in the endowment fund).

Current Restricted Gifts. The Guide states that all current restricted gifts and other income should be reported in the year in which received (or pledged). Traditionally such income has been recorded only to the extent actually expended, on the theory that it is not income until expended for the restricted purpose.

Now, under the new rules, if a donor makes a contribution for a current restricted purpose of $50,000 but the organization expends only $40,000 during the current year, the full $50,000 would still be reported as income. This is contrary to the practice provided in the Audit Guides for colleges and hospitals.* Both these types of institutions would report as "income" only the amount which had actually been expended ($40,000) during the year. See pages 106–115 for a comprehensive discussion of the various alternatives for reporting current restricted income.

Building Fund Gifts. These gifts would be reported in the fixed asset fund. As was noted above, however, the Guide does not prohibit combining the fixed asset fund and the current unrestricted fund. If this combining is done, restricted building fund gifts would then be reported in the current restricted fund.†

Endowment Fund Gifts. As noted above, these gifts would be reported in a separate endowment fund, and only legally restricted gifts would be reported here.

* See Chapters 14 and 15.
† If a significant amount of building fund gifts were received, the title of the fund would probably have to be changed, or possibly two separate funds used (i.e., current restricted fund and restricted building fund gifts).

Timing of Reporting of Gifts

Current unrestricted and restricted gifts are reported as income in full in the year for which the gift *is intended.* If the donor is silent as to his intent, the presumption is that the gift is intended for the year in which made. Where it is appropriate to defer recording the gift as income to a future period (because of a donor timing restriction) the gifts would be reported in the Balance Sheet as a "deferred credit." (See Figure 13–3, on page 202.)

In many instances, of course, there will be some question as to the donor's intent. For example, if a calendar-year organization normally solicits contributions in the late Fall of the year with the clear understanding in its solicitation literature that the amounts raised will be used for the organization's upcoming year beginning January 1, it is reasonable to presume that contributions raised are intended for the future year and those received before December 31 should not be reported as income. On the other hand, if a large unsolicited gift is unexpectedly received toward the end of the year (say, on December 15), the entire amount of this gift should be recorded as income in the current year. The fact that the contribution is an extraordinarily large one and that it occurs toward the end of the year does not justify deferring its recognition as income. There must be clear evidence that the donor intended the gift for a future period in order to justify excluding it from income in the year in which it is received (or pledged).

Bequests. A special problem occurs with respect to bequests. Often the organization will be notified that it is a beneficiary under a will but a significant period of time will elapse before the organization receives the cash. The exact amount of the bequest may not be known until shortly before it is received.

The question frequently asked is when to record a bequest as income. The general answer is to record a bequest at the time the organization is first reasonably certain of the amount it will receive. If the organization is informed that it will receive a fixed dollar amount, the gift should be recorded at the time it is so informed, recognizing the gift as income of the appropriate fund.

If the organization is informed that it will receive a percentage of an estate and that its share will definitely exceed a certain amount, then this "certain" amount would be recorded with an adjustment when the final distribution is made. On the other hand, if the organization is told only that it is a beneficiary and that there will be a sizable payment, the amount of which cannot be estimated, no amount should be recorded although footnote disclosure should be made.

Pledges

Pledges represent assets and should be recorded as an asset. The same is true with allocations from the United Fund campaigns that have been made but not received in cash at the end of the period. Appropriate provision for uncollectible pledges should be established based on prior experience.

Investment Income

All unrestricted investment income (dividends and interest) must be reported directly in the current unrestricted fund in the revenues section. Endowment income which has been restricted to a specified purpose would be reported directly in the current restricted fund. Investment income from current restricted fund investments or plant fund investments is normally considered "restricted" and would be reported in the fund generating the income.

Gains or Losses on Investments

Gains or losses (and appreciation or depreciation where investments are carried at market; see below) on *unrestricted* investment funds would be reported in the current unrestricted fund, in the revenue section. Gains or losses (and appreciation or depreciation) on endowment funds are usually considered to be restricted and would be reported directly in the endowment fund. Likewise, gains or losses on current restricted fund investments and plant fund investments would normally be reported in the respective fund.

As can be seen in Figure 13–1 (page 193), gains or losses on investments are reported in the "revenues" section of the Statement of Support, Revenues and Expenses, and Changes in Fund Balances. Prior to the issuance of the Guide, gains or losses on endowment funds were typically added directly to the fund balance of that fund and not reported as income (i.e., revenue).

Where an organization carries its investments at market, the unrealized appreciation or depreciation would also be reported in the "revenues" section of this statement. It would not be appropriate, for example, to report a realized gain in the "revenues" section and then the unrealized appreciation (representing the increase in market value during the year) at the bottom of the statement after the caption "Excess of revenues over expenses." When an organization decides to carry investments at market, then its appreciation (or depreciation) is "revenue" and is reported in the same manner as realized gains or losses.

Total Return Concept

Where the board wishes to transfer some of the realized or unrealized gains on endowment fund investments to the current unrestricted fund (and assuming it has the legal right to do so under the law), the transfer must be shown below the caption "Excess of support and revenues over expenses." It is not permissible to treat this transfer as income in the revenues section. This can be seen in Figure 13–1 where a transfer of $50,000 from the endowment fund has been reported. For a more complete discussion of accounting under the total return investment concept, see pages 94 to 104.

Carrying Value of Investments

The Guide provides that an organization can carry its investments either at market or at cost. Previously, marketable securities could be carried only at cost or, in the case of donated securities, at the fair market value at the date of receipt. This is an important change which many organizations will want to consider carefully.

Carried at Cost.   If an organization carries its investments at cost, market value should be disclosed in the financial statement. If the market value of the portfolio as a whole is less than cost and such decline is of a permanent nature, it may be necessary to write down the portfolio or to provide a provision for loss. This same approach can be taken with respect to an individual investment where there is a permanent impairment.   But note that this is necessary only where the decline is of a "permanent" nature; short-term fluctuations normally do not require a provision.

Carried at Market.   If the organization carries its investments at market, it must do so for all of its investments.   It may not pick and choose which investments to carry at market.   Unrealized appreciation or depreciation would be reported in the same manner as gains or losses on investments are reported.   See the discussion on gains and losses above.

Fixed Asset Accounting

Prior to the issuance of the Guide, the practices followed by voluntary health and welfare organizations in handling fixed assets included every conceivable combination of methods.*   The Guide, however, has changed this with dramatic suddenness.   It provides that an organization must capitalize its fixed assets *and* must follow depreciation accounting procedures.   This means that this category of organization will be following fixed asset accounting practices similar to those followed by business entities.

Reason for Depreciation.   In discussing the question of depreciation accounting, the Guide states:

The relative effort being expended by one organization compared with other organizations and the allocation of such efforts to the various programs of the organization are indicated in part by cost determinations.   Whenever it is relevant to measure and report the cost of rendering current services, depreciation of assets used in providing such services is relevant as an element of such measurement and reporting process.   Although depreciation can be distinguished from most other elements of cost in that it requires no

---

* See Chapters 6 and 7 for a comprehensive discussion of fixed assets and depreciation accounting.

current equivalent cash outlay, it is not optional or discretionary. Assets used in providing services are both valuable and exhaustible. Accordingly, there is a cost expiration associated with the use of depreciable assets, whether they are owned or rented, whether acquired by gift or by purchase, and whether they are used by a profit-seeking or by a not-for-profit organization.

Where depreciation is omitted, the cost of performing the organization's services is understated. Depreciation expense, therefore, should be recognized as a cost of rendering current services and should be included as an element of expense in the Statement of Support, Revenue, and Expenses of the fund in which the assets are recorded and in the Statement of Functional Expenditures. *

There are, of course, many strong arguments for not recognizing depreciation and these are discussed at some length in Chapter 7. However, for this category of organization these arguments are fairly moot because the Guide requires that depreciation accounting be followed. If depreciation accounting is not followed, the CPA will be required to qualify his opinion.

Retroactive Recording. Of course, this does not mean that every $10 purchase must be capitalized and depreciated. The cut-off point is left to the organization to determine and many may conclude that this cut-off should be fairly high to minimize record keeping. While obviously each organization will have to make its cut-off decision based on its size and extent of fixed asset activity, the author would think most organizations would establish a cut-off of between $100 and $250.

The Guide also recognizes that there will be some initial implementation problems when the Guide becomes effective (for years beginning after July 1, 1974). It provides that the organization should reconstruct the amount of fixed assets and accumulated depreciation as though the organization had followed this accounting principle all along.

Most voluntary health and welfare organizations do not have large amounts of fixed assets. Normally their assets consist of furniture, equipment, and sometimes vehicles; only occasionally do they own real property. While it might seem that the organization would have to reconstruct its fixed asset records from the date of its original incorporation, it would appear the spirit

---

* Page 12 of the Guide.

of the Guide would be met if the organization reconstructed its fixed asset and depreciation records only for assets still in service and not fully depreciated. For example, furniture and fixtures are typically depreciated over a ten-year period. As of July 1, 1974, the earliest fixed asset purchases which would be still undepreciated would be acquisitions made in the year 1964. There would seem little need to reconstruct fixed asset additions prior to 1964 since they would be fully depreciated at July 1, 1974. Of course, if the organization had a significant amount of fully depreciated assets it would be appropriate to record both the asset and the full depreciation.

The Guide also provides that if an organization is unable to reconstruct its cost basis for its fixed assets (or the fair market value at the date of receipt in the case of donated fixed assets), it may use a "cost" appraisal. A cost appraisal differs from a current value appraisal in that the appraiser attempts to determine what the asset would have cost at the time it was originally purchased, and not at today's cost.

Fixed Assets Where Title May Revert to Grantors. Some organizations purchase or receive fixed assets under research or similar grants in which, at the completion of the grant period, title to these fixed assets reverts to the grantor.

Should these assets be recorded and depreciated? Typically the grant period closely approximates the useful life of these assets and the grantor in fact seldom asks for their return. The right to reclaim these assets usually is in the grant award mainly to protect the grantor in the event the grant is prematurely terminated. Under these circumstances, fixed assets, whether purchased or donated, should be recorded as an asset and depreciated as with any other asset. If the aggregate amount of these assets which might have to be returned were material, disclosure of the relevant facts would, of course, be appropriate.

Donated Services

Donated services are not normally recorded except where their omission would make the financial statements misleading. If this would be the case, donated services would still only be recorded when:

1. There is "a clearly measurable basis for the amount."
2. The "organization exercises control over the employment and duties" of the person donating the services.
3. "The services performed are a normal part of the agency's program. . . ." *

Certain categories of services would not normally be recorded; these include supplementary efforts of volunteers which are in the nature of services to beneficiaries of the organization, volunteers assisting in fund-raising drives, and professional personnel assisting in research and training activities without pay.

But where all of the requirements listed above are met, and where the amounts are material, there is no option. Donated services must be recorded or the CPA will be required to qualify his opinion.

Donated Materials

Donated materials are normally recorded as a contribution at their fair market value, appropriately disclosed. The principal exception would be where the amounts are not significant or where there is no readily measurable basis for valuing such materials. In addition, donated materials that merely pass through the hands of the organization to a beneficiary are normally not recorded since the organization is merely acting as an agent for the donor.

Donated Securities

Donated securities are treated in the same way as donated cash; that is, if the donated securities are to be used for a donor-specified purpose or endowment then the gift would be recorded directly in the appropriate fund at the fair market value at the date of receipt. If the gift is not restricted by the donor, then, of course, the gift would be recorded directly in the current unrestricted fund in the same manner as any other cash gift.

* Page 21 of the Guide.

Donated Equipment and Fixed Assets

Donated fixed assets would be recorded at their fair market value as revenue of the fixed asset fund, provided a separate fixed asset fund were used. If, on the other hand, the donated asset will be sold shortly after receipt and the cash received therefrom will be unrestricted, then these fixed asset gifts would be recorded in the current unrestricted fund at the time of initial receipt.

Appropriations

The board is permitted to "appropriate" or designate a portion of the unrestricted fund balance for some special and specific purpose. This appropriation or designation, however, would be reported only in the fund balance section of the Balance Sheet. The appropriation or designation may *not* be shown as a deduction on the Statement of Support, Revenues and Expenses, and Changes in Fund Balances.

Accordingly, it is not appropriate for an organization to charge expenditures directly against "appropriated" balances. The expenditure must be included in the Statement of Support, Revenues and Expenses, and Changes in Fund Balances. All an appropriation does is to allow the board to designate *in the fund balance section* of the Balance Sheet how it intends to spend the unrestricted fund balance in the future.

For example, the unrestricted current fund balance of the National Association of Environmentalists of $135,516 (Figure 13–3) could be split into several amounts, representing the board's present intention of how it plans to use this amount. Perhaps $50,000 of it is intended for Project Seaweed, and the balance is available for undesignated purposes. The fund balance section of the Balance Sheet would appear:

Fund balance:
Designated by the board for
  Project Seaweed . . . . $ 50,000
Undesignated, available for
  current purposes   85,516
                                        $135,516

As monies are expended for Project Seaweed in subsequent periods, they would be recorded as an expense in the Statement of Support, Revenues and Expenses, and Changes in Fund Balances. At the same time the amount of the fund balance designated by the board for Project Seaweed would be reduced and the amount "undesignated" for current purposes would be increased by the same amount. See pages 50–56 for a comprehensive discussion of appropriation accounting techniques.

FINANCIAL STATEMENTS

The Guide provides for three principal financial statements:

1. Statement of Support, Revenues and Expenses, and Changes in Fund Balances (Figure 13–1, page 193)
2. Statement of Functional Expenses (Figure 13–2, page 200)
3. Balance Sheet (Figure 13–3, page 202)

The statements presented in the Guide are for illustrative purposes only and the Guide points out that variations from the ones presented may be appropriate. However, as noted below, expenses must be reported on a functional basis and supporting services such as management and general, and fund raising must be separately disclosed. Further, the Guide indicates that the major categories of expenses going into each of the functional classifications must also be disclosed, either in a formal Statement of Functional Expenses (Figure 13–2) or in notes to the financial statements.

Statement of Support, Revenues and Expenses, and Changes in Fund Balances

Figure 13–1 shows a Statement of Support, Revenues and Expenses, and Changes in Fund Balances for the National Association of Environmentalists. This is the format shown in the Guide with some modifications (discussed below).

Functional Classification of Expenses. Traditionally, nonprofit organizations have reported in terms of amounts spent for salaries, rent, supplies, etc. (i.e., a natural expense classification). This

NATIONAL ASSOCIATION OF ENVIRONMENTALISTS

STATEMENT OF SUPPORT, REVENUES AND EXPENSES, AND CHANGES IN FUND BALANCES
For the Year Ended December 31, 1974

	Current Funds		Fixed Asset Fund	Endowment Fund	Total All Funds
	Unrestricted	Restricted			
Support:					
Contributions and gifts	$213,000		$10,000		$223,000
Bequests	60,000			$ 21,500	81,500
Total support	273,000		10,000	21,500	304,500
Revenues:					
Membership dues	20,550				20,550
Research projects	89,500	$38,400			127,900
Advertising income	33,500				33,500
Subscriptions to nonmembers	18,901				18,901
Dividends and interest income	14,607				14,607
Appreciation of investments				33,025	33,025
Total revenues	177,058	38,400		33,025	248,483
Total support and revenues	450,058	38,400	10,000	54,525	552,983
Expenses:					
Program services:					
"National Environment" magazine	108,240		2,260		110,500
Clean-up month campaign	124,308		2,309		126,617
Lake Erie project	83,285	26,164	5,616		115,065
Total program services	315,833	26,164	10,185		352,182
Supporting services:					
Management and general	30,355		3,161		33,516
Fund raising	5,719		250		5,969
Total supporting services	36,074		3,411		39,485
Total expenses	351,907	26,164	13,596		391,667
Excess (deficit) of revenues over expenses	98,151	12,236	(3,596)	54,525	161,316
Other changes in fund balance:					
Equipment acquisitions from unrestricted funds	(30,000)		30,000		–
Transfer of endowment fund gains	50,000			(50,000)	–
Fund balance, beginning of year	17,365	5,915	67,266	230,010	320,556
Fund balance, end of year	$135,516	$18,151	$93,670	$234,535	$481,872

Fig. 13–1.   Income statement in the columnar format recommended in the AICPA Audit Guide for Voluntary Health and Welfare Organizations.

Guide takes a major step forward when it states that the organization exists to perform services and programs and therefore should be reporting principally in terms of its individual program activities or functions. Figure 13–1 shows the expenses of the

National Association of Environmentalists reported on a functional basis. This type of presentation requires management to tell the reader how much of its funds were expended for each program category and the amounts spent in supporting services, including fund raising.

Further, the Guide states that this functional reporting is not optional. The Statement of Support, Revenues and Expenses, and Changes in Fund Balances must be prepared on this functional or program basis or the CPA will be required to qualify his opinion, stating that the statements were not prepared in accordance with generally accepted accounting principles.

Many organizations will have to develop reasonably sophisticated procedures to be able to allocate expenses between various categories. An excellent reference source is the revised edition (1974) of *Standards of Accounting and Financial Reporting for Voluntary Health and Welfare Organizations,* discussed on pages 206–209. Also, United Way of America has published a comprehensive book to guide "human service organizations in identifying their program classifications. This book is referred to as *UWASIS— United Way of America Services Identification System.*

Fund-Raising Expenses Disclosed.- The Statement of Support, Revenues and Expenses, and Changes in Fund Balances must also clearly disclose the amount of supporting services. These are broken down between fund raising and other management and general expenses. This distinction between supporting and program services is required, as is the separate reporting of fund raising. Absence of either the functional reporting approach or information on fund raising would result in a qualified opinion by a CPA.

Columnar Presentation. The statement presentation is in a columnar format and, as can be observed in Figure 13–1, includes *all* four funds on one statement. This represents a significant departure from the statement format recommended in the Audit Guide for hospitals (discussed in Chapter 15), and from past practice. This format, however, is very similar to the format recommended in earlier chapters of this book.

It should be noted that this statement provides a complete picture of all activity of this organization for the year—not just the activity of a single fund. Further, by including a "total all funds" column on the statement, the reader is quickly able to see the total activity and does not have to himself add together several funds to get the total picture. This represents a major advance in nonprofit accounting.

The illustrated financial statements in the Guide show figures in the "total all funds" column for both the revenues and expenses categories. The illustrated statements do not, however, show figures in this total column for the caption "Excess of revenues over expenses" or for the captions that follow (i.e., other changes, fund balance beginning of year, fund balance end of year). The reason these totals were omitted is that the authors of the Guide were troubled by adding unrestricted and restricted revenues and expenses together to get a total. This is a continuation of the historic reluctance many accountants have shown in adding together what they feel are apples and oranges.

At the same time, the Guide's authors felt that they had to show total expenses for all funds because depreciation was being reported in a separate column, and, as noted above, depreciation is an expense which has to be reported as part of the functional expenses for the period. Only by showing a total of the expenses of the several columns would the reader see the total expense picture. Thus, somewhat reluctantly, the authors included a "total all funds" column for the expenses (and revenues). They chose not to include a total column for the "excess of revenues" and the "fund balances" captions because of their concern that the reader might misinterpret these amounts.

It seems somewhat inconsistent that while the Guide shows revenues and expenses in total, it does not show the net of these two amounts or the fund balances at the beginning and end of the year. However, nothing in the Guide indicates a prohibition from showing total-all-funds amounts for these other captions, as has been done in Figure 13–1. The author believes that usage will eventually result in almost universal acceptance of total-all-funds figures for these captions.

Unrestricted Activity in Single Column.   One of the most significant features of this presentation is that all legally unrestricted revenues and expenses are reported in the single column, "current unrestricted" fund. The use of a single column in which all unrestricted activity is reported greatly simplifies the presentation and makes it more likely that "grandmother" will be able to comprehend the total picture of the organization. Further, a number of interfund transfers are eliminated because under the earlier Audit Guide separate board-designated funds were permitted whereas here the organization is *required* to combine all unrestricted activity in this single column.

Many organizations, of course, will want to continue to keep board-designated accounts within their bookkeeping system. This is fine. But, for reporting on the activity for the year, all unrestricted funds must be combined and reported as indicated in this illustration.

While not recommended, there would appear to be no prohibition to an organization's including additional columns to the *left* of this total "unrestricted" column to show the various unrestricted board-designated categories of funds which make up' the total unrestricted fund column. However, where an organization does so it must clearly indicate that the total current unrestricted fund column represents the total unrestricted activity for the year and that the detailed columns to the left are only the arbitrarily subdivided amounts making up this total. Probably an organization is better advised to show such detail in a separate supplementary schedule, if at all.

Current Restricted Column. The "restricted" column represents those amounts which have been given to the organization for a specified purpose other than for endowment or fixed asset additions. It should be observed that the amounts reported as revenues in this fund represent the total amount the organization received during the year, and not the amount of such funds that was actually expended. As noted earlier in this chapter, gifts or grants which have time restrictions placed on them by the donor and could not be expended during the current period would not be reported as revenues but would be shown as deferred income on the Balance Sheet.

Use of Separate Fixed Asset Fund. The Guide provides for the use of a separate plant fund, although, as noted earlier, it does not require its use. The organization could combine the fixed asset fund with the current unrestricted fund and report such activity as part of that fund. This, of course, has certain advantages since it would reduce the number of columns (thus helping "grand-mother") and would eliminate the need for certain interfund transfers.

One of the reasons why this separate plant fund was presented is that the industry committee * objected strongly to the fixed asset· capitalization and depreciation accounting requirements. One argument expressed against depreciation was a concern that certain organizations had to budget their income and expenses exclusive of depreciation. For this reason the industry committee was reluctant to follow depreciation accounting practices, but agreed to do so provided the depreciation provision was reported directly in a separate fixed asset fund column, and not in the un-restricted fund column. Thus in Figure 13–1 the depreciation for this organization is reflected entirely in the plant fund column.

Another argument many make against combining the plant fund with the unrestricted fund is that fixed assets are often pur-chased with donor-restricted gifts. There is a legal question of whether the original restrictions remain with the fixed assets once purchased. In the event of sale many believe the cash proceeds would remain restricted, and for this reason feel it inappropriate to combine the two funds.

Appreciation of Investments.   This organization has elected to carry its investments at market. Obviously this means that the organization must reflect appreciation (or depreciation) on its Statement of Support, Revenues and Expenses, and Changes in Fund Balances. In this instance the net appreciation of invest-ments was $33,025. Assuming there were no sales or purchases of investments during the year, this amount would have been determined by comparing the market value of the investments at the end of the year with the market value at the beginning of the year. Normally, however, there will be some realized gain or loss during the year. While there is no technical objection to reporting the realized gain or loss separate from the unrealized appreciation (or depreciation), there seems little significance to this distinction. See page 94 for a discussion of the reasons why.

---

* Joint Liaison Committee of the National Health Council, the National Assem-bly for Social Policy and Development, Inc., and the United Way of America.

Activity of Restricted Funds Reported as Revenues and Expenses.
It is significant to note that the Guide has reported changes in the
three restricted funds (current restricted fund, endowment fund,
and fixed asset fund) in an income statement format and has
reported the excess of revenues over expenses of these restricted
funds. In the past many have argued that such restricted fund
activity should not be reported in an income statement format but
rather as "changes" in fund balance without any indication of the
net change for the year. (See Figure 12–5 and the accompanying
discussion in Chapter 12.)

This change is significant because it now permits the reader to
see the total activity of the organization—both restricted and unrestricted. Thus the Guide appears to be saying that we have a
single entity on which we are reporting as distinct from several
subentities for which there is no total. In this example, the total
excess of revenues over expenses was $161,316, whereas the ac-
tivity of the unrestricted funds resulted in an excess of only
$98,151.* Certainly the reader has a right to know of these other
amounts in a manner which will permit seeing a total picture.

Other Changes in Fund Balance. This section represents interfund transfers. Since all unrestricted funds are reported as a
single fund there are very few such transfers. In this illustration
$30,000 of equipment was purchased from current unrestricted
funds. Since all fixed assets are reported in the fixed asset fund,
this $30,000 has to be transferred from the current unrestricted
fund to the fixed asset fund.

The second transfer shown in Figure 13–1 is a transfer of endowment fund gains from the endowment fund to the current
unrestricted fund. This transfer was made under a "total return"
approach.†

---

* As noted on page 195, however, the illustrated statements in the Guide
did not include figures in the total column for the excess of revenues over expenses.

† See pages 94 to 103 for a comprehensive discussion of transfers under the
total return concept of endowment funds investments.

Statement of Functional Expenses

Figure 13–2 is a statement which analyzes functional or program expenses and shows the natural expense categories which go into each functional category. It is primarily an analysis to give the reader insight as to the major types of expenses involved.

Obviously in order to arrive at the functional expense totals shown in the Statement of Support, Revenues and Expenses, and Changes in Fund Balances an analysis must be prepared which shows all of the expenses going into each program category.

The Statement of Functional Expenses merely summarizes this detail for the reader. In many instances the allocation of salaries between functional or program categories should be based on time reports and similar analyses. In other instances the allocation will be made on the basis of floor space. Obviously each organization will have to develop time and expense accumulation procedures that will provide the necessary basis for allocation.

The Guide would seem to give some leeway to an organization whose principal expenses are salaries and only one or two other major expenses. Under those circumstances it might be possible to present this information in notes to the financial statements rather than in a separate statement.

Depreciation. In the illustrative financial statements in the Guide, depreciation expense is shown as the very last item on the statement and all other expenses are subtotaled before depreciation is added. This presentation was illustrated in the Guide because of the concern of many nonprofit organizations in showing depreciation as an expense. By subtotaling all expenses before adding depreciation, the Guide emphasizes the somewhat different nature of depreciation expense. The author disagrees and for this reason has included depreciation among the other expense categories in Figure 13–2. Either presentation is acceptable.

NATIONAL ASSOCIATION OF ENVIRONMENTALISTS

STATEMENT OF FUNCTIONAL EXPENSES

For the Year Ended December 31, 1974

	Total All Expenses	Program Services				Supporting Services		
		"National Environment" Magazine	Clean-up Month Campaign	Lake Erie Project	Total Program	Management and General	Fund Raising	Total Supporting
Salaries	$170,773	$ 24,000	$ 68,140	$ 60,633	$152,773	$15,000	$3,000	$18,000
Payroll taxes and employee benefits	22,199	3,120	8,857	7,882	19,859	1,950	390	2,340
Total compensation	192,972	27,120	76,997	68,515	172,632	16,950	3,390	20,340
Printing	84,071	63,191	18,954	515	82,660	1,161	250	1,411
Mailing, postage, and shipping	14,225	10,754	1,188	817	12,759	411	1,055	1,466
Rent	19,000	3,000	6,800	5,600	15,400	3,000	600	3,600
Telephone	5,615	895	400	1,953	3,248	2,151	216	2,367
Outside art	14,865	3,165	11,700	–	14,865	–	–	–
Local travel	1,741	–	165	915	1,080	661	–	661
Conferences and conventions	6,328	–	1,895	2,618	4,513	1,815	–	1,815
Depreciation	13,596	2,260	2,309	5,616	10,185	3,161	250	3,411
Legal and audit	2,000	–	–	–	–	2,000	–	2,000
Supplies	31,227	–	1,831	28,516	30,347	761	119	880
Miscellaneous	6,027	115	4,378	–	4,493	1,445	89	1,534
Total	$391,667	$110,500	$126,617	$115,065	$352,182	$33,516	$5,969	$39,485

Fig. 13–2. An analysis of the various program expenses showing the natural expense categories making up each of the functional or program categories.

Balance Sheet

Figure 13–3 shows a Balance Sheet for the National Association of Environmentalists. The statement illustrated in the Audit Guide presents the more conventional Balance Sheet format in which each fund is reported as a separate sub-Balance Sheet. Figure 4–2 on page 39 is an example of a typical Balance Sheet. Figure 13–3 has been presented in a columnar format because the author feels this presentation is more meaningful to most readers. The Guide does not prohibit a columnar presentation but indicates that care must be taken to ensure that the restricted nature of certain of the funds is clearly shown.

Comparison Column. In Figure 13–3 we have shown the totals for the previous year to provide a comparison for the reader. Obviously in a columnar presentation it is practical to show this comparison with the previous year for only the "total all funds" column, although it is possible also to show a comparison for a second column, as is illustrated on page 165.*

Designation of Unrestricted Fund Balance. While it is a little more awkward to show when the Balance Sheet is presented in a columnar fashion as in Figure 13–3, it is still possible to disclose the composition of the unrestricted fund balance of $135,516. This is shown earlier in this chapter, on page 191.

Investments Carried at Market. As previously noted, the National Association of Environmentalists carries its investments at market rather than at cost. The Guide indicates that where this is done the statement should disclose the unrealized appreciation (or depreciation). This particular organization has disclosed this information in footnotes to the financial statements rather than on the face of the statement itself.

---

* Many accountants object to including this total comparison column, saying that sufficient information on the nature of the restricted portions is not reported. There is some validity to this argument but the author feels this total column is preferable to no comparison.

NATIONAL ASSOCIATION OF ENVIRONMENTALISTS

BALANCE SHEET
December 31, 1974 and 1973

| | December 31, 1974 | | | | | December 31, 1973— |
| | Current Funds | | Endowment Funds | Fixed Asset Funds | Total All Funds | Total All Funds |
	Unrestricted	Restricted				
ASSETS						
Current assets:						
Cash	$ 52,877	$22,666	$ 8,416	$ 2,150	$ 86,109	$ 11,013
Savings accounts	50,000				50,000	
Accounts receivable	3,117				3,117	918
Investments, at market	76,195		226,119		302,314	269,289
Pledges receivable	4,509	1,000			5,509	769
Total current assets	186,698	23,666	234,535	2,150	447,049	281,989
Fixed assets, at cost				111,135	111,135	72,518
Less: Accumulated depreciation				(19,615)	(19,615)	(6,019)
Net fixed assets				91,520	91,520	66,499
Total assets	$186,698	$23,666	$234,535	$ 93,670	$538,569	$348,488
LIABILITIES AND FUND BALANCES						
Current liabilities:						
Accounts payable	$ 48,666	$ 1,015			$ 49,681	$ 25,599
Deferred income	2,516	4,500			7,016	2,333
Total current liabilities	51,182	5,515			56,697	27,932
Fund balance	135,516	18,151	$234,535	$ 93,670	481,872	320,556
Total liabilities and fund balances	$186,698	$23,666	$234,535	$ 93,670	$538,569	$348,488

Fig. 13–3.   A Balance Sheet prepared in columnar format.

RECOMMENDED SIMPLIFIED PRESENTATION

While the Audit Guide for voluntary health and welfare organizations significantly strengthens both the accounting and reporting principles for this category of organizations, there are several further steps that the Guide might have taken which would have aided in the reader's comprehension of these statements. Most of the improvements the author recommends involve elimination of detailed reporting on a fund-by-fund basis.

Figures 13–4 and 13–5 show such a simplified Statement of Income, Expenses, and Changes in Fund Balances, and the Balance Sheet for the National Association of Environmentalists. The principal change has been to eliminate the reporting on each fund, and to report only on the entity as a whole.* This does not mean that it is not important to inform the reader of the amount of restricted resources which have been received and are unspent at the end of the year. Obviously this is important. What is not of particular importance, however, is the detail of all of the transactions that took place during the year or even of the composition of the restricted assets at the end of the year. Rather, the interested reader should be primarily concerned with the amount of restricted funds remaining at the end of the year. This is clearly shown in the detail presented in the fund balance section of the Balance Sheet (Figure 13–5).

Not Generally Accepted

The Audit Guide states that "the financial statements should reflect unrestricted and restricted funds separately." † For this reason it would appear that the statements shown in Figures 13–4 and 13–5 cannot be considered generally accepted at this time. If restricted funds were material in amount—as here—an independent auditor would be required to qualify his opinion.

---

* There have been a number of other changes, including a change in some of the captions (principally the substitution of the word "income" for the words "support and revenues"). Note also that because we have presented all funds together there is no need to show interfund transfer.

† Page 33 of the Guide.

NATIONAL ASSOCIATION OF ENVIRONMENTALISTS

STATEMENT OF INCOME, EXPENSES, AND CHANGES IN FUND BALANCE

Year Ended December 31, 1974

Income:

Contributions and gifts	$223,000	
Bequests	81,500	
Membership dues	20,550	
Research projects	127,900	
Advertising income	33,500	
Subscriptions to nonmembers	18,901	
Dividends and interest income	14,607	
Appreciation of investments	33,025	
Total income		$552,983

Expenses:

Program services:

"National Environment" magazine	110,500	
Clean-up month campaign	126,617	
Lake Erie project	115,065	
Total program services		352,182

Supporting services:

Management and general	33,516	
Fund raising	5,969	
Total supporting services		39,485
Total expenses		391,667

Excess of income over expenses	161,316
Fund balance, beginning of year	320,556
Fund balance, end of year	$481,872

Fig. 13–4. A simplified Statement of Income and Expenses in which no distinction is made between restricted and unrestricted funds.

NATIONAL ASSOCIATION OF ENVIRONMENTALISTS
BALANCE SHEET

	December 31	
	1974	1973
ASSETS		
Current assets:		
Cash	$ 86,109	$ 11,013
Savings accounts	50,000	
Investments, at market.	302,314	269,289
Accounts receivable	3,117	918
Pledges receivable.	5,509	769
Total current assets	447,049	281,989
Fixed assets, at cost	111,135	72,518
Less: Accumulated depreciation	(19,615)	(6,019)
Net fixed assets	91,520	66,499
Total assets	$538,569	$348,488

LIABILITIES AND FUND BALANCES

Current liabilities:		
Accounts payable.	$ 49,681	$ 25,599
Deferred income	7,016	2,333
Total current liabilities	56,697	27,932
Fund balance:		
Restricted by donors for:		
Endowment.	234,535	230,010
Fixed asset purchases	2,150	1,617
Current purposes	18,151	5,915
Total restricted	254,836	237,542
Unrestricted:		
Invested in fixed assets	91,520	66,499
Designated for Project Seaweed.	50,000	
Undesignated, available for current use	85,516	16,515
Total unrestricted	227,036	83,014
Total fund balance.	481,872	320,556
Total liabilities and fund balance	$538,569	$348,488

Fig. 13–5.   A simplified Balance Sheet in which restricted funds are disclosed only in the fund balance section.

CONCLUDING COMMENTS ON THE GUIDE

The AICPA Audit Guide for voluntary health and welfare organizations is a significant step forward in reporting for a major category of nonprofit organizations. Its relatively direct approach will add greatly to the ability of the nonaccountant reader to understand the financial statements.

The requirement of reporting expenses on a functional or program basis should have major impact on these organizations because functional reporting will emphasize the purpose of the organization's existence. In reporting on this basis the reader will be given a basis for judging how effectively the organization's resources have been used.

The Guide has also eliminated much of the confusion caused by fund accounting in the past by reporting restricted and unrestricted funds on a single statement. Thus the Guide seems to confirm what most nonaccountants have always known (but which accountants tend to forget): each organization is a single entity, not a collection of separate entities.

THE EVOLUTION OF STANDARDS

In 1964, two national organizations in their respective fields of health and social welfare, the National Health Council and the National Assembly for Social Policy and Development, published a book for use by affiliated organizations to assist them in establishing uniform standards of accounting and reporting. This book, *Standards of Accounting and Financial Reporting for Voluntary Health and Welfare Organizations,* was one of the first major attempts to analyze the needs of the readers of financial statements of voluntary health and welfare organizations and to prescribe standards of both accounting and reporting for member organizations. It was written because prior thereto contributors could not compare the financial statements of member organizations since each organization followed accounting principles it felt appropriate and each had a different concept of what the reader of financial statements should be told. The standards of accounting and reporting prescribed in this book provided a framework which, when followed, made it possible for readers to make meaningful comparisons of the financial statements of several organizations.

While the standards prescribed were initially seen as being applicable only to the member organizations of these two national organizations,* this book's influence was felt by all voluntary health and welfare organizations, in part because until recently there was no other definitive source of accounting principles, or reporting standards, to which they could refer.†

A number of the accounting principles recommended in this 1964 book were controversial and were not uniformly accepted by accountants or by nonprofit organizations.** Nevertheless the book provided a set of "standards" which had great impact on nonprofit accounting, particularly for voluntary health and welfare organizations. In large part because of this influence and because many accountants found some of the principles recommended by Standards‡ difficult to accept, it became necessary for the authors of Standards and the accounting profession to reach agreement on appropriate principles for such organizations.

---

* There are many well-known organizations associated with the National Health Council or the National Assembly for Social Policy and Development. These include, among others, the American Cancer Society, Boy Scouts of America, National Jewish Welfare Board, YMCA, the American Red Cross, and The Salvation Army.

† The reader should be aware of the 1974 AICPA Audit Guide discussed earlier in this chapter.

** The two major areas with which many CPAs had difficulty were the handling of fixed assets and the form of recommended financial statements. Standards recommended that all fixed assets be written off as purchased but then later capitalized and reported in the Balance Sheet. This is the "write-off, then capitalize" method discussed on page 64 . It is contrary to the way commercial organizations handle fixed assets and many could not accept such a contrary treatment. Further, to many this method was just too complicated to be understood.

The form of financial statement recommended, the Summary of Financial Activities, was a unique form of financial statement in which all income and expenditures of the organization were reported, regardless of source or restriction. While this concept was excellent, the format of the statement was just too complicated and hard to understand and few readers—including CPAs—really comprehended the information it contained.

‡ To the end of this chapter reference to "Standards" refers to *Standards of Accounting and Financial Reporting for Voluntary Health and Welfare Organizations,* published in 1964. "Revised Standards" refers to the 1974 edition.

Accordingly two committees were formed: a Committee of CPAs under the AICPA and a separate Industry Committee formed by the authors of Standards and referred to as the Joint Liaison Committee. * These Committees worked together over a several-year period to reconcile the differences between Standards and practices which CPAs felt represented "generally accepted accounting principles." At the conclusion of this period, the AICPA published in 1974 its Audit Guide, discussed earlier in this chapter. While the Joint Liaison Committee was not enthusiastic about all of the principles contained in the Audit Guide, they were able to endorse it and to urge their members and affiliated organizations to adhere to its principles.

Accordingly, in 1974 the second edition of *Standards of Accounting and Financial Reporting for Voluntary Health and Welfare Organizations* was published. † It was revised to conform with the AICPA Audit Guide and there are no significant differences in accounting and reporting principles between the two publications.

INFLUENCE OF STANDARDS ON THE AUDIT GUIDE

Without question, Standards had a significant impact on the accounting and reporting principles prescribed in the AICPA Audit Guide. Perhaps the most important impact was from Standards' insistence that an organization must present on a single financial statement all of its activities for the year, both unrestricted and restricted. Without the influence of Standards and the efforts of the Joint Liaison Committee, the Audit Guide would

---

* This Committee consisted of representatives of the original two national organizations sponsoring Standards, and representatives of the United Way of America.

† United Way of America joined the National Health Council and the National Assembly for Social Policy and Development, Inc. in the sponsorship of the second edition. In 1974, United Way of America was in the process of completing a major book, *Accounting and Financial Reporting—A Guide for United Ways and Not-For-Profit Human Service Organizations*. The accounting principles and reporting formats recommended in this book are consistent with those in both the Audit Guide and Revised Standards. In addition, it offers considerable advice, including a comprehensive chart of accounts, forms, and documentations specifically addressed to this category of nonprofit organizations. It can be obtained from United Way of America, Alexandria, Va. 22314.

have followed pretty much the format recommended in the Hospital Audit Guide. As discussed in Chapter 15, the Audit Guide for hospitals recommends reporting all unrestricted funds together in one statement but reporting restricted funds in separate statements. This makes it difficult for the reader to see the total picture.

A Useful Reference

This book provides considerable assistance to the reader and offers much more detailed instruction than does the Audit Guide. The Audit Guide is intended to be only an outline of principles for the CPA's guidance. Revised Standards is intended to be a manual for the accountant within an organization applying these principles. It is an important reference book for the organization following the principles outlined in the AICPA Audit Guide.*

---

* It can be obtained from the National Health Council, New York, N.Y. 10019.

14

Colleges and Universities

Among the most influential types of nonprofit institutions are colleges and universities. The extent of their influence is suggested by the fact that there are more than eight million students currently attending institutions of higher learning. There are approximately 2,500 colleges and universities and they must depend in large part on support from gifts and contributions from alumni and the general public. These institutions have the same need to report on their activities and to effectively communicate their financial needs as do other nonprofit organizations. The problems of reporting are complicated for these institutions by their historical reliance on fund accounting techniques. The purpose of this chapter is first to outline and discuss the accounting principles which are generally accepted for colleges and universities, and then to offer suggestions on how to simplify the financial statements to help the reader more easily understand them.

AUTHORITATIVE PRONOUNCEMENTS

The American Council on Education published in 1953 *College and University Business Administration,* of which a substantial portion deals with the principles of accounting and reporting. Republished in 1968,* this book was until 1973 generally accepted as

* *College and University Business Administration,* Revised Edition, American Council on Education, Washington, D. C., 1968.

210

the most authoritative source of accounting and reporting principles applicable to colleges and universities. Because of its wide use, it has become generally known by the acronym "CUBA." This acronym will be used throughout this chapter and refers to the 1968 edition.

AICPA Audit Guide

In 1973 the Committee on College and University Accounting and Auditing of the American Institute of Certified Public Accountants issued an Audit Guide for use by CPAs in their examination of the financial statements of these institutions. As with the other industry guides* it contains not only guidance to the CPA on auditing procedures, but also a comprehensive discussion of accounting and reporting principles for such institutions. Accordingly, the Audit Guide has now become the authoritative source for principles of accounting and reporting for colleges and universities.† Throughout this chapter the principles outlined herein will be as discussed in this Audit Guide except where the author indicates his preference for alternative treatment.

To a large extent this Audit Guide has codified principles of accounting and reporting discussed in CUBA. In fact, a number of representatives of the National Association of College and University Business Officers (NACUBO) worked with the AICPA Committee throughout the development of this Audit Guide so that the Guide represents a joint effort of both the accounting profession and college and university business officers.

NACUBO "Administrative Service"

The 1968 edition of CUBA has now been superseded by a looseleaf administrative service titled "College and University Business Administration—Administrative Service," published by NACUBO. The Audit Guide for colleges and universities has been incorporated as a part of this Service.

---

* See Chapter 13 for a discussion of the Audit Guide for voluntary health and welfare organizations and Chapter 15 for the Audit Guide for hospitals.

† See page 177 for a discussion of the significance of Audit Guides and their relationship to generally accepted accounting principles.

Changes in terminology of the captions of the financial statements, interpretations of the Audit Guide, and other changes as occur from time to time will be reflected on a current basis in this Service. In mid-1974 a number of changes in financial statement captions and terminology for current fund revenues and expenditures were recommended by a joint committee consisting of industry representatives and members of an AICPA task force. These changes have been reflected in the Administrative Service. For this reason readers interested in seeing the latest industry and AICPA recommended financial statement formats should refer to this Service rather than to the Audit Guide.

FUND ACCOUNTING

Fund accounting is followed by colleges and universities in a classical manner and no other type of institution is as wedded to fund accounting. This results from an historic reliance on outside gifts, many of which involved restrictions, and thus the need to keep track of these restricted resources. Also, because of a continuing reliance on outside financial help, these institutions often felt it prudent to set aside funds from current unrestricted gifts to function as endowment funds and thus to provide future endowment income. All of this accented the use of fund accounting and the resulting problem of communicating to the nonaccountant reader of the financial statements.

Classification of Funds

Generally the number of major fund groupings is limited to five: *

1. Current funds
   a. Unrestricted
   b. Restricted

---

* There is a sixth fund group—agency funds. These are funds that are in the custody of the institution but do not belong to it. An example would be funds belonging to student organizations on deposit with the institution. Agency funds are not discussed or illustrated in this chapter because they are not funds of the institution. Reference should be made to the Audit Guide and to the Administrative Service by interested readers.

2. Loan funds
3. Endowment and similar funds
4. Annuity and life income funds
5. Plant funds
   a. Unexpended
   b. Renewal and replacement
   c. Retirement of indebtedness
   d. Investment in plant

Within these major groupings there are often several subgroupings. Figure 14–1 (pages 218–219) shows the format of Statement of Changes in Fund Balances for Mary and Isla College and the subgrouping of both current and plant funds can be seen.

Current Funds.   These are the funds that are available for the general operations of the institution. Usually a distinction is made between those current funds that are unrestricted and those that are restricted by an outside party for a current purpose. Generally each type of activity for the year is presented in a separate column, with the columns side by side in the financial statements.

The balance in the current *restricted* fund represents the unexpended balance of amounts which have been received for a specific current purpose and, in theory, these amounts would have to be returned if the institution were not to use the funds for the restricted purpose.

The balance in the current *unrestricted* fund represents only that amount which the board has chosen to leave in this fund. As is discussed below, the board can transfer into and out of the current unrestricted fund and there is little significance to the balance in this fund at any given time. Unfortunately, few non-accountant readers understand this and many mistakenly assume that a low current unrestricted fund balance is an indication the organization is in poor financial condition, which may or may not be the case. This can be seen in Figure 14–3 (page 226), in which the ending balance of $160,000 suggests that Mary and Isla College is in dire financial straits. Notice, however, immediately above this ending balance that the board has chosen to transfer $600,000 from this fund to other funds.

Loan Funds. These are funds which are available for granting loans to students and, to a lesser extent, to faculty. These funds are not available for other uses. The principal of restricted gifts where only the income can be used for loans should be shown as part of the endowment fund, and income as earned and available for loans should be transferred to the loan fund.

Endowment Funds. This fund grouping includes three types of funds classified as endowment and similar funds:

1. Endowment funds, where the donor has stipulated that the principal is to be kept intact in perpetuity and only the income therefrom can be expended either for general purpose or for a restricted purpose.
2. Term endowments, where the donor has provided that upon the passage of time or the happening of a specific event the endowment principal can then be utilized either for a specific purpose or for the general operation of the institution. Term endowments are usually not reported separately in the principal financial statement except where they are sizable.
3. Quasi-endowment, where the board, as distinct from the donor, has set aside unrestricted current funds to be used as endowment. Quasi-endowment funds are also known as "Board-Designated Endowment," or "Funds Functioning as Endowment." The amount of quasi-endowment funds should be clearly shown in the financial statements or notes thereto.

Annuity or Life Income Funds. These are amounts where only the principal, and not the income to be earned thereon, has been given to the institution. The income is usually reserved by the donor for a specified period of time and the institution agrees to pay either a specified sum or the actual income earned to the donor for this period. The principal of these gifts represents an asset owned by the institution but until the income or annuity restrictions lapse, clearly these amounts do not represent funds which have the same value as unrestricted funds. For this reason these amounts should not be combined with endowments or other funds for reporting purposes.

Plant Funds.　Plant funds consist of four subgroupings:

1. Unexpended funds. These funds are amounts which are to be used for plant additions or modernizations. Such funds will also include cash and other investments which have been transferred to this fund for plant purposes.
2. Funds for renewal or replacement. These funds represent amounts transferred from current funds for renewal or replacement of existing plant. Such amounts represent a form of funding in lieu of depreciation. In reporting, often these funds are combined with unexpended funds.
3. Funds for retirement of indebtedness. These are the amounts set aside by the Board for debt service (interest and principal) often under a mandatory contractual arrangement with the lender. These funds can also include amounts set aside by the Board at its discretion.
4. Investment in plant. This represents the cost of plant including land and equipment. Actual cost, or market value at date of gifts is used.

All plant or fixed assets are reported in the plant fund. The current funds show plant activities to the extent that funds for additions, renewal, or replacement and retirement of indebtedness are transferred from the current fund to the plant fund. Also, the current fund will show plant activities to the extent that equipment purchases charged directly through current fund expenditures will subsequently be recorded in the plant fund as additions to the net investment in plant.

While the Guide illustrates the use of all four subgroupings, some institutions combine several or all of these for reporting purposes, showing the balances of each subgrouping only in the Balance Sheet.

THE THREE PRINCIPAL FINANCIAL STATEMENTS

Three principal financial statements are used by colleges and universities, as follows:

1. Statement of Changes in Fund Balances (Figure 14–1, pages 218–219).
2. Balance Sheet (Figure 14–2, pages 224–225).

3. Statement of Current Funds, Revenues, Expenditures, and Other Changes (Figure 14–3, page 226).

There are frequently other supporting statements which provide detail that should tie in with these three principal statements. While the supporting statements provide information which the board or other specific users of the statement may want, it is important not to confuse the general reader of the financial statements by providing more detail than is appropriate. The discussion in this chapter will be confined to the three principal statements listed above. A reader interested in further information should refer to CUBA and the Administrative Service.

It is important to recognize the premise from which the Guide has prescribed accounting and reporting principles. The Guide states:

> Service, rather than profits, is the objective of an educational institution; thus, the primary obligation of accounting and reporting is one of accounting for resources received and used rather than for determination of net income.°

Thus it is essential to recognize that the Guide does not attempt to prescribe accounting and reporting principles that would assist the reader in understanding whether the institution had an excess of revenues over expenditures for the period. This is not its purpose. Its purpose is only of "accounting for resources received and used."

The key, then, to understanding college financial statements is to recognize what type of transaction is included in each of these three statements, and to understand the principles of fund accounting. The following paragraphs describe the type of transactions in each of these principal statements. A description of some of the accounting and reporting principles appears in a later section of this chapter.

Statement of Changes in Fund Balances

The most important of the three financial statements is the Statement of Changes in Fund Balances. This statement summarizes all of the activity of the institution for the entire period.

° Page 5 of the Guide.

Figure 14–1 shows the Statement of Changes in Fund Balances for Mary and Isla College.

Notice that this format essentially follows an income statement format (i.e., revenues less expenditures equals net change for the year). This is a significant change from the format of the Statement of Changes in Fund Balances previously recommended by CUBA. That form of statement was the more typical Statement of Changes in Fund Balances in which the first line was the balance at the beginning of the year, then the additions were shown, then the deductions, and finally, the fund balance at the end of the year. An example of this superceded format can be seen in Figure 12–5 on page 156.

The significance of the new format is that it presents a reasonably concise summary of the net change in the institution for the entire year. While most business officers (and many accountants) flinch at the comparison, this "net change" has much the same significance as "excess of revenues over expenditures," particularly when all funds are viewed together.

Total All Funds. The illustrative financial statements in the Audit Guide do *not* show a "total all funds" column, as is illustrated in Figure 14–1, and the Guide discourages such a total column. The Guide indicates, however, that the use of a total column is permitted provided care is taken to ensure that the restricted nature of certain of the funds is clearly shown. As has been repeatedly noted, the author recommends the use of a total column and accordingly has included one in this and subsequent illustrations.*

Revenues and Other Additions. The reader should note that while this statement is in an income statement format, the captions are not pure. Observe that the caption is "Revenues and other additions." The "other additions" are a number of items which do not constitute revenue in a traditional accounting sense, but which are added to the fund balance of a particular fund.

* Those readers not familiar with the arguments for and against the inclusion of such a "total all funds" column will find a discussion on pages 149–151.

MARY AND

STATEMENT OF CHANGES

For the Year

	Current Funds		Loan
	Unrestricted	Restricted	Funds
Revenues and other additions:			
Educational and general revenues.	$3,260,000		
Auxiliary enterprises revenues	125,000		
Gifts and bequests—restricted		$400,000	$10,000
Grants and contracts—restricted		200,000	
Investment income—restricted		10,000	
Realized gains on investments.			
Interest on loans receivable			5,000
Expended for plant facilities			
Retirement of indebtedness			
Total.	3,385,000	610,000	15,000
Expenditures and other deductions:			
Educational and general expenditures	2,300,000	550,000	
Auxiliary enterprises expenditures	95,000		
Refunded to grantors		10,000	
Expended for plant facilities			
Retirement of indebtedness			
Interest on indebtedness.			
Disposal of plant facilities			
Loans written off.			3,000
Total	2,395,000	560,000	3,000
Net increase/(decrease) before transfers.	990,000	50,000	12,000
Transfers among funds—additions/ (deductions):			
Mandatory:			
Principal and interest	(220,000)		
Renewals and replacements	(50,000)		
Unrestricted gifts allocated	(600,000)		
Portion of unrestricted quasi-endowment funds investment gains appropriated	40,000		
Total	(830,000)		
Net increase/(decrease) for the year	160,000	50,000	12,000
Fund balance, beginning of year	650,000	85,000	84,000
Fund balance, end of year	$ 810,000	$135,000	$96,000

Fig. 14—1.   An example of a Statement of Changes in Fund Balances in

ISLA COLLEGE

IN FUND BALANCES

Ended June 30, 1974

| Endowment and Similar Funds | Plant Funds | | | | Total All Funds |
	Unexpended	Renewal and Replacement	Retirement of Indebtedness	Investment in Plant	
					$ 3,260,000
					125,000
$ 160,000	$ 65,000				635,000
					200,000
5,000	20,000	$ 10,000			45,000
150,000					150,000
					5,000
				$ 1,000,000	1,000,000
				170,000	170,000
315,000	85,000	10,000		1,170,000	5,590,000
					2,850,000
					95,000
					10,000
	900,000	100,000			1,000,000
			$170,000		170,000
			50,000		50,000
				85,000	85,000
					3,000
	900,000	100,000	220,000	85,000	4,263,000
315,000	(815,000)	(90,000)	(220,000)	1,085,000	1,327,000
			220,000		
		50,000			
550,000	50,000				
(40,000)					
510,000	50,000	50,000	220,000		
825,000	(765,000)	(40,000)		1,085,000	1,327,000
4,210,000	1,200,000	150,000	100,000	21,615,000	28,094,000
$5,035,000	$ 435,000	$110,000	$100,000	$22,700,000	$29,421,000

the basic format recommended by the AICPA Audit Guide (see page 216).

In this illustration the "other additions" are the $1,000,000 expended for plant facilities, and the $170,000 for retirement of indebtedness.* As is illustrated in Figure 14–4, the author recommends eliminating such "nonrevenue" additions from this financial statement in order to provide a pure revenue and expenditure classification.

In this presentation certain information is presented in summary form. For example, the $3,260,000 shown as educational and general revenues include a number of categories of income, including all unrestricted gifts, and investment income. The detail of this $3,260,000 is shown in the Statement of Current Funds, Revenues, Expenditures, and Other Changes (Figure 14–3). For this reason this second statement (or one containing similar information) is necessary in order for the reader to see some detail of the sources of income of the institution.

The *restricted* gifts and bequests reported in the current restricted fund represents the total amount which has been received during the year, and not the amount actually expended. It will be observed that in the Statement of Current Funds, Revenues, Expenditures, and Other Changes (Figure 14–3) the amount reported in that statement as revenues is the exact amount actually expended. This inconsistency in presentation causes considerable reader confusion. For a more complete discussion of the principles followed in reporting current restricted funds the reader should refer to pages 106–115.

Expenditures and Other Deductions.   As with the "Revenues and other additions" caption, there are also a number of nonexpense categories included in this caption. In part that is why the word "expenditure" is used instead of the word "expense." "Expenditure" implies disbursement whereas "expense" implies accrual basis "cost." The principal nonexpense categories are the $1,000,000 expended for plant facilities and $170,000 of retire-

---

* Many would also argue that the gifts, bequests, capital gains, and other "revenue" in the funds other than the current unrestricted fund are also "other additions." They feel that these amounts are not revenue and are only additions to the fund balance which should not be looked upon as revenue. The author disagrees and feels that such amounts do represent revenue. Note that the same basic format is used in the Audit Guide for voluntary health and welfare organizations (see Figure 13–1) and the authors of that Guide consider the "revenue" caption appropriate.

ment of indebtedness. It may be noted that both of these items are also shown in the "Revenue and other additions" section of this statement, but in different fund columns. If these were eliminated in both sections, the amounts shown as revenues and expenditures would represent fairly pure amounts.

As in the revenue section there is no detail shown for the $2,300,000 of educational and general expenditures. Again, this is because these amounts are reported in more detail in the Statement of Current Funds, Revenues, Expenditures, and Other Changes (Figure 14–3).

Net Increase (Decrease) Before Transfers.   This caption is *not* included in the illustrated Statement of Changes in Fund Balances in the Audit Guide, perhaps in part because the authors of the Guide were reluctant to imply that these amounts represented anything similar to "excess of revenues over expenditures," which certainly they are not. Yet it does seem useful for the reader to know what the results of each fund's activity were before the transfers are made between funds. For example, observe that the net increase in the current unrestricted fund before transfers was $990,000. Without this subtotal most readers would probably focus on the $160,000 net increase after transfers.

Those who argue against this subtotal point out that some of the transfers are required under mandatory debt arrangements and have many of the characteristics of an expenditure. They feel that the reader focusing on the $990,000 is likely to be misled into thinking that this is truly the amount available for expenditure by the Board.

The Guide does not prohibit such a subtotal and in fact several members of the Audit Guide Committee felt that the Guide's illustrated statements should include this subtotal. The author believes this caption is useful and would encourage all colleges and universities to include it.

Transfers Among Funds.   Transfers among funds have been properly separated from the revenues and expenditures sections of the statement. As will be seen in Figure 14–3, this is not so on the Statement of Current Funds, Revenues, Expenditures, and Other Changes. On that statement "mandatory" transfers are reported as part of the caption "Expenditures and mandatory transfers." See the discussion on mandatory transfers below.

The transfer from the endowment fund of a portion of the quasi-endowment fund investment gains (under the total return concept) is properly shown as a transfer and not up in the revenues section (where many institutions would prefer to show such amounts). See Chapter 8 for a complete discussion of the total return concept, and the proper accounting thereof.

While there are a number of transfers reported in this section of the statement, the use of a total-all-funds column greatly helps the reader to see that these transfers have no effect on the net results of activity for the institution as a whole. This is important for the reader to recognize; otherwise he is likely to become hopelessly mired in confusing detail.

Net Increase (Decrease) for the Year. The inclusion of this caption is quite important because, appropriately, it tells the reader what the net change was for the year in each fund and, where the total-all-funds column is also provided, for the institution as a whole.

The reason this caption reads as it does, instead of "Excess of revenues over expenditures," is that the various arbitrary transfers between funds essentially destroy the purity of such a caption. For this reason the authors of the Guide had to devise a caption which would not suggest to the reader that this "net change" in any given fund represented "Excess of revenues over expenditures." This was also necessary because, with the use of four separate plant funds, several of the nonrevenue and nonexpenditure transactions (retirement of indebtedness and expenditure for plant facilities) were transactions to which the caption "Excess of revenues over expenditures" would not be appropriate. However, the caption "Excess of revenues over expenditures" would be appropriate if it were associated only with the total-all-funds column. See pages 236–245 for a number of suggestions for simplifying the financial statements so that, among other things, the "Excess of revenues over expenditures" caption might then be appropriate.

Balance Sheet

Figure 14–2 shows the Balance Sheet for Mary and Isla College in a columnar format. The Balance Sheet, as illustrated in the Guide and prepared by most institutions, is set up in a typical format where the assets are on the left side of the page and the liabilities and fund balances are on the right side, with major fund groupings presented as separate Balance Sheets within the Balance Sheet. The illustrations on pages 39 and 250–251 are examples of this type of Balance Sheet. The Guide permits the use of a columnar presentation as an acceptable alternative, although it does caution against cross-footing the columns to a total "unless all necessary disclosures are made, including interfund borrowings." * While the columnar format used in Figure 14–2 is not used as widely, the author prefers it because of the ease in seeing the overall picture of the institution. At the same time it must be recognized that the columnar format can be misleading if the reader does not recognize the restricted nature of most of the assets.

Statement of Current Funds, Revenues, Expenditures, and Other Changes

Figure 14–3 shows the Statement of Current Funds, Revenues, Expenditures, and Other Changes for Mary and Isla College. This is a very difficult statement for most readers to understand or to correctly interpret. It is an attempt to show on one statement all of the activity involving "current" funds—that is, the funds available for current use by the college in performing its primary objectives. Since the institution uses both restricted and unrestricted funds in carrying out its current objectives, it is necessary to include both types of funds in this statement.

It is important to note, however, that this statement "does not purport to present the results of operations or the net income or loss for the period as would a Statement of Income or a Statement of Revenues and Expenses." † In fact it does not even purport to

---

* *Audits of Colleges and Universities,* AICPA, 1973, page 57.
† Page 55 of the Guide.

MARY AND

BALANCE

June 30,

	Current Funds		Loan
	Unrestricted	Restricted	Funds
ASSETS			
Current assets:			
Cash	$ 910,000	$285,000	$16,000
Short-term investments	930,000		
Accounts receivable	18,000		80,000
Inventories	20,000		
Prepaid expenses	25,000		
Total	1,903,000	285,000	96,000
Long-term investments			
Invested in plant			
Interfund receivable (payable)	(410,000)	(150,000)	
Total assets	$1,493,000	$135,000	$96,000
LIABILITIES AND FUND BALANCE			
Current liabilities:			
Accounts payable	$ 573,000		
Current portion of debt			
Tuition deposits	110,000		
Total	683,000		
Long-term debt			
Fund balances:			
Restricted		$135,000	$50,000
Unrestricted	810,000		46,000
Total	810,000	135,000	96,000
Total liabilities and fund balance	$1,493,000	$135,000	$96,000

Fig. 14–2. An example of a columnar presentation of a Balance the AICPA

ISLA COLLEGE

SHEET

1974

Endowment and Similar Funds	Plant Funds				Total All Funds
	Unexpended	Renewal and Replacement	Retirement of Indebtedness	Investment in Plant	
$ 310,000	$ 20,000	$ 60,000			$ 1,601,000
	400,000	50,000	$100,000		1,480,000
					98,000
					20,000
					25,000
310,000	420,000	110,000	100,000		3,224,000
4,215,000					4,215,000
				$23,450,000	23,450,000
510,000	50,000				
$5,035,000	$ 470,000	$110,000	$100,000	$23,450,000	$30,889,000
	$ 35,000				$ 608,000
				$ 170,000	170,000
					110,000
	35,000			170,000	888,000
				580,000	580,000
$2,025,000	210,000	$110,000		22,700,000	25,230,000
3,010,000	225,000		$100,000		4,191,000
5,035,000	435,000	110,000	100,000	22,700,000	29,421,000
$5,035,000	$ 470,000	$110,000	$100,000	$23,450,000	$30,889,000

Sheet for a small college using fund accounting recommended in Audit Guide.

MARY AND ISLA COLLEGE

STATEMENT OF CURRENT FUNDS, REVENUES, EXPENDITURES, AND OTHER CHANGES

For the Year Ending June 30, 1974

	Current Fund Unrestricted	Current Fund Restricted	Total
Revenues:			
Educational and general:			
Student tuition and fees.	$1,610,000		$1,610,000
Governmental appropriations.	400,000		400,000
Governmental grants		$200,000	200,000
Gifts.	900,000	340,000	1,240,000
Endowment income	350,000	10,000	360,000
Total educational and general	3,260,000	550,000	3,810,000
Auxiliary enterprises	125,000		125,000
Total revenues	3,385,000	550,000	3,935,000
Expenditures and mandatory transfers:			
Educational and general:			
Instruction	1,100,000		1,100,000
Research	300,000	550,000	850,000
Academic support	200,000		200,000
Student services	100,000		100,000
Operation and maintenance of plant	500,000		500,000
Institutional support.	100,000		100,000
	2,300,000	550,000	2,850,000
Mandatory transfers for:			
Principal and interest	200,000		200,000
Renewals and replacements	50,000		50,000
Total educational and general	2,550,000	550,000	3,100,000
Auxiliary enterprises:			
Expenditures	95,000		95,000
Mandatory transfer for principal and interest	20,000		20,000
Total expenditures and mandatory transfers	2,665,000	550,000	3,215,000
Other transfers and additions:			
Excess of restricted receipts over transfers to revenues		60,000	60,000
Refunded to grantors		(10,000)	(10,000)
Unrestricted gifts allocated to other funds	(600,000)		(600,000)
Portion of quasi-endowment gains appropriated	40,000		40,000
Net increase in fund balance	$ 160,000	$ 50,000	$ 210,000

Fig. 14–3. An example of a Statement of Current Funds, Revenues, Expenditures, and Other Changes for a small college in the format recommended by the AICPA Audit Guide.

report all of the unrestricted activity for the year. Excluded from this statement are transactions involving board-designated funds (i.e., board-designated endowment funds) which have been set aside for purposes other than current operations, and restricted funds which are not directly for a "current" purpose. This statement attempts only to show the reader the revenues and expenditures used for current operations, and the amounts transferred to other funds either by board action or under agreement with outside parties. To further complicate matters (and thus to confuse the reader) all of the amounts reported on this statement are also reported in total on the Statement of Changes in Fund Balances (Figure 14–1). For all of these reasons, it is not appropriate to look upon this statement as a Statement of Revenues and Expenditures; it is not, for it contains transactions which are extraneous to revenue and expenditure transactions in the conventional accounting sense. Since very few nonaccountant readers are likely to be aware of the limitations of this statement and what it purports to show, most readers are not able to properly interpret it. As is discussed later in this chapter, the author would expect that eventually this statement will find so little acceptance that it will be replaced with a more meaningful statement.

Column Headings. Three column headings are used on this statement: current unrestricted, current restricted, and total. The amount shown in the current unrestricted column represents all of the current unrestricted fund activity for the year, including transfers in and out.

The major categories of revenues and expenditures on this statement can be seen also in the Statement of Changes in Fund Balances (Figure 14–1). Note that the total educational and general revenues of $3,260,000 is the same amount shown on that statement, as is the total educational and general expenditures of $2,300,000. While there is no such subtotal, the thoughtful reader who is trying to learn what the net results were for the year is likely to make just such a subtraction; if he does he will observe that there is an excess of revenue over expenses of $960,000.*

---

* This $960,000 is different from the $990,000 net increase before transfers discussed above because the $960,000 excludes auxiliary activities.

Restricted Fund Column. The restricted fund column is quite confusing because the amount *reported* as "revenue" is exactly the amount expended for the restricted purposes indicated. Note the $550,000 of revenue and the $550,000 of expenditures. Colleges follow the practice of reporting on this statement restricted revenues only to the extent expended for the restricted purposes. As is discussed above, this approach is very complicated and difficult for most readers to understand. For example, note that the amount reported as revenues in the Statement of Changes in Fund Balances is $610,000 rather than $550,000. The careful reader who tries to trace the figures back and forth between these two statements is bound to become confused.

Further complicating the figures shown in the restricted fund column is the need to report the "net increase" in fund balance for the restricted fund for the year, and the obvious necessity of having that net increase "agree" with the net increase reported on the Statement of Changes in Fund Balances. It will be noticed that the net increase shown in both statements for this restricted fund is $50,000. Yet, since the only revenue which is reportable in the Statement of Current Funds, Revenues, Expenditures, and Other Changes is the amount actually expended (under the accounting principles followed), there has to be a "balancing figure" to reflect the net change in the restricted fund during the year. This can be seen at the bottom of Figure 14–3 where $60,000 has been indicated as the excess of restricted receipts over transfers to revenues. This figure plus the amount reported as "refunded to donors" net down to the "net increase" for the year. Obviously only the most knowledgeable accountant will comprehend these gymnastics.

The total column is required on the Statement of Current Funds, Revenues, Expenditures, and Other Changes in order to show the reader the total current fund activity, i.e., the total activity for the year handled by funds which are available for current use.

Unrestricted Revenues. Looking only at the unrestricted column, the reader is shown the complete revenue picture. *All* unrestricted contributions, bequests, investment income, and other revenue *must* be reported in this section. The only exception is capital gains, discussed below. If the institution receives a large unexpected gift on the last day of the year and it wishes to utilize these funds for board-designated endowment, it may do so but it must first report the receipt of this gift in the revenues section. Prior to the issuance of this Guide the board had the option of reporting such gifts directly in the Statement of Changes in Fund Balances, but this is no longer permitted.

It should also be observed that all unrestricted investment income (i.e., dividends and interest) must be reported in this section. The use of an "income stabilization reserve" is no longer permitted. All investment income that is unrestricted must be reported here, in the year in which it is earned.

Expenditures and Mandatory Transfers.   Included in this caption are mandatory transfers. Mandatory transfers are those transfers which are required under debt or under agreement with outside parties. The most typical mandatory transfer involves debt service, i.e., interest on indebtedness *and* repayment of debt principal. In Figure 14–3 the amount of such principal and interest was $220,000 ($200,000 under educational and $20,000 under auxiliary activities). Also, some institutions are required under contractual arrangements to put aside in a renewal and replacement fund certain amounts every year. Mary and Isla College is making a mandatory transfer of $50,000.

The important point to note here is that while these transfers are "required" the nature of these transactions is not that of an *expenditure* in a conventional accounting sense. Debt repayment, while requiring an expenditure of cash, is not considered an expenditure in an accounting sense any more than the proceeds from a bank borrowing is considered income. Thus, these mandatory transfers tend to frustrate the reader who is trying to learn what excess, if any, there was of revenues over expenditures in a traditional sense. This cannot be determined without some rearrangement of the figures shown in this statement.

Yet, keep in mind that it is not intended that this statement be looked at for purposes of determining an excess of income over expenditures. It is intended only to show the activity of the current funds, and these mandatory transfers obviously represent activity that reduced the available current funds.

Note also that there were mandatory transfers under the sub-category of "auxiliary enterprises." Auxiliary enterprises are those activities which are not central to the principal objectives of the institution, i.e., educating students. Typical auxiliary activities would be the dormitory system and the food service activities. The dormitory operation involves borrowing of funds on a long-term basis and often involves repayment through room charges. As can be seen in Figure 14–3, such auxiliary enterprises are reported separately within that statement.

Other Transfers and Additions.   In addition to mandatory transfers, the board obviously has the right to make transfers to its other funds. These "other transfers" are shown separately at the bottom of the Statement of Current Funds, Revenues, Expenditures, and Other Changes, under this caption. The distinction between mandatory and other transfers is simply to indicate to the reader which transfers were required and which ones were truly a board decision. In the case of Mary and Isla College there are two transfers: the transfer of $600,000 of unrestricted gifts to other funds and the $40,000 transferred from the endowment and similar fund of gains on board-designated endowments under the total return concept.*

Excess of Revenues over Expenditures.   It is important to observe that the reader is not shown a figure representing an excess of revenues over expenditures for the year, or, for that matter, the excess of revenues over expenditures and mandatory transfers for the year. The only total that is reported is the final figure on the statement, net increase in fund balances. If the reader tries to draw some conclusion from this "net increase" amount, he will obviously be drawing an erroneous conclusion since this net amount can be controlled by the board. It has no significance other than being the amount the board has chosen to leave in this fund.

The Guide does not specifically prohibit a caption "Excess of revenues over expenditures and mandatory transfers" and this is one improvement that some institutions should perhaps consider. However, with the inclusion of mandatory transfers which are

---

* See pages 94–104 for a discussion of this accounting approach to handling investment fund gains.

themselves a mixture of expenditures and nonexpenditures in an accounting sense, there is, of course, some question as to the significance of even that net amount. On the other hand, this net excess of revenues over expenditures and mandatory transfers would probably give the reader a little more accurate indication of what took place than does the final caption "Net increase in fund balance."

Significance of this Statement.   As the reader can undoubtedly surmise by this point, this statement does not tell the reader what the results of activities were for the year. Certainly the reader should not focus on the net increase for the year and he must also be very careful if he focuses on the total expenditures and mandatory transfers caption. For these reasons this statement probably serves relatively little purpose. It does serve a purpose at present, however, in that it provides some detail of the revenues and expenditures categories that go into the totals which are shown in the Statement of Changes in Fund Balances (Figure 14–1). As has been suggested, the author feels that the Statement of Current Funds, Revenues, Expenditures, and Other Changes will not survive too many years because of its limited usefulness. The authors of the Guide recognized this, too, and indicated that the information shown on this statement could be presented in other ways.

ACCOUNTING PRINCIPLES

Summarized below are the accounting principles prescribed by the Audit Guide for colleges and universities, a number of which were discussed above.

Accrual Basis

The Guide concludes that accrual basis of accounting is normally necessary for financial statements prepared in accordance with generally accepted accounting principles. Investment income should be recorded on an accrual basis unless unrecorded amounts would not be material. Also, revenues and expenditures relating to a summer session should be reported in the fiscal year in which the summer session principally occurs.

Encumbrance Accounting

Implicit in the use of accrual basis accounting is the presumption that the only amounts to be recorded as expenditures will be those for which materials or services have been received and used as of the balance sheet date. Some institutions in the past have followed a governmental accounting approach in which expenditures were charged at the time purchase orders or other commitments were issued, without regard to the actual date of receipt. This is another form of "appropriation" accounting which is discussed in detail on pages 50 to 55.

The Guide states quite clearly that encumbrance accounting is not acceptable and that such amounts should not be reported either as expenditures or as liabilities in the Balance Sheet. If the institution wishes to designate or allocate a portion of the unrestricted current fund balance, it may do so but such designation would appear only in the fund balance section of the Balance Sheet.*

Unrestricted Gifts

All unrestricted gifts, donations, and bequests are recorded as revenue in the current unrestricted fund in the year received. While the board is free to designate any portions of such unrestricted gifts or bequests as "board-designated endowment," such gifts must nonetheless be reported initially in the current unrestricted fund. After being so reported, these amounts may then be transferred by the board, as it wishes, to the endowment and similar funds.

Current Restricted Gifts

Restricted gifts for current purposes are reported in their entirety in the Statement of Changes in Fund Balances. However, as has been previously discussed, the amount of current

---

* See page 191 for a discussion of fund balance designations.

restricted gifts reported as revenues in the Statement of Current Funds, Revenues, Expenditures, and Other Changes would be only the amount which had been actually expended for such restricted purposes during the year. Thus, depending on which statement the reader is looking at, he would see either the total amount received during the year or the total amount which had actually been expended.

Other Restricted Gifts

All other categories of legally restricted gifts would be reported directly in the fund to which they applied. If a donor made a contribution to the endowment fund it would be reported directly in that fund (assuming that the donor had made clear his intention, presumably in writing).

Pledges

The Guide is permissive with respect to handling pledges. The institution may record such amounts but if the institution elects not to do so, it must disclose in the footnotes the amount of uncollected pledges as of the financial statement date if they are material.

Investment Income from Unrestricted Funds

All investment income (dividends and interest) must be reported directly in the current unrestricted fund in the revenues section. Prior to the issuance of the Guide the use of an income stabilization reserve was permitted. This is no longer considered acceptable and all investment income must be reported in the year in which earned.

Endowment fund investment income is normally considered unrestricted income unless the donor has specified the restricted use for which the investment income is to be used. Accordingly, unrestricted endowment fund income should be reported directly in the current unrestricted fund.

Restricted Investment Income

All restricted investment income would be reported directly in the fund to which such investment income pertains. For example, the investment income from surplus plant funds temporarily invested would normally be reported in the plant fund.

Gains or Losses on Investments

Gains or losses (and appreciation or depreciation where investments are carried at market; see below) are normally considered adjustments of the carrying value of the investment and are reported in the Statement of Changes in Fund Balances in the fund holding the investment which gave rise to the gain. This means, therefore, that gains on board-designated endowment funds which are reported as part of the "endowment and similar funds" would be reported in that fund in the revenues and other additions section of the Statement of Changes in Fund Balances.

Where an organization carries its investments at market, the unrealized appreciation or depreciation would be reported in the same manner as the realized gains or losses.

Carrying Value of Investments

The Guide provides that a college or university can carry its investments at either market or cost. Previously investments could be carried only at cost or, in the case of donated securities, at the fair market value at the date of receipt. This is an important change which many institutions will want to consider carefully. If an institution so elects, however, it must carry all of its investments at market. It cannot carry some at market and some at cost.

Total Return Concept

Where the board wishes to transfer some of the realized or unrealized gains on endowment and similar fund investments to the current unrestricted fund (and assuming the board has the legal right to do so) the transfer must be shown in the non-mandatory transfer section of the Statement of Current Funds, Revenues, Expenditures, and Other Changes. In the Statement of Changes in Fund Balances the transfer would also be shown in the transfer section. It is not permissible to treat this transfer as income in the revenue section in either statement. This can be seen in Figure 14–1 where a transfer of $40,000 from the endowment and similar funds has been reported in the current unrestricted fund. For a more complete discussion of the accounting under the total investment concept, see pages 94–104.

Fixed Asset Accounting

The Guide follows the CUBA approach to handling fixed assets and requires that all fixed asset purchases be capitalized and carried on the Balance Sheet. This means that a college or university cannot "expense" its fixed asset purchases in the year in which acquired.

Depreciation Accounting

The Guide reaffirms the position historically taken by colleges and universities of not following depreciation accounting procedures. The Guide in discussing depreciation states:

Depreciation expense related to depreciable assets comprising the physical plant is reported neither in the Statement of Current Funds, Revenues, Expenditures, and Other Changes nor in the Statement of Changes in Unrestricted Current Funds Balance. The reason for this treatment is that these statements present expenditures and transfers of current funds rather than operating expenses in conformity with the reporting objectives of accounting for resources received and used rather than the determination of net income. Depreciation allowance, however, may be reported in the Balance Sheet and the provision for depreciation reported in the Statement of Changes in balance of the investment-in-plant fund subsection of the plant funds group.*

This statement, of course, very succinctly states that it is not the Guide's intention to present financial statements that will show the cost of operations, and therefore there is no need to report depreciation. The author disagrees with this conclusion.

* Pages 9–10 of the Guide.

It should be observed, however, that in the last sentence quoted above provision has been made for reporting of depreciation in the plant fund column of the Statement of Changes in Fund Balances. Where depreciation is so reported and where a total-all-funds column is also presented, effectively depreciation is presented in the financial statements as a whole. This can be seen in Figure 14–4.

SIMPLIFIED SET OF STATEMENTS

The principles of accounting and reporting presented so far in this chapter are those recommended by the Guide, and are followed by most colleges and universities. While the format is technically correct, in the author's opinion these statements are deficient in that the average reader, not knowledgeable in either accounting or college reporting, will have considerable difficulty in understanding exactly what has taken place during the year. A large part of the difficulty arises because of the use of separate columns for each fund, normally without a total column, making it difficult for the reader to see an overall picture. This derives from the legal accountability such institutions have to see that funds entrusted to them for specific uses are expended in the manner designated by the donor. This legal accountability, however, does not mean that the institution must report to the public on a detailed separate statement basis for each fund grouping. There is no reason why financial statements cannot be presented in a format which will permit the reader to see the overall picture.*

* Other accountants have also indicated the need for an overall financial statement that shows the total operations of the entity in a meaningful manner. In a report of the Committee on Accounting Practice on Not-for-Profit Organizations of the American Accounting Association published in early 1971 that Committee stated on page 137:

"Another significant shortcoming of financial statements in the college and university and municipal areas, as measured against the standard of relevance, can be characterized as the lack of emphasis on organizational reporting. As noted in the preceding section, these organizations emphasize fund entity accountability in most instances almost to the complete exclusion of over-all accountability for the organization.

"A fundamental objective of accounting should be that of disclosing how a group of resources directed by a co-ordinated managerial group has been used to

The premise that a set of financial statements for a college should not show results of operations certainly has to be questioned. True, the college is not expected to make a "profit" in the commercial sense, but it is expected over a period of time to take in enough money to be able to sustain its operations. If it doesn't, clearly it is headed for serious trouble. It may very well be that the financial plight that many private institutions are presently in can be traced, at least in part, to financial reporting that really does not tell it "as it is."

Further, college financial statements as prescribed in the Guide give very little useful information to the reader or trustee as to cost of operating the institution. Most institutions, for example, have a number of educational programs—different colleges within the university, different departments, etc. It would appear that the trustees should be told what the costs are for each type of major program of the institution; otherwise, though they are charged with the responsibility for the institution, they have no way of really making a judgment.

An All-Inclusive Statement of Activities

Figure 14–4 shows an all-inclusive Statement of Revenues, Expenses, and Changes in Fund Balances for Mary and Isla College. A number of things should be noted about this statement.

Restricted versus Unrestricted. Observe that we have included, on this all-inclusive statement, activities broken out in only two categories: unrestricted and restricted. Included in the restricted column are all funds which were restricted by outside persons. This includes current restricted funds, loan funds, true endowment funds, and plant funds which have been restricted by others (other than the investment in plant itself). Investment in plant has been included in the unrestricted fund column because these assets are available for the purposes for which the institution was

___

accomplish the goals of the entity. Since the upper level management group in all instances is responsible for the performance of the organization as a whole—and because externally interested groups must evaluate it as a whole—it seems imperative that these organizations develop reporting practices that would draw the elements of the financial data together in a meaningful manner for the total operating entity."

MARY AND ISLA COLLEGE

STATEMENT OF REVENUES, EXPENSES, AND CHANGES IN FUND BALANCES

For the Year Ended June 30, 1974

	Unrestricted	Restricted	Total
Operating revenues:			
Tuition and fees	$ 1,610,000		$ 1,610,000
Governmental appropriations . .	400,000		400,000
Research grants		$ 190,000	190,000
Auxiliary activities	125,000		125,000
Total operating revenues . .	2,135,000	190,000	2,325,000
Operating expenses:			
Educational:			
Engineering	930,000		930,000
Arts	410,000		410,000
Business	625,000		625,000
Research.	300,000	550,000	850,000
Supporting:			
Administrative	495,000		495,000
Fund raising.	90,000		90,000
Auxiliary activities	95,000		95,000
Total operating expenses . .	2,945,000	550,000	3,495,000
Excess of operating expenses over revenues . .	(810,000)	(360,000)	(1,170,000)
Other revenues:			
Gifts and bequests	900,000	635,000	1,535,000
Investment income	350,000	47,000	397,000
Realized and unrealized appreciation.		150,000	150,000
Total other revenues.	1,250,000	832,000	2,082,000
Excess of revenues over expenses	440,000	472,000	912,000
Fund balance, beginning of year. .	26,671,000	1,838,000	28,509,000
Transfer between funds	(220,000)	220,000	
Fund balance, end of year	$26,891,000	$2,530,000	$29,421,000

Fig. 14—4. An example of an all-inclusive Statement of Revenues, Expenses, and Changes in Fund Balances, in the format recommended by the author.

formed—that is, for educational purposes. Whatever restrictions were originally attached to the contributions which were used to purchase these assets, the conditions have been fulfilled by virtue of the purchase of these assets. Accordingly, fixed assets have been considered "unrestricted." *

The advantage of this simplified presentation with only two categories of funds—unrestricted and restricted—is that the reader quickly sees the total activity without a lot of potentially confusing detail. At the same time there is full disclosure that certain of the revenues and expenses during the year resulted from transactions which the board had only partial control over.

Total Column. Another striking feature of this statement is that we have combined the unrestricted and restricted columns to show a total column. This helps the reader to see total activity for the year. There are many valid arguments for not including such a total, but, as the author has indicated elsewhere, these arguments are not as important as the need for the reader to see the total picture of the institution. In this instance, it is hard to imagine a reader not understanding that certain of the revenues and expenses shown are restricted and not available for unrestricted use.

Functional Reporting. This statement is set up on a functional basis; that is, all expenses have been classified by program or function which the funds have been used to accomplish. The principal purpose of a college is, of course, educational. Note that we have clearly indicated the amounts which have been spent directly for this purpose, and we have broken these amounts into three categories to represent the three individual programs offered by Mary and Isla College (i.e., engineering, arts, and business). Also, we have indicated the amounts spent on research, another major program of this institution. Certain expenses are related to the overall administration of the school and these are also shown separately, as are fund-raising expenses.

Depreciation. Although it is not obvious from this statement, we have included $500,000 of depreciation as an expense and allocated this expense among the various programs. There are many

---

* This is the same position taken in the hospital Audit Guide. See Chapter 15.

arguments for and against depreciation but once it is concluded that a set of statements should attempt to reflect the "cost" of performing a particular service the question becomes basically moot. Depreciation is a cost and should be reflected. Otherwise the trustees are only kidding themselves if they think they know what each of the college's programs is costing.*

The college Audit Guide provides for institutions to record debt service (i.e., repayment of principal and interest) as a charge to the current unrestricted fund. Debt repayment is not an "expense" as generally thought of, and this has been eliminated in the simplified financial statements. Likewise, since we have included a depreciation charge of $500,000, the simplified statements exclude the "write off" of fixed assets of $85,000 reflected in Figure 14–1.

Excess of Revenues over Expenses. Included on this statement is clear indication of what the excess of revenues over expenses was for the year. This is in keeping with the author's strong belief that the trustees and other interested readers must know what the net results were for the year. Not to do so is sticking one's head in the sand and pretending that the principles of survival applicable to all organizations somehow do not apply to a college or a university.

Operating Revenue Excludes Other Revenue. In this statement we have reported gifts and investment income after reporting operating revenue and expense, to assist the reader in seeing what the results of operations were, exclusive of such other, non-operating revenue. Note that this "other revenue" is reported before the caption "Excess of revenues over expenses."

Restricted Grants Recorded in Year Received. The college Audit Guide provides for reporting in the Statement of Current Funds, Revenues, Expenditures, and Other Changes restricted revenues only to the extent expended during the year. This, of course, causes considerable confusion, as has been previously noted. In Figure 14–4 restricted income is reported in the year received

---

* See Chapter 7 for a more complete treatment of the pros and cons of recording depreciation. Also, see page 187 for discussion in the Audit Guide for voluntary health and welfare organizations.

unless the terms of the restriction are such that the funds could not have been expended during that year.*

Transfers Between Funds. By including all unrestricted funds in a single column, the number of transfers between funds has been significantly reduced. In this instance the only transfer reported is the amount required to be set aside in a restricted fund under the debt agreement.

Functional Analysis of Expenses

Figure 14–5 provides an analysis of the natural expense categories going into the functional expenses reported on the Statement of Revenues, Expenses, and Changes in Fund Balances (Figure 14–4).

Note that each of the functional categories on the Statement of Revenues, Expenses, and Changes in Fund Balances appears also on the Statement of Functional Expenses and that the figures on both statements agree with each other in total.

For simplicity in presentation, the number of natural expense categories has been somewhat limited in this illustration. Nevertheless, the reader is given considerable information about the natural expenses which go into each of the functional categories. This gives the reader a chance to make his own judgments as to the appropriateness of these amounts.

Comparison with Prior Years. We have not shown a comparison with the previous year's figures but this could have been done. Typically there would have been a second "total expenses" column for the natural expense category comparison with the preceding year. Likewise, the unit cost information at the bottom of this report would also have been presented for the preceding year.

Unit Cost Information. Another important piece of information contained on this statement is a unit cost of providing educational and supporting services for each of the several functional categories. While one might argue whether these particular unit

* See Chapter 9 for a more complete description of the principles of recognizing revenues in the year in which they were received.

MARY AND
STATEMENT OF
For the Year

	Educational		
	Engineering	Arts	Business
Salaries and related benefits	$ 450,000	$ 180,000	$ 350,000
Scholarships.	50,000	10,000	20,000
Operation of physical plant, exclusive of depreciation and salaries	150,000	100,000	100,000
Depreciation.	200,000	70,000	95,000
Library books.	30,000	10,000	10,000
Supplies	40,000	30,000	40,000
Interest.			
Other.	10,000	10,000	10,000
Total	$ 930,000	$ 410,000	$ 625,000
Student population.	350	250	300
Cost per student	$ 2,657	$ 1,640	$ 2,083

*Excluding fund raising and research.

Fig. 14–5.   An example of a Functional Analysis of

cost data are *the* appropriate data for this institution, they should give the reader an indication of the kinds of information which can be presented on a unit cost basis.*

Balance Sheet

Figure 14–6 shows the Balance Sheet for Mary and Isla College. It follows the basic presentation shown for the Statement of Revenues, Expenses, and Changes in Fund Balances. †

* In presenting unit cost information on this statement, the author does not intend to imply that this suggestion is something new. Many studies have been made in the past to develop appropriate unit cost measurements. However, to the author's knowledge, no college or university includes such data in its published annual report.

† The reader is cautioned against trying to compare this Balance Sheet with the one shown in Figure 14–3. While the ending fund balance (for all funds) has been deliberately shown in both statements as $29,421,000, this has been merely for purposes of illustration, to make the reader's job somewhat easier. In reality the two amounts would not be the same because we are applying different

ISLA COLLEGE

FUNCTIONAL EXPENSES

Ended June 30, 1974

		Supporting		
Research	Administrative	Fund Raising	Auxiliary Activities	Total Expenses
$720,000	$275,000	$40,000	$30,000	$2,045,000
				80,000
70,000	50,000	10,000	20,000	500,000
50,000	50,000	25,000	10,000	500,000
				50,000
10,000	40,000	15,000	25,000	200,000
	50,000			50,000
	30,000		10,000	70,000
$850,000	$495,000	$90,000	$95,000	$3,495,000
	900		900	900
	$ 550		$ 105	$ 2,839*

Expenses in the format recommended by the author.

It should be observed that the fund balance section of this statement breaks out the unrestricted and restricted fund balances according to the purposes for which they are to be used. Note that in the unrestricted fund balance we have indicated the amount invested in plant assets ($23,450,000) and the amount in investment funds ($3,010,000). This aids the reader in seeing how the fund balance is being utilized. Observe, also, that the amount available for current use is only $431,000.

Again, many would take exception to the use of the total column reported on this statement. Nevertheless the author feels that it is appropriate for the trustee or other interested reader to see the total resources available.

accounting principles. For example, depreciation is being recorded in this revised format and this would result in a lower "fund balance." Also we have, again deliberately, shown our net plant assets as the same amount in both statements whereas in the earlier statement this amount was the gross amount; in Figure 14–6 it is the "net" amount after applying the accumulated depreciation.

MARY AND ISLA COLLEGE
BALANCE SHEET
June 30, 1974

	Unrestricted	Restricted	Total
ASSETS			
Current assets:			
Cash	$ 1,220,000	$ 381,000	$ 1,601,000
Short-term investments	1,480,000		1,480,000
Accounts receivable	18,000		18,000
Student loans		80,000	80,000
Other current assets	45,000		45,000
Total current assets	2,763,000	461,000	3,224,000
Long-term investments			
(at market)	2,146,000	2,069,000	4,215,000
Plant assets:			
Land	500,000		500,000
Land improvements	2,900,000		2,900,000
Buildings	29,675,000		29,675,000
Equipment	4,660,000		4,660,000
	37,735,000		37,735,000
Accumulated depreciation. . . .	(14,285,000)		(14,285,000)
Net plant assets	23,450,000		23,450,000
Total assets	$28,359,000	$2,530,000	$30,889,000
LIABILITIES AND FUND BALANCE			
Current liabilities:			
Accounts payable.	$ 608,000		$ 608,000
Tuition deposits	110,000		110,000
Current portion of long-term			
debt	170,000		170,000
Total current liabilities . . .	888,000		888,000
Long-term debt, due 1975–78. . .	580,000		580,000
Total liabilities	1,468,000		1,468,000
Fund balances:			
Available for current use.	431,000		431,000
Invested in plant assets.	23,450,000		23,450,000
Endowment funds	3,010,000	$2,025,000	5,035,000
Other restricted funds		505,000	505,000
Total fund balances	26,891,000	2,530,000	29,421,000
Total liabilities and fund			
balances.	$28,359,000	$2,530,000	$30,889,000

Fig. 14–6. An example of a columnar Balance Sheet in the format recommended by the author.

Statement of Changes in Financial Position

These simplified statements are deficient in one particular respect. They do not provide the reader with information on financial transactions not affecting revenues, expenses, or the fund balance that took place during the year. For example, there is no information on resources used for acquisition of plant, or detail on how such acquisitions were financed. On the other hand, the AICPA Audit Guide Statement of Changes in Fund Balances (Figure 14–1) clearly provides this type of information.

Where significant nonrevenue or nonexpense transactions occur, consideration should be given to either including details of such transactions in a footnote or including a separate Statement of Changes in Financial Position. The Statement of Changes in Financial Position is not illustrated because it is a format widely used by profit-oriented organizations in their financial statements. Readers wishing more information on this format should refer to APB Opinion Number 19.

Conclusion

Undoubtedly these revised simplified statements have weaknesses, particularly when viewed from the perspective of traditional college financial statement presentations. However, the author believes that present college financial statements are seriously deficient because most nonaccountant readers cannot understand them. Since the purpose of financial statements must be to communicate, thoughtful college trustees should encourage their business managers to experiment with simpler presentations, perhaps along the lines suggested above.

15

Hospitals

A very important nonprofit institution that has not been discussed so far is the hospital.* By and large hospitals tend to be more complex than other nonprofit organizations because they effectively operate a number of separate but related businesses all within the hospital framework. Yet in spite of their greater complexity, the financial and reporting problems of nonprofit hospitals are in very large measure similar to those of other large nonprofit organizations. Their similarity lies principally in their common problem of presenting meaningful financial statements, and in their need to communicate with the general public.† Fund accounting is normally used by voluntary nonprofit hospitals and as with most organizations using fund accounting, there is often difficulty in preparing statements in a straightforward manner that will allow readers to see the overall financial picture in a clear and concise manner. Unlike most nonprofit organizations, hospitals vitally affect the lives of the general public and are coming under increasing public pressure and governmental control. The fact that a hospital's activities are complex doesn't mean that the financial statements must be complex or hard to understand.

* Not all hospitals are nonprofit. There are about 850 proprietary hospitals out of a total of about 7,100. These proprietary hospitals are smaller in size with an average of about 70 beds each. About 2,650 hospitals are local, state and federal institutions and the balance of 3,600 are nonprofit, nongovernmental.

† Hospitals also raise funds from the general public but a decreasing proportion of their total revenue comes from this source. About 90% of their revenue comes from patient revenues, including Blue Cross and governmental assistance.

Hospitals are also faced with reporting to groups other than contributors because a substantial amount of their resources comes from third party arrangements such as Blue Cross, Medicare, Medicaid, etc. This also influences financial reporting.

In 1972 the Committee on Health Care Institutions of the American Institute of Certified Public Accountants issued an Audit Guide recommending auditing and reporting standards to be followed by independent auditors in making examinations of the financial statements of hospitals. Included in this Guide is a discussion of accounting principles and reporting standards that should be applied to all hospitals. While some hospitals were not following all of these principles at the time issued, this Guide represents an important pronouncement on hospital accounting and financial statements and all hospitals that have audits made by certified public accountants will be expected to adopt these principles.* This chapter summarizes the accounting and reporting principles outlined in this Guide.

The principles of accounting and reporting presented in this Guide are, in the author's opinion, applicable to most nonprofit organizations as well as to hospitals. Many of the principles of accounting recommended in earlier chapters are included in this Guide. Furthermore, while the form of reporting is not in the author's recommended columnar format, it is relatively straightforward, particularly when compared to the form of reporting used by many nonprofit organizations. While there are still a few accounting and reporting principles that may be disagreed with,† this Guide goes a long way toward presenting the financial activities of a nonprofit organization in a meaningful and straightforward manner.

---

* As discussed on page 178, an Audit Guide does not represent the establishment of accounting principles. Only the Accounting Principles Board of the AICPA normally issues authoritative pronouncements of accounting principles. However, an Audit Guide does represent the considered opinions of a committee of the AICPA and their views obviously carry great weight with certified public accountants. Accordingly, whenever an organization deviates from the principles outlined in an Audit Guide, the burden is on the CPA to justify such deviation as being in accordance with generally accepted accounting principles if an unqualified opinion is to be given by the CPA on the financial statements.

† The principal disputed area is the use of a separate Statement of Changes in Fund Balances in which all restricted fund activities are reported. The author believes it preferable to show all such activity in a single Statement of Revenues, Expenses, and Changes in Fund Balances, in a columnar format. An example of this presentation is shown in Figure 15–5. As will be discussed, if this approach

FUND ACCOUNTING

Fund accounting is usually followed since hospitals receive restricted gifts and endowments. The fund groupings provided in the Guide differ somewhat from the fund grouping most non-profit organizations have traditionally followed. The principal difference is that only two major fund groupings áre permitted: the unrestricted fund and restricted funds. Here are the fund groupings:

Unrestricted Fund	Restricted Funds
Current	Specific Purpose
Board-Designated	Plant Replacement and Expansion
Plant	Endowment

While the unrestricted fund is divided into three parts, they are not individually considered separate funds. There is only one unrestricted fund and that is the total of the three parts. All reporting for the unrestricted fund is on the total of the three parts. The three restricted funds, however, are reported separately for each subgrouping. Here is a description of each of the funds.

Unrestricted Fund

All funds not restricted by donors or outside parties are included in this fund grouping. The unrestricted fund may be divided into the following three parts.

Current. The current portion represents the working capital of the hospital. The amounts included in this subgrouping are the unallocated general funds of the institution. Generally the current portion will consist of current assets, current liabilities, and any deferred credits.

---

were followed the principle of recognizing restricted fund income only to the extent expended, would, of course, not be appropriate since such unexpended income would be reported in the restricted fund column. Another change that the author recommends is reporting contributed plant and equipment as nonoperating income in the Statement of Revenues and Expenses rather than as an addition to the unrestricted fund balance in the Statement of Changes in Fund Balances. Notwithstanding the above comments, the Guide on the whole represents an important step in defining accounting principles and reporting techniques that will go a long way toward strengthening nonprofit reporting.

Board-Designated. All board-designated assets are included in this subgrouping, including board-designated endowment or investment assets, board-designated assets for specific purposes and board-designated plant replacement assets.

Plant. The plant portion represents the actual investment in plant assets, land, building, leasehold improvements and equipment. It should be particularly noted that the plant portion is included as part of the unrestricted fund grouping because the segregation of plant assets into a separate fund implies the existence of restrictions on their use or disposition. Also if plant assets were shown as part of the restricted fund grouping there would be mechanical problems of showing short- and long-term liabilities related to such assets without distorting working capital. In addition, there is the usual problem of presenting depreciation when funds are separated.

Restricted Funds

All contributions, gifts or income which are restricted by the donor or grantor (as distinct from the board) are included in this fund grouping. Three subgroupings are used.

Specific Purposes Fund. All donor-restricted funds other than plant or endowment are placed in this fund until such time as the restrictions lapse, either through passage of time or by the expenditure for the specified purpose. At that time such funds are transferred to the unrestricted fund. This is discussed under "restricted contributions" below.

Plant Replacement and Expansion Funds. All restricted cash and other assets given to the hospital for plant or fixed asset purchases are included in this fund. Revenues received from third parties who specify that part of the revenue is to be used for plant additions will also be transferred into this fund. Note that the plant assets themselves are not included in this fund; only cash and other assets that will eventually be used to purchase plant assets are included.

Endowment Funds. All donor-designated gifts that are to be held for the production of income are included in this fund. Such endowments may be permanent in nature or may be term endowments. Term endowments should be disclosed separately in the financial statements and taken into income when the term expires.

FINANCIAL STATEMENTS

Four primary financial statements are used by hospitals:

Balance Sheet
Statement of Revenues and Expenses
Statement of Changes in Fund Balances
Statement of Changes in Financial Position

JOHNSTOWN

BALANCE SHEET
December 31,

ASSETS

UNRESTRICTED

Current assets (in total)	$ 1,500,000
Board-designated funds:	
Cash	50,000
Investments	475,000
Property, plant and equipment	10,000,000
Less depreciation	(4,400,000)
Total	$ 7,625,000

RESTRICTED

Specific-purpose

Cash	$ 100,000

Plant replacement and

Cash	25,000
Investments	100,000
Pledges	75,000
	$ 200,000

Endowment

Cash	$ 25,000
Investments..........................	5,000,000
	$ 5,025,000

Fig. 15–1.   An example of a Balance Sheet in the

In addition to these four statements, additional supplementary schedules may be appropriate for certain of the users of the statements. These schedules might include Patient Service Revenue, Expense by Functional Divisions, etc.

Balance Sheet

As previously noted, there are two principal fund groupings—unrestricted and restricted. The Balance Sheet of a hospital therefore shows these two groupings separately. Figure 15–1 shows an example of the layout of the Balance Sheet in somewhat abbreviated form.

HOSPITAL

(CONDENSED)

1974

LIABILITIES AND FUND BALANCES

FUNDS

Current liabilities (in total)	$1,200,000
Deferred third-party reimbursement	100,000
Long-term debt	400,000
Fund balance	5,925,000
Total	$7,625,000

FUNDS

fund

Fund balances	$ 100,000

expansion fund

Fund balance	$ 200,000
	$ 200,000

fund

Fund balances:

Permanent	$4,500,000
Term	525,000
	$5,025,000

---

format recommended for hospitals by the Guide.

It should be noted that on this Balance Sheet there is a single fund balance figure representing all unrestricted funds. The reader does not have to wonder what the total resources available to the board are. It is clearly shown. At the same time, the Guide suggests that the composition of the unrestricted fund be shown. On a less abbreviated balance sheet the composition could be shown right on the statement. For example, in our illustration this would look like this.

Fund balances:

Unallocated	$ 200,000
Board-designated investment fund	300,000
Board-designated specific operating purposes	125,000
Board-designated equipment fund	100,000
Property, plant and equipment	5,200,000
	$5,925,000

Alternatively, this information could be shown at the bottom of the Statement of Changes in Fund Balances, or possibly in the notes to the financial statements. The important thing, however, is that the reader sees a total of all these unrestricted resources. Normally it is not necessary to include a separate statement showing the changes in these individual elements making up the total unrestricted fund balance since these internal actions have no significance except as they affect the balances at the end of the year.

The restricted funds are themselves broken down into three self-balancing subfund groupings. Notice that the "plant replacement and expansion fund" contains no plant assets. This fund merely accumulates restricted funds until such time as they are used for actual plant purchases. At that time the amount involved is transferred to the unrestricted fund.

Statement of Revenues and Expenses

Figure 15–2 shows an example of the Statement of Revenues and Expenses contemplated by the Guide. This statement is easy to read and understand because it shows all unrestricted income on one statement with a minimum of confusing detail.

JOHNSTOWN HOSPITAL

STATEMENT OF REVENUES AND EXPENSES
For the Year Ended December 31, 1974

Patient service revenue	$5,000,000
Allowance and uncollectable accounts (after deduction of related gifts of $30,000)	(1,000,000)
Net patient service revenue	4,000,000
Other operating revenue (including $50,000 from specific-purpose funds)	100,000
Total operating revenue	4,100,000
Operating expenses:	
Nursing services	1,800,000
Other professional services	1,300,000
General services	1,000,000
Fiscal services	200,000
Administrative services (including interest of $18,000).............	500,000
Provision for depreciation.................................	200,000
Total operating expenses	5,000,000
Loss from operations	(900,000)
Nonoperating revenue:	
Unrestricted gifts and bequests.............................	600,000
Income from unrestricted endowment funds	300,000
Income and gains from Board-designated funds	50,000
Total nonoperating revenue	950,000
Excess of Revenues over Expenses.........................	$ 50,000

Fig. 15–2. An example of a Statement of Revenues and Expenses in the format recommended for hospitals by the Guide.

Notice the simplicity of the basic statement arrangement:

Patient Revenue	$ 4,000,000
Other Operating Revenue	100,000
Operating Expenses	(5,000,000)
Nonoperating Revenue	950,000
Excess of Revenues over Expenses	$ 50,000

Since this statement includes all unrestricted revenues and expenses there should be a minimum of reader confusion resulting from the use of fund accounting. This form of financial statement, while intended for hospitals, is equally applicable to other nonprofit organizations.*

Statement of Changes in Fund Balances

The third basic statement for hospitals shows the changes in fund balances for all fund groupings. Figure 15–3 shows an example of this statement in the format recommended in the Guide. Figure 15–4 shows the same statement in the format preferred by the author, where a columnar format is used.

Some of the transfers on this statement may confuse the reader: first, the transfer from the plant replacement and expansion fund to the unrestricted fund of $100,000, and second, the transfer from the unrestricted fund to the plant replacement fund of $75,000. The basic concept is that all plant fund assets belong on the unrestricted fund statement, but cash and other assets restricted by others should be carried in a separate restricted fund until expended. At the time these funds are used to purchase fixed assets the amount must then be transferred to the unrestricted fund balance. The reverse is true where portions of operating revenues have been restricted, usually by third party payors, for fixed asset additions. An example would be where Blue Cross allowed in the rate reimbursement formula an amount which the hospital could expend only for certain types of medical equipment. The full amount received from Blue Cross is initially recorded in the unrestricted fund as operating revenue since services have been provided which gave rise to the income. The portion of this revenue that is restricted by Blue Cross for medical equipment is then transferred to the restricted plant, replacement and expansion fund until expended.

---

* An alternative columnar format of Statement of Revenues and Expenses is provided in the Guide. In this format, three columns and a total column are provided. The three columns are headed: "operations," "other" and "plant." The total column would show the same amounts as in Figure 15–2. The purpose of this alternative format is to provide detail on these unrestricted funds. The author does not recommend this alternative approach since these extra columns tend to complicate the statement presentation without providing meaningful information.

JOHNSTOWN HOSPITAL

STATEMENT OF CHANGES IN FUND BALANCES

	Year Ended December 31,	
	1974	1973

UNRESTRICTED FUNDS

Balance, beginning of the year	$5,750,000	$5,630,000
Excess of revenues over expenses.	50,000	80,000
Donated medical equipment	100,000	10,000
Transferred from plant replacement and expansion fund to finance property, plant and equipment expenditures	100,000	80,000
Transfers to plant replacement and expansion fund to reflect third-party payor revenue	(75,000)	(50,000)
Balance, end of the year.	$5,925,000	$5,750,000

RESTRICTED FUNDS

Specific-purpose fund:

Balance, beginning of the year	$ 80,000	$ 75,000
Restricted gifts and bequests.	65,000	45,000
Net gain on sale of investments.	5,000	—
Transferred to other operating revenue and to offset allowances	(50,000)	(40,000)
Balance, end of the year	$ 100,000	$ 80,000

Plant replacement and expansion fund:

Balance, beginning of the year	$ 95,000	$ 85,000
Restricted gifts and bequests	100,000	25,000
Income from investments	10,000	10,000
Net gain on sale of investments.	20,000	5,000
Transferred to unrestricted funds	(100,000)	(80,000)
Transferred from unrestricted funds	75,000	50,000
Balance, end of the year	$ 200,000	$ 95,000

Endowment fund:

Balance, beginning of the year	$4,825,000	$4,645,000
Restricted gifts and bequests	100,000	150,000
Net gains on sale of investments	100,000	30,000
Balance, end of the year.	$5,025,000	$4,825,000

Fig. 15–3. An example of a Statement of Changes in Fund Balances in the format recommended for hospitals by the Guide.

JOHNSTOWN HOSPITAL

STATEMENT OF CHANGES IN FUND BALANCES
For the Year Ended December 31, 1974

			Restricted	
	Unrestricted	Specific Purposes	Plant Replacement and Expansion	Endowment
Balance, beginning of the year	$5,750,000	$ 80,000	$ 95,000	$4,825,000
Excess of revenues over expenses	50,000			
Restricted gifts and bequests		65,000	100,000	100,000
Donated medical equipment	100,000			
Income from investments			10,000	
Net gain on sale of investments		5,000	20,000	100,000
Additions to plant fund from plant replacement and expansion fund	100,000			
Portion of reimbursement of third-party payers restricted to replacement of equipment	(75,000)		(100,000)	
Transferred to other operating revenue and to offset allowances		(50,000)	75,000	
Balance, end of the year	$5,925,000	$100,000	$200,000	$5,025,000

Fig. 15–4. An example of a columnar Statement of Changes in Fund Balances in the format preferred by the author.

Statement of Changes in Financial Position

The fourth basic statement recommended by the Guide for hospitals is the Statement of Changes in Financial Position.

The Accounting Principles Board of the American Institute of CPAs requires that this statement or its equivalent be included as a basic financial statement. An illustration is not presented since this statement is not peculiar to nonprofit organizations. If the reader wants to study this statement, reference should be made to the Guide and to APB Opinion No. 19.

ACCOUNTING PRINCIPLES

Generally Accepted Accounting Principles

Generally accepted accounting principles are applicable to hospitals. As a result, the opinions of the Accounting Principles Board are also applicable to hospitals except where they are clearly inappropriate and hospitals must conform their accounting practices to such opinions in order to receive unqualified opinions from the CPAs.

Accrual Basis

The accrual basis of accounting should be used by hospitals. This means that a number of valuation reserves must be established. Hospitals, for example, normally record all receivables for patient services at the gross amount of the billing. In a substantial number of instances the hospital will ultimately settle the bill for a lesser amount. Part of this lesser settlement will be because of charity cases, and part will be because of special arrangements with third party payors such as Blue Cross, Medicare, etc. Traditionally hospitals have recorded their receivables at the gross amount and then recorded the actual allowance at the time of settlement. Accrual accounting requires that an estimate of this allowance be set up at the time of billing. Accrual accounting also requires that receivables be recorded at the time services are rendered and not at the time the patient is discharged.

Accrual accounting requires much the same type of valuation judgments be made for those contracts which are subject to periodic adjustment. The hospital must make its best estimate of these adjustments on a current basis and reflect these amounts in the Statement of Revenues and Expenses. To the extent that the subsequent actual adjustment is more or less than the estimate, such amount should be reflected in the accounts of the period in which the final adjustment becomes known.

Investment income should also be recorded on an accrual basis. The same is true with investment income from trusts held by outside trustees. That amount can also be estimated and should be recorded.

Unrestricted Contributions

Unrestricted contributions and bequests must be included as nonoperating revenue in the Statement of Revenues and Expenses in the year received. It is not permissible for the board to place restrictions on these amounts and then to include them as restricted fund income. The donor is the only person who can place restrictions on gifts. If no legally binding restrictions are placed on the gift it must be reported in the Statement of Revenues and Expenses.

Restricted Contributions

Contributions and bequests restricted by the donor must be shown on the Statement of Changes in Fund Balances in the year received in the appropriate subfund. If the gift is for a current, but restricted, purpose, it is recorded in the restricted fund and then, as expended for the designated purchase, is transferred to the Statement of Revenues and Expenses. The mechanics of this transfer can be seen in Figures 15–2 and 15–3. Notice that in the Statement of Changes in Fund Balances $65,000 of restricted gifts and bequests have been received and added to the specific purposes fund; $50,000 has then been transferred from the specific purposes fund to the Statement of Revenues and Expenses and is recorded in that statement as part of "other operating revenue," and the $50,000 is shown parenthetically.

Term endowment gifts should also be included in the Statement of Changes in Fund Balances. At the time such term endowments become legally unrestricted, the amount of the term endowment (plus any capital gains accumulated therewith) should be shown as nonoperating income on the Statement of Revenues and Expenses.

Pledges

Pledges should be recorded, less an appropriate estimate for the uncollectible portion. Pledges made for unrestricted purposes should be recorded in the accounts in the same manner as any other unrestricted gift. Restricted pledges should be handled as restricted gifts.

Grants

Restricted grants should be treated as a restricted contribution and be recorded in the Statement of Changes in Fund Balances. Unrestricted grants, or grants that by their terms are fully expended within the year of receipt, would be shown directly in the Statement of Revenues and Expenses. If the purpose of the grant is to provide for charity cases, then the grant should be netted against the "allowances and uncollectible accounts" line. This can be seen in Figure 15–2. If the grant is for a specific activity or function other than payment for services provided to specific patients, the grant would be shown as part of "other operating income." If the gift is for the general operations of the hospital and is not restricted in any way, it should be included as a nonoperating revenue.

Donated Services

Donated services should be recorded only when an employer-employee relationship exists and when there is an objective basis for valuing the services rendered. Thus the services of most volunteers are not recorded. There are many hospitals, however, run by religious organizations where the majority of the employees are unpaid. In that instance it is appropriate to record the value of these donated services.

Donated Materials

Donated materials that are normally purchased by the hospital should be recorded as nonoperating revenue in the Statement of Revenues and Expenses. The use of these materials would be accounted for in the same manner as any purchased material.

Donated Property and Plant

Donated property, plant, and equipment should be recorded at fair market value on the Statement of Changes in Fund Balances as a direct addition to the Unrestricted Fund balance. It would not be recorded as a gift on the Statement of Revenues and Expenses. There is an example of this on the Statement of Changes in Fund Balances shown in Figure 15–3.

The reason why the Guide recommends recording here rather than on the Statement of Revenues and Expenses is, apparently, that such gifts not being in the form of cash, are a form of restricted gift. As such the board does not have the same use of the gift as it would if it were in the form of cash. Since donated medical equipment, for example, could be sizable in any one year, many are concerned that such gifts would distort the Statement of Revenues and Expenses.

Investments

Investments should be carried at cost, and not at market value.* The market value of all investments should be shown parenthetically on the balance sheet or in the notes. If market is less than cost and a permanent impairment of value exists, then cost should be written down to market. Where investment funds are pooled, gains or losses and income should be distributed to each fund on the basis of the number of units each fund holds, and not on a cost basis. If unrestricted fund investments are pooled with restricted funds, income and gains and losses should be distributed

* The Audit Guide for hospitals is in direct conflict with the Guides for colleges and for voluntary health and welfare organizations, which provide that investments can be carried at either cost or market (i.e., fair value). The author believes it is only a matter of time before this conflict is resolved and hospitals are also permitted to carry their investments at market.

currently in order to record such amounts in the Statement of Revenues and Expenses.

Investment Income

Investment income from all unrestricted funds should be included in the nonoperating revenues section of the Statement of Revenues and Expenses. Investment income from endowments, which is not restricted by the terms of the endowment, should also be added to nonoperating revenues. Endowment income, which is restricted for a specific purpose, should be added to the restricted funds for specific purposes. Investment income on restricted funds for specific purposes and plant replacement and expansion fund is normally added to the restricted fund balances.

Capital Gains and Losses

Capital gains or losses on unrestricted funds should be recognized as nonoperating revenue in the year in which such gains or losses are realized. Gains or losses on restricted investment funds normally would be added to the principal of such funds on the Statement of Changes in Fund Balances. If, however, such gains on restricted funds are legally unrestricted, then they would also be shown on the Statement of Revenues and Expenses.

Funds Held in Trust by Others

Occasionally a donor will give to an outside trustee an endowment fund, the income from which is to be given by the trustee to the hospital. In such circumstances the principal of the trust should not be recorded on the hospital's books, but if the terms of the trust are such that the hospital has a legal right to the income, the hospital should record the income on an accrual basis, and not on a cash basis.

Property, Plant, and Equipment

Property, plant, and equipment should be recorded in the Unrestricted Fund at cost, or at fair market value in the case of donated property. Where historical cost records are not available an appraisal at "historical cost" should be made and these amounts recorded.

Depreciation

Depreciation should be recognized in hospital financial statements, and the amount of depreciation should be shown separately in the Statement of Revenues and Expenses.

Provision for Replacement

Provisions for replacement or expansion of plant are not charges against the Statement of Revenues and Expenses but represent a board decision to set aside certain funds for this purpose. Such provisions should be treated as allocations of the unrestricted fund balance. On the Balance Sheet such amounts would be shown as part of the board-designated funds. See the example in Figure 15–1.

Appropriations

Appropriations of the unrestricted fund balance can be made by the board at its discretion since there are no restrictions on the use of this fund.* Appropriations are, however, only designations of the unrestricted fund balances and should not be reflected as an expense in the Statement of Revenues and Expenses. All expenditures in subsequent periods for the purpose of the appropriation are handled in exactly the same manner as all other expenditures and are reported in the Statement of Revenues and Expenses. The assets representing the appropriation are shown as part of the board-designated funds on the asset side of the Balance Sheet.

Third Party Reimbursement Timing Differences

For purposes of calculating rate reimbursement from third parties, accelerated depreciation may be used whereas for financial statement purposes the straight line method may be followed. The use of accelerated depreciation in this circumstance results in a larger reimbursement in the early years. In subsequent years, when accelerated depreciation is less than straight line depreciation, the reverse is true. The amount of additional revenue arising from this accelerated method of depreciation for rate re-

* See Chapter 5 for a full discussion of accounting for appropriations.

imbursement purposes should be "deferred" and not recognized in income in the year received. This deferred income should be subsequently recognized over the years when the allowable depreciation for reimbursement purposes will be less than that for book purposes on a straight line basis.

The accounting principles followed are similar to those generally used in following deferred tax accounting. Of course, if depreciation does not directly enter in the reimbursement formula, as for example in a negotiated contract in which a factor for depreciation not based on actual costs is used, then timing differences do not arise and no deferral is necessary. Other types of timing differences should also be accounted for on a deferred basis. Examples are pension costs and vacation accruals.

For example, using a very simple illustration, assume that an asset is purchased having a cost of $10,000, and a life of five years. The hospital depreciates this asset over a five-year period, and assuming no salvage value, charges depreciation of $2,000 a year. In the rate reimbursement formula for Blue Cross, however, depreciation is taken on the accelerated sum-of-the-year's digits method.* This results in larger depreciation in the first several years, offset by lower depreciation in the last several. Here is a comparison of the depreciation on both bases:

Year	Straight Line Method	Sum-of-the-Year's Digits Method	Difference Book Greater (less)
1	$ 2,000	$ 3,333	($1,333)
2	2,000	2,667	(667)
3	2,000	2,000	—
4	2,000	1,333	667
5	2,000	667	1,333
	$10,000	$10,000	$ —

* The sum-of-the-year's digits method of calculating depreciation is a method in which the amount of depreciation in a given year is calculated by multiplying a "fraction" times the cost of the asset (less salvage value, if any). This "fraction" is calculated by taking the number of years of remaining life as the numerator and the sum of the year's digits over the asset's total life as the denominator. The denominator remains constant from year to year, but the numerator decreases each year. In the illustration above, the fraction for the first year is 5/15. The numerator (5) is the number of remaining years of life. The denominator (15) is the sum of the number "5", "4", "3", "2" and "1", or 15. The fraction for the second year is 4/15, the fraction for the third year is 3/15 and so forth.

Now if Blue Cross were effectively reimbursing the hospital for 100 per cent of the cost of this equipment (which is normally not the case), the amount received in years 1 and 2 in excess of the straight line depreciation should be deferred to years 4 and 5 when an amount less than straight line will be received. This is merely an attempt to match revenues and the related expenses.

In practice, Blue Cross will not represent the only source of revenue, and therefore will not be reimbursing the hospital for 100 per cent of the cost of the equipment. Therefore, in calculating the amount to defer, the hospital should compare the amount received from Blue Cross (or any third party payor) with the amount that would have been received if the rate reimbursement formula used depreciation calculated on a straight line basis.

Patient Revenues

The amount of income shown as patient revenues should be the full amount at established rates regardless of whether the hospital expects to collect the full amount. The amount of allowance for charity and the amount of discount given third party payors should be shown as part of "allowances and uncollectible accounts." In this way the reader is in a position to see what portion of the hospital's full rate structure is being collected.

Bad Debts

At the time of recording revenues (at full rates, as noted above) the hospital should estimate the portion that will not be collected, such as charity cases, etc. This amount would be shown as part of the "allowances and uncollectible accounts" and deducted from revenue in the Statement of Revenues and Expenses. Subsequent bad debts should also be shown as a further adjustment of the allowances and uncollectible accounts line.

RECOMMENDED SIMPLIFIED STATEMENT

In previous chapters we have shown how it is possible through the use of a columnar format to combine the activities of all funds on one statement. The same approach is possible with hospital financial statements. Figure 15–5 shows how the columnar format could be applied to the Johnstown Hospital.

As will be observed in this illustration, the reader can quickly see the total activity of the hospital, including all activity in the restricted funds. He will see, for example, that there were substantial restricted gifts received during the year, as well as restricted investment income and gains. As has been noted in other chapters, many argue that there is a real danger that the reader will be misled by showing such restricted income on the same page as unrestricted income, particularly where a "total" or, as here, a "combined all funds" column is shown. Such persons believe that the reader is not likely to appreciate the significance of these restricted funds and will, mistakenly, assume that the board has available for general purposes all of the income shown on the statement, including restricted income. However, as has been discussed repeatedly throughout this book, the author recognizes these risks but feels that they are less important than the risk that the reader will not understand or grasp the total picture of the institution when separate statements are presented for each fund.

In this columnar format, several principles of reporting have been followed that differ from the Guide. Notice that donated medical equipment has been shown as nonoperating revenue rather than being added directly to the fund balance on a separate Statement of Changes in Fund Balances. Presumably the board accepted this equipment because it felt it would contribute to the hospital, and accordingly it should be reflected as nonoperating revenue.

Another change is that restricted gifts for specific purposes have been shown in the unrestricted fund column to the extent that such gifts were actually expended during the year. Likewise the amount reported as specific purpose gifts is only the net amount not expended during the year. By contrast, the Guide provides that such income will be shown in its entirety in the specific purposes fund and then transferred to the unrestricted fund and reported as "other operating revenue." This appears to be awkward, and is difficult for the reader to understand. Also, it is difficult, in part, because gifts are reported in three different places in the Statement of Revenues and Expenses (gifts under "nonoperating revenue," gifts as a deduction from "allowances," and gifts transferred from specific purpose funds in the other

JOHNSTOWN HOSPITAL

STATEMENT OF REVENUES, EXPENSES, AND CHANGES IN FUND BALANCES
For the Year Ended December 31, 1974

	Unrestricted	Specific Purpose Fund	Restricted Plant Replacement and Expansion Fund	Endowment Fund	Combined All Funds
Patient service revenues	$5,000,000				$ 5,000,000
Allowances and uncollectible accounts	(1,030,000)				(1,030,000)
Net patient service revenue	3,970,000				3,970,000
Other operating revenue	50,000				50,000
Total operating revenue	4,020,000				4,020,000
Operating expenses:					
Nursing services	1,800,000				1,800,000
Other professional services	1,300,000				1,300,000
General services	1,000,000				1,000,000
Fiscal services	200,000				200,000
Administrative services (including interest of $18,000)	500,000				500,000
Provision for depreciation	200,000				200,000

Total operating expenses	5,000,000				5,000,000
Loss from operations	980,000				(980,000)
Nonoperating revenue:					
Gifts and bequests	680,000	$ 15,000	$100,000	$ 100,000	895,000
Investment income	320,000		10,000		330,000
Realized gains on sale of investments	30,000	5,000	20,000	100,000	155,000
Donated medical equipment	100,000				100,000
Total nonoperating revenues	1,130,000	20,000	130,000	200,000	1,480,000
Excess of revenues over expenses	150,000	20,000	130,000	200,000	500,000
Fund balance, beginning of the year	5,750,000	80,000	95,000	4,825,000	10,750,000
Interfund transfers, net	25,000		(25,000)		—
Fund balance, end of the year	$5,925,000	$100,000	$200,000	$5,025,000	$11,250,000

Fig. 15–5. An example of a Statement of Revenues, Expenses, and Changes in Fund Balances for all funds in the format recommended by the author.

operating revenue). In the suggested simplified format, all gifts are reported as nonoperating revenue.

In our illustration, the amount shown as unrestricted gifts and bequests is $680,000 compared to $600,000 shown in the Statement of Revenues and Expenses in Figure 15–2. Fifty thousand dollars of this difference is restricted fund gifts which were expended during the current year for operating purposes and the remaining $30,000 are gifts which were previously netted against "allowances and uncollectible accounts" in the operating revenue section.

Another change that has been made is that the two partially offsetting plant fund transfers have been netted and shown without explanation. If the details of such transfers are important they could be shown in a footnote where the risk of confusion would be minimized. Also, observe that the fund balances at the beginning and end of the year have been shown on this statement, thus eliminating the need for a separate Statement of Changes in Fund Balances. This should help the reader to understand the statements. Also, in the process of combining the two statements, the caption "Excess of revenues over expenses" has been somewhat de-emphasized by not showing it as the last line on the statement. This is appropriate since emphasis on excess of revenue is relatively less important in nonprofit reporting.

CONCLUSION

The Hospital Guide published by the American Institute of Certified Public Accountants represents a significant step forward in establishing realistic accounting principles and reporting standards. The most important concept in this Guide is that there are only two types of funds—restricted and unrestricted, and that all unrestricted funds should be reported together. This is a very important principle. This Guide should be studied by all nonprofit organizations.

At the same time some suggestions have been offered to simplify the statements even further. The major recommendation is to combine the Statement of Revenues and Expenses and the Statement of Changes in Fund Balances in a columnar format and to modify certain of the accounting and reporting principles.

16

Accounting Standards for Other Types of Organizations

In the preceding chapters we have discussed the Audit Guides issued by the American Institute of Certified Public Accountants for use by accountants in their examinations of voluntary health and welfare organizations, colleges and universities, and hospitals. The Guides applicable to the latter two categories deal specifically with those types of institutions, though some of the principles involved can be applied to other, similar organizations. The Audit Guide for voluntary health and welfare organizations, on the other hand, is addressed to a much broader category of organization. This Guide will have great influence on accounting for other types of nonprofit organizations because there are so many organizations directly affected.

This chapter discusses first the features and general implications of the three Audit Guides, enumerating five areas in which the author believes they will have their greatest impact. This is followed by an evaluation of the applicability of the Guides to several types of organizations to which they are not specifically addressed. In each instance, the author's conclusions as to the most applicable Guide and the principles to be applied to special accounting problems are given with supporting reasons.

* For the Audit Guide definition of these organizations, see page 178.

GENERAL FEATURES OF THE THREE GUIDES

Applicability for All Nonprofit Organizations

At first it might appear that the three Audit Guides are applicable only to the types of organizations to which they are addressed, but in fact these Guides will greatly affect all categories of nonprofit organizations. The three Guides, collectively, discuss almost all of the accounting and reporting problems encountered by nonprofit organizations of all types—including those not directly addressed by the Guides. For this reason thoughtful accountants will have to give considerable weight to the solutions offered by the Guides to these common problems. It will be very difficult for the CPA to express an unqualified opinion on an accounting or reporting treatment which is contrary to that recommended in one or more of these three Audit Guides. The Guides can therefore be expected to have a major impact on all nonprofit organizations.

Consistency Among the Guides

Three separate committees were involved in writing the Guides. Some attempt was made toward conformity, but different industry practices and customs and the differing perspectives of the committees resulted in a number of principles that are not completely consistent. On some points, however, the Guides are consistent. On others, two of the three Guides are in agreement, therefore suggesting how a particular issue is likely to be eventually resolved. Figure 16–1 summarizes the major accounting and reporting principles and the positions taken in each of the three Guides.

There are, of course, a number of differences among the Guides, particularly in financial statement format. However, if one takes a broad overview of the three Guides and looks at the basic underlying accounting and reporting principles he will find that there are more areas of consistency than of inconsistency. Most of the differences among the Guides are in the cosmetics of the financial statement presentation.

Accounting or Reporting Principles	Hospitals	Colleges	Voluntary Health and Welfare
1. Accrual basis accounting required	Yes	Yes	Yes
2. All unrestricted fund activity—including board-designated funds—must be reported together	Yes	No	Yes
3. All unrestricted contributions must be reported together in income statement*.	Yes	Yes	Yes
4. Current restricted contributions reported in full in year received rather than in year expended	No	Yes†	Yes
5. Pledges *must* be recorded if material	Yes	No	Yes
6. Contributed services must be recorded under certain circumstances	Yes	Yes	Yes
7. Unrestricted dividend and interest income must be reported in the unrestricted fund in the income statement.	Yes	Yes	Yes
8. Capital gains on legally unrestricted investment funds must be reported in the unrestricted fund in the income statement	Yes	No	Yes
9. Transfers between funds reported in the income statement	No	Yes	Yes**
10. Use of a separate fixed asset or plant fund allowed	No	Yes	Yes
11. Fixed assets must be capitalized	Yes	Yes	Yes
12. Fixed assets must be depreciated and the depreciation charge reported in the income statement	Yes	No	Yes
13. Appropriations or encumbrances can be charged against expenses	No	No	No
14. Appropriations or encumbrances can be reported as a liability on the balance sheet	No	No	No
15. Transfers under the "total return" concept of reporting endowment fund gains must be reported as a transfer in the "transfer" section of the statement	Not discussed	Yes	Yes

*As is discussed fully in Chapter 14, college financial statements do not include an "income" statement. However, for purposes of showing the consistency of accounting and reporting principles among the three guides, the author has considered the Statement of Changes in Fund Balances as the equivalent of an "income" statement.

†But only in the Statement of Changes in Fund Balances. In the Statement of Current Funds, Revenues, Expenditures, and Other Changes, current restricted revenue is reported only to the extent expended.

**But only after the caption "Excess of revenues over expenses."

Fig. 16-1. Comparison of accounting and reporting principles prescribed in the new Audit Guides.

Important Principles Evolving from the Guides

There are five areas where the author believes the Guides will have great impact on all categories of nonprofit organizations. These are discussed below.

1. *All legally unrestricted contributions reported in a single "income" statement.*

The most important and far reaching change is that each of the three Guides now requires nonprofit organizations covered by these Guides to record all legally unrestricted contributions in a single income statement so that the reader can see the total amounts received.* Previously it was common for boards of trustees to "designate" certain categories of legally unrestricted contributions for some specific purpose and then disclose these contributions only in separate income statements for the "designated" funds. As a result, the casual reader who was unaware of this practice would see a bleak picture when he looked at what appeared to be a statement of operations. In fact, the organization may very well have received substantial amounts of unrestricted contributions which the board had designated for some purpose other than recurring operations and thus not included in general funds. All unrestricted contributions must now be reported in the general fund income statement.

2. *Summarizing all other unrestricted activity on one statement.*

Each of the three Guides also requires that all other unrestricted revenues and expenses be reflected in this single income statement. Again, there are three different styles of statement format but each attempts to tell the reader what the *total* unrestricted revenues and the *total* unrestricted expenses were for the year.

---

* The "purist" would argue that the college Audit Guide does not require that contributions be reported in an "income" statement since college financial statements do not include an "income" statement as such. This is certainly technically correct. At the same time the college Audit Guide does require all legally unrestricted contributions to be reported in the current unrestricted fund. While the Guide goes on at considerable length to point out that college financial statements do not include "an income statement," the knowledgeable reader looking at a financial statement will find *all* unrestricted contributions reported in this single fund. For this reason, it seems appropriate to consider this principle as being applicable to all categories of organizations, including colleges.

What these three Guides are saying is that board-designated funds must be reported together with other unrestricted funds so that the reader will see the total picture. Effectively (except for colleges), the use of board-designated funds, while permitted for bookkeeping purposes, is not permitted for reporting purposes.

Perhaps it is not so obvious, but in including all categories of unrestricted income, the Guides are saying that investment income (dividends and interest) must also be reported in this "income" statement. In the case of hospitals and voluntary health and welfare organizations, capital gains arising from *unrestricted* investments must be included too.

The Audit Guide for voluntary health and welfare organizations presents a statement format that clearly emphasizes the organization as a whole: this format provides not only for reporting all unrestricted activity together but also for reporting all *restricted* income and expenses on the same statement. This columnar statement presentation can be seen in Figure 13–1 (page 193) and is the most desirable.

3. *Fixed assets and depreciation accounting.*

The recording of fixed assets in the financial statements and the taking of depreciation have stirred up controversy in nonprofit accounting for years. All three Guides now require that fixed assets be recorded and reported in the Balance Sheet, and two of the Guides (those for hospitals and voluntary health and welfare organizations) require that fixed assets be depreciated over their useful lives. The Guide for colleges requires capitalization of fixed assets but does not require depreciation.*

All of this means, of course, that for all practical purposes all categories of nonprofit organizations should be recording fixed assets, and depreciation accounting practices should be followed (with the possible exception of institutions that are similar in structure to that of a college). There is no longer any basis in accounting literature to conclude that fixed assets should be written off when purchased. And, where there is a charge for

---

* Even in the Guide for colleges there is permissive language allowing depreciation in the plant fund column of the Statement of Changes in Fund Balances. The acceptance of depreciation accounting by two of the Guides and the emphasis on cost of services (discussed below) will put increased pressure on colleges to follow depreciation accounting in the future.

services, there is a presumption that financial information should disclose the cost of the services rendered, and depreciation is part of that cost.

4. *Carrying investments at market.*

Significantly, both the college and the voluntary health and welfare Guides state that investments may now be carried at market or fair value. This is not a requirement but rather an acceptable alternative to carrying investments at historical cost. Many institutions with large endowment funds may find carrying investments at market value is more meaningful than carrying them at cost. Except for hospitals, discussed below, all nonprofit organizations may now do so.

The hospital Audit Guide does not provide for carrying investments at market and is in direct conflict with the other two Guides on this issue. Eventually the accounting profession must come to grips with this conflict because many hospitals may feel that the subsequent release of these other two Guides gives them license to also carry investments at market.

5. *An increased emphasis on programs of the organization.*

Traditionally, nonprofit organizations have reported in terms of the amounts spent for salaries, rent, supplies, etc. The voluntary health and welfare Guide takes a major step forward when it states that the organization exists to perform services and programs and therefore should be reporting principally in terms of its individual program activities or functions. Figure 13–1 (page 193) is an example of an organization reporting on a program or functional basis. This type of presentation tells the reader how much of the organization's funds were expended for each program category and the amount spent in supporting services, including fund raising.

The Guides for hospitals and colleges also require reporting on a functional basis but in a somewhat different format. Neither *requires* the separate reporting of supporting services (i.e., management and general, and fund raising) from program services. Because of the large number of voluntary health and welfare organizations, the requirement for functional reporting in the format shown in Figure 13–1 will have the greatest impact. In time this format of functional reporting may well become the format which nonprofit organizations in general will be expected to follow.

We turn now to a discussion of the applicability of the three Audit Guides to several types of nonprofit organizations which are not specifically addressed by these Guides. For each type of institution, the author gives his conclusions as to the most applicable accounting principle and identifies the Guide that best applies to the special accounting problems of that category of nonprofit organization.

PRIVATE FOUNDATIONS

Type of Organization

The term "private foundation" is used here as defined in the Tax Reform Act of 1969. The tax aspects of private foundations are discussed in considerable detail in Chapter 23. For the most part, such organizations do not solicit funds from the public but receive their income mainly from endowment income. Occasionally they receive new gifts but, by definition, from a relatively few individuals.[*]

Guide Most Applicable[†]

The voluntary health and welfare Guide would appear to be the Guide most applicable to private foundations with respect to the "program" side of the foundation's activities. The college Guide would appear to have applicability to the endowment fund aspects because, like colleges, foundations often have large endowment funds.

---

[*] Community foundations are one exception.

[†] The AICPA has established a "task force" to consider accounting problems of private foundations. The author doubts, however, that this group will issue any definitive rules because the AICPA is no longer the rule-making body of the accounting profession. The Financial Accounting Standards Board (FASB) took over this function on July 1, 1973, and, in the author's opinion, is unlikely to consider accounting problems of nonprofit organizations for many years, in view of other, more pressing problems. This task force was, however, at the date of publication, in the process of preparing a position paper in which the task force has interpreted the three earlier Guides and the applicability of the principles therein to private foundations. The author (who is a member of this task force) would expect this position paper to be consistent with the positions taken in this chapter.

Special Accounting Problems

Recording of Grants.   There are several accounting problems which are somewhat peculiar to private foundations. The most important deals with the reporting of unpaid grants. Often private foundations will award a grantee institution monies payable over a several-year period. Most frequently these subsequent payments are dependent upon satisfactory performance or compliance with the original grant agreement, and as such, the "liability" for payment is somewhat "conditional." The accounting questions relate to timing of recording of these grant liabilities.

Some foundations prefer to treat payments to grantee institutions on a "cash" basis. That is, they will not record as an expense of the current year amounts which by their terms are not payable until future years. Likewise, no obligation for payment is recorded on the Balance Sheet for these unpaid amounts. Other foundations, on the other hand, record as an expense and as a liability the full commitment at the time the grantee institution is informed of the foundation's intention to make such payments.

Still other foundations (but much fewer in number) record both as an expense and as a liability amounts which the board of trustees has "appropriated" for particular areas of interest. This board action usually occurs before grantees have been selected and really is a nonbinding action indicating only where the trustees would like to see the foundation spend its money. Where such "appropriations" are recorded, the foundation effectively treats as an expense the amount which the board has concluded it will spend in a given area. This is the recording at time of appropriation as distinct from recording at the time of grant awards.

While sound accounting arguments can be made for both the first and second approaches and a sound business reason advanced for the last approach, the author believes that the most appropriate treatment for private foundations is the second approach: record both as an expense and a liability all amounts which grantee institutions have been informed they will receive. However, disclosure should be made of the various amounts of the total liability payable in specific future years. While in some instances such amounts will ultimately not be paid, these are usually infrequent and the unpaid amounts should be restored to income (as a reduction of expenses) in the year in which it becomes apparent that the foundation will not be making these payments.

The first approach discussed above—that is, treating payments on a "cash" basis—has the defect of being cash basis accounting whereas most of the reasons for using accrual basis accounting apply here. Further, private foundations preparing their financial statements in accordance with generally accepted accounting principles have to follow accrual basis accounting, and the first method would not appear to meet this criterion.

The third approach—recording as an expense at the time of an appropriation when specific commitments have not yet been made—would also appear to fail the "generally accepted accounting principles" test. As is noted in Chapters 13, 14, and 15, appropriation accounting is not acceptable and this third approach is basically appropriation accounting. The reader should refer to the appropriate pages of these earlier chapters, and to Chapter 5, for a more extended discussion of the reasons for this position.

Investments at Market. Private foundations typically have large endowment portfolios. Under the new Audit Guide investments can be carried at market or fair value, or at cost. It would appear that carrying at market or fair value is more meaningful to most readers of such financial statements, and the author would encourage foundations to do so. Reference should be made to pages 92–94 for a discussion of appropriate accounting and reporting procedures.

Distinction Between Principal and Income. One accounting distinction that private foundations often make in their fund balance section is the distinction between principal and income. This distinction appears to be arbitrary and, except where legal restrictions are involved, probably serves little purpose. Typically where such distinctions are made, the original principal and usually all capital gains thereon are maintained separately from the accumulated unspent income arising from investment of this principal. Particularly with the Tax Reform Act of 1969 and its requirement that minimum distributions be made (which will have the effect of dipping into capital gains and principal if dividend and interest income is not sufficient) this distinction between principal and income seems even less meaningful. The author recommends that in the absence of legal restriction these two amounts be combined and simply recorded as "fund balance." Where there are legal restrictions, the fund balance should be appropriately disclosed either in footnotes or as illustrated in Figure 13–5 (page 205).

PRIVATE ELEMENTARY AND SECONDARY SCHOOLS

Type of Organization

Private elementary and secondary schools are those institutions which provide education below the college and university level and which are supported by tuition and contributions from private sources. Excluded from this category are publicly supported school systems.

Guide Most Applicable

The National Association of Secondary Schools has recommended that the accounting principles prescribed for colleges and universities be followed. For this reason the college and university Audit Guide is clearly applicable to these institutions.

On the other hand, in the past many private elementary and secondary schools have not followed the heavy emphasis on fund accounting outlined in the college Guide but have used the principles followed by less well endowed organizations such as voluntary health and welfare organizations. For this reason, it would appear that there is some latitude for these schools, and they are free to follow the accounting and reporting principles prescribed in the voluntary health and welfare Audit Guide.

Special Accounting Problems

Competency of Bookkeeping Staff. The most difficult accounting problem many of these institutions have does not relate to accounting principles per se but rather to not having adequate bookkeeping and accounting capability to prepare *meaningful* financial statements on a monthly basis. The boards of such organizations should consider carefully their need for timely financial information and whether their present staffing arrangement can realistically meet this need. Where it appears that this is not possible, the board will have to consider the potential risks involved in not receiving timely and complete financial information. See Chapter 19 for a discussion of the alternatives to having a full-time bookkeeper.

RELIGIOUS ORGANIZATIONS OTHER THAN CHURCHES

Type of Organization

The term "religious organizations," as contemplated here, excludes individual churches, which are discussed below. Organizations that exist to service the particular needs of an organized religion on a regional or national basis would be included, as would organizations involved in the national administration of churches.

Guide Most Applicable

Typically such organizations receive a substantial amount of their income from the public or their constituency in the form of contributions and where this is so, the voluntary health and welfare Guide is applicable and probably mandatory. Where the principal support is from program services, and contributions are only a minor portion of the total, this Guide would not be mandatory but the principles outlined therein are sound and should still be applied.

Functional reporting would appear to be particularly appropriate (whether mandatory or not) since the board should be concerned with continually stressing to its membership the services being performed.

Special Accounting Problems

Allocations from Other Organizations.   Religious organizations frequently receive allocations from affiliated local or regional organizations. Usually the allocation is established by the "parent" organization at the beginning of the fiscal year but is paid by the local organization at varying times throughout the year. An accounting question often arises as to timing of income recognition. Should it be at the beginning of the year when the allocation is determined, at the time it is paid, or pro rata throughout the year?

Recognition normally should be on a pro rata basis throughout the year since the services being rendered are presumably also throughout the year. This is the method prescribed in the voluntary health and welfare Guide. Of course, unpaid allocations at the end of the year must be reviewed for collectibility.

Fixed Assets and Depreciation.   Fixed assets should be recorded and depreciation accounting practices followed for all of the reasons outlined in the voluntary health and welfare Guide (see page 187).

CHURCHES

Type of Organization

Here we are talking about individual parishes or churches as distinct from religious organizations discussed above. Typically all of the support comes as contributions directly from the membership.

Guide Most Applicable

The principles outlined in the voluntary health and welfare Guide are generally appropriate except for fixed asset accounting discussed below.

Special Accounting Problems

Fixed Assets and Depreciation.   Fixed assets and depreciation accounting is one of the more difficult areas for individual churches because of the complexity of keeping track of fixed assets and depreciation accounting procedures. Most churches do *not* record fixed assets and even fewer follow depreciation accounting practices. Accordingly, for the time being, the author believes that churches have an option of capitalizing fixed assets in their financial statements or simply reporting expenditures in the period made. Likewise, those few churches that do capitalize their fixed assets have the option of following or not following depreciation accounting practices, although carrying a fixed asset completely out of line with its current value is not recommended.*

Cash Basis Accounting. Many churches keep their records on a cash or a modified cash basis of accounting,† again mainly for ease of record keeping. This is probably appropriate for interim financial statement purposes, but if at the end of the accounting period there are any *material* amounts of unrecorded liabilities or assets (such as pledges receivable), these should be reflected on the financial statements. The key word here is "material." It is not suggested, for example, that accrual entries be made to record uncollected dividends or interest on investments if such amounts would not, in the aggregate, significantly change the results of the year's activities. Perhaps the easiest way to determine whether accruals are needed is to ask whether the board might make different decisions if it saw financial statements in which all accruals were recorded. If yes, then they are "material."

Competency of Bookkeeping Staff. Another related problem is that churches often have bookkeeping problems. Typically the treasurer of a small church will be the person actually keeping the records himself, with the result that the quality of the record keeping and financial statements is directly related to his competency and the amount of time available. Also, in such circumstances the deficiency in internal accounting control should be recognized. See Chapter 20 for a discussion of a desirable segregation of duties where feasible.

---

* The author believes, however, that it will only be a matter of time before churches will be required to capitalize and depreciate their fixed assets *if* they want an unqualified opinion from a CPA stating that the financial statements are prepared "in accordance with generally accepted accounting principles."

† Cash basis and modified cash basis accounting are discussed in Chapter 3.

MUSEUMS

Type of Organization

Museums (as contemplated here) include all nongovernmental, private institutions which maintain a collection exhibited to the public either with or without a charge.

Guide Most Applicable

Many museums have a staff organization very similar to that of colleges and universities in that the curatorial staff is usually accorded privileges and perquisites similar to a professorial staff of a university. For this reason the college Audit Guide is often considered appropriate for museums.

Nonetheless, the author feels that museums wishing to follow the accounting or reporting principles outlined in the voluntary health and welfare Guide are very much at liberty to do so. As is indicated in Chapter 14, college accounting and reporting principles are difficult for the typical reader to understand and where a museum is concerned with public understanding of its financial statements it should give serious consideration to the desirability of reporting formats other than the one prescribed in the college Audit Guide.

Special Accounting Problems

Carrying the Collection as an Asset. The most difficult question is whether to place a value on the "collection" and to record it as an asset in the financial statements. The dominant practice is to report the expenditure for collection acquisitions at the time they are purchased and not to "capitalize" them. Few museums reflect a value on their balance sheet for their collection. While this is the prevailing practice, the author believes institutions also have the option of capitalizing the collection and reflecting it on the balance sheet, and this is the preferable treatment.

Where To Report the Cost of Acquisitions. Where the museum does not capitalize its acquisitions at the time acquired, a related question is where to report the cost—in the Statement of Revenue or in the Statement of Changes in Fund Balances.

If the acquisition is reported in the Statement of Revenue, effectively the board is saying that acquiring the collection is a continuing part of the operations of the museum and part of the operating budget. Alternatively, if reported in the Statement of Changes in Fund Balances, the board is saying that acquisitions are part of the "principal" of the museum and should not be reported as though they were part of its operations. Further, this approach often assumes restricted gifts are used for such acquisitions, and typically restricted funds are accounted for only in a Statement of Changes in Fund Balances. The prevailing practice is to simply charge acquisitions against the fund balance in the Statement of Changes in Fund Balances.

Alternatively, if a museum were to follow the author's recommendation of using the voluntary health and welfare Audit Guide format (Figure 13–1), acquisitions would be presented in a combined Statement of Revenues, Expenses, and Changes in Fund Balances. If this were done the reader would see a total picture of all acquisitions, whether from restricted funds or from unrestricted funds. The format recommended in this Guide could be modified to distinguish between operating and acquisition expenses, as illustrated below:

	Unrestricted	Restricted	Total
Revenues	$ 500,000	$125,000	$ 625,000
Operating expenses	(450,000)	(25,000)	(475,000)
Excess of revenues over operating expenses	50,000	100,000	150,000
Acquisitions of collection	(40,000)	(85,000)	(125,000)
Excess of revenues over operating expenses and acquisitions	10,000	15,000	25,000
Fund balance beginning	100,000	50,000	150,000
Fund balance ending	$ 110,000	$ 65,000	$175,000

Recording Donated Collections.   Another related question is the handling of donations to the collection: Should a value be established and recorded for these gifts? The answer is "yes," although obviously there are valuation problems.

Donations to the collection should be recorded as a contribution in the same manner as cash contributions even where a museum follows the prevailing practice of simply charging collection costs against the fund balance as purchased. The value recorded as a contribution would also be recorded as an expenditure in the same manner as any other acquisition (see above). While this may appear to be just a lot of needless bookkeeping (recording of the gift as income followed by the write-off as expense), this presentation will show the reader the value of the total gifts received during the year.

This is not to minimize the valuation problem; perhaps one practical solution is to use the value reported by the donor for tax purposes provided that valuation is not obviously overstated.

Recording Sales from the Collection. From time to time museums sell from their collection in order to raise funds for other acquisitions. Where the item sold has not been capitalized the entire proceeds of such sale should be reported as revenue. This revenue should be reported in the same statement as purchases are reported.

Where the museum does reflect the value of its collection on its Balance Sheet, the difference between the sales proceeds and the original cost (or assigned value in the case of donated works) would be reported as a "gain" or "loss" from the sale.

Depreciation and Appreciation of Collection. Where fixed assets are capitalized, depreciation accounting practices are not followed with respect to collections because generally these assets increase rather than decrease in value with the passage of time. However, where it is determined that the carrying value (i.e., cost) will substantially exceed the fair market value for such assets, they should, of course, be written down. It is not appropriate to periodically write up the value of the collection to current market value.

Fixed Asset Accounting. Fixed assets other than the collection should be capitalized and reflected on the balance sheet (i.e., it is not appropriate to expense fixed assets as purchased). While the college Guide does not provide for depreciation of such fixed assets (and accordingly it is not mandatory) the author recommends that museums depreciate their fixed assets.

Recording of Pledges. College principles do not require recording pledges in the financial statements. Museums frequently receive a substantial portion of their revenue from gifts from the public, and where this is so the author recommends that pledges be recorded and revenue be recognized in the year in which the pledge was made. See the discussion in Chapter 13.

Functional Reporting. The author also recommends functional reporting wherever possible. Museums have a very real need to convince their membership and the public of the value of services being rendered and to the extent that functional accounting helps to tell this story museums are wise to follow such reporting techniques.

LIBRARIES

Type of Organization

Libraries as contemplated here are all nonprofit, nongovernmental libraries. Libraries run by governments usually follow fund accounting principles common to government and municipalities.

Guide Most Applicable

Libraries have considerable similarity to museums in that both are open to the public and have works on exhibit; they differ principally in that the function of the library is the exhibition of work created by others while museums often have considerable scholarly activity by the museum staff to interpret the significance of the collection. Consequently, there is less compelling reason to consider the college Guide as being the most applicable and the author feels that in most instances the accounting and reporting procedures prescribed in the voluntary health and welfare Guide are the more appropriate.

Special Accounting Problems

Recording a Value for Books. As with museums, the collections of libraries are usually not recorded as an asset on the financial statement. There would appear to be no real objection to doing so, however, and in fact, strong arguments could be made.

When the collection is recorded as an asset, depreciation accounting practices are probably appropriate since most books are dated. While it is difficult to establish a composite life for all types of books, a 3- to 7-year life is probably not unreasonable. Of course, where a library has a type of collection which is likely to maintain its value over a considerable period of time, depreciation would be at a reduced rate.

As with works of art, donations of library books should be appropriately valued and recorded as contributions (and then reported as expenditures if the library does not capitalize them). Fixed assets other than the collection of books should be recorded as an asset and depreciated over a reasonable period of time.

ASSOCIATIONS AND PROFESSIONAL SOCIETIES

Type of Organization

Associations and professional societies include membership organizations that have been formed for other than a social purpose. They include trade associations, engineering societies, business leagues, and the like. Dues or other fees charged to members are the main source of revenue for these organizations.

Guide Most Applicable

The voluntary health and welfare Guide is the most appropriate although few associations have significant amounts of restricted funds, and thus fund accounting techniques are usually not appropriate.

Special Accounting Problems

Reporting on a Functional Basis.   An association or professional society can exist only so long as the membership is convinced the services being rendered justify the dues and other payments being made by the members. There must be a return for their money. This means the association has a real need to communicate to the members. Functional reporting * is one of the most

---

* Functional reporting is discussed on pages 199 to 200.

effective ways of doing so since it requires the board to define the association's programs, and then to report on this basis.

Reporting of Sections or Groups.   Many national and regional professional societies are organized with separate sections, groups, or units operating in various parts of the country, more or less autonomously. Usually, these semi-autonomous sections or groups are legally part of the main organization and the board of directors has legal responsibility for their activities and financial affairs.

The question often asked is: Should the financial affairs of these sections and groups be reported with those of the main organization? The answer is "yes" although there are often problems in doing so. Typically the financial affairs of these units are handled locally by a volunteer treasurer and the quality of bookkeeping varies considerably. Often there is difficulty in getting the unit treasurers to submit financial information on a timely basis and in a uniform manner. Nevertheless, professional societies and associations should include in their statements the financial activity of all units for which the board has legal responsibility.

Use of Appropriation Accounting.   Associations and professional societies often follow appropriation accounting techniques but, in doing so, frequently do not observe the accounting rules that must be followed. See pages 50–56 for a comprehensive discussion of appropriation accounting procedures.

Separate Charitable Organization.   Many trade associations and professional societies are organized as noncharitable tax-exempt organizations * so they can engage in political activities and attempt to influence legislation. As such, contributions received are not tax-deductible by the donor. Often these organizations will set up a second, separate organization which is charitable in nature and which can receive tax-deductible contributions. This charitable organization must carefully conduct its affairs so that all of its activities are for "charitable" purposes. Usually the boards of both organizations are substantially the same and both organizations occupy the same quarters (with appropriate intercompany charges).

* These are referred to as 501(c)(6) organizations under the Internal Revenue Code and are discussed on page 384.

The reporting question is: Should the financial statements of the two organizations be combined? The answer is "yes" because the distinction between the two organizations is basically a legal one and the members have a right to see the total financial picture of both organizations. In fact, the members may not even be aware of the existence of the second organization.

CLUBS

Type of Organization

Clubs include many types of organizations ranging from small social clubs that meet informally to much larger clubs that have their own buildings and property. Country and city clubs are typical of the latter category.

Guide Most Applicable

Of the three Guides, the voluntary health and welfare Guide is the most applicable. Many clubs do not have restricted funds and as such often do not need to follow fund accounting principles.

Special Accounting Problems

Initiation Fees and Capital Stock. Most clubs charge a fee to new members—either an initiation fee, or payment for capital shares, or a combination of the two. Should such amounts be treated as revenue and reported as part of the excess of revenue over expenses for the period?

Payment for capital shares is not revenue and should be reported as a direct addition to the fund balance of the organization. Normally there is provision for redemption of capital shares or the right of direct transfer of ownership to others.

Initiation fees that are not payments for capital shares are often considered as contributions and reported as revenue. Alternatively, some argue that such fees are similar to capital stock payments and represent the new member's share of total members' equity and should be reported as a direct addition to the fund balance as contributed capital.* The author recommends that the first approach be followed and that the initiation fee be looked on as additional revenue and reported in the income statement. In this way the reader sees all "revenue" that the club receives. Since initiation fees are not returnable, clearly such fees represent revenue to the club, albeit revenue of a different type than revenue from sales of goods.

Fixed Asset Accounting. Clubs having buildings and other major fixed assets should capitalize these assets and follow depreciation accounting practices. Most clubs with such facilities have a need to know the cost of particular services being rendered, in part to be sure their pricing structure is recovering all the costs. As is discussed in Chapter 7, depreciation is a cost and must be considered whenever it is necessary to know the cost of a product or service, especially when separate fees are billed, such as for swimming pool privileges. To do otherwise is to leave the club membership with an inadequate understanding of the cost of particular services. Further, if nonmembers are served by the club and "unrelated business income" is generated (see below), depreciation is an expense which is deductible in arriving at taxable income.

"Unrelated Business." Many clubs provide services not only to their membership but also to guests of members and in some instances to the public at large. If "unrelated business income" becomes sizable it can jeopardize the club's tax-exempt status, as well as create taxable income (see Chapter 23). Accordingly, it is very important that clubs keep track of revenue from nonmembers and the applicable expenses. This usually involves a fairly elaborate reporting and bookkeeping system, and most clubs are well advised to get competent advice from a CPA.

---

* This is the approach taken in *Uniform System of Accounts for Clubs*, published by Club Managers Association of America, 1967.

PART IV

CONTROLLING THE NONPROFIT ORGANIZATION

17

The Importance of Budgeting

A budget, like motherhood, is something very few would argue against. Yet, the art of preparing *and using* budgets in a meaningful manner is completely foreign to most nonprofit organizations. It is not that the treasurer or board is unaware of their importance, but more that they lack the skill necessary to apply budgeting techniques, and often are reluctant to use a budget as a tool to control the financial activities. The purpose of this chapter is to discuss the importance of budgeting, the art of skillfully preparing a useful budget, and equally important, the art of actually using the budget to control.

THE BUDGET: A PLAN OF ACTION

A budget is a "plan of action." It represents the organization's blueprint for the coming months, or years, expressed in monetary terms. This means the organization must know what its goals are before it can prepare a budget. If it doesn't know where it is going, obviously it is going to be very difficult for the organization to do any meaningful planning. All too often the process is reversed and it is in the process of preparing the budget that the goals are determined.

So the first function of a budget is to record, in monetary terms, what the realistic goals or objectives of the organization are for the coming year (or years). The budget is the financial plan of action which results from the board's decisions as to the program for the future.

The second function of a budget is to provide a tool to monitor the financial activities throughout the year. Properly used, the budget can provide a bench mark or comparison point which will alert the board to the first indication that their financial goals won't be met. For a budget to provide this type of information and control four elements must be present:

(1) The budget must be well-conceived, and have been prepared or approved by the board.

(2) The budget must be broken down into periods corresponding to the periodic financial statements.

(3) Financial statements must be prepared on a timely basis throughout the year and a comparison made to the budget, right on the statements.

(4) The board must be prepared to take action where the comparison with the budget indicates a significant deviation.

Each of these four elements will be discussed in this chapter.

Steps for Preparation

It was noted above that a budget should represent the end result of a periodic review by the board or by the membership of the organization's objectives or goals, expressed in monetary terms. Often the budget process is a routine "chore" handled by the treasurer to satisfy the board that the organization has a budget, which the board, in turn, routinely ratifies. Frequently, such budgets are not looked at again until the following year, at the time next year's budget is prepared. This type of budgeting serves little purpose and is worth little more than the paper it is written on. A budget, to be effective, must be a joint effort of many people. It must be a working document which forms the basis for action.

Here are the basic steps that, in one form or another, should be followed by an organization in order to prepare a well-conceived budget:

1. A list of objectives or goals of the organization for the following year should be prepared. For many organizations this process

will be essentially a re-evaluation of the relative priority of the existing programs. Care should be taken, however, to avoid concluding too hastily that an existing program should continue unchanged. Our society is not static and the organization that does not constantly re-evaluate and update its program is in danger of being left behind.

2. The cost of each objective or goal listed above should be estimated. For continuing programs, last year's actual expense and last year's budget will be the starting point. For new programs or modifications of existing programs, a substantial amount of work may be necessary to accurately estimate the costs involved. This estimating process should be done in detail since elements of a particular goal or objective may involve many categories of expense and salaries.

3. The expected income of the organization should be estimated. With many organizations, contributions from members or the general public will be the principal income and careful consideration must be given to the expected economic climate in the community. A year when unemployment is high or the stock market is down is a poor year to expect "increased" contributions. With other organizations the amount of income will be dependent on how successful they are in selling their program. Possibly some of the programs can be expanded if they are financially viable, or contracted if they are not. Organizations are often overly optimistic in estimating income. This can prove to be the organization's downfall if there is no margin for error, and realism must be used or the budget will have little meaning.

4. The total expected income should be compared to the expense of achieving the objectives or goals. Usually the expected expenses will exceed income, and this is where some value judgments will have to take place. What programs are most important? Where can expected costs be reduced? This process of reconciling expected income and expense is probably the most important step taken during the year because it is here that the program's blue print for the coming year is fixed.

It is important that consideration be given to the reliability of the estimated income and expense figures. Is it possible that expenses have been underestimated or that income has been overestimated? If expenses have been underestimated by 15 per cent and income has been overestimated by 10 per cent, there will be a deficit of 25 per cent, and unless the organization has substantial cash reserves it could be in serious difficulty. If the organization has small cash reserves or with little likelihood of getting additional funds quickly, then a realistic safety margin should be built into the budget.

5. The final proposed budget should be submitted to the appropriate body for ratification. This may be the full board or it may be the entire membership. This should not be just a formality but should be carefully presented to the ratifying body so that, once ratified, all persons will be firmly committed to the resulting plan of action.

The steps listed above may seem so elementary that there is no need to emphasize them here. But elementary as they are, they are often not followed and the resulting budget serves very little value to the organization.

Responsibility for Preparation

There has been very little said about "who" should follow these steps in preparing the budget. The preparation of a budget involves policy decisions. While the "treasurer" may be the person best qualified to handle the figures, he may or may not be the person to make policy decisions. For this reason, a "budget committee" should consist of persons responsible for policy decisions. Usually this means that the board should either itself act as the budget committee, or it should appoint a subcommittee of board members.

This doesn't mean that the detailed estimated cost studies for various programs can't be delegated to staff members. But the decision as to what are the goals and their relative priority has to be a board-level function.

Take, for example, a private, independent school. At first glance there might not appear to be many board-level decisions to make. The purpose of a school is to teach and it might seem that the budget would be a most routine matter. But there are many decisions that have to be made. For example:

1. Should more emphasis be placed on science courses?
2. Should the school get a small computer to help teach computer science?
3. Should the school hire a language teacher for grades 2–4?
4. Should the school increase salaries in the coming year and try to upgrade the staff?
5. Should the athletic field be resodded this year?
6. Should a fund raiser be hired?

7. Should the music program be expanded?

8. Should tuition be increased?

These questions and many more face the board. Undoubtedly they may rely on the paid staff to make recommendations, but the board is responsible for policy and the budget represents "policy." This responsibility cannot be delegated.

MONTHLY AND QUARTERLY BUDGETS

Many organizations have no real difficulty in preparing an annual budget. The real problem comes in trying to divide the budget into meaningful segments that can be compared to interim financial statements prepared on a monthly or quarterly basis. Some organizations attempt to do this by dividing the total budget by twelve and showing the resulting amounts as a monthly budget, which is then compared to actual monthly income and expense. While this is better than not making any budget comparison, it can produce misleading results when the income or expenses do not occur on a uniform basis throughout the year. Consider the following abbreviated statement of a small church:

	Annual Budget	Three Months Ending March 31	
		Annual Budget ÷ 4	Actual
Contributions	$ 120,000	$ 30,000	$ 35,000
Less Expenses	(120,000)	(30,000)	(30,000)
Excess	—	—	$ 5,000

The logical conclusion that might be drawn is that the church will have a surplus at the end of 12 months of approximately $20,000—four times the quarterly excess of $5,000. If this conclusion were reached the temptation would be to slacken off on unpaid pledge collection efforts and to be a little less careful in making purchases. This would be a very serious mistake if, in fact, the normal pattern of pledge collections were such that $36,000 should have been collected in the first quarter instead of the $35,000 actually received. A monthly or quarterly budget can produce misleading conclusions unless considerable care is taken in preparing it.

Allocating an Annual Budget to Monthly or Quarterly Periods

One of the best and easiest ways to allocate an annual budget into shorter periods is to first analyze the actual income and expense for the prior year, and then allocate this year's budget based on last year's actual expenses.

To illustrate, assume the church's income last year was $100,000 but is expected to be $120,000 this year. A budget for the new year could be prepared as follows:

	Actual Last Year	Percent of Last Year's Total	New Budget
Income:			
First quarter	$ 30,000	30%	$ 36,000
Second quarter	25,000	25%	30,000
Third quarter	25,000	25%	30,000
Fourth quarter	20,000	20%	24,000
	$100,000	100%	$120,000

In this illustration we have assumed that the increase in income of $20,000 will be received in the same pattern as the prior year's income was received. If this assumption is not correct, then adjustment must be made for the anticipated income which will depart from past experience. For example, if it is anticipated that a single gift of $10,000 will be received in the first quarter and the other $10,000 will be received in about the same pattern as last year's income, the calculations to arrive at a new budget would be somewhat different, as shown below:

	Actual Last Year	Percent of Last Year's Total	New Budget Other Than Special	Special Gifts	Total Budget
First quarter	$ 30,000	30%	$ 33,000	$10,000	$ 43,000
Second quarter	25,000	25%	27,500	—	27,500
Third quarter	25,000	25%	27,500	—	27,500
Fourth quarter	20,000	20%	22,000	—	22,000
	$100,000	100%	$110,000	$10,000	$120,000

If at the end of the first quarter income of only $35,000 had been received compared to a budget of $43,000, it would be apparent that steps should be taken to increase contributions or the church will fall short of meeting its budget for the year.

The expense side of the budget should be handled in the same way. Generally, expenses tend to occur at a more uniform rate, although this is not always so. In many ways the expense side of the budget is more important than the income side since it is easier to increase expenditures for things that weren't budgeted than to raise additional contributions. If the budget is regularly compared to actual expenditures for deviations, it can be an effective tool to highlight unbudgeted expenditures.

The budget should probably be prepared on a monthly rather than on a quarterly basis to reduce the time lag before effective action can be taken. If a monthly basis appears to be too cumbersome, consideration could be given to bimonthly budgets and statements. However, if the organization's cash position is tight, monthly statements become almost a necessity.

ILLUSTRATIVE EXPENSE BUDGET

The Valley Country Club is a good example of an organization that has to be very careful to budget its income and expenses. While the club has a beautiful club house and a fine golf course, all of its money is tied up in these fixed assets and there is no spare cash to cover a deficit. Accordingly each fall when the board starts to wrestle with the budget for the following year it is aware that it cannot afford the luxury of a deficit. Since the budget is so important, the entire board sits as a budget committee to work out the plans for the following year. The treasurer, with the help of the club manager, prepares a worksheet in advance of the budget meeting. This worksheet indicates the actual expenses for the current year to date, the estimate of the final figures for the year, and the current year's budget to show how close the club will come. The board through discussion and debate attempts to work out a budget for the coming year. Figure 17–1 shows the worksheet for the expense budget.

In looking at this worksheet notice first that the expenses are grouped by major function so that the board can focus attention

THE VALLEY COUNTRY CLUB

WORKSHEET FOR PREPARING 1974 EXPENSE BUDGET
(in thousands)

	Actual Current Year			Budget Current Year	Budget for New Year		
	To Date (10 Months)	Estimate Balance Of Year	Estimate For Year		Proposed Minimum	Proposed Maximum	Final
Maintenance of greens and grounds:							
Salaries and wages...............	$ 47	$ 3	$ 50	$ 46	$ 50	$ 65	$ 55
Seeds, fertilizer and supplies.........	14		14	13	14	14	14
Repairs, maintenance and other	12	2	14	10	10	15	15
Maintenance of clubhouse:							
Salaries and wages...............	20	4	24	23	24	28	26
Supplies, maintenance and repair	10	1	11	12	11	11	11
Golf activities:							
Salaries and wages...............	10		10	11	12	20	20
Tournament costs	14		14	15	15	15	15
Golf cart maintenance	8		8	5	5	5	5

Swimming pool expenses:							
Salaries and wages..........	4		4	4	5	10	5
Supplies and maintenance	2		2	1	2	2	2
General and administrative salaries	35	6	41	40	44	51	44
Property taxes	33	7	40	38	42	42	42
Other expenses	41	7	48	40	40	50	50
Total, excluding restaurant	250	30	280	258	274	328	304
Restaurant expenses:							
Food and beverages	96	13	109	67	110	150	130
Salaries and wages:							
Kitchen	32	6	38	30	45	60	50
Dining room	20	4	24	19	26	39	32
Bartender.....	11	2	13	10	14	19	16
Supplies, repairs and maintenance......	13	4	17	8	15	25	18
Total restaurant	172	29	201	134	210	293	246
Total expenses	$422	$59	$481	$392	$484	$621	$550

Fig. 17–1. Worksheet used in preparing an expense budget for a country club.

on the activities of the club. The alternative presentation would have been to list expenses by type—salaries, supplies, food, etc.— but this doesn't tell the board how much each of the major activities is costing.

There are three columns for the proposed budget—the minimum, the maximum, and the final amount. As the board considers each item it records both the minimum and the maximum it feels is appropriate. No attempt is made at the beginning to fix a "final" budget amount. Instead all budget items are considered, listed as to the minimum and maximum cost, and totals arrived at. It is only after all items have been considered, and only after a preliminary review of potential income has been made, that the board is in a position to make a judgment.

After the board has completed this worksheet showing final figures for the year, the next step is to break down the budget into monthly budgets. As with many organizations, the Valley Country Club's expenses (and income) are seasonal. In this case, the budget is broken down into monthly segments assuming that the expenses will be incurred in the same pattern as they were for the current year, in the manner discussed earlier.

TIMELY INTERIM STATEMENTS

The most carefully thought out budget will be of little value if it is not compared throughout the year with the actual results of operations. This means that the interim financial statements must be prepared on a timely basis.

What is timely? This largely depends on the organization and how much "slippage" or deviation from budget the organization can afford before serious consequences take place. If the cash balance is low an organization can't afford the luxury of not knowing where it stands on a timely basis. Guidelines are dangerous, but if an organization is unable to produce some form of abbreviated monthly or quarterly financial statement within 20 days of the end of the period the likelihood is that the information is "stale" by the time it is prepared. If twenty days is the length of time it takes then the board should plan to meet shortly after the twentieth of the month so as to be able to act on deviations while there is still time to act.

This is not to suggest that monthly financial statements are always appropriate for nonprofit organizations. But even if prepared on a bimonthly or quarterly basis, they should still be prepared on a timely basis.

Importance of Budget Comparison

The financial statement should also show the budget, and for the same period of time. Interim figures for the three months cannot easily be compared to budget figures for twelve months. The budget must also be for three months. Last year's actual figures for the same period may also be shown, although this added information could detract from the reader seeing the deviation from the current year's budget.

Figure 17–2 shows the Valley Country Club Statement of Income and Expense for both the month of June and for the 6 months, with budget comparisons to highlight deviations from the budget.

This financial statement gives the reader a great deal of information about the club's activities for the two periods. It should have the effect of alerting the reader to the fact that unless something happens, there may be a deficit for the year. For instead of having a small excess for June, there was a deficit of $6,200, and instead of having an excess of $7,500 for the six months, there was a deficit of almost $5,000. The board member reading the statement should be concerned about these deviations from the budget. This form of presentation makes it easy to see deviations. He can quickly pinpoint all unfavorable deviations and can then explore the reasons for them and determine the action that must be taken to prevent their recurrence.

Notice that both the current month and the year-to-date figures are shown on this statement. Both are important. The month gives a current picture of what is happening, which cannot be learned from the six-month figures. If only the six-month statements were shown the reader would have to refer to the previous month's statement showing the first five months to see what happened in June. Likewise, to show only the month, with no year-to-date figures, puts a burden on the reader. He will have to do some calculating using previous monthly statements to get

VALLEY COUNTRY CLUB

STATEMENT OF INCOME AND EXPENSES, AND COMPARISON WITH BUDGET

For the Month of June and the 6 Months Ending June 30, 1974

	Month			6 Months		
	Actual	Budget	Deviation Favorable (Unfavorable)	Actual	Budget	Deviation Favorable (Unfavorable)
Income:						
Annual dues	$15,650	$17,000	($1,350)	$ 81,900	$ 90,000	($ 8,100)
Initiation fees	2,100	2,000	100	6,600	4,500	2,100
Greens fees	4,750	4,000	750	11,000	8,000	3,000
Swimming	3,300	3,000	300	2,300	2,000	300
Other	6,710	8,000	(1,290)	18,250	14,000	4,250
Total, excluding restaurant	32,510	34,000	(1,490)	120,050	118,500	1,550
Restaurant	37,850	34,000	3,850	168,500	180,000	(11,500)
Total income	70,360	68,000	2,360	288,550	298,500	(9,950)
Expenses:						
Maintenance of greens and grounds	14,650	12,000	(2,650)	37,650	36,000	(1,650)
Maintenance of clubhouse	3,450	3,000	(450)	18,100	19,000	900
Golf activities	13,500	10,000	(3,500)	19,500	16,000	(3,500)
Swimming pool	3,400	3,000	(400)	5,100	4,000	(1,100)
General and administrative	4,200	3,700	(500)	24,150	22,000	(2,150)
Payroll taxes	3,700	3,500	(200)	23,500	21,000	(2,500)
Other expenses	4,150	5,000	850	19,560	20,000	440
Total, excluding restaurant	47,050	40,200	(6,850)	147,560	138,000	(9,560)
Restaurant	29,550	27,000	(2,550)	145,650	153,000	7,350
Total expenses	76,600	67,200	(9,400)	293,210	291,000	(2,210)
Excess of income over (under) expenses	($ 6,240)	$ 800	($7,040)	($ 4,660)	$ 7,500	($12,160)

Fig. 17–2. Statement of Income and Expenses for both the month and year to date, showing a comparison to budget.

his own total to see where the club stood cumulatively. Year-to-date budget comparisons are often more revealing than monthly comparisons because minor fluctuations in income and expenses tend to offset over a period of months. These fluctuations can appear rather large in any one month.

Restaurant Operation

Restaurant income and expenses have been shown "gross" in the statements. It would be equally proper for the club to show net income for the club before the restaurant operation was considered. Here is how this would look:

Income (excluding restaurant)	$ 120,050
Expenses (excluding restaurant)	147,560
Excess of expenses over income excluding restaurant	(27,510)
Restaurant	
Gross income	168,500
Expenses	(145,650)
Net restaurant income	22,850
Excess of expenses over income	$ (4,660)

Another possibility is to show only the net income of the restaurant in the statements, perhaps in the income section. In condensed form here is how the statements would look:

Income	
Other than restaurant	$ 120,050
Restaurant net income	22,850
Total income	142,900
Expenses (other than restaurant)	(147,560)
Excess of expenses over income	$ (4,660)

Either presentation, or the one in Figure 17–2, is acceptable. The appropriate presentation depends on the importance of highlighting the restaurant activities.

Variable Budget

One technique that is often used in budgeting an operation where costs increase as the volume of activity increases is to relate the budgeted costs to income. For example, the final expense budget (Figure 17–1) and the relationship to budgeted income for the restaurant operation is as follows:

	Amount	Percent of Income
Income	$290,000	100%
Food and beverages	$130,000	45%
Salaries and wages		
Kitchen	50,000	17
Dining room	32,000	11
Bartender	16,000	6
Supplies, repairs and maintenance........	18,000	6
	$246,000	85%

If all costs increase proportionately as income increases, then it is a simple matter to create new budget figures each month based on actual income. Using the six-month figures shown in Figure 17–2, our budget comparison for the restaurant activity for the six-month period would look like this:

	Actual	Variable Budget	Deviation from Variable Budget	Deviation from Original Budget Shown in Figure 17–2
Income	$168,500	$180,000 *	$(11,500)	$(11,500)
Expenses (in total)	145,650	143,225 †	(2,425)	7,350
Net	$ 22,850	$ 36,775	$(13,925)	$ (4,150)

* Original budget for six months.
† 85% of actual income for the six months, based on the relationship of budgeted expenses to budgeted income as shown above.

The significant observation here is that while the original budget comparison in Figure 17–2 showed an unfavorable deviation from budget of only $4,150, the unfavorable deviation using this variable budget is significantly higher, $13,925. Obviously if the variable budget is accurate, then the club manager has not been watching his costs carefully enough.

The financial statements would show only the variable expense budget. The original expense budget would not be used. This kind of budget is more difficult to work with because each month the treasurer or bookkeeper has to recalculate the expense figures to be used based on actual income. At the same time by doing so, a meaningful budget comparison can then be made. It is very difficult otherwise for the board to judge the restaurant's results.

One final observation about this variable budget. Certain costs are not proportional to income. For example, the club cannot have less than one bartender or one chef. Accordingly, in preparing a variable budget sometimes the relationships that are developed will not be simple percentage relationships. For example, perhaps the relationship of bartender salary will be, say, $5,000 plus 5 per cent of total income over $75,000. If so, then if restaurant income is $350,000, the budget will be $18,750 ($5,000 + 5 per cent of $275,000).

Narrative Report on Deviations from Budget

It will be noted that much of the detail shown in the budget (Figure 17–1) has not been shown on the interim financial statement (Figure 17–2). If the board felt it appropriate, supporting schedules could be prepared giving as much detail as desired. Care should be taken, however, not to request details that won't be used since it obviously takes time and costs money to prepare detailed supporting schedules.

It may be that a more meaningful supporting schedule would be a narrative summary of the reasons for the deviations from budget for the major income and expense categories. The club manager, in the case of the Valley Country Club, would probably be the one to prepare this summary. The amount of detail and description that he might put in this summary would vary from account to account. Clearly the report should only discuss reasons for the major deviations. This report should accompany the financial statement so that questions raised by the statement are answered immediately. Figure 17–3 shows an example of the type of summary he might prepare to explain the expense deviations from budget (in part).

This type of report can be as informal as you want to make it as long as it conveys why there have been deviations from the original budget. But it should be in writing, both to ensure that the board knows the reasons, and to force the club manager to

---

VALLEY COUNTRY CLUB

CLUB MANAGER'S REPORT TO THE BOARD
EXPENSE DEVIATIONS FROM BUDGET, JUNE 1974

Maintenance of greens and grounds ($2,650)

As you will recall, April and May were fairly wet months. This coupled with other unfavorable soil conditions required that we treat about 25% of the course with a fungicide which had not been budgeted ($1,850). We also had some unexpected repairs to the sprinkler system ($1,500). For the six months to date we have exceeded budget by only $1,650 and I am confident that our annual budget will not be exceeded.

Maintenance of clubhouse ($450)

We had scheduled painting the Clubhouse for May but because of the rains were not able to get it done until this month. Year-to-date expenses are $900 under budget.

Golf activities ($3,500)

After the budget had been approved the Board decided to have an open tournament with a view toward attracting new membership. With promotion and prizes this came to $2,850. So far the membership committee has received thirteen new applications for membership.

Fig. 17–3. An example of a narrative report prepared by the manager of a country club explaining why certain major deviations have occurred from budget.

face squarely his responsibility to meet the projected budget. This report is a form of discipline for him.

Action by the Board

The best-prepared budget serves little purpose if the board is unwilling to take action once it becomes apparent that expenses are exceeding budget or that income has not been as high as anticipated. To be useful, the budget must be a planning device that everyone takes seriously; otherwise its usefulness is truly limited. There must be follow-up action.

The type of reporting discussed in this chapter will give the board information on where the plan is not being followed. But the board must be prepared to take action when the deviations are serious. Perhaps all that will be appropriate is for the board to discuss the budget deviations with the club manager. If the club manager knows that the board fully expects him to come within his budget, he will take appropriate action. If some matters are beyond his control he may suggest alternatives to the board for their action.

The board must be prepared to take action to modify their plans if it becomes apparent that the budget cannot be met. If the organization has substantial resources to fall back on, it can afford to accept some deviations from the original budget without serious financial consequences. For most organizations, this is not the case. The board must be willing to face unpleasant facts once it becomes apparent from interim financial statements that corrective action must be taken. Many budgets fail, not because there is not enough information available to the board, but because the board fails to take aggressive, corrective action. In these instances, the board is not fulfilling its responsibilities and the budget is a meaningless formality.

A FIVE-YEAR MASTER PLAN

So far our discussion has centered on budgeting techniques for the current year. Almost as important, and quite related, are the techniques for planning even further into the future than the twelve-month period most budgets use. As will be discussed more fully in the next chapter, organizations must be constantly alert to changing conditions which may alter their goals or objectives and thus their sources of income. Otherwise they may find themselves in unexpected financial difficulty. One of the more effective ways organizations can avoid the unexpected is to prepare, and periodically update, a five-year master plan. The purpose of this five-year plan is to force the board to look ahead and anticipate not only problems but goals and objectives that they want to work toward achieving.

The development of a five-year plan requires considerable effort. While the treasurer can be the person who initiates and pushes the board toward developing such a plan, he cannot single-handedly be the one to prepare it. As was discussed earlier on budget preparation, to be effective any plan of action involving the organization's program and allocation of resources must be developed by all of the people who will have to live with the resulting plans. To unilaterally prepare a five-year plan risks the strong possibility that the treasurer's conception of the important objectives are not truly representative of the conceptions of the rest of the board.

Suggested Procedures

There is no "standard" way to go about preparing a five-year plan. Probably the best way to start is to set up a committee of say, three persons. As with the budget committee discussed earlier in this chapter, the persons chosen for this five-year planning committee should be persons who are in policy-making roles within the organization. There is little point in putting a person on this committee who is not both knowledgeable and influential within the organization. Otherwise the resulting document will be of relatively little value to the organization.

Setting Goals.   Before meeting as a committee, each member should be instructed to take five sheets of paper, each representing one of the five years. On each sheet the member should list all of the goals or objectives that he sees as being important for that year. He can be as specific or as general as he wants. The important thing is to get down his thoughts as to what the organization should be doing during that year, particularly as they might be different from what is being done currently. No consideration should be given at this point to dollar costs—only goals or objectives.

Once each member of the committee has independently prepared his conception of the future goals or objectives of the organization, the committee should meet and discuss these projections jointly. There may or may not be initial agreement among the three, and if not, there should be extended discussions to try to establish a plan of objectives that all members can agree on as being reasonable. If, after extended discussions, the committee cannot agree on these broad objectives, they should go back to the board for direction. All of this is *before* any figures have been associated with each specific objective or goal. The organization must decide what its goals or objectives are before it starts worrying about costs.

Estimating Costs. Once the committee has agreed upon objectives for each of the five years, then it is appropriate to start to estimate the costs involved in reaching each of these goals. This can be difficult because there are always many unknowns and uncertainties as to the details of how each goal will be accomplished. Nevertheless, it is important that the best estimate be made by the committee. Clearly the treasurer is a key person in this estimating process. Among other things, it is up to him to try to factor inflation and realism as to costs into these figures.

After the committee has associated dollar costs with each objective for the five years, the next step is to add up the total to see how much income will have to be raised. Notice that until this point, no real consideration has been given to how the goals will be financed. This is important because in long-range planning an organization should set its objectives and then look for the means to reach them. If the objectives are good ones which the membership or public will agree should be accomplished, the financial support should follow. An organization gets into difficulty when it does not periodically reevaluate its direction and thus finds itself out of step with our rapidly changing society. So the procedure to follow is first to define the objectives and goals, then to associate dollar amounts with each, and ·finally to determine how to raise the necessary income. It must be in this order.

Plan for Income. This final step of determining how the income will be raised is usually not as difficult as it may sound provided the goals and objectives are ones that the board and the membership believe are sound. It is possible that as a result of this five-year plan new sources of income may be required. Perhaps a foundation will be approached, or perhaps a major capital improvement fund drive will be started. There are many possibilities. The important thing is that the organization has no right to exist except as it serves societal or members' interests. So if the organization keeps up with the times it should be able to get sufficient support to achieve its objectives; if it does not, this is clear evidence that the objectives or goals are not sufficiently important to justify support. At that point the organization should either change its goals or should seriously consider the desirability of discontinuing its existence.

Illustrative Master Plan

The result of this whole process is a master plan that should guide the board in its planning. It should be reviewed at least every year or two and should be updated and extended so that it represents, at all times, a five-year plan for the future. Figure 17–4 shows an example of a simple master plan for the Center for Development of Human Resources. The Center for Development of Human Resources is one of many organizations that has come into existence in the last few years to help individuals "grow" through interaction in study groups. The center has a professional staff organizing and running programs, which are held in a rented building.

Note that on this master plan the "center" has indicated future expenses not in terms of the type of expenses (salaries, rent, supplies, etc.) but in terms of the goals or objectives of the organization. This distinction is important because the center pays salaries and other costs only to further some goal or objective. Thus, in a master plan it is entirely appropriate to associate costs with each goal or objective. This means that a certain amount of allocation of salaries between goals will be necessary.

Another observation is that the format of this master plan did not start off with the traditional approach of showing income and then deducting expenses. Instead, the goals or objectives were stated first and only after the organization agreed on what it wanted to do did it start to work on how to raise the necessary income. This point has been emphasized because the organization does not exist to raise money and pay expenses; it exists to accomplish certain objectives, and unless these are spelled out clearly and are constantly kept in mind the organization may lose sight of the reason for its existence.

No attempt was made in this master plan to balance the amounts of income and expense except in a general way. In each year there is an indicated surplus. This recognizes that while the board has made its best guess as to how it will raise its income, there are a great many unknowns when working with a five-year budget. As each year passes and this five-year plan is updated (and extended) the sources will become more certain, as will costs, and these figures will be refined and adjusted. The

CENTER FOR THE DEVELOPMENT OF HUMAN RESOURCES

MASTER PLAN—1975 THROUGH 1979

	1975	1976	1977	1978	1979
Goals or objectives:					
Develop and run management program	$ 17,000	$ 22,000	$ 25,000	$ 27,000	$ 30,000
Reprogram receptive listening program	12,000	–	–	–	–
Continue receptive listening program	35,000	35,000	45,000	45,000	45,000
Work with other "centers" across country	–	12,000	15,000	15,000	15,000
Develop and run child day care training centers	8,000	15,000	20,000	20,000	20,000
Explore Project "A"	20,000	10,000	–	–	–
Run other programs	40,000	45,000	50,000	55,000	55,000
Purchase building for center	–	150,000	–	–	–
Total	132,000	289,000	155,000	162,000	165,000
Sources of income:					
Contributions from members	60,000	45,000	60,000	60,000	60,000
Special gifts and legacies	10,000	10,000	–	–	–
Building fund drive	–	100,000	–	–	–
Program fees:					
Management	10,000	15,000	18,000	20,000	22,000
Receptive listening	30,000	35,000	45,000	45,000	45,000
Child care	–	5,000	10,000	10,000	10,000
Other	38,000	40,000	45,000	45,000	45,000
Foundation grants:					
Child care	10,000	–	–	–	–
Building fund	–	50,000	–	–	–
Total	158,000	300,000	178,000	180,000	182,000
Projected surplus	$ 26,000	$ 11,000	$ 23,000	$ 18,000	$ 17,000

Fig. 17–4. An example of a five-year master plan which emphasizes the objectives and goals of the organization.

important thing, however, is that the board has set down what it plans to do in the future, and how it now expects to be able to finance such plans.

CONCLUSION

A budget can be an extremely important and effective tool for the board in managing the affairs of the organization. However, to prepare a meaningful budget the organization must know where it is heading and its goals and objectives. Priorities change and this means that many people should be involved in the budget preparation and approval process to insure the resulting budget is fully supported. Once prepared, the budget must be compared to actual results on a timely basis throughout the year to insure that the board knows where deviations are occurring. Equally important, the board must promptly take corrective action if unfavorable deviations occur. The foundations of a sound financial structure are a well-conceived budget, a timely reporting system, and a willingness by the board to take corrective action.

The importance of planning into the future cannot be overemphasized. In this fast-moving age, worthy nonprofit organizations can quickly get out of step with the times, and when this happens contributions and income quickly disappear. A five-year master plan is one technique to help ensure this won't happen.

18

Avoiding Bankruptcy

"Bankruptcy?" "It can't happen to us!" These are famous last words. Of course it can. Don't think that your organization is immune to all of the ills that can befall any organization whether it is a commercial or a nonprofit one. Insolvency will be the fate of many organizations that are today vigorous and healthy. An organization's importance and reputation will not by themselves protect it. Avoiding bankruptcy takes effort and real skill.

EARLY RECOGNITION OF PROBLEMS

While the final responsibility for the financial health of the organization is the board's, the treasurer is the person charged with watching both the day-to-day and the long-term financial picture. Without doubt one of the most important functions of the treasurer is to recognize potential problems while there is still time to act. While it might seem like a simple task to recognize that the organization is in, or is headed for financial trouble, the fact is that many organizations hide their heads in the sand like ostriches and fail to recognize the symptoms at a time when they might be able to do something.

The reason why recognizing that there is a problem on a timely basis is so important, is that most nonprofit organizations have so little cash. They cannot afford the luxury of waiting until after the problem has fully manifested itself, because if they do, they may run out of cash.   If there are substantial reserves in the bank, most small organizations can afford several years of deficits before they really have to become concerned about the future.   But few organizations have this amount of cash reserves.   Organizations usually have enough cash for only three or four months' operations if all income ceased.

There is no perpetual life for nonprofit organizations.   And this is as it should be.   Nonprofit organizations have a privileged place in our society.   Most have been granted certain tax privileges which means that society as a whole has a right to demand that they perform their function in the public interest.   If the organization fails to be responsive, no matter how "worthwhile" their program may be when viewed objectively from afar, the organization will have a short life.   This is as true of churches and religious organizations as it is of other types.   The organization must be responsive, and the contributor is the final judge of whether it is or not.   This means the treasurer must be alert to indications that the health of the organization may be declining either as shown in historical financial statements, or as projected into the future.

Historical Statements as a Guide

Many look upon past financial statements only as an historical bookkeeping record, which has little significance for the future. This is a mistake.   Often there is a clear indication in these statements of potential problems for the future.   This can often be seen by comparing several years' statements, because relationships may become obvious that were not apparent when looking at only one year's statements.

An example can best illustrate this point.   The five-year master plan of The Center for Development of Human Resources was discussed in the last chapter.   Let us now look at the Center's five-year historical financial statements.   They are shown in Figure 18–1.

This statement offers a great deal of information to the observant treasurer and should help him in anticipating problems. The obvious and most serious problem revealed is that there has been a large deficit in 1973 which, if repeated, would wipe out

CENTER FOR THE DEVELOPMENT OF HUMAN RESOURCES

SUMMARY OF INCOME, EXPENSES, AND CASH BALANCES
RESULTING FROM CASH TRANSACTIONS
For the Five Years Ended December 31, 1973

	1969	1970	1971	1972	1973
Income:					
Contributions	$ 53,000	$ 65,000	$ 56,000	$ 66,000	$ 49,000
Program fees	46,000	48,000	48,000	50,000	52,000
Other	3,000	3,000	2,000	3,000	2,000
Total income	102,000	116,000	106,000	119,000	103,000
Expenses:					
Salaries	68,000	72,000	76,000	78,000	80,000
Rent	14,000	16,000	18,000	20,000	24,000
Supplies	9,000	10,000	14,000	18,000	22,000
Other	3,000	3,000	4,000	5,000	6,000
Total expenses	94,000	101,000	112,000	121,000	132,000
Excess of income over (under) expenses	8,000	15,000	(6,000)	(2,000)	(29,000)
Cash balance, beginning of the year	34,000	42,000	57,000	51,000	49,000
Cash balance, end of the year	$ 42,000	$ 57,000	$ 51,000	$ 49,000	$ 20,000

Fig. 18–1. An example of a five-year Statement of Income, Expenses, and Cash Balances which can assist the reader in spotting trends.

the organization. But beyond this obvious observation, a number of other important clues can be seen. Note first the relationship between expenses and program fees over the years. From 1969 to 1973 expenses have gone up almost 40 per cent, but program fees have gone up only 13 per cent. Either the organization is not charging enough for its programs, or the programs are not responsive to the membership and therefore attendance is down. Alternatively, perhaps the center has gotten too sophisticated in its programming, with too many paid staff for the size of fees that can be charged. These are the kind of questions that have to be asked.

Another question that should concern the treasurer is why contributions have fluctuated so much from year to year. Is there significance in the decline in gifts received from $66,000 in 1972 to $49,000 in 1973? Does this represent a strong "vote" by the membership that they are not interested in the programs of the center, or that something is wrong? This question concerned the treasurer and after some digging, this is what he found:

Year	Recurring Contributions	Special or One-Time Gifts	Total
1969	$43,000	$10,000	$53,000
1970	45,000	20,000	65,000
1971	47,000	9,000	56,000
1972	55,000	11,000	66,000
1973	49,000	—	49,000

From this analysis it is easy to see what happened. The center had been living off special, or one-time, gifts and these gifts were not received in 1973. Most of the special gifts had come from half a dozen people, some now deceased. It is obvious that the earlier five-year summary did not tell the whole story and the treasurer recast this statement showing these special gifts separately. Figure 18–2 shows in condensed form these revised statements.

CENTER FOR THE DEVELOPMENT OF HUMAN RESOURCES

SUMMARY OF INCOME AND EXPENSES
For the Five Years Ended December 31, 1973

	1969	1970	1971	1972	1973
Recurring income:					
Contributions	$43,000	$ 45,000	$ 47,000	$ 55,000	$ 49,000
Program fees	46,000	48,000	48,000	50,000	52,000
Other	3,000	3,000	2,000	3,000	2,000
Total	92,000	96,000	97,000	108,000	103,000
Expenses (total)	94,000	101,000	112,000	121,000	132,000
Excess of expenses over recurring income	(2,000)	(5,000)	(15,000)	(13,000)	(29,000)
Special nonrecurring gifts	10,000	20,000	9,000	11,000	—
Excess of income over (under) expenses	$ 8,000	$ 15,000	($ 6,000)	($ 2,000)	($ 29,000)

Fig. 18–2. A five-year Statement of Income and Expenses in which nonrecurring special gifts are shown separately to highlight continuing income.

From this statement it is easy for the treasurer and the board to see that they had been living off special gifts in every year except 1973. Obviously hard decisions had to be made as to whether the center should count on receiving such special gifts in the future and if not, how expenses could be cut or additional income gained.

Analysis of Interim Statements

It is not necessary (or wise) to wait for the completion of a full year's activities before starting to draw conclusion from the trends that should be obvious to the careful analyst. Figure 18–3 illustrates a worksheet showing a comparison of actual with budget for three months, and a projection for the entire year by assuming that the experience for the first three months compared to budget is a good indication of what can be expected for the next nine months.

Based on this worksheet it is obvious that unless something happens to change the pattern, instead of being ahead of budget the center is headed for a deficit of $23,000. As will be recalled, the center had only $20,000 in cash at the beginning of the year, and obviously cannot afford to have a deficit of $23,000! The board can hardly spend money it does not have, and yet it appears that some time during the fourth quarter this is exactly what is going to happen.

The point should be obvious. If the treasurer does not stay on top of the finances of his organization, he may find that the organization is in serious trouble after it is too late to do anything about it.

Treasurer's Duty To Sound the Alarm

With all of these warning signs, the treasurer must call for help as loud as he can! The treasurer's job is to call the situation to the attention of the board, and to offer suggestions if he has any. The real responsibility of solving the problem, however, is not his, but the board's. Of course, the treasurer should be prepared to offer recommendations on how to solve the problem. He is the person closest to the finances and he will probably have some sound ideas. But under the laws of most states, it is the

CENTER FOR THE DEVELOPMENT OF HUMAN RESOURCES
WORKSHEET SHOWING CALCULATION OF PROJECTED INCOME AND EXPENSES
For the Year 1974

	3 Months to March 31			9 Months April to December		12 Months	
	Actual	Budget	Percentage Actual to Budget	Budget	Projected Based on Actual*	Budget	Projected
Recurring income:							
Contributions	$18,000	$20,000	90%	$38,000	$ 34,200	$ 58,000	$ 52,200
Program fees	17,000	18,000	95%	42,000	39,900	60,000	56,900
Other	500	500	100%	1,500	1,500	2,000	2,000
Total	35,500	38,500	92%	81,500	75,600	120,000	111,100
Expenses:							
Salaries	22,000	21,000	105%	63,000	66,100	84,000	88,100
Rent	6,000	6,000	100%	18,000	18,000	24,000	24,000
Supplies	4,500	2,500	180%	7,500	13,500	10,000	18,000
Other	1,000	500	200%	1,500	3,000	2,000	4,000
Total	33,500	30,000	111%	90,000	100,600	120,000	134,100
Excess of income over (under) expenses	$ 2,000	$ 8,500		($ 8,500)	($ 25,000)	—	($ 23,000)

*I.e.: percentage actual to budget for three months times budget for nine months (90% x 38,000 = $34,200).

Fig. 18–3. An example of a worksheet projecting income and expenses for the year based on only the first three months' actual experience.

board itself that is responsible for the continuation of the organization.

There is another very practical reason for calling for help as loudly as possible. Sometimes calling attention to a problem is all that is really necessary to start the wheels in motion to solve it. Perhaps some of the members who have been lax in making contributions or attending programs will start doing so.

REMEDIAL ACTION

Once the board has been forced to recognize the problem, what are the alternatives or courses of action that can be taken? There are perhaps six or seven, some of which may not be available to all organizations.

Increasing Contributions

The most obvious solution to most organizations' financial problems is to raise additional contributions. This is usually much easier said than done. If there are many small donors, it is not realistic to expect that the organization will be able to increase contributions by a very large amount. Unless the organization really motivates the donor, his contributions tend to remain fairly constant from year to year except for small increases attributable to general cost of living increase, his increased income, etc.

This is not as true with donors making large contributions. If the organization can sell its program, often these larger donors will make additional special contributions. The key is that the organization must convince these large donors that the extra amount it needs to solve this year's crisis will not be needed again next year. This means that in presenting its case, the organization must be able to show how it can and will avoid a similar difficulty next year. Otherwise, to the donor it will appear that he is not really helping to solve the problem but only to postpone it.

Credibility is an important aspect of the ability to raise additional funds. The board will have a greater chance of success if over the years it has presented meaningful financial statements to all donors and has not created doubts about the true financial condition. But even with good statements, an organization that is in serious difficulty will probably find that the first place to look is not at contributions. Contributions can be increased but usually the response rate is too slow and the amounts too modest.

Increasing Fees

Another source of increased income is raising fees charged for services being rendered. Modest increases usually can be "sold" if there has not been a recent increase. Most people recognize the effect of inflation. At the same time, increasing fees may decrease the number of persons using the services.

For example, in the case of the Center for the Development of Human Resources, if the board were to increase charges by only 10 per cent effective April 1, almost $4,000 would be added to income assuming nobody dropped out as a result of the increase. This represents 20 per cent of the projected deficit for the year. If the programs are worthwhile, the board should be able to convince the membership that the alternative to increasing fees is discontinuing the organization's activities. If the board is unable to "sell" this, then perhaps they should question the need for these programs.

Cutting Expenses

If it appears that there will be a deficit, and this deficit cannot be covered by increasing income, then it must be covered by reducing expenses. This is always difficult for the board of a nonprofit organization to accept. Somehow the board finds it difficult to accept the fact that sometimes an organization cannot do all that it wants to do, no matter how worthy.

Whatever the reason, nonprofit organizations seem to have particular difficulty in recognizing that as with any individual, they must spend within their means. This is one reason why the treasurer can offer only suggestions but not final solutions. The board has to wrestle with the policy question of which programs are in fact most "indispensable." The treasurer may have his suggestions, but if he forces these upon the organization without the board's full concurrence, his suggestions either will not "stick" or he will find his efforts are sabotaged. Remember that nonprofit organizations, unlike commercial ones, are heavily depend-ent on volunteer help and these volunteers must be in agreement with what is going on or they will stop volunteering their time and effort.

The conclusion is obvious. When the organization is threat-ened with insolvency the board must either raise income or cut expenses. Cutting expenses, however unpleasant, is often the only practical solution to an immediate crisis.

Borrowing

One source of emergency funds that many organizations use is the bank. They will borrow to cover short-term emergency needs, particularly when they have fluctuations in their income. Short-term borrowing is fine if used only to cover fluctuating in-come, and if the treasurer is sure that there will be income from which to pay these monies back. On the other hand, what should not be done without some serious thought is to mortgage the organization's physical property to raise money to pay current operations. It is one thing to borrow money for capital additions but it is an entirely different thing to borrow money which will be used for the day-to-day operations of the organization. If this becomes necessary, the treasurer and board should consider very carefully how they can reasonably expect to repay these loans. If repayment is in doubt, then the board must seriously consider the future of the organization, and why they are prolonging its life.

Keep in mind that the board of a nonprofit organization has a responsibility to act prudently on all matters. If they mortgage the "cow" to pay for its fodder with the full knowledge that they are going to have to sell the "cow" to pay the bank back, perhaps they should sell the "cow" to start with.

Many times a bank will lend funds to an organization on the basis of the members of the board being well known and influen-tial in the business community. This often means an organiza-tion will be able to borrow money when the banker may have some doubts about repayment. He knows, however, that the board members will not let the organization default. The board members should carefully consider the repayment problem. They will not want their personal reputations tarnished by subsequent difficulties with the bank.

Applying for Foundation Grants

Another source of financial help that many organizations should consider are grants from foundations. There are approximately 25,000 foundations in the United States and under the Tax Reform Act of 1969 these foundations are required to distribute a minimum of 6 per cent of their assets every year. While there are limitations as to whom such money can be given, generally any nonprofit organization that is itself a tax-exempt organization (which excludes social clubs) and is not a "private foundation" can receive grants from foundations. Most people think of foundations as being only the large ones—the Ford Foundation, the Carnegie Foundation, etc. While these giant foundations are giving millions of dollars to worthwhile organizations every year, there are thousands of lesser known foundations that are also granting millions.*

In trying to find foundations to approach, an advantage may be gained where members of the board already know one or more of the trustees of the foundation. There is no question that the chances are increased if the board's message can be informally presented to individual members of the foundation's board of trustees in advance of their considering the formal request. This does not mean that such personal contacts can assure success, but it certainly will increase their chances.

Obviously each foundation receives many more requests than it can possibly handle, so it is important that application be made only to those whose stated interests coincide with the organization's. There is no point in wasting time in submitting a request for funds that will not receive serious consideration because it is outside of the foundation's scope of interest.

The formal application itself is very important. There are no standard forms as such to fill out. Instead, the application should

* *The Foundation Directory,* published by The Foundation Library Center, is a good source of information. Included in the 1971 edition were listings on over 5,000 foundations. They are listed geographically by state. Included in each listing is a brief description of the foundation, the size of its fund, the amount of grants made and the purposes for which the foundation will consider making a grant.

outline succinctly and with feeling what the objectives of the organization are. It should document why the foundation's gift would be of significant help *and* how it would further the foundation's stated objectives. Keep both of these points in mind— *why* their grant would be significant, and *how* it would further their stated objectives. An application which cannot answer both of these points is defective.

The application should contain evidence that the board is effective and that the foundation won't be wasting its money if they make a grant. Obviously it should contain complete financial information in a format that clearly indicates that the board has financial control of the organization. In the case of the Center for the Development of Human Resources, they would include their five-year summary of income and expenses, their budget for the current year, their projections based on the first quarter's results and a projection for five years. This five-year projection is important to show that the crisis is truly under control, or will be under control, and that the foundation's grant will not necessarily have to be a continuing one.

The application should specify quite explicitly how the money will be used. Most foundations will not consider requests for money that will be merely added to the "pot" and used for general purposes. In the 1971 edition of *The Foundation Directory* this point is emphasized:

Fund-raisers need to be warned that at least the larger foundations do not usually make grants toward the operating budgets of agencies, whether national or local, or for individual need. Many foundations have accepted the doctrine that their limited funds should be used chiefly as the venture capital of philanthropy, to be spent in enterprises requiring risk and foresight, not likely to be supported by government or private individuals. In their fields of special interest they prefer to aid research, designed to push forward the frontiers of knowledge, or pilot demonstrations, resulting in improved procedures apt to be widely copied.

Support for current programs, if it comes at all from foundations, must usually be sought from the smaller organizations, and especially those located in the area of the agency, well acquainted with its personnel and its needs. Most small foundations, and some larger ones, restrict their grants to the local community or state. Immense variety exists; the interests and limitations of each foundation need to be examined before it is approached.

Care must be taken to plan exactly how these funds will be used. This should not be done hastily. It takes many months to get foundation help and an organization that has not carefully thought out its needs may find that when it receives the grant it really would have preferred to spend the money in some other way. Foundations look with disfavor on organizations that ask that their grants be used for different purposes than originally specified.

Another thing to keep in mind is that many foundations like to make grants on a matching basis. That is, they will make the grant at such time as the organization has raised an equal or greater amount from other sources. This is in line with many foundations' concern that recipients not become dependent on foundation help.

Timing is important. Many foundations will make grants only once or twice a year. This means that unless the application is received on a timely basis there may be a long delay before there is an answer. Foundation grants are not very likely to get an organization out of an immediate cash bind. But foundations can be very helpful to the organization that truly plans for its future and knows what it wants and how to accomplish its objectives. For these organizations, foundation help should be carefully considered because there are monies available.

Merging With Another Organization

One of the alternatives that the board must consider if bankruptcy looms on the horizon is the possibility that the organization should merge with another organization having similar or at least compatible objectives. This, obviously, is not a course of action that is appealing but if the alternative is bankruptcy, then the only real question is how the objectives and programs of the organization can best be salvaged. It is probably better to have a combined program with another organization than to have no program at all. If the board doubts that this is true, then clearly the reason for the continued existence of the organization is in doubt and perhaps bankruptcy is the appropriate answer.

Where do you look for other candidates for merger? There is no easy answer. Basically you have to know the field that your organization is working in, and then you have to approach all possible candidates. Do not hesitate to do so, for it may turn out that there are other organizations in similar financial straits, which if combined with yours would make the resulting organization stronger than either was before. Keep in mind that unless you personally know the board members of the other organization you are not likely to know of their problems before you approach them. Perhaps they are also looking for a merger candidate.

There are other considerations which must be taken into account. One of the more important is to determine if any of your donor-restricted funds contain restrictions that would prohibit use by a combined organization. Hopefully the board would find a compatible organization with similar enough goals and objectives so that any restricted funds could be effectively used. If there are problems in this area, ask the original donor for permission to change the restrictions.

Another consideration is, of course, how the merged organization can accomplish the organization's objectives more effectively at less cost than as a separate entity. Perhaps this will not be the case, but rather that they have more resources and therefore can afford to subsidize the program. The chances are, however, that there will be some opportunity for cost saving, perhaps through sharing staff, or facilities, or a combination of both. The board, however, should be sure that it looks very carefully before it leaps. It must analyze the other organization's financial statements and their five-year plan very carefully. It serves very little purpose to trade one set of problems for another if several years from now the combined organization will again be on the verge of bankruptcy.

CONFRONTING BANKRUPTCY

Another possibility is that the board will conclude that the organization has accomplished the purposes for which it was set up, or that times have changed and the original objectives are no longer appropriate. If so, perhaps the humane thing to do is to let the organization "die" but in a controlled manner so as not to leave a trail of debts behind it. Although this may not seem like a very practical suggestion at first, it is one that must be considered by every thoughtful board member. If the members are not supporting the organization, then why not? If it is only a momentary problem of poor economy, it is perhaps appropriate to try to wait for better times. But the board must be cautious in drawing this conclusion. It must not get so emotionally involved in the mechanics of the organization's programs that it loses sight of the need to respond to today's conditions, which are different from yesterday's. In this "throw away" society that we are in, nonprofit organizations are not exempt, and those that do not serve society's current needs will find that bankruptcy will always be close by.

As the board gets closer and closer to bankruptcy, the individual members of the board, as well as the treasurer, have to consider carefully the steps that should be taken to ensure that actual bankruptcy as such does not take place. No board wants to incur financial obligations that they cannot meet. This includes salary obligations. As the time for going out of existence looms, consideration must be given to an orderly dismissal of the staff with appropriate termination benefits to help them over the period of relocation. This is expensive, because once the decision to terminate operations is made, sources of income will dry up promptly. This means that the board cannot wait until the bank account is empty to face these difficult decisions. If they do, either the board members themselves are going to personally face the prospects of making sizable contributions to cover their moral obligations, or they are going to leave unpaid debts and recriminations. Most board members have personal reputations at stake and this last alternative is not very attractive.

One area that must be carefully watched as cash gets low is the payment of withholding taxes to the various governments. Usually the federal government can sue the treasurer himself and all other persons responsible for nonpayment of such withholding taxes. These amounts are not the funds of the organization but are held in escrow until paid to the government. To use these funds to pay other bills is a very serious offense that can result not only in recovery from the treasurer, but also subject him to a fine and/or imprisonment.

Another consideration, if it is decided to discontinue operations, is that any funds or other assets that remain must either be given to another exempt organization or to the state. This is true for all tax-exempt organizations except social clubs. Obviously when thinking about discontinuing operations competent legal help is needed to consider all ramifications. Timing is of major importance. The point at which operations will be discontinued must be anticipated and this must be before the bank account is empty. Very few board members want the stigma of having been on a board of an organization that actually went bankrupt and could not pay its bills.

CONCLUSION

This chapter has discussed the ever-present threat of bankruptcy almost all nonprofit organizations face at one time or another. It was noted that one of the characteristics of such organizations is that they receive support only so long as they serve the needs of the public or their members. Since most organizations find it difficult to build up large cash reserves, they must be responsive.

If they are not, support will drop and unless the organization responds quickly, it could very well find itself on the verge of actual bankruptcy.

The treasurer's role of eliminating the unexpected was discussed, and several techniques reviewed to help the treasurer stay on top of the current financial situation. It was emphasized that when trouble looms the treasurer's first and most important responsibility is to call "loud and clear" so that the board can take appropriate action. It is the board that must take action.

Most organizations in financial trouble find that it is difficult to increase income by any substantial amount in a short period of time. Accordingly, when financial troubles loom, one of the first things the board must do is to cut back on its rate of expenditures. If some of the budgeting techniques discussed in the previous chapters have been followed, the board will have plenty of warning that it must cut expenses and should be able to avoid actual bankruptcy.

It may very well be that the board will find, however, that the organization is not viable, and that the reason for its continuation no longer exists. When this occurs, it is important that the board take action on a timely basis to either merge it into another more viable organization, or to actually discontinue operations and dissolve the organization in a controlled manner. It is also important to constantly remember that a nonprofit organization does not have a perpetual life. It can continue to exist only so long as it serves a worthwhile purpose which its members or the public will support.

19

Small Organizations—Obtaining the Right Bookkeeper

Obtaining and keeping the right bookkeeper is the key to making life easy and routine for the treasurer of small organizations.* For, unless he wants to spend a substantial portion of his time and effort in keeping the records himself, he will need a good bookkeeper. There is nothing difficult about bookkeeping as such, but the details can become most wearisome to the busy volunteer treasurer. The time they consume can detract from the treasurer's other responsibilities, particularly that of planning. For most nonprofit organizations, a part or full-time bookkeeper will be hired.

The problem of finding the right bookkeeper is compounded for nonprofit organizations because traditionally such organizations pay low salaries to all of their staff, including the bookkeeper. This frequently results in the organization getting someone with only minimum qualifications. This appears to be false economy. A good bookkeeper can help the organization save money and can free the time of the volunteer treasurer.

Often the other staff in the organization are extremely dedicated individuals interested in the particular program of the organization and are willing to accept a lower than normal salary.

---

* This chapter deals only with the bookkeeping problems of relatively small organizations. Larger organizations are not discussed because to a very large extent they are run like commercial organizations.

But the bookkeeper is seldom dedicated to the program of the organization as such. She (or he) has been hired to provide bookkeeping services and often has no special interest in the program of the organization.

LEVEL OF BOOKKEEPING SERVICES NEEDED

The first step in obtaining a bookkeeper is to determine what bookkeeping services are needed. Depending on the size of the organization, there are a number of possibilities. If the organization is very small and only 15–25 checks are issued a month, the treasurer will probably find that a "checkbook" type set of records will be all that is required or appropriate. If so, he may very well keep the records himself and not try to find someone to help him. In this case the "bookkeeping problem" is merely one of finding enough time to keep the checkbook up-to-date and to prepare financial statements on a timely basis. While the problem of finding this time is not to be underestimated, still the bookkeeping problems are largely under control.

Secretary as Bookkeeper

For many organizations, the number of transactions is too large for the treasurer to handle himself but not large enough to justify a full-time bookkeeper. If the organization has a paid full- or part-time secretary, often some of the bookkeeping duties are delegated to her. Usually this means having the secretary keep the "checkbook" or perhaps a simple cash receipts and cash disbursements ledger.* At the end of the month the treasurer will usually summarize these cash records and prepare the financial statements. While this means the treasurer will still have a lot of work to do, the work has been reduced significantly by having the secretary keep the basic records. This is a very practical approach for small organizations with very limited staff and not too many transactions.

---

* Chapter 26 discusses both a checkbook system of bookkeeping and a simple cash basis bookkeeping system. A secretary could probably keep most of the records in these two systems with a minimum of instruction.

Volunteer as Bookkeeper

Another possibility for the small organization is to find a volunteer within the organization who will help keep the records. While this can occasionally be effective it often turns out to be less than satisfactory. There is less control over the activities of a volunteer bookkeeper and it is difficult for the treasurer to insist that the records be kept on a timely basis. After all, volunteer bookkeepers are just that—volunteers—with all the rights and privileges that go with volunteers. Volunteers have to work around their own schedules and it is difficult to insist that they perform their duties on as strict a basis as with full-time employees. Another problem with volunteers is that their tenure tends to be short. Keeping a set of books is hard work, and while a volunteer bookkeeper's enthusiasm may be great at the beginning, it tends to diminish in time. The result is that there are often delays, clerical errors, and eventually the need to get another bookkeeper. The volunteer bookkeeper is not a good solution. If the treasurer cannot handle the bookkeeping then he should use a paid secretary or consider hiring a part-time bookkeeper.

Part-Time Bookkeepers

In considering a part-time bookkeeper, the first question is how much time is required. Is the job one that can be handled on a one-day-a-month basis, two-days-a-month, two-days-a-week? For most small organizations the answer will probably be only a day or two a month, or at the most, a day a week. Where do you go to find a good, part-time bookkeeper? This can be difficult.

Some of the best potential may be found among mothers with school children who were full-time bookkeepers at one time. Since a part-time bookkeeping job can easily fit into a flexible schedule permitting the mother to be home before and after school, this can be a very good arrangement if the bookkeeping needs are not more than 15–20 hours a week.

If the organization wants someone at its office for a full day each week or during hours not suitable for a mother with school children, then perhaps a retired bookkeeper or accountant will be the next best bet. However, it is difficult to find a competent retired person. Many persons will apply who have an impressive background but very little practical bookkeeping experience. An example might be a retired assistant treasurer of a large and well known organization. Typically, he had bookkeeping back in school forty years ago, but never used his bookkeeping. While he may have a sophisticated knowledge of business, he is not competent as a bookkeeper, and often finds the detail boring and his interest is short-lived. Also, the hourly rate such persons may demand will probably be higher than that commanded by a competent bookkeeper. An ad in a local newspaper is probably the best place to start to look for a qualified person.

Full-Time Bookkeepers

For larger or growing organizations, there is a point when a full-time bookkeeper is needed.

An advertisement in the newspaper is probably the best approach. The ad should be explicit and should indicate salary, and the type of experience and competence this person will need. It should also indicate the type of organization since some applicants will not be interested in working for a nonprofit organization.

Alternatively, an employment agency can be used. The principal advantage of a good agency is a saving of time and effort of the treasurer. They will place the ad in the paper and will do the initial weeding out of the obvious misfits before forwarding the potential candidates to the organization for review. They also know the job market and will probably be in a good position to advise on the "going" salary. They should also be able to help in checking references.

These agencies charge a fee which usually the organization ends up paying, and this can be from two to six weeks' pay. The question that the treasurer must ask is, is it worth this amount for the help an agency can give? There is no sure answer to this question. In many instances their help is most valuable. On the other hand some agencies do very little screening and the organization ends up with almost the same work that it would have had without the agency.

Often a friend of the treasurer knows of someone who is look-ing for a job and while there is no reason not to consider such a person, the treasurer should also interview others.

If the organization has an outside auditor, he may be able to help. Get his advice, and before actually hiring a bookkeeper, let him talk with the candidate. While he cannot guarantee that the right person is hired, he is more likely to be able to judge the candidate's technical skills and background than the treasurer is.

PERSONALITY CHARACTERISTICS

There are several personality characteristics that good book-keepers often have that the treasurer should be aware of. Obvi-ously a good bookkeeper is usually a very meticulous and well organized person. This often means that the bookkeeper will become impatient with other members of the staff who are slow in providing the required information or who are sloppy in pro-viding all of the necessary details. To the rest of the staff the bookkeeper often appears to be a "nit picker." Obviously if the bookkeeper is not diplomatic, this can be annoying to the rest of the staff, but these are desirable qualities that the treasurer should not discourage.

Another desirable characteristic is that the bookkeeper will often be critical of the spending patterns of the organization, particularly if she feels the organization is not being frugal. This tendency to be critical of spending habits can be a very helpful trait which the treasurer should not discourage. The bookkeeper sees all of the spending of the organization and is bound to have an opinion about how wisely expenditures are made. She may not be correct in her conclusion because her vantage point is quite limited. Yet, from the treasurer's standpoint, the book-keeper acts as a watchdog for him and will often have some good ideas. He should act on them when she does.

ALTERNATIVES TO BOOKKEEPERS

Outside Preparation of Payroll

One thing that can be done to either relieve the burden on the bookkeeper or to minimize the time requirements is to let a bank or a service bureau handle the payroll. This is particularly effective where employees are paid the same amount each payroll period.

Some banks will handle the complete payroll function and will use their own bank checks. This eliminates the need for the organization to prepare a bank reconciliation. Others will prepare the payroll but use the organization's checks, which after being cashed are returned to the organization. Some will prepare the payroll tax reports, others will not. Banks usually have a minimum fee which ranges from $15 to $20, for each payroll. If there are more than about 20 employees, this amount increases. While the charge may seem high, the time saved can be considerable. Remember that in addition to the payroll preparation the bank will also keep cumulative records of salary paid to each employee and will prepare the various payroll tax returns, W–2 forms, etc.

The use of a bank or service bureau works best where the payroll is regular and routine in amount . . . that is, where there are not a lot of hourly employees, or changes in rates between periods. While a bank can handle such changes, the "input" to the bank is such that the organization would be faced with the need to have someone act as a payroll clerk to assemble the information for the bank, and this takes time. If there are a lot of changes each period, it may be just as easy for the bookkeeper to handle the complete job and not use an outside service bureau or bank.

Service Bureau Bookkeeping Records

Another possibility is to have a service bureau keep all the bookkeeping records. If there is any volume of activity, a service bureau can often keep the records at less cost than an organization can hire a bookkeeper. For example, there are some service bureaus that will key punch information from original documents such as the check stubs, invoices, etc. They can then prepare a cash receipts book, cash disbursement book, general ledger, financial statements, etc., all automatically. All the organization has to provide is the basic information. The costs for such services vary widely depending on the volume and type of records and the geographic area in which the organization is located.

Once a treasurer starts to think about going to a service bureau, he should get some outside professional advice on whether it is practical or not. While talking to the service bureau will provide information on costs, etc., he must keep in mind that the service bureau will be trying to sell him their services and will not tell him of all the problems he will encounter or the other alternatives he could consider. So if a treasurer wants to study these alternatives he should seek the advice of a CPA. If the organization has no CPA, they should hire one for the express purpose of getting advice on this one area.

Accounting Service

There is another alternative, and that is to hire an outside accounting service to perform the actual bookkeeping. Many CPA's and public accountants provide bookkeeping services for their clients. Under this arrangement the accountant has one of his staff do all of the bookkeeping and he takes the responsibility for reviewing the work and seeing that it is properly done. The accountant usually prepares financial statements monthly or quarterly.

There are still some functions the organization itself usually must perform. The organization will normally still have to prepare its own checks, vouchers, payroll, depositing of receipts and billings. This means that normally it cannot delegate 100 per cent of the bookkeeping to an outside accounting service.

The cost of this type of service is its principal disadvantage. The accountant is in business and has overhead and salaries to pay, including salaries for his employees when they are not busy. All of these costs are considered in establishing his hourly rates. These rates are generally about twice what it costs to hire a competent bookkeeper on a full-time basis. This means that they will range from $10–25 an hour. Nevertheless, it may still be cheaper to hire an accountant than to have someone on the payroll. The outside accountant is paid only as needed. If he works 10 hours a month, that is all he is paid for. Also, these services are performed by experienced staff, and there is no problem of competency.

One of the problems with this type of service is that the accountant cannot be in two places at the same time. The chances are that at the time you are ready for him to come in, several other clients will also be ready. This can result in some delay, although usually not an excessive amount.

TIMING IN HIRING A REPLACEMENT

One question that is frequently asked is when should a replacement be hired if the present bookkeeper is leaving. Should there be an overlap in employment so that the retiring bookkeeper can indoctrinate the new one and if so, how long a period of overlap is appropriate? Or is it better to have no overlap at all?

It is appropriate to have some overlap, but it should be fairly short. While the present bookkeeper may not agree, a good bookkeeper can pick up another bookkeeper's set of books and procedures fairly quickly. A bookkeeper can usually get oriented to the broad outlines of the procedures within a few days. While he may not have picked up all of the details that he will have to learn, most of these details are going to be learned by experience and not from having the former bookkeeper tell him about them. Also, the new bookkeeper will tend to be confident of his own ability to do things better than the last bookkeeper. This means that too long an overlap period will grate on the nerves of the new bookkeeper.

For most organizations, it is probably best to keep the overlap short and recognize that things will not be entirely smooth for a month or two. Unless the organization is willing to have an overlap period of at least a month, it must expect that it will take some time for the new bookkeeper to get his feet on the ground.

SUMMARY

The bookkeeping needs of nonprofit organizations vary widely. At the one extreme is the small organization which has so few transactions that the treasurer himself is able to handle all the bookkeeping. On the other extreme is the large national organization that has an accounting or bookkeeping staff of many persons which is run exactly like a commercial organization. In between these two extremes is every conceivable combination of full- and part-time bookkeeping need.

A number of sources for bookkeepers were discussed. Often in small organizations, a paid secretary will keep some simple records for the treasurer. Until the records get voluminous, this can be quite satisfactory. On the other hand, "volunteer" book-keepers are seldom satisfactory because of rapid turnover and the problem of control. It was suggested that part-time bookkeeping jobs could be particularly attractive to mothers with children in school who might want to earn some extra money. This, of course, assumes previous bookkeeping experience. The proce-dures to follow in looking for both part- and full-time bookkeep-ers were discussed and the importance of paying the going salary was emphasized. The use of banks or service bureaus was also suggested as one way to reduce the work load for the book-keeper. Finally, it was suggested that while some overlap in bookkeepers is necessary, this overlap period should be relatively short.

20

Small Organizations—Providing Internal Control

"SPINSTER ADMITS EMBEZZLEMENT OF TEN THOUSAND DOLLARS." "TRUSTED CLERK STEALS $50,000." These headlines are all too common and many tell a similar story—a trusted and respected employee in a position of financial responsibility is overcome by temptation and "borrows" a few dollars until payday to meet some unexpected cash need. When payday comes some other cash need prevents repayment. Somehow the employee just never catches up, and borrows a few more dollars, and a few more and a few more.

The reader's reaction may be, "Thank goodness, this kind of thing could never happen to my organization. After all, I know everyone and they are all honest, and besides who would think of stealing from a nonprofit organization?" This is not the point. Very few who end up as embezzlers start out with this intent in mind. Rather they find themselves in a position of trust and opportunity and when personal crises arise, the temptation is too much. Nonprofit organizations are not exempt, regardless of size. There is always a risk when a person is put in a position where there is an opportunity to be tempted.

The purpose of this chapter is to outline some of the practical procedures that a small organization can establish to help minimize this risk and thus safeguard the organization's physical assets. For purposes of this discussion the emphasis is on smaller organizations where one or two persons handle all the bookkeeping. This would include many churches, country clubs, local fund-raising groups, YMCA's, etc. Internal control for larger organizations is not discussed here because controls for such organizations can become very complicated and would require many chapters. The principles, however, are essentially the same. Setting up a set of internal controls requires an understanding of the basic principles plus a great deal of common sense. Larger organizations will probably want professional help in setting up a strong set of controls. Readers who are interested in this subject should refer to the Bibliography (pages 551–555).

REASONS FOR INTERNAL CONTROL

Internal control is a system of procedures and cross checking which in the absence of collusion minimizes the likelihood of misappropriation of assets or misstatement of the accounts and maximizes the likelihood of detection if it occurs. For the most part internal control does not prevent embezzlement but should insure that, if committed, it will be promptly discovered. This likelihood of discovery usually persuades most not to allow temptation to get the better of them. Very few first-time embezzlers are so desperate that they would steal if they really expected to be promptly caught.

There are several reasons for having a good system of internal controls. The first, obviously, is to prevent the loss through theft of some of the assets. A second reason, equally important, is to prevent an "honest" employee from making a mistake that could ruin his life. An employer has a moral responsibility to avoid putting undue temptation in front of his employees. Internal controls are designed to help remove the temptation.

Aside from this moral responsibility of the employer there is also a responsibility of the board to the membership and to the general public to safeguard the assets of the organization. The board has an obligation to use prudence in protecting the assets. If a large sum were stolen and not recovered it could jeopardize the program of the organization. Furthermore if only a small amount were stolen it would be embarrassing to the members of the board. In either case, the membership or the public would certainly want to know why internal control procedures had not been followed by the board.

FUNDAMENTALS OF INTERNAL CONTROL

The very simple definition of the purpose of internal control noted above relates to small organizations and emphasizes the fraud aspects. For larger organizations this definition would have to be expanded to include a system of checks and balances over all paper work to insure that there was no intentional or unintentional misstatement of the accounts.* For purposes of this discussion, however, the emphasis is on the physical controls over the organization's assets, principally cash.

One of the most effective internal controls is the use of a budget which is compared to actual figures on a monthly basis. If deviations from the budget are carefully followed up by the treasurer or executive director, the likelihood of a large misappropriation taking place without being detected fairly quickly is reduced considerably.† This type of overall review of the financial statements is very important, and every member of the board should ask questions about any item which appears out of line either with the budget or with what he would have expected to have been the actual figures. Many times this type of probing for reasons for deviations from the expected has uncovered problems.

---

* The American Institute of Certified Public Accountants in an official pronouncement, Statement on Auditing Standards No. 1, has defined internal control as follows:

"Internal control comprises the plan of organization and all of the co-ordinate methods and measures adopted within a business to safeguard its assets, check the accuracy and reliability of its accounting data, promote operational efficiency, and encourage adherence to prescribed managerial policies. This definition possibly is broader than the meaning sometimes attributed to the term. It recognizes that a system of internal control extends beyond those matters which relate directly to the functions of the accounting and financial departments." Copyright 1973 by the American Institute of Certified Public Accountants, Inc.

† Chapter 17 discusses budgeting techniques.

SOME BASIC CONTROLS

There are a number of other basic internal controls that are probably applicable to many, if not most, small nonprofit organizations and these are discussed below. However, it must be emphasized that these are only basic controls and should not be considered all-inclusive. Establishing an effective system of internal control requires knowledge of the particular organization and its operations. The controls discussed below should give the reader, however, some indication of the nature of internal control and act as a starting point for establishing an appropriate system.

In this discussion we will be considering the division of duties for a small organization, The Center for the Development of Human Resources, whose financial statements were discussed in Chapter 18. As will be recalled, this organization sponsors seminars and retreats and has a paid staff to run its affairs. The office staff consists of:

An executive director
The executive director's secretary
A program director
A bookkeeper

The officers of the Center are all volunteers and usually are at the Center at irregular times. The executive director, treasurer, president and vice president are check signers. With this background let us now look at each of eleven controls in detail and see how each applies to this organization.

Control Over Receipts

The basic objectives in establishing internal control over receipts is to obtain control over the amounts received at the time of receipt. Once this control is established, procedures must be followed to ensure that these amounts get deposited in the organization's bank account. Establishing this control is particularly difficult for small organizations because of the small number of persons usually involved.

1. *Prenumbered receipts should be issued for all money at the time first received. A duplicate copy should be accounted for and a comparison eventually made between the aggregate of the receipts issued and the amount deposited in the bank.*

The purpose of this control is to create a written record of the cash received. The original of the receipt should be given to the person from whom the money was received; the duplicate copy should be kept permanently. Periodically, a comparison should be made of the aggregate receipts issued, with the amount deposited. The receipts can be issued at the organization's office, or if door-to-door collections are made, a prenumbered receipt can be issued as amounts are received by the collector. Hopefully, all contributors will learn to expect a receipt for cash payments.

It is important that both the duplicate copy and the original be prenumbered in order to provide control over the receipts issued. If a receipt is "voided" by mistake both the original and the duplicate should be kept and accounted for. In this way there will be complete accountability over all receipts that have been issued.

In our illustration, the Center receives a fair amount of cash at its seminars and retreats on weekends when the bookkeeper and treasurer are not available. One of the participants is designated as the fee collector for that session and he in turn collects the fees and issues the receipts. After he has collected all of the fees he turns the duplicate copy of the receipts (along with all unused receipt forms) and the cash collected to the program director. He also prepares and signs a summary report of the cash collected, in duplicate. He mails one copy of this report directly to the treasurer at his home in an envelope provided, and the duplicate is turned over to the program director. The program director in turn counts the money, agreeing the total received with the total of the duplicate receipts, and with the summary report. The program director puts the money in the safe for the weekend and on Monday morning gives the money, the duplicate receipts and the copy of the summary report to the bookkeeper for depositing. The bookkeeper in turn deposits the money from each program separately, and files the duplicate receipts and summary report for future reference. Once a month the treasurer compares his copy of each summary report with the deposits shown on the bank statement.

2. *Cash collections should be under the control of two people wherever possible, particularly where it is not practicable to issue receipts.*

In the illustration in the previous paragraph, control was established over cash collections by having the person collecting at each seminar issue receipts and a summary report. The program director, in turn, also had some control since he knew how many persons attended and was able to compare the amount collected with the amount that should be collected. This provided dual control.

There are many instances, however, where cash collections are received when it is not appropriate to give a receipt. Two examples are church "plate" collections on Sundays, and coin canisters placed in stores and public places throughout the community for public support. To the extent that only one person handles this money, there is always a risk. The risk is not only that some of it will be misappropriated, but also that someone may erroneously think it has been. This is why it is recommended that two people be involved.

With respect to church plate collections, as soon as the money has been collected, it should be locked up until it can be counted by two people together. Perhaps the head usher and a vestryman will count it after the last service. Once counted, both should sign a cash collection report. This report should be given to the treasurer for subsequent comparison with the deposit on the bank statement. The cash should be turned over to the bookkeeper for depositing intact.

This procedure will not guard against the usher dipping his hand into the "plate" before it is initially locked up or counted, but the ushers' duties are usually rotated and the cumulative risk is low. But the bookkeeper and treasurer normally have access to such funds on a regular and recurring basis. This is why their function of counting these cash receipts should be controlled by having a second person involved. This is not because they are not trusted; it is to insure that no one can think of accusing one of them.

Canisters containing cash which are placed in public places

should be sealed so that the only way to get access to the cash is to break the canister open. Of course, someone could take the entire canister, but if the canister is placed in a conspicuous place —near the cash register, for example, this risk is fairly low. These canisters should be serially numbered so that all canisters can be accounted for. When the canisters are eventually opened, they should be counted by two people using the same procedure as with plate collections.

3. *Two persons should open all mail and make a list of all receipts for each day. This list should subsequently be compared to the bank deposit by someone not handling the money. Receipts in the form of checks should be restrictively endorsed promptly upon receipt.*

Two persons should open the mail; otherwise there is a risk that the mail opener may misappropriate part of the receipts. This imposes a heavy burden on the small organization with only a few employees but it is necessary if good internal control is desired.* One alternative is to have mail receipts go to a bank lock box and let the bank do the actual opening of the mail.

The purpose of making a list of all checks received is to ensure that a record is made of the amount that was received. This makes it possible for the treasurer to later check to see if the bookkeeper has deposited all amounts promptly.

Checks should be promptly endorsed since once endorsed there is less likelihood of misappropriation. The endorsement should be placed on the check by the person first opening the mail.

In theory if the check has been made out in the name of the organization, no one can cash it. But experience has shown that if someone were clever enough, he could probably find a way to cash it. On the other hand, once endorsed with the name of the bank and account number it is very difficult for the embezzler to convert the check to his own use.

In our illustration at the Center, the secretary to the executive director together with the bookkeeper jointly open all mail and

---

* Organizations that have their financial statements audited by CPAs will find that the CPA cannot give an unqualified opinion if internal control is considered inadequate. See pages 359 and 360.

place the rubber stamp endorsement on the check. They then make a list, in duplicate, of all checks received, with one copy of the list going to the bookkeeper with the checks for depositing. They both sign the original of the list, which goes to the executive director. The executive director obtains this copy because he wants to see what amounts have been received. At the end of the month, he turns over all of these lists to the treasurer who then compares each day's lists with the respective credit on the bank statement.

4. *All receipts should be deposited in the bank, intact and on a timely basis.*

The purpose of this control is to insure that there is a complete record of all receipts and disbursements. If an organization receives "cash" receipts, no part of this cash should be used to pay its bills. The receipts should be deposited, and checks issued to pay expenses. In this way there will be a record of the total receipts and expenses of the organization on the bank statements.

This procedure does not prevent someone from stealing money but it does mean that he will have to use a check to get access to the money. This leaves a record of the theft and makes it more difficult for a person to cover up.

In our illustration, it should be noted that the bookkeeper deposits each day's mail receipts intact, and also deposits, separately, the receipts from each seminar. On some days she has two or three deposits. By making the deposits separately the treasurer at the end of the month is then able to compare his copy of the summary of seminar receipts and the daily mail receipts to the bank statement. This comparison by the treasurer does not take more than a few minutes each month but it provides excellent internal control over receipts and it also gives him assurance that the bookkeeper is depositing all receipts daily.

Control Over Disbursements

The basic objective in establishing internal controls over disbursements is to ensure that a record of all disbursements is made and that only authorized persons are in a position to withdraw funds. The risk of misappropriation can be significantly reduced if procedures are established to minimize the possibility that an expenditure can be made without leaving a trail or that an unauthorized person can withdraw money.

5. *All disbursements should be made by check and supporting documentation kept for each disbursement.*

This control is to insure that there will be a permanent record of how much and to whom money was paid. No amounts should be paid by cash, with the exception of minor petty cash items. For the same reason no checks should be made payable to "cash." Checks should always be payable to a specific person, including checks for petty cash reimbursement. This makes it more difficult to fraudulently disburse funds.

At the Center, the bookkeeper is the one who prepares all checks for payment of bills. Before she will prepare a check, however, the vendor's invoice must be approved by the executive director. If the purchases involved goods that have been received at the Center she also insists that the person who received the goods indicate that he did receive them, right on the vendor's invoice.

The bookkeeper is not a check signer since, if she were, she could fraudulently disburse funds to herself and then cover them up in the books. The check signers are the executive director, the treasurer, the president, and the vice president. Normally the executive director signs all checks. Checks of more than $1,000 require two signatures, but these are very infrequent. The executive director carefully examines all supporting invoices, making sure that someone has signed for receipt of the goods before he signs the check. After he has signed the check, he personally marks each invoice "paid" so that he won't inadvertently pay the same invoice twice. His secretary mails all checks to the vendor as an added control over the bookkeeper. By not letting the bookkeeper have access to the signed checks, the bookkeeper is not in a position to profit from preparing a fraudulent check to a nonexistent vendor.

6. *If the treasurer or check signer is also the bookkeeper, two signatures should be required on all checks.*

The purpose of this control is to insure that no one person is in a position to disburse funds and then cover up the disbursement in the records. In part, this recommendation is designed to protect the organization, and in part, to protect the treasurer.

Two signatures on a check provide additional control only so long as the second check signer also examines the invoices or supporting bills behind the disbursement before he signs the check. The real risk of having dual signatures is that both check signers will rely on the other and will review the supporting bills in such a perfunctory manner that there is less control than if only one person signed but realized he had full responsibility.

Two signatures should also be required on checks of very large amounts even when the treasurer is not the bookkeeper, and for transfers out of a savings account. This gives some added protection that the treasurer won't be able to abscond with the entire assets of the organization.

As was noted before, the bookkeeper at the Center is not a check signer. This reduces the need for the second signature on checks except for the ones over $1,000. Where the second signature is required for those large checks the treasurer is usually the second signer. He very carefully inspects all bills involving such payments although he is usually well aware of the purchase in advance because of the size. The Center has a safe deposit box at the bank, and two signatures are also required for access. The same persons who are authorized to sign checks have access to this box.

7. *A person other than the bookkeeper should receive bank statements directly from the bank and should reconcile them.*

This control is to prevent the bookkeeper from fraudulently issuing a check to himself and, as bookkeeper, covering up this disbursement in the books. While the bookkeeper may not be a check signer, experience has shown that banks often do not catch forged check signatures. The bookkeeper usually has access to blank checks and could forge the check signer's signature. If the bookkeeper were to receive the bank statements he could remove the fraudulent and forged cancelled check and then destroy it, covering up the fraud through the books.

In most smaller organizations the bank statement and cancelled checks should go directly to the treasurer and he should prepare the bank reconciliation.* In those situations where the

---

* In large organizations the control can be even more effective where the division of duties is such that an employee who is not a check signer *or* bookkeeper can prepare the bank reconciliation. Obviously, it is possible for a check signer to fraudulently make out a check to himself and then, if he has access to the re-

treasurer is also the bookkeeper the bank statements should go directly to another officer to reconcile. The treasurer should insist on this procedure to protect himself from any suspicions of wrong-doing.*

In the Center's case, the bank statement and cancelled checks are mailed directly to the treasurer's home each month. He usually spends half a day at the Center's offices on the Saturday after receiving the bank statement. He prepares the complete bank reconciliation. At this time he also compares the lists of mail and program receipts he has received throughout the month to the deposits shown on the bank statement.

Other Areas of Control

8. *Someone other than the bookkeeper should authorize all write-offs of accounts receivable or other assets.*

This control is to insure that if the bookkeeper has embezzled accounts receivable or some other assets he will not also be in a position to cover up the theft by writing off the receivable or asset. If he is unable to write such amounts off, someone will eventually ask why the "receivable" has not been paid and this

---

turned checks, to remove the cancelled check. However, if he doesn't also have a means of covering up the disbursement, sooner or later the shortage will come out. The person reconciling the bank account is not in a position to permanently "cover up" a shortage although he could hide it for several months. For this reason, it is preferable to have neither a check signer or the bookkeeper prepare the reconciliation.

* In those situations where the treasurer or other officer does not have the time to prepare the reconciliation, then, as a minimum procedure, he should receive the unopened bank statement directly from the bank. He should look at each check returned by the bank to be sure he recognizes both the payee and the purpose of the check. If there is a check he does not recognize, he should raise a question about it. After this review, which usually doesn't take very much time, he can turn the bank statement and checks over to the bookkeeper (or treasurer) to reconcile. The completed bank reconciliation should be returned to the treasurer (or other officer) for his review. His review of the completed reconciliation should consist of reviewing the reconciling items, comparing the balance "per bank" to the bank statement, and the balance "per books" to the general ledger.

This alternative procedure should only be used where it is not practical for the treasurer or other officer to actually prepare the bank reconciliation. While this alternative procedure can be effective, it does not offer the protection that comes from having someone independent of the bookkeeper actually perform all of the steps of a bank reconciliation.

should trigger correspondence that would result in the fraud being discovered.

Generally, write-offs of small receivables should be approved by the treasurer (provided he is not also the bookkeeper), but if they are large in amount they should be submitted to the board for approval. Before any amount is written off, the treasurer should make certain that all appropriate efforts have been made, including, where appropriate, legal action. He must constantly keep in mind his fiduciary responsibility to take all reasonable steps to make collection.

The Center only very rarely has accounts receivable. It does have, however, many pledges receivable. Although the Center would not think of taking legal action to enforce collection * it does record those pledges as though they were receivables. Very occasionally the bookkeeper has to call the treasurer's attention to a delinquent pledge. He, in turn, usually calls the delinquent pledger himself in an effort to evaluate the likelihood of future collection. Once a year he submits a written report to the board advising them of delinquent pledges, and requesting formal approval to write them off. The board discusses each such delinquent pledge before giving its approval.

9. *Marketable securities should be kept in a bank safe deposit box or held by a bank as custodian.*

This control is to insure that securities are protected against loss by fire or theft or from bankruptcy of a brokerage house. For most organizations, marketable securities represent long-term rather than short-term investments and they should not be kept in a safe in the organization's office or at the broker's office. The organization should provide the maximum protection for these assets. Either a bank should keep these securities as custodian or they should be kept in the bank safe deposit box under dual signature control. Safeguarding investments is discussed more fully on pages 378 to 380.

In our illustration, the Center does not have very much in the way of investment funds. What endowments the Center has it keeps in a bank common stock fund. This is a form of mutual

---

* Pledges are discussed more fully in Chapter 9.

fund which the bank set up to handle investments on a pooled basis for a number of nonprofit organizations. All decisions at the Center to put money into or take money out of this bank fund are made by the executive committee of the board. The bank insists that the executive committee's minutes accompany any request for withdrawals of or additions to the Center's shares in this fund. There are no share certificates as such although the bank sends quarterly statements to the treasurer showing the number of shares the Center has.

10. *Fixed asset records should be maintained and an inventory taken periodically.*

This is to insure that the organization has a complete record of its assets. This permanent record should contain information such as a description of the asset, cost, date acquired, location, serial number, and similar information. This information will provide a record of the assets that the employees are responsible for. This is particularly important in nonprofit organizations where turnover of employees and officers is often high. This also provides fire insurance records. An example of the type of fixed asset record that should be kept is shown in Chapter 27 (Figure 27-3).

11. *Excess cash should be maintained in a separate bank account. Withdrawals from this account should require two signatures.*

Where an organization has excess cash which will not be needed for current operations in the immediate future, it should be placed in a separate bank account to provide an added safeguard. Frequently this separate account will be an interest-bearing savings account. The bank should be advised that the signatures of two officers are required for all withdrawals. Normally in such situations withdrawals are infrequent, and when they are made the funds withdrawn are deposited intact in the regular current checking account. In this way all disbursements are made from the regular checking account.

Obviously in this situation the officers involved in authorizing a withdrawal should not do so without being fully aware of the reasons for the need of these funds. Approval should not be perfunctorily given.

FIDELITY INSURANCE

One final recommendation. Fidelity insurance should be carried. The purpose of fidelity insurance is to insure that if a loss from embezzlement occurs the organization will recover the loss. This insurance does not cover theft or burglary by an outside person. It provides protection only against an employee's dishonesty. Having fidelity insurance also acts as a deterrent because the employees know that the insurance company is more likely to press charges against a dishonest employee than would a "soft hearted" and embarrassed employer.

There is only one "catch" to this type of coverage. The organization has to have good enough records to prove that an embezzlement has taken place. This means that this coverage is not a substitute for other internal controls. If the theft occurs but the employer doesn't know it or if there is no proof of the loss, fidelity insurance will not help.

This protection is not expensive since the risk is usually low. Of course, the risk varies from one organization to another, and thus the premium will vary. In the case of the Center, their fidelity policy covering losses of up to $100,000 costs them about $200 annually. In any case the cost is relatively so little that prudence dictates that all nonprofit organizations, except possibly the very smallest, have this coverage.

Sometimes employees feel that a lack of confidence is being expressed in them if the organization has fidelity insurance. The treasurer should assure them that this is not the case, and that fidelity insurance is similar to fire insurance. All prudent organizations carry such coverage.

CONCLUSION

Internal control as discussed in this chapter for small organizations is a system of procedures which in the absence of collusion minimizes the likelihood of misappropriation of assets or misstatement of the accounts, and if it has occurred maximizes the likelihood of detection. These controls largely depend on a division of duties such that no one person is in a position to both misappropriate assets and to cover up the theft in the records. These controls are very important even in a smaller organization where it is difficult to provide for this division of duties. One of the principal reasons often overlooked for having good internal control is to remove temptation from normally honest employees.

Even the smallest organization should be able to apply the eleven internal controls that have been recommended in this chapter. The board should insist that these and similar controls be established. It has a responsibility to insist that all practical measures be taken to protect the organization's assets. Otherwise the board is subject to severe criticism if an embezzlement were to occur. Fidelity insurance was also recommended.

The controls discussed in this chapter are basic ones and should not be considered all-inclusive. A complete system of internal control encompasses all of the procedures of the organization. If the organization is a large or complex one, or if it has peculiar problems or procedures, the board will want to retain the services of a professional to help set up and monitor the effectiveness of internal control. The next chapter discusses the services that the certified public accountant can provide, including assistance in establishing internal controls.

21

Independent Audits

Related to the internal controls discussed in Chapter 20 is the question whether the books and records should be audited, and if so, by whom. Like many other decisions the board has to make, this is a value judgment for which there are no absolute answers. Audits cost money, and therefore the values to be derived must be considered carefully.

FUNCTIONS AND LIMITATIONS

An audit is a series of procedures followed by an experienced professional accountant used to test, on a selective basis, transactions and internal controls in effect, all with a view to forming an opinion on the fairness of the presentation of the financial statements for the period. An audit is not an examination of every transaction that has been recorded; it is a series of tests designed to give the accountant a basis for judging how effectively the records were kept and the degree of reliance he can place on the internal controls. The end result of an audit is the expression of an opinion.

Several things should be underscored. The auditor does not examine all transactions. If he were to do so the cost would probably be prohibitive. He does look at what he believes is a representative sample of the transactions. In looking at these selected transactions, he is as concerned with the internal control and procedures that were followed as he is with the legitimacy of the transaction itself. If internal controls are good the extent of his testing can be limited. If controls are weak, he will have to examine many more transactions to be satisfied. In smaller organizations where internal controls are often less effective, he must examine proportionately more transactions.

Another point that should be made is that for the most part he can only examine and test transactions that have been recorded. If a contribution has been received but not deposited in the bank or recorded in the books, there is little likelihood that he will discover it. This is why the last chapter emphasized that controls should be established over all receipts at the point of receipt and all disbursements should be made by check. In this way a record is made and the auditor has a chance of testing the transaction.

The end product of the audit is not a "certificate" that every transaction has been properly recorded, but an expression of an opinion by the auditor on the fairness of the presentation of the financial statements. The auditor does not guarantee accuracy; the bookkeeper may have stolen $100, but unless this $100 is material in relation to the financial statements as a whole, the auditor is not likely to discover it.

Auditor's Opinion Explained

Here is a typical opinion prepared by a certified public accountant which in this case is on the financial statements of the National Environmental Society.

In my opinion, the accompanying balance sheet and the related statement of income and expense present fairly the financial position of National Environmental Society at December 31, 1974, and the results of its operations for the year, in conformity with generally accepted accounting principles applied on a basis consistent with that of the preceding year. My examination of these statements was made in accordance with generally accepted auditing standards and accordingly included such tests of the accounting records and such other auditing procedures as I considered necessary in the circumstances.

This opinion is very carefully worded, and each phrase has significance. The wording has evolved over a period of time and is designed to tell the knowledgeable reader what responsibility the auditor takes and does not take. Since this opinion is the end product of an audit it is important to know exactly what the opinion means. Let us look at the opinion phrase by phrase to see what is being said.

Identification of Statements. "In my opinion the accompanying balance sheet and the related statement of income and expense . . ."

The auditor is carefully identifying the statements on which he is giving an opinion—the "accompanying" balance sheet and statement of income and expense. He is saying that these statements and only these statements are the ones he is referring to.

Statements Present Fairly. "In my opinion . . . present fairly the financial position . . . at December 31 and the results of its operations for the year . . ."

Here the auditor is saying the statements "present fairly." He is not saying they are correct, or that they are accurate. He is saying that they present "fairly." What does "fairly" mean? It means that there is no *material* misstatement of these statements. The statements may not be 100 per cent accurate, but they are not materially inaccurate. The question of what is "material" cannot really be answered with any definiteness since this is largely a subjective question, and in part depends on what figures you are looking at.*

Accounting Principles Followed. ". . . in conformity with generally accepted accounting principles . . ."

Here the auditor is defining the principles of accounting which have been followed—"generally accepted accounting principles." These words have specific meaning and refer to both published pronouncements by the American Institute of Certified Public Accountants and to general usage by similar organizations. Where there have been pronouncements of accounting principles by the AICPA, the auditor is saying here that these principles have been followed. Where there have been no pronouncements, the auditor

---

* The SEC in referring to reporting requirements for SEC filings defines "material" as ". . . the information . . . [about] which an average prudent investor ought reasonably to be informed before purchasing the security registered."

is saying that the principles followed are those generally used by similar organizations. Chapters 2–9 discuss some of the principles generally accepted as they relate to nonprofit organizations. If an opinion is issued without these specific words "in accordance with generally accepted accounting principles" the reader should be on his guard.

Principles Consistently Followed. ". . . applied on a basis consistent with that of the preceding year . . ."

The accountant is saying here that there have been no changes in accounting principles or in the application of these principles during the current year and the reader can compare last year's statements to this year's statements and know that they are comparable in this respect. If there have been changes, the auditor always has to spell out or make reference to these changes in his opinion.

Audit Standards Followed.   "My examination was made in accordance with generally accepted auditing standards . . ."

Here the auditor is spelling out in technical language how he conducted his examination. There is a whole body of literature and pronouncements which define "generally accepted auditing standards." These include standards of training, proficiency, independence, planning, supervision of staff, evaluation of internal control, and obtaining evidential matter to support the audit conclusions. They also provide that the auditor must perform certain specific tests where applicable.

Essential Tests.   There are two specific tests which cannot be omitted by the auditor: confirmation of accounts receivable, and observation of physical inventories. Confirmation of accounts receivable involves writing to those owing money (or making pledges) to the organization and asking them to confirm that they do, in fact, owe the organization. Observation of physical inventories involves going out and physically verifying the existence of the inventory. Both of these tests can require substantial amounts of the auditor's time, and often an organization will ask the auditor to eliminate these tests to save time and cost. If omitted, however, and if receivables or inventories are material, the auditor will not be able to say that his examination has been made in accordance with generally accepted auditing standards. He will not be able to express an opinion on the financial statements "taken as a whole." He may or may not be able to then express a "piecemeal" * opinion on specific items within the statement.

Extent of Audit Tests. ". . . and accordingly included such tests of the accounting records and such other auditing procedures as I considered necessary in the circumstances."

This phrase says that in addition to all other auditing requirements spelled out in official pronouncements, the auditor has performed whatever additional tests he believes should be performed.

Adequacy of Internal Control Over Contributions

The auditor must be satisfied that internal control over contributions is such as to ensure that all contributions received have been recorded. Internal control was discussed in the last chapter, but one control in particular should again be noted. Normally two persons should open all mail to prevent misappropriation. In the absence of adequate internal control, the CPA is required to qualify his opinion.

Qualified Opinions

A "qualified" opinion is an opinion in which the independent auditor takes exception to some specific aspect of the financial statements as presented, or is unable to form an unqualified opinion because of some contingency which might affect the financial statements. The independent auditor will spell out in his opinion exactly what the nature of the qualification is. A qualification with respect to presentation can result because generally accepted accounting principles were not followed, or because they were not consistently followed. A qualification because of a material

---

* A piecemeal opinion is an opinion where the auditor states that while he cannot express an opinion on the statements as a whole, he is able to express an opinion on certain specific accounts in the statements. An example might be where he was satisfied with the cash account, but not with accounts receivables. He would not express an opinion on the statements as a whole but would give an opinion on the cash balances shown.

uncertainty results when neither the auditor or anyone else is in a position to know the ultimate outcome of a pending transaction which affects the financial statements. A law suit against the organization is a good example.

Adverse Opinion. An "adverse" opinion results when, in the opinion of the auditor, the financial statements taken as a whole do not present fairly the financial position in conformity with generally accepted accounting principles. The distinction between a "qualified" opinion and an "adverse" opinion is primarily one of materiality.

Disclaimer. A "disclaimer" of opinion results when the auditor is unable to form an opinion on the financial statements. This could be the result of limitations on scope of the examination, uncertainties about the outcome of some event that would affect the financial statements in a very material way, or because the records were inadequate and it was not possible to form an opinion. When an auditor gives a disclaimer he will spell out the reasons for the disclaimer in his opinion.

Any qualification detracts from the credibility of the financial statements. Since one of the functions of an auditor's opinion is to add credibility to the financial statements, an opinion other than a "clean" or unqualified opinion will detract and raise questions about the statements. Wherever it is possible for an organization to take corrective action to eliminate the qualification, it should do so.

BENEFITS OF AN INDEPENDENT AUDIT

Audits are not free. This means that the board has to evaluate the benefits to be derived from an audit and the cost of this professional service. What are the benefits that can be expected from an audit? There are four: credibility of the financial statements; professional assistance in developing meaningful financial statements; professional advice on internal control, administrative efficiency and other business matters; and assistance in tax reporting and compliance requirements.

Credibility of the Financial Statements

We have already touched on credibility. This is the principal benefit of having an independent CPA express his opinion on the financial statements. Unfortunately, over the years, there have been many instances where nonprofit organizations have been mismanaged and the results buried in the financial statements in a manner that made it difficult, if not impossible, for the reader of the statements to discern.

It has been noted that the purpose of financial statements is to communicate in a straightforward and direct manner what has happened. The presence of an auditor's opinion helps in this communication process because an independent expert, after an examination, tells the reader that the financial statement presents fairly what has happened. Nonprofit organizations are competing with other organizations for the money of their members or of the general public. If an organization can tell its financial story accurately and completely and it is accepted at face value, the potential contributor is more likely to feel that the organization is well managed.

Meaningful Statements

Another benefit of having professional help is that the auditor is an expert at preparing financial statements in a format that will be most clear to the reader. All too often financial statements are poorly organized and hard to understand. The CPA has had years of experience in helping organizations prepare financial statements in clear and understandable language.

Advice on Internal Control and Other Matters

Another benefit is that the CPA will be in a position to advise the board on how to strengthen internal controls, and simplify the bookkeeping procedures. As an expert, he can also assist the board in evaluating the competency of the organization's bookkeeper or accountant. He will also be able to help the organization when it comes time to hire someone for these positions.

He has had experience in dealing with many different types of organizations and is likely to have a number of general business suggestions. Typically, he will periodically meet with the treasurer or executive director to discuss the problems of the organization and business conditions in general. Many boards meet with the CPA annually to ask questions and to be sure that the organization has picked his brains. This meeting also provides the CPA with an opportunity to call any potential problems to the board's attention.

Assistance in Tax Reporting and Compliance Requirements

As is discussed in Chapters 23–25, almost all nonprofit organizations are required to submit some form of report to one or more agencies of a state government and the IRS. These reports are almost always technical in format and unless the treasurer is an accountant, he will probably require assistance by an expert. The CPA is an expert, and can either offer advice on how to prepare the returns or can actually prepare them.

SELECTING A CERTIFIED PUBLIC ACCOUNTANT

Like doctors and lawyers, certified public accountants do not advertise. They depend on word of mouth to spread their reputation. Accordingly when it comes time to choose a CPA, talk with your banker, attorney, and fellow members of the board. The chances are that collectively they will know many CPA's practicing in your locality and will know of their reputations. Talk also with officers of other nonprofit organizations. They will probably have had some experience which may be of help.

In any professional relationship, the interest and willingness of the CPA to serve the organization is one of the most important factors to consider in making a selection. It is always difficult to judge which of several CPA's have the greatest interest in helping the organization. In large part the treasurer will have to make his decision from impressions formed in personal interviews.

One of the more effective ways to gain an impression of the CPA is to send him financial statements before interviewing him.

Then, at the time of the interview, he should be asked for his comments on the statements. If he has done his homework, it will be obvious in his response.

During this personal interview, let him take a look at the records so that he can get a general impression of the amount of time he will spend, and thus his fee. For the most part the treasurer's judgment should not be swayed significantly by the fee range estimated unless it is out of line with the other CPA's. Like a doctor or lawyer, the accountant expects to receive a fair fee for his services and there are plenty of places to cut corners when it comes to professional services. The organization is largely dependent on the honesty and professional reputation of the accountant to charge a fair fee.

Cost of an Audit

What does it cost to have an audit? This is a difficult question to answer because most CPA's charge on an hourly basis. If the organization's records are in good shape and up to date the time will be less. There is no way to know how much time will be involved without looking at the records and knowing something about the organization.

The hourly rates vary, depending on the individual assigned and his experience. Most examinations involve a combination of experienced and inexperienced staff members. In 1974 the hourly rates ranged from $18–$75, with an overall average effective rate of between $20–$28 an hour. This average rate is a composite. Most of the time spent on any audit will be by less experienced staff members whose billing rates will be lower than for the CPA in charge.

The only accurate way to find out what it will cost to have an audit is to call a CPA and ask him to make an estimate. Even then it will be difficult for him to know all the problems he may encounter and he will probably hedge on his estimate by indicating that while it is his best estimate the final amount might be more or less. Keep in mind that he is providing a professional service just as does a doctor or a lawyer.

Sometimes an organization will shop around in an effort to find the CPA that will charge it the least. While understandable, this makes about as much sense as choosing a doctor based on the rate he charges for an office visit. You get what you pay for. Since the salaries paid these men by the various firms are pretty much the same at any given level of competence, each CPA firm will charge about the same amount per hour for a staff member's services. The variable is the length of time it will take to perform the examination. Since the treasurer is not likely to be in a position to judge the quality of the work, he takes a risk if he chooses a professional accountant solely on the basis of an estimated fee. Choosing a CPA should be on the basis of reputation and willingness to serve the organization.

The "Big Eight" Accounting Firms

Many smaller organizations tend to feel that the major accounting firms, including the "big eight," won't be interested in serving a smaller nonprofit organization. This is not the case with most of these firms. There should be no hesitation in soliciting their interest, as well as smaller firms.

PUBLIC ACCOUNTANTS

So far we have talked about the advantages of bringing in a "certified public accountant." There are also "public accountants" in many states. What does the difference in title mean?

The certified public accountant is the "professional." He has been licensed by the state after proving his competency by passing a rigorous two-and-a-half-day examination, meeting certain educational requirements, and in most states, working for another CPA for a period of time. The CPA is continually accountable to the state. Only a CPA can join the American Institute of Certified Public Accountants.

The public accountant may or may not be licensed by the state. Where he is licensed, there are usually no examinations to pass or educational requirements to meet, and for the most part he can practice without experience. Nevertheless, the public accontant is often quite competent and can provide good and effective service to his clients, particularly in keeping the records or preparing financial statements. If an organization is going to hire an accountant to help keep the records, the public accountant may well be the right person to hire. But, as a general rule, it should retain a certified public accountant if it wants an audit to be made.

THE AUDIT COMMITTEE

Many smaller organizations do not feel they can afford a CPA (or a public accountant) and yet want some assurance that all disbursements have been made for properly approved purposes. One solution to this is to set up an "audit committee" consisting of several members of the board or of the membership. The purpose of this audit committee is usually to review all disbursements "after the fact" to make sure that all have been properly approved and documented. This review can take place at any time, but for convenience sake it is usually done some time after the payment has been made. This committee may meet on a monthly or bimonthly basis and review all transactions since the last meeting. They may also review bank reconciliations, marketable securities bought, sold and on hand, and any other matter which could be "sensitive."

The advantage of an audit committee is that it strengthens internal control significantly with little cost. This is particularly important where internal control is weak because it is not practical to segregate duties as much as might be desired.

The weakness of an audit committee is that it can become so routine and perfunctory that the committee does little effective auditing and is merely a rubber stamp. Probably the best way to see that this doesn't happen is to rotate the responsibility. Perhaps the past president, past treasurer and a member chosen from the board would constitute an effective and knowledgeable audit committee. Since both the president and treasurer have limited tenure, the audit committee would also automatically change with time.

There is also a risk that the board will get a false sense of security with an audit committee. The committee members are usually not trained accountants and might very well miss clues that a CPA would see. Also, this committee is essentially looking at only disbursements and is making no test of receipts. All of this means that an audit committee has some limitation although it clearly is better to have such a committee than to have no committee at all.

SUMMARY

We have discussed the principal advantages of retaining a certified public accountant to make an audit of nonprofit organizations. In addition to providing "credibility" to the financial statements, the CPA also can provide advice for improving the format of the financial statements to make them more effective in communicating to the reader. He can offer suggestions to improve internal controls and administrative efficiency. In addition, in this increasingly complex society of rules and reports, he is an expert and can help an organization comply with the many reporting requirements.

The importance of hiring the right CPA was discussed and some suggested procedures to follow were outlined. As with any professional, it is important to find a CPA who is interested in serving your organization. This is largely a personal judgment and one that each organization has to make based on interviews and the reputation of the accountant. The difference between a "public accountant" and a "certified public accountant" was discussed. While there are many competent public accountants, the CPA is the professional and therefore is the accountant that should be hired if an audit is needed. The use of an audit committee was suggested as one way in which internal control could be strengthened.

22

Investments

Some nonprofit organizations have an investment program to manage resulting from receipt of endowment funds and other restricted gifts. In addition, some organizations also have excess cash in their general fund which can be invested. Together all of these investment funds can be very sizable. They are usually invested in publicly traded securities, although occasionally part may be invested in real estate or in mortgages.

One of the practical problems faced by the nonprofit organization is how to handle its investment program where there are a number of separate funds, each with amounts available for investment. The question that arises is whether investments should be made on a separate fund-by-fund basis or whether all investments should be pooled together in one pot. This chapter discusses the concept of pooling of investments and shows how to keep the appropriate records. Some sources of investment advice are given, along with the considerations a treasurer must take into account in providing physical safeguards over the securities themselves.

POOLING VERSUS INDIVIDUAL INVESTMENTS

Typically, most organizations have a number of different individual funds, each having cash that can be invested. These individual funds may include board-designated endowment funds, as well as donor-designated endowment funds. Within these fund groupings there are frequently many individual "name" funds. All of this means that a nonprofit organization can have a number of separate accounting entities which have assets invested in marketable securities. This is where some practical problems arise.

The organization can, of course, invest the money of each individual fund in specific securities and keep track of the actual income and gain or loss associated with these specific investments. If it does so, there is no question about the amount of income, or the gain or loss associated with each separate fund.

But for many organizations, the cash available for investment in each fund is not large enough to make individual purchases. If purchases were made on an individual fund basis there probably would be little diversification. Yet the aggregate of the investable assets of all individual funds could be sizable enough to provide a good portfolio if all of the assets were invested together as an investment pool.

This is what many organizations do. They pool all of their investment funds together and prorate the resulting income and gains or losses.

Example of Individual Investments for Each Fund

An example will illustrate the difference in these two approaches. The Johnstown Museum has investments aggregating about $200,000. It follows the approach of making specific investments for each fund. What the portfolio looked like at December 31, 1973 is shown at the top of the next page.

As is typical, some of the individual investments have done better than others but on an overall basis, market value is a third above cost. Since the museum keeps track of its portfolio by individual fund, the gain or loss and the income for each of these funds are based on the actual investments in each fund. As can be seen the board-designated endowment fund had income of $3,900, and if the organization were to sell all of these investments there would be a capital gain of $55,000. On the other hand, the R. A. Adler Fund has had a decline in value of $25,000.

One of the problems of making investments on an individual fund basis is that there are usually some amounts of cash which

	Cost	Market 12/31/73	Income Year 1973
Board-designated endowment fund			
1,000 shares of Stock A	$ 20,000	$ 45,000	$1,400
500 shares of Stock B	20,000	40,000	1,500
1,000 shares of Stock C	40,000	50,000	1,000
Uninvested cash	15,000	15,000	
	95,000	150,000	3,900
Endowment fund—W. H. Miller			
1,000 shares of Stock D	9,000	31,000	1,500
100 shares of Stock E	5,000	3,000	100
Uninvested cash	1,000	1,000	
	15,000	35,000	1,600
Endowment fund—R. A. Adler			
500 shares of Stock F	37,500	12,500	500
Uninvested cash	2,500	2,500	
	40,000	15,000	500
Total all funds	$150,000	$200,000	$6,000

are too small to be individually invested. In this case the Johnstown Museum has a total of $18,500 of uninvested cash in all of its funds, which is large enough that it should be put to work.

Example of Pooled Investments

There is a fair amount of paper work involved in keeping track of specific investments by individual funds. Pooling all investments and putting them into one pot eliminates the need to keep track of the individual purchases by specific fund. It also provides a larger investment fund which helps to cushion the effect of any single poor investment decision. In the case of the 500 shares of stock F, which has declined in value, the effect on the R. A. Adler Fund is devastating. It is worth a fraction of its original $40,000. On the other hand, if stock F had been pooled with the other stocks, the effect on the Adler Fund would have been only a prorata portion. Likewise, the large gain on stock D in the Miller Fund would have been spread over all of the funds. The principal advantage of pooling is that it spreads the risk uniformly over all of the pooled funds. A second advantage is that the total uninvested cash is usually lower. And, as noted above, a third advantage is simplified record keeping.

Let us now examine how these funds would have looked if the museum had been on a pooled basis. For the sake of simplicity it is assumed that no investments have been sold since the original principal was established in each fund and that all funds were established on the same date, January 1, 1969. Accordingly, each fund has been assigned "shares" on the basis of one share for each dollar transferred to the investment pool. Here is what the individual funds would look like at December 31, 1973:

	Number of Shares	Cost	Market 12/31/73	Income for 1973
Board-designated fund	95,000	$ 95,000	$126,666	$3,800
Endowment fund				
W. H. Miller	15,000	15,000	20,000	600
R. A. Adler	40,000	40,000	53,334	1,600
	150,000	$150,000	$200,000	$6,000
Per share		$1.00	$1.33	$.04

The number of shares in each fund represents the original amount pooled as, in this example, $1.00 per share. The market value per share is simply the aggregate portfolio market value (including uninvested cash) divided by the number of shares (i.e., $200,000 ÷ 150,000 shares = $1.33). The market value for each individual fund is the value per share of $1.33 times the number of shares in each fund. Likewise, the overall per-share income of $.04 is first calculated ($6,000 ÷ 150,000 shares) and then the individual fund income amounts are arrived at by multiplying $.04 times the number of shares.

When a comparison is made of the market value of each fund on a pooled basis to the market value on an individual investment basis, it will be seen that there are significant differences. The Adler Fund is the most conspicuous example because the market on the pooled basis is now $53,334 compared to only $15,000 before.

Distribution of the income on a pooled basis is also based on shares, and as can be seen the Adler Fund is again a beneficiary of this method.

CALCULATING SHARE VALUES IN POOLED INVESTMENTS

The discussion above has been centered on a relatively simple illustration showing the principles involved in pooling. It was assumed that all of the funds pooled their money on the same date, and accordingly each fund received shares with a "cost" of the same amount per share. In practice this doesn't happen except for the single date when the pool is set up. At subsequent dates the market value per share will be higher or lower, and additions or withdrawals to and from the pool must obviously be at the then existing per-share market value.

Let us look at the transactions that took place in the Johnstown Museum portfolio in 1974:

March 31: The board transferred $40,500 from the general fund to the board-designated fund.

August 10: The board finds it transferred more than it should have and needs to redeem some of its shares. It transferred $14,300 from the board-designated fund back to the general fund as of the end of the calendar quarter.

December 31: The board received a large contribution for addition to the R. A. Adler Fund.

Figure 22–1 shows a calculation of the share values at the end of each of the calendar quarters. The market value of the portfolio is determined, based on actual market values on these dates plus all uninvested cash.

Generally, organizations calculate share values only at the end of the calendar quarter. If the board wants to buy or redeem shares during a period between quarters, the value of the shares purchased or redeemed is based on the value at the end of the quarter in which the request to purchase or redeem is made. Thus, if the board decides to redeem some of the shares in the board-designated fund on August 10, the transaction does not take place until the next date on which share values are calculated. In this case, this would be the end of the quarter, September 30. If the board wanted to calculate share values on August 10, the transaction could be effected on that date.

JOHNSTOWN MUSEUM

CALCULATION OF SHARE VALUES FOR PURPOSES
OF PURCHASING AND REDEEMING SHARES

By Quarter for 1974

Date	Shares Outstanding Before Purchase or Redemption	Market Value Before Purchase or Redemptions	Value Per Share	Shares Purchased (Redeemed) This Date		Shares Outstanding After Purchase or Redemption	Market Value After Purchase or Redemption
				Shares*	Amount		
12/31/73	150,000	$200,000	$1.33	—	—	150,000	$200,000
3/31/74	150,000	202,500	1,35	30,000	$40,500	180,000	243,000
6/30/74	180,000	252,000	1.40	—	—	180,000	252,000
9/30/74	180,000	257,400	1.43	(10,000)	(14,300)	170,000	243,100
12/31/74	170,000	238,000	1.40	10,000	14,000	180,000	252,000

*The number of shares purchased or redeemed is determined by dividing the amount invested or withdrawn by the value per share.

Fig. 22–1. A worksheet showing how to calculate share values for a pooled investment fund.

Cost Basis Accounting

Although nonprofit organizations may carry their investments at either cost or market,* most keep their books on a "cost" basis. For organizations on a cost basis, marketable securities cannot be "written up" to reflect the market value of the portfolio. However, when a stock is sold, the realized gain or loss should be recorded.

There is no difficulty in determining the amount of gain or loss when individual stocks are purchased for a specific fund. It is quite clear which fund realized the gain or loss. On pooled investments, however, each fund shares in all realized gains or losses on a prorata basis. This presents a mechanical problem of allocation. From a practical standpoint, this allocation is usually not made each time a stock is sold unless such sales are made very infrequently. Instead, these gains or losses are accumulated and allocated at the end of the quarter, or at the end of the year if there has been no change in the number of shares outstanding.

An illustration may be helpful. Assume the following transactions take place during 1974:

March 10: 500 shares of Stock F are sold for $12,500 with a cost of $37,500, and a loss of $25,000.

August 15: 500 shares of Stock C are sold for $30,000 with a cost of $20,000, and a gain of $10,000.

September 15: 100 shares of Stock E are sold for $4,000 with a cost of $5,000, a loss of $1,000.

At the end of the first and third quarters the loss of $25,000 and net gain of $9,000 are allocated on the basis of shares as shown in the following statement.

---

* Both the Audit Guide for voluntary health and welfare organizations and the Audit Guide for colleges and universities permit the carrying of investments on a market value basis. See pages 90–93 for a more complete discussion.

| | March 31 | | September 30 | |
	Shares Outstanding *	Gain/(Loss) Allocated	Shares Outstanding *	Gain/(Loss) Allocated
Board-designated fund ..	95,000	($15,833)	125,000	$6,250
Endowment fund:				
W. H. Miller	15,000	(2,500)	15,000	750
R. A. Adler	40,000	(6,667)	40,000	2,000
	150,000	($25,000)	180,000	$9,000
Gain (loss)	($25,000)		$9,000	
Per share	($.16666)		$.05	

* The purchase and redemption of shares in Figure 22–1 have also been reflected here, but notice that the allocation is based on the number of shares before purchases or redemptions on that date.

Here is the balance in each of the individual funds at December 31, 1974, taking into consideration both gains and losses and purchases and redemptions shown in Figure 22–1:

	Number of Shares	Book Cost	Market Value (i.e. Share Value Times Number of Shares)
Board-designated fund	115,000	$111,617	$161,000
Endowment fund:			
W. H. Miller	15,000	13,250	21,000
R. A. Adler	50,000	49,333	70,000
	180,000	$174,200	$252,000

Each of these amounts was calculated at December 31, 1974, as follows:

	Shares	Book Cost
Board-designated fund		
December 31, 1973 balance	95,000	$ 95,000
March 31, allocation of loss	—	(15,833)
March 31, purchase of shares	30,000	40,500
September 30, allocation of gain (net)	—	6,250
September 30, redemption of shares	(10,000)	(14,300)
December 31, 1974 balance	115,000	$111,617

	Shares	Book Cost
W. H. Miller		
December 31, 1973 balance	15,000	$ 15,000
March 31, allocation of loss	—	(2,500)
September 30, allocation of gain (net)	—	750
December 31, 1974 balance	15,000	$ 13,250
R. A. Adler		
December 31, 1973 balance	40,000	$ 40,000
March 31, allocation of loss	—	(6,667)
September 30, allocation of gain (net)	—	2,000
December 31, purchase of shares	10,000	14,000
December 31, 1974 balance	50,000	$ 49,333

It should be emphasized that while the calculation of share values for purposes of purchases and redemptions of shares is based on the market value of the portfolio at date of valuation, this calculation is only for purposes of this purchase or redemption and is not recorded in the books. The books are kept on a cost basis adjusted only for realized gains or losses.*

ALLOCATION OF POOLED INCOME

There has been no discussion of the handling of income and interest received on pooled funds, but the mechanics of allocation are exactly the same as with the allocation of gains or losses. Generally, allocation of income is also made on a quarterly basis, although some organizations allocate on an annual basis. Investment income is usually not added back to the principal of the fund and reinvested. It is expended for the purposes specified by the donor or added to the general fund in the case of board-designated endowment funds. This means that as income is received it is put into a separate account. At the end of each quarter, it is allocated to each fund on a share basis. An organization could, of course, allocate more often than quarterly but this would complicate the bookkeeping.

Once the mechanics of these calculations are established they should not cause difficulty. It is important to formalize these

---

* Of course if an organization elects to carry its investments at market, then the books would be periodically adjusted to reflect unrealized gains and losses.

calculations in work sheets which should be made part of the records of the organization.

PROFESSIONAL INVESTMENT ADVICE

Let us turn now to a practical nonaccounting question. Where should an organization go to get good investment advice? The answer is clear: to a professional, to someone who knows the market, and is in the business of advising others.

You may feel that this skirts the question. Yet many medium and some large organizations try to outguess the market on their own and they usually don't succeed. They make all of the investment mistakes that many individuals do. They tend to rely on their own intuition and try to outguess the professionals. This doesn't make sense when an individual's own money is involved, and it makes even less sense when the money belongs to a nonprofit organization.

Sometimes the board, recognizing its fiduciary responsibilities, will tend to be too conservative in its investment policy, and will purchase high-grade, low-interest-bearing bonds. This conservatism can be almost as risky as purchasing a highly volatile stock, as many holders of bonds discovered in recent years when high interest rates depressed bond prices. This is why professional advice is needed.

There are a number of places to go for professional advice. If the total investments are relatively small in size (say, under $100,000), many organizations find that a no-load mutual fund or a bank common stock fund is the answer.* In both cases the organization is purchasing expertise when it pools its funds with those of many other people. Mutual funds offer a convenient way to obtain investment management when the organization has a minimum amount to invest.

---

* If an organization has under $100,000 to invest, the board should carefully consider the nature of the funds being invested before buying common stocks. If the funds available are to be invested for only a short period of time, or if investment income is essential, then the organization should not be investing in common stocks. Instead, a savings account is probably more appropriate.

There are several hundred mutual funds with different investment goals and varying degrees of risk. A good place to start looking for a mutual fund is the Forbes Magazine annual review of mutual funds published each August. This review gives a great deal of comparative information which should help pinpoint several funds to study.

Bank commingled or common stock investment funds are a form of mutual fund. One of the advantages of using a bank fund is that the reputation of the bank is involved and they pay close attention to the investments made. They are often more conservative than mutual funds in their investment decisions, but this may be appropriate when one considers the fiduciary nature of nonprofit organizations.

If the investment fund is larger in size (over $100,000) the organization may prefer to select a professional to advise on specific stocks and bonds to purchase for its own portfolio. Most brokers are pleased to offer this service. On the other hand many nonprofit organizations are reluctant to entrust investment decisions to the broker who handles the actual purchasing because he is wearing two hats. This can be avoided by going to one of the many investment advisory services that are available which do not themselves handle the actual purchasing or selling.

A list of investment advisory services can usually be found in the classified telephone directory. Bear in mind that, as with all professionals, the investment advisor's reputation should be carefully checked. The bank's trust department is usually also happy to give advice on investment decisions. The point to emphasize is that investment decisions should be made by professionals in the investment business and not by amateurs (this is as true of investments as it is of medicine!). And remember, too, that even professionals make errors in judgment.

The professional advisor will charge a fee which is generally calculated on the basis of a percentage of the monies invested. The larger the investment fund, the lower the rate charged. This rate will vary depending on the size of the fund, but frequently is in the range of $\frac{1}{2}$ to 1 per cent annually. The rate structure follows pretty closely the structure that investment advisors charge mutual funds.

SAFEGUARDING INVESTMENT SECURITIES

The physical safeguarding of an organization's investment securities is as important as making the right decision as to which stocks to buy or sell. This is often overlooked. There are three areas with which to be concerned. The first is to be sure the stock certificates aren't lost or misplaced through carelessness or poor handling. The second is that they are not lost through misappropriation by an employee. The third is that the stockbroker doesn't lose the certificates or, worse yet, go bankrupt. Let's look at the risks in each of these three areas.

Careless Handling. If the organization keeps the certificates in its possession, the certificates should be kept in a bank safe deposit box. They should be registered in the name of the organization. The organization should also maintain an investment register which shows the certificate number as well as cost and other financial information.* There should be limited access to the safe deposit box and it is wise to require the presence of two persons (preferably officers) whenever the box is opened.†

Some organizations become careless in handling the certificates because they are registered in their name. They know they can "stop transfer" if the certificates are lost. While this is usually true, most transfer agents will require the registered owner to post a bond before a replacement certificate is issued. The purpose of the bond is to protect the agent from any loss that might result from misuse of the lost certificate. The bond can be purchased from an insurance company, but it is expensive, ranging between 1 and 4 per cent of the market value of the lost certificate on the date the replacement certificate is issued. This is a high price to pay for carelessness.

Embezzlement. An organization must always be concerned that someone having access to stock certificates may be tempted to steal them. While the certificates may be registered in the

---

* An example of an investment register is shown on page 499.
† It is also wise for the board to establish an investment committee charged with the responsibility for authorizing all investment transactions. If an outside advisor is retained, this committee should still review the outside advisor's recommendations before they are accepted. It is not wise to delegate complete authority to an outside advisor to act without prior review by the investment committee.

organization's name, there is an underworld market for stolen certificates. Furthermore, if the loss is not discovered promptly and the transfer agent advised to "stop transfer," the organization's rights may be jeopardized.

The best control is to have the broker deliver the stock certificate directly to a custodian bank for safekeeping. When the stock is sold, the bank is then instructed to deliver the certificate to the broker. In this way, the organization never handles the certificate. The use of a custodian bank provides excellent internal control. There is, of course, a charge for this custodian service which usually ranges from $10–12 annually per issue held, plus a transaction charge of $10–15 for each purchase or sale. There is usually a minimum annual charge of $150–250.

Leaving Certificates With Brokers. Some organizations leave their certificates at the broker's office in his custody. This has certain risks. One is that the broker will temporarily lose track of the certificates if his back office falls behind in their paper work or incorrectly records the certificates in the wrong account. If this happened there might be some delay before the broker straightened out his records. This is a risk that cannot be completely avoided since the broker must buy or sell the stock. But it increases if the organization also has him hold the certificate in safekeeping. As long as the broker doesn't go bankrupt, the worst that is likely to happen is that there will be a delay in getting the certificates when the organization wants them. This risk can be minimized by making inquiries as to the broker's reputation for handling his back office problems.

The other risk is the broker going bankrupt while he is holding the stock. Provided he has not fraudulently hypothecated the stock, a broker's bankruptcy should not result in a loss to an organization. However, there could be considerable delay before the stock is released by a court. On the other hand, if the broker has, without the consent of the organization, pledged this stock for his own borrowings there is a possibility of actual loss. While the organization might be able to take both civil and criminal action against the broker, this would be of little consolation if he were bankrupt. The first $50,000 of such losses, however, would be recovered from the federally chartered Securities Investor Protection Corporation.

While these risks might be relatively small, a nonprofit organization has a fiduciary responsibility to act with more than ordinary care and judgment. Accordingly, it would be prudent for an organization to have the broker deliver the stock certificates in the organization's name, either to a custodian bank or to the organization.

Conclusion

The board of a nonprofit organization has an obligation to act prudently in all of its actions. When it comes to handling investments, very few boards are competent to make informed professional decisions. Accordingly, professional advice should be obtained to ensure that the organization's investments are wisely made. For very small organizations often this can be accomplished by choosing a mutual fund or bank common stock fund. For larger organizations a professional advisor should be retained.

The board should not overlook its responsibility for security of its stock certificates. The most effective arrangement is to have the broker deliver all certificates to a custodian bank. In this way neither the employees of the organization or the broker have access to the certificates.

PART V

TAX AND
COMPLIANCE REPORTING
REQUIREMENTS

23

Principal Federal Tax and Compliance Requirements

Congress has imposed an income tax on all individuals and organizations with few exceptions. Those organizations that are exempt from such tax are known as "exempt" organizations. Generally nonprofit organizations are "exempt" organizations if they meet certain specific criteria as to purpose for which formed and their source of income is related to that purpose. But even "exempt" organizations can be subject to tax on certain portions of their income, and if they are a "private foundation" they are subject to a number of very specific rules as well as certain "excise taxes." The purpose of this chapter is to discuss generally the types of organizations that are exempt and the general provisions of the rules governing such organizations from a tax standpoint.

This discussion is intended only to give the reader a general understanding of the tax rules and is not intended to be a complete discussion of the law and the tax regulations. Each organization should consult with its own tax accountant or attorney about its own status and any specific problems it may have.

ORGANIZATIONS "EXEMPT" FROM TAX

The Internal Revenue Code provides exemption from tax for certain very specific organizations. The most widely applicable of these exemptions are:

1. "Corporations, and any community chest, fund or foundation, organized and operated exclusively for religious, charitable, scientific, testing for public safety, literary, or educational purposes, or for the prevention of cruelty to children or animals, no part of the net earnings of which inures to the benefit of any private shareholder or individual, no substantial part of the activities of which is carrying on propaganda, or otherwise attempting to influence legislation, and which does not participate in, or intervene in (including the publishing or distributing of statements), any political campaign on behalf of any candidate for public office." 501(c)3 *

2. Clubs organized and operated exclusively for pleasure, recreation, and other nonprofitable purposes, no part of the net earnings of which inures to the benefit of any private shareholder. 501(c)7

3. "Business leagues, chambers of commerce, . . . not organized for profit . . ." 501(c)6

4. "Corporations organized for the exclusive purpose of holding title to property, collecting income therefrom, and turning over the entire amount thereof, less expenses, to an organization which itself is exempt . . ." 501(c)2

There are other exempt organizations, but the ones listed above are the organizations primarily applicable to nonprofit organizations. Most organizations fall under the first exemption, the "501(c)3" exemption. It should be noted that there are four purposes that organizations exempt under Section "501(c)3" can have: religious, charitable, scientific, or educational. This covers organizations such as churches, hospitals, schools, community funds, museums, medical research organizations, YMCAs, etc.

The other exemption most applicable to this discussion is the second one pertaining to social clubs, "501(c)7." This would include country clubs, swim clubs, women's clubs and any social clubs operated exclusively for pleasure and recreation.

Further Categories of Exempt Organizations

The Tax Reform Act of 1969 created two general categories of "exempt" organizations with different rules and benefits for each: "private foundations," and "other than a private foundation." For

---

* References are to specific sections of the Internal Revenue Code from which the quotation was taken. Exempt organizations often refer to their type of exemption by reference to this section.

purposes of this discussion, organizations other than a private foundation are referred to as "publicly supported organizations."

> "Publicly supported organizations"—these are the organizations that receive public support and there are a minimum of rules that apply to these organizations. An individual donor can normally deduct from his own taxable income contributions up to 50 per cent of his adjusted gross income.

> "Private foundations"—these are organizations that do not receive broad public support. Private foundations are subject to many restrictions on their activities and are subject to certain taxes including a tax on failure to distribute income. Normally an individual donor can only deduct contributions up to 20 per cent of his adjusted gross income unless the private foundation makes qualifying distributions within 2½ months of the end of the fiscal year.

Publicly Supported Organizations

A "publicly supported organization" is defined for this discussion as a "501(c)3" * organization that is not a private foundation.† There are three principal categories of organizations that are not private foundations. These three categories are as follows:

1. Organizations organized exclusively for religious, charitable, scientific, literary or educational purposes that normally receive a substantial portion of their receipts from direct or indirect contributions from the general public or from a governmental unit. Also excluded are churches, educational institutions with a faculty and student body, hospitals and medical research organizations related to a hospital.

2. Organizations that meet both of the following "mechanical" tests, based on actual "support" during the previous four years:

* Organizations exempt under another section of the law, such as social clubs, business leagues, etc. are not private foundations.

† There are some organizations that are not private foundations which do not receive broad public support. However, these organizations are subject to the same rules that organizations receiving broad public support are subject to; accordingly, in order to assist the reader in distinguishing between private foundations and other than private foundations, the title "publicly supported" organizations will be used throughout this discussion to refer to all "501(c)3" organizations not private foundations.

(a) The organization receives not more than one third of its support from gross investment income, and

(b) The organization receives more than one third of its support from a combination of:

    (1) Contributions, gifts, grants, membership fees, except from "disqualified persons," * and

    (2) gross receipts from admissions, sale of merchandise, performance of services, all of which must be in an activity related to the organization's exempt purpose. Excluded from gross receipts are any amounts from any one person, governmental unit, or company in excess of $5,000 or 1 per cent of total support (whichever is greater).

3. Organizations organized and operated exclusively for the benefit of an exempt publicly supported organization.

Mechanical Test. Most organizations that receive broad public support will qualify under the first category.† There are many other organizations, however, that do not receive broad public support which will nevertheless qualify for the non-private foundation status under the so-called "mechanical" test. This mechanical test is complicated because of the limitation on support from "disqualified" persons and receipts from individual sources. Here are several examples that show how these mechanical tests work.

Example 1:

Contributions:

Individual gifts of less than $5,000	$75,000	
Gift from Mrs. Stanneck	50,000	$125,000
Investment income		55,000
Total income (support)		$180,000

Test 1: Investment income must be less than one third of total support.

---

* A disqualified person is basically a substantial contributor, or a foundation manager, or a person having a sizable interest in a corporation which is itself a substantial contributor. A substantial contributor is a person who has contributed in either the current or a prior year $5,000, if that amount at the time of the contribution was 2 per cent or more of total contributions received since formation of the foundation. A foundation manager is any officer, director, or trustee of the foundation.

† There is a specific mathematical test for determining whether an organization receives broad public support. For the sake of clarity it has been omitted here.

$$\frac{\text{Investment income}}{\text{Total support}} \quad \frac{55,000}{180,000} = 30.6\%$$

Investment income is less than 33.3 per cent and therefore this test is met.

Test 2: Total qualified support must be more than one third of total support.

$$\frac{\text{Individual gifts}}{\text{Total support}} \quad \frac{75,000}{180,000} = 41.6\%$$

Qualified support is more than 33.3 per cent and therefore this test is met. Since the organization meets both of these tests, it is not considered a private foundation; therefore it is a "publicly supported organization."

Example 2:

Contributions:		
Individual gifts of less than $5,000	$110,000	
Gifts from "disqualified" persons	140,000	$250,000
Gross receipts from services:		
Receipts of less than $6,600 per donor *	90,000	
Receipts of more than $6,600 per donor	160,000	250,000
Investment income		160,000
Total income (support)		$660,000

* $6,600 is 1 percent of total support of $660,000. If total support had been less than $500,000, then the limitation would have been $5,000.

Test 1: Investment income must be less than one third of total support.

$$\frac{\text{Investment income}}{\text{Total support}} \quad \frac{160,000}{660,000} = 24.2\%$$

Investment income is less than 33.3 per cent and therefore this test is met.

Test 2: Total qualified support must be more than one third of total support.

$$\frac{\text{Qualified support (\$110,000 + \$90,000)}}{\text{Total support}} \quad \frac{200,000}{660,000} = 30.3\%$$

Qualified support is less than 33.3 per cent and therefore this test is not met. Accordingly this organization is a "private foundation."

These examples are presented only to show generally how these rules are applied. There are a number of exceptions to these rules and each organization should consult with legal or tax counsel to determine exactly how these rules affect it. Also, keep in mind that this mechanical test is applied only to organizations with four years' experience. Younger organizations having at least one year's experience can obtain a "temporary" exemption until they have four years' experience, at which time the above tests are applied.

Facts and Circumstances Test.   For newly formed organizations, or for organizations that do not meet one of the three categories of publicly supported organizations listed above, the Internal Revenue Service is allowed to apply a "facts and circumstances" test. If all the "facts and circumstances" indicate that the organization is, in fact, a publicly supported organization, the IRS can classify it as a publicly supported organization. However, even here the IRS requires that an organization show it can reasonably expect to obtain at least 10 per cent of its support from qualified public sources.

REGISTRATION AND REPORTING

Initial Registration

All charitable organizations except churches and certain organizations having annual gross receipts of less than $5,000 must comply with Internal Revenue Service notification requirements before they are considered "exempt" from tax. After reviewing the "notification" received from the organization, the IRS sends an "exemption" letter confirming the tax-exempt status of the organization.

For charitable organizations the "notification" should be on Form 1023. Other categories of exempt organizations (social clubs, business leagues, etc.) must also file a notification but different forms are used.

A second notification is required for those charitable organizations claiming not to be private foundations. If an organization fails to apply for this "not a private foundation" status, then it will be presumed to be a private foundation, with all of the consequences associated with this status. Churches are exempt from this second notification requirement as are charitable organizations with annual gross receipts of less than $5,000.

Annual Information Returns

Almost all exempt organizations are required to file annual information returns. The principal exceptions to this reporting requirement are churches and certain religious organizations, and certain organizations having gross receipts of $5,000 or less.

This annual information return includes information on income, receipts, contributions, disbursements, assets and liabilities, and names and addresses of substantial contributors.

These information returns must be filed by the fifteenth day of the fifth month after the end of the fiscal year (May 15 for calendar year organizations). There is a penalty of $10 a day on an organization that fails to file this return. Extensions of time for filing can usually be obtained if there is good reason why the return cannot be filed on a timely basis, but application for extension must be made before the filing deadline. These returns do not require certification by an outside auditor.

In addition to this return, all exempt organizations having unrelated business income of $1,000 or more must file a separate tax return and pay taxes at regular corporate rates on all taxable income over $1,000. Unrelated business income is discussed later on in this chapter. Chapter 24 discusses the annual reporting forms principally used by exempt nonprofit organizations.

PRIVATE FOUNDATIONS

There are many specific rules and taxes that apply to private foundations which are not applicable to publicly supported organizations. The most important are:

1. A 4 per cent excise tax on investment income.
2. All net income (as defined) must be distributed.
3. Excess business holdings must be disposed of.

4. Certain transactions are prohibited, and if made, are considered "taxable expenditures."

5. An annual report must be published.

Excise Tax on Investment Income

The Tax Reform Act of 1969 established a 4 per cent excise tax on net investment income. Net investment income includes not only dividends, interests and royalties but also net capital gains and losses.* For purposes of calculating gain on investments acquired prior to December 31, 1969, the fair market value at December 31, 1969 is considered the tax basis or "cost." In calculating net investment income, reasonable expenses can be deducted. An example of the excise tax applied to a private foundation that had stocks and bonds which were acquired both before and after December 31, 1969, follows:

		Taxable Income
Dividends and interest		$ 10,000
Sale of stock A for $45,000 purchased in 1967, at a cost of $20,000, but having a market value at December 31, 1969 of $30,000		
Proceeds	$ 45,000	
December 31, 1969 value	(30,000)	
Gain		15,000
Sale of stock B for $20,000 purchased in 1968 at a cost of $15,000, but having a market value at December 31, 1969 of $25,000		
Proceeds	$ 20,000	
December 31, 1969 value	(25,000)	
Difference, not recognized for tax purposes. No loss is recognized if using the December 31, 1969 market value creates a loss	$ (5,000)	
Sale of stock C for $15,000 purchased in 1970 at a cost of $20,000		
Proceeds of sale	$ 15,000	
Cost	(20,000)	
Loss		(5,000)
Net		20,000
Less investment advisory fees and other expenses		(2,000)
Net investment income		$ 18,000
Tax at 4%		$ 720

* Capital losses can be offset only against capital gains and not against investment income.

It is obviously important to keep accurate accounting records of the cost basis for all investments as well as an accurate segregation of any expenses applicable to investment income. With respect to investments acquired prior to December 31, 1969, it is obviously also important to keep a record of the fair market value as of December 31, 1969.

Tax Consequences of Gifts of Securities

On investments received by gift subsequent to December 31, 1969, the contributor's tax basis is the "cost" basis which must be used when the investment is ultimately sold for purposes of calculating taxable gain. For investments received prior to December 31, 1969, the basis is the higher of fair market value at December 31, 1969 or contributor's tax basis. In most instances the fair market value would be higher. Thus a private foundation must obtain at the time a gift of securities is received, a statement from the donor stating his tax basis.* This is very important and great care should be taken to obtain this information promptly upon receipt of the gift. At a later date the donor may be difficult to locate or he may have lost his tax records. Since donated securities are recorded for accounting purposes at fair market value at date of receipt, the foundation must keep supplementary memo records of the donor's tax basis.

Here is an illustration of how two gifts of the same marketable security can have different tax consequences to the private foundation. Both gifts made in 1974 involve 100 shares of stock A.

Gift 1—very low basis:

Mr. Jones acquired his 100 shares of stock A in 1933 when the company was founded. His cost was only 10 cents a share, and therefore his basis for these 100 shares was only $10. Market value on the date of gift was $90 a share, or a total of $9,000. The tax basis to Mr. Jones of $10 carries over to the private foundation. If the foundation later sells the stock for $10,000 it will pay a 4 per cent tax on $9,990 ($10,000 sales proceeds less $10 tax basis), or a tax of $399.60.

* If a donor contributes a gift of $50,000 or more to an exempt organization, he is required to file a statement within 90 days with the IRS on Form 4629 stating the fair market value of such gift. Form 4629 does not provide for reporting the taxpayer's basis. It should be noted that this Form is filed with the IRS, and not with the exempt organization.

Gift 2—very high basis:

Mr. Smith acquired his 100 shares of stock A in 1970 at a cost of $110 a share or a total of $11,000. The market value on the date of his gift was also $90 a share, or a total of $9,000. If the private foundation later sells this stock for $10,000 it will have neither a taxable gain or loss. In this instance the donor's basis of $110 a share carries over to the foundation for purposes of calculating taxable gain, but for purposes of calculating *loss,* the fair market value at date of gift ($90 a share) becomes the tax basis. Since the sales price ($100) is more than the fair market value at the date of gift ($90), but less than the donor's cost ($110) there is no gain or loss recognized.

As can be seen from this example, in one instance the private foundation had to pay a tax of $399.60 and in the other instance had no tax. To the extent a private foundation has capital losses, they can be offset against capital gains in the same year. If there are no capital gains to offset such losses, the losses cannot be offset against investment income. Capital losses cannot be carried over to another year.

Distribution of Income

A private foundation is required to make "qualifying distributions" of at least the "distributable amount" by the end of the year following the year of receipt. Qualifying distributions are those amounts paid to accomplish the exempt purposes of the foundation. If this is not done, taxes are imposed which ultimately have the effect of taxing 100 per cent any amount not so distributed.

The "distributable amount" is the higher of (a) adjusted net income or (b) minimum investment return, both less 4 per cent excise tax. Adjusted net income for this purpose means gross income, including unrelated trade or business income and investment income, less expenses related directly thereto. "Adjusted net income" excludes gifts and contributions and long-term capital gains.

Minimum investment return for 1974 has been arbitrarily set at 5½ per cent * of the fair market value of all the foundation's assets

---

* This applies to organizations formed before May 27, 1969. The 1974 percentage for organizations formed after this date is 6. These percentages change each year.

which are not used in directly carrying out the exempt purpose. Cash equal to 1½ per cent of the total foundation's assets are deemed to be used in carrying out the exempt purpose, and are deducted for this calculation. This means that if a foundation has marketable securities and cash with a market value of $1,000,000 it must make minimum qualifying distributions of 5½ per cent of $985,000 ($1,000,000 less 1½ per cent of $1,000,000) or $54,175 regardless of its actual income. If, for example, actual investment income were only $30,000, the foundation would still have to make qualifying distributions of $54,175.

It should be emphasized that contributions or gifts are not included in the calculation of "distributable amount." This means that the private foundation will not have to make qualifying distributions out of principal provided its investment income plus contributions and gifts equal the distributable amount. In the illustration in the preceding paragraph, if contributions to the foundation were, say, $50,000, the distributable amount would still be $54,175. It would appear that these requirements will have little effect on private foundations that receive continuing contribution support and have a continuing program.

Here is an illustration showing how these calculations work. In the A. C. Williams Foundation financial statements, shown on the next page, the distributable amount is the higher of adjusted net income or minimum investment income. Using the figures given, this is calculated as follows:

Adjusted net income:

Investment income	$ 30,000
Unrelated business income	20,000
Less expenses related to unrelated business income	(10,000)
	$ 40,000

Minimum investment income:

Average fair market value of securities and cash	$1,000,000
Less 1½% of above amount for cash deemed to be used in carrying out the exempt purpose	(15,000)
Net, subject to stipulated minimum investment return	985,000
Stipulated rate of return	5½%
	$ 54,175

Distributable amount—the higher of:

Adjusted net income	$40,000
Less 4% excise tax	(4,000)
	$36,000

or

Minimum investment income	$54,175
Less 4% excise tax	(4,000)
	$50,175

Thus the distributable amount is $50,175. Qualifying distributions were $70,000, which exceeds the distributable amount by $19,825, and the requirement has thus been met. This $19,825 excess can be carried over for 5 years to meet the requirements of a year in which there is a deficiency. Where there is such a carryover, the order of application of the amounts distributed would be: current year, carryover from earliest year, carryover from next earliest year, and so forth.

A. C. WILLIAMS FOUNDATION

SUMMARY OF RECEIPTS AND EXPENDITURES

Receipts:

Contributions	$140,000	
Investment income	30,000	
Unrelated business income	20,000	
Long-term capital gains	10,000	$ 200,000

Expenditures:

For exempt purposes	70,000	
Expenses of unrelated business	10,000	
4% Excise tax*	4,000	84,000
Net		$ 116,000

ASSETS

Cash		$ 30,000
Marketable securities		970,000
Fund balance		$1,000,000

---

*This tax is paid in the current year based on investment income in the prior year. In this case investment income including capital gains in the prior year was $100,000.

Excess Business Holdings

A private foundation is not allowed to own a stock interest in a corporation if the stock it owns together with the stock owned by "disqualified" persons * would exceed 20 per cent of the voting stock.

Here is an example. Mr. Scotty owns together with his family 15 per cent of the voting stock in the A. M. Scotty Company, and he is a "substantial" contributor to the "Scotty Foundation" and thus is a "disqualified person." The maximum amount of stock that the Scotty Foundation can own is 5 per cent (20 per cent maximum less 15 per cent). There are several minor exceptions to this general rule, and there is a transitional period for foundations to dispose of their pre-1969 "excess" holdings. Failure to comply with these rules will result in taxes which can be as high as 200 per cent of the value of the excess stock held.

Prohibited Transactions (Taxable Expenditures)

There are several categories of transactions that private foundations may not engage in. They cannot engage in "self-dealing," make investments that jeopardize their exempt purpose, or make expenditures for certain purposes. If such transactions are made they become "taxable expenditures." There is an excise tax on both the foundation and the foundation manager making these taxable expenditures which is initially 10 per cent and 2½ per cent respectively, but is increased to 100 per cent and 50 per cent if corrective action is not taken.

Self-dealing. The law prohibits private foundations from having transactions with "disqualified" persons,* or foundation managers. These prohibited "self-dealing" transactions include the sale, leasing, or lending of property or money, the furnishing of goods or services on a basis more favorable than to the general public, or the payment of unreasonable compensation. All transactions involving one of these persons should be examined very closely to make absolutely certain they do not involve "self-dealing."

---

* A "disqualified person" is defined in the footnote on page 386.

Investments That Jeopardize Exempt Function. The law provides that the foundation may not make investments that jeopardize the exempt function of the foundation. Thus, the foundation is expected to use a "prudent trustee's approach" in making investments. Examples of investments that probably would not be prudent would be investments made on margin, commodity future transactions, trading in warrants, etc.

Prohibited Expenditures. The law provides that a foundation may not make expenditures to carry on propaganda to influence legislation or the outcome of a public election. It also prohibits making a grant to an individual for travel or study unless it can be shown the grant was a tax-exempt scholarship to be used at an educational institution, or was a tax-exempt prize in recognition of a specific achievement, or was a grant for the purpose of achieving a specific product or report. The law also provides no grant shall be made to another *private* foundation unless the granting foundation exercises expenditure control over the grant to see that it is expended solely for the purposes granted. Finally, the law prohibits a private foundation from making any grant for any purpose other than a charitable purpose.

Annual Reports

In addition to the annual information return (Form 990–PF) filed with the IRS, every private foundation having assets of $5,000 is required to file a special annual report, usually on Form 990–AR. Chapter 24 discusses this annual report and illustrates a completed form.

A private foundation must also publish a notice in a newspaper broadly circulated in the county where its principal office is located stating that a copy of this annual report is available for inspection by anyone desiring to see it at the organization's office within six months of date of publication.

PRIVATE "OPERATING" FOUNDATION

Private "operating" foundations are private foundations that actively carry out program activities which are the exempt function for which the organization was founded. This is in contrast to private foundations that act only as a conduit for funds and have no operating program as such. These private operating foundations have most of the characteristics of publicly supported organizations but do not meet the tests outlined for such organizations, discussed earlier in this chapter.

Qualifying Tests

In addition to expending substantially all (85 per cent) of its income directly for the active conduct of its exempt function, a private foundation, to be a private "operating" foundation, must meet one or more of the following tests:

1. It devotes 65 per cent or more of its assets to its exempt function.
2. Two thirds of its "minimum investment return" (see page 392) is devoted to its exempt function.
3. It derives 85 per cent or more of its support other than investment income from the general public and from five or more exempt organizations, no one of which provides more than 25 per cent. In addition not more than 50 per cent of its total support is from investment income.

Advantages

The advantage of being a private operating foundation is that the minimum distribution rules which private foundations are subject to do not apply, and the contributor receives the same tax treatment for his contribution as he would receive if the foundation were a publicly supported organization. See page 401.

UNRELATED BUSINESS INCOME

Virtually every exempt organization, including churches and clubs, is subject to normal corporate taxes on its unrelated business income. There is a transitional rule for churches which exempts them from this tax on unrelated businesses owned before 1970, but starting in 1976 these businesses will also be subject to this tax. Churches are currently subject to such taxes on any businesses acquired after 1969 and on any unrelated business income arising from "debt-financed" transactions.

Definition

There is always difficulty in knowing exactly what is unrelated business income. Here is the way the law reads:

"The term 'unrelated trade or business' means . . . any trade or business the conduct of which is not substantially related . . . to the exercise or performance by such organization of its charitable, educational, or other purpose or function constituting the basis for its exemption . . ." (Sec. 513(a) of the Internal Revenue Code).

". . . the term 'unrelated business income' means the gross income derived by any organization from any unrelated trade or business . . . regularly carried on by it, less the deductions . . . which are directly connected . . ." (Sec. 512(a)(1) of the Internal Revenue Code).

There are two key phrases in these definitions. The first is "unrelated" trade or business, and the second is "regularly carried on." Both must be present. It is not difficult to determine if the business in question is "regularly carried on," but it is difficult to know what is truly unrelated. The burden, however, is on the exempt organization to justify exclusion of any income from this tax.

Exclusions. There are a few exemptions to this tax. They include, among others, income from research activities in a hospital, college, or university, income from a business in which substantially all the people working for the business do so without compensation, and income from the sale of merchandise donated to the organization. There are special rules for social clubs which are discussed on page 404.

Also excluded from unrelated business income is passive investment income such as dividends, interest, royalties, rents from real property and gains on sale of property. However, rents which are based on a percentage of the net income of the property are considered "unrelated." Private foundations must still pay the 4 per cent excise tax on these items of passive income.

Advertising Income. One of the categories of unrelated business income which was clearly spelled out in the 1969 Act was income from advertising. Many exempt organizations publish magazines that contain advertising. While this advertising helps to pay the cost of the publication, which may itself be an exempt function, this advertising is nevertheless considered to be "unrelated business income." The advertising is not directly part of the exempt function, and therefore is taxable. The fact that the activity helps pay for exempt functions is not enough. It must be itself part of the exempt function. This is the distinction that must be made.

Caveats. As is indicated in the above quotation from the tax law, the organization is allowed to deduct the costs normally associated with the unrelated business. This places a burden on the organization to keep its records in a manner that will support its business deductions. Overhead can be applied, but the organization must be able to justify both the method of allocation and the reasonableness of the resulting amount. Also keep in mind that if after all expenses and allocation of overhead, the organization ends up with a loss, it will have to be able to convincingly explain why it engages in an activity that loses money. Logically no one goes into business to lose money and if there is a loss the allocation of expenses to that business is immediately suspect.

Tax Rates on Unrelated Business Income

Unrelated business income is taxed at the same rates as net income for corporations. This means that after a special $1,000 exemption, the first $25,000 of net income will be taxed at 22 per cent, and the balance at 48 per cent.* All exempt organizations having gross income from unrelated business activities of $1,000 or more are required to file Form 990-T within 2½ months of the end of the fiscal year (March 15 for calendar year organizations). Extensions can be obtained if applied for before the due date of the return.

---

* Rates in effect in 1974.

Need for Competent Tax Advice

From the above discussion, it should be obvious that taxes on unrelated business income are sizable and can apply to most organizations. It must be emphasized that every organization contemplating an income-producing activity should consult with competent tax counsel to determine the potential tax implications of that activity.

SUMMARY OF INDIVIDUAL TAX DEDUCTIONS

Nonprofit organizations depend to a very large extent on individual contributions for support. To the extent that a contributor receives a tax deduction for his contribution, he is more inclined to be generous in his contribution. Accordingly the tax deductibility of a contribution is of real importance. Figure 23–1 summarizes the general rules applicable to common types of contributions. There are many involved rules and exceptions and the figure should be used only as an overall guide.

SOCIAL AND RECREATION CLUBS

One of the types of organizations which are granted exemption from tax are "clubs organized and operated exclusively for pleasure, recreation, and other nonprofitable purposes, no part of the net earnings of which inures to the benefit of any private shareholder." The key words when considering tax implications for social clubs is the phrase "no part of the net earnings of which inures to the benefit of any private shareholder."

The members are the shareholders. If they operate the club in such a way that part of the fixed costs are paid for by nonmembers or the general public, then clearly there is a benefit to the members even though there may be no "net profit" as such. Thus a country club that rents out its facilities to non-members for an amount greater than its out-of-pocket costs is receiving income which benefits the membership by reducing the charges the members would have to pay to maintain the facilities.

This jeopardizes the tax-exempt status of the club, and also subjects the club to corporate income tax on this income from

DEDUCTIBILITY OF GIFT FOR INDIVIDUALS

Type of Property Contributed	Publicly Supported Organization*	Private Foundation†
Cash	100% up to total limitation	Same
Property held less than 6 months	Cost only	Same
Securities and real property held more than 6 months	Fair market value	Fair market value less 1/2 of the appreciation
Tangible personal property not created or produced by donor	Fair market value if used by the charity in its exempt function Fair market value less 1/2 of the appreciation if not used by the charity in its exempt function	Fair market value less 1/2 of the appreciation
Taxable personal property created or produced by donor (including inventory, art, books, etc.)	Cost	Same
Total limitation	50% of contribution base (which is usually adjusted gross income) except that long-term capital gain property is limited to 30%	20% of contribution base
Carry-over limitations	5 years	No carryover

*Including a private operating foundation. See pages 396–397 for definition.

†For purposes of donor's deductibility, the private foundation would be considered a publicly-supported organization if the private foundation makes qualifying distributions of 100% of its contributions and 100% of its "distributable" income (see page 392), both within 2-1/2 months of the end of its fiscal year.

Fig. 23–1. Tax deductibility by individual donors of gifts to charitable organizations.

non-members as unrelated business income. Both have serious implications for social clubs. In the first instance, the club could lose its tax-exempt status and find all of its net income was subject to tax as well as finding limitations on accumulation of retained earnings. In the second instance, the club could find it had substantial tax to pay even though it had an overall loss for the year. While to some extent these problems have always been present, the Tax Reform Act of 1969 tightened up the rules under which all social clubs must live if they want to maintain tax-exempt status.

Exempt Status

The first concern that a social club must have if it intends to receive income from non-members is what implication such income will have on the organization's tax exempt status. Significant use of the club by the non-members can result in loss of the club's tax exemption. Effective July 1, 1971, the IRS established guidelines * for determining whether a social club has significant revenues from the non-members. These guidelines provide that the club will be considered to meet its exempt status if gross receipts from non-members do not exceed the greater of 5 † per cent of total gross receipts or $2,500.

"Total gross receipts" includes receipts from normal and usual activities of the club, including charges, admissions, membership fees, dues, and assessments and excludes initiation fees, capital contributions, investment income and certain unusual or non-recurring income.

Receipts from Non-Members.   Gross receipts from non-members are the amounts not paid by members and amounts paid by members involving non-bona fide guests. Amounts paid by a member's employer can, depending on the situation, be considered as

---

* As of May, 1974, these rules had not been finally adopted by the IRS. However it is expected that the final rules will be substantially the same as those outlined in this chapter. Social clubs should consult competent tax counsel to determine how these rules, as finally adopted, affect them.

† A bill has been introduced into Congress that would allow receipts from non-members of up to 15 per cent of gross receipts. At date of publication it was uncertain whether this bill would be passed. Clubs having such non-member income should obtain advice from tax counsel.

paid by a member or as paid by a non-member. See the discussion below.

The problem of determining whether someone using the club is a bona fide guest of a member has proved troublesome. Most clubs take the position that under club rules the facilities may be used only by members and their guests and that these rules are rigidly adhered to. The Internal Revenue Service has taken the position that, in many situations, the member's participation in, or connection with, a function is so limited that the member is merely using his membership to make the club facilities available to an outside group. In effect, they hold that in many instances the member merely acts as a sponsor.

If a member's charges are reimbursed by his employer, the income will be member income provided that the guests are in attendance due to a personal or social purpose of the member, or due to a direct business objective or relationship of the member in his work for the employer. If there is no direct relationship between the business objective or purpose of the activities of the particular employee-member, the reimbursement will be considered non-member income. The distinction is where the member has a direct interest in the company function as contrasted with a situation where the member is merely serving as a sponsor to permit the company to use the facilities.

There are also guidelines to help determine if group functions hosted by members at which guests are present constitute member or non-member receipts. In groups of eight or fewer individuals it is assumed that all non-members are guests. In larger groups, it is assumed that all non-members are bona fide guests provided 75 per cent of the group are members. In all other situations the club must substantiate that the non-member was a bona fide guest. In the absence of adequate substantiation it will be assumed such receipts are non-member receipts, even though paid for by the members.

Substantiation Requirements. In order to rely upon the above assumptions regarding group functions, clubs must maintain certain records. Where the "8 or fewer" rule or the "75 per cent member rule" noted above is used, it is necesary to document only the number in the party, the number of members and the source of the payments. For all other group occasions involving club use by non-members, even where a member pays for the use, the club must maintain records containing the following information if it wishes to substantiate that such receipts are not "non-member" receipts:

1. Date
2. Total number in the party
3. Number of non-members in the party
4. Total charges
5. Charges attributable to non-members
6. Charges paid by non-members

In addition, the club must obtain a statement signed by the member indicating whether he has been or will be reimbursed for such non-member use and, if so, the amount of the reimbursement. Where the member will be reimbursed, or where the member's employer makes direct payment to the club for the charges, the club must also obtain a statement signed by the member indicating (a) name of his employer, (b) amount of the payment attributable to the non-member use, (c) non-member's name and business or other relationship to the member (or if readily identifiable, the class of individuals—e.g., sales managers), and (d) business, personal or other purpose of the member served by the non-member use. Figure 23–2 shows the type of form used by some clubs.

Record-keeping requirements for other activities such as providing guest rooms, parking facilities, steam rooms, etc., have not been specifically set forth. Clubs must be careful to see, however, that their record-keeping procedures provide information regarding member and non-member use of these facilities.

A careful study of the implications of these rules will show that all social clubs must be extremely careful not to receive, even inadvertently, very much non-member income. If the 5 per cent "guideline" established by the Internal Revenue Service is exceeded, clearly the exempt status of the club may be questioned.

Unrelated Business Income

In addition to jeopardizing its exempt status, a social club must also be concerned with the tax implications of receiving receipts

Member's Statement on Use of Private Dining Room

Income tax regulations require the following information to be furnished with respect to each use of a private dining room by more than 8 persons unless at least 75% of those present are Club members.

....
(Name and account number of member reserving room) (Date of use)

1. Do you expect to be reimbursed by any person or organization, including your own employer (or partnership), for the charges for the party or function for which you are reserving this room? Yes ☐ No ☐

   If your answer to Question 1 is "Yes", and it is your employer or partnership which will reimburse you, please answer Question 2 below. If your answer to Question 1 is "No", **or** if you will be reimbursed by a person or organization other than your employer or partnership, please disregard Question 2 entirely, and merely sign this form in the space provided below.

2. If you expect to be reimbursed by your **employer or partnership,** please enter below the name of your employer or partnership and complete **either** A or B below:

   Name of employer or partnership ....

   A. Is the room to be used for your own direct business objectives? Yes ☐ No ☐

   If your answer is "Yes"

       (i) What is the business relationship of your guests to you? (Check applicable items.)

           ☐ Customers or clients, or prospective customers or clients.
           ☐ Suppliers of goods or services.
           ☐ Fellow employees or partners.
           ☐ Other (describe)* ....

           ....

       (ii) Is entertainment of persons of the above class one of your duties as an employee or partner? Yes ☐ No ☐

   B. Is the room to be used merely for the accommodation of your employer or partnership (as distinguished from your own direct business objectives)? Yes ☐ No ☐

....
(Signature of Member) (Date)

*If the guests cannot be readily classified, please list on the back of this form their names and the business relationship of each to you.

The items below this line are to be completed by the Club.

Number served   .... Total Charges $.................

Number of Non-Members   .... Charges for Non-Members $.................

Fig. 23–2. Typical statement completed by club members when they entertain guests at their club.

from non-members since such receipts constitute unrelated business income. Social clubs are subject to tax at regular corporate tax rates on their unrelated business income. This is calculated on a somewhat different basis than for other types of exempt organizations. The total income of the club from all sources except for exempt function income (dues, fees, etc., paid by the members) is subject to tax. This means that income from non-members, as well as investment and other types of income, is subject to tax. Deductions are allowed for expenses directly connected with such income, including a reasonable allocation of overhead. As with other exempt organizations, there is a specific deduction of $1,000 allowed.

It is possible for a social club to have an overall loss but still have a substantial amount of unrelated business income. Here is an example of a country club where this is the case:

	Exempt	Unrelated	Total
Interest on taxable bonds	—	$ 10,000	$ 10,000
Membership fees	$ 100,000	—	100,000
Golf and other fees	40,000	20,000	60,000
Restaurant and bar	200,000	50,000	250,000
Total income	340,000	80,000	420,000
Direct expenses	(320,000)	(30,000)	(350,000)
Overhead	(60,000)	(20,000)	(80,000)
Net income (loss)	$ (40,000)	$ 30,000	$ (10,000)

As can be seen from this illustration, this club will have taxes to pay on $30,000 of income, which at the current corporate tax rates would be approximately $7,400.* It should also be noted that the club has probably jeopardized its tax-exempt status because it has non-member income substantially in excess of 5 per cent.

One of the real burdens for social clubs is to keep their bookkeeping records in such a manner that it is possible to not only determine direct expenses associated with non-member income,

---

* $30,000 less, $1,000 special exclusion, taxed at 22 per cent on first $25,000 of taxable income, plus 48 per cent on the remaining $4,000, or a total tax of $7,420.

but also to provide a reasonable basis of allocation between member and non-member activities. Even the largest of corporations has difficulty in making allocation of overhead between functions, so the problems of allocation for social clubs should not be passed over lightly. If, for example, the $50,000 of "unrelated" deductions claimed above were challenged by the Internal Revenue Service, the club would pay 48 cents tax on each dollar of expenses disallowed. This is why a social club needs to get professional advice on setting up appropriate records.

24

Principal Federal Tax Forms Filed

In the last chapter it was noted that while nonprofit organizations may be exempt from most federal taxes, they must file annual information returns with the Internal Revenue Service. With few exceptions, all exempt organizations other than private foundations are required to file Form 990 annually. Private foundations are required to file Form 990–PF. In addition, private foundations are also required to prepare and publish "an annual report," and all nonprofit organizations having "unrelated business" income must file Form 990–T. Both private foundations and organizations having unrelated business income will probably have taxes to pay at the time of filing. This chapter discusses these four principal returns and comments on some of the less obvious points that the preparer must be aware of in filling out these forms.

FORM 990—RETURN OF ORGANIZATION EXEMPT FROM INCOME TAX

Who Must File

All nonprofit organizations exempt from income tax must file Form 990 except the following:

1. Churches
2. Exclusively religious activities of any religious order

3. A church-sponsored mission society
4. Organizations other than private foundations with gross receipts of $5,000 or less *
5. Private foundations (they file Form 990–PF)

This means that most nonprofit organizations must file this return, including social clubs, educational institutions, and membership organizations. The return is due not later than the fifteenth day of the fifth month after the end of the fiscal year (May 15 for calendar year organizations), and there is a penalty of $10 a day for failure to file unless it can be shown that there was a reasonable cause for not doing so.

Contents of Form 990

This return consists of three parts:

Part I   Completed by all filing organizations.
Part II†   Completed by all filing organizations having gross receipts of $10,000 or more.
Schedule A†   Completed by all 501(c)3 filing organizations (see page 384) except private foundations.

Gross receipts means the total amount received during the year, including contributions, investment income, proceeds from the sale of investments, and sale of goods, before the deduction of any expenses or costs including the cost of investments or goods sold. This means that if an organization received contributions of $5,000 and had gross receipts from the sale of marketable securities of $5,100 it would have to complete Part II, even though the cost (or other basis) of these marketable securities might have been $5,000, leaving a net profit on the sale of only $100. Thus most organizations will have to prepare Part II.

---

* However, all organizations having gross receipts of less than $5,000 must in their first year file a return indicating that their gross receipts are less than $5,000. In subsequent years, no return is required provided gross receipts do not exceed $5,000.

† Under certain circumstances the IRS will accept other reporting forms in lieu of Part II and Schedule A.

Form **990**	**Return of Organization Exempt From Income Tax**	**1973**
Department of the Treasury Internal Revenue Service	Under section 501(c) of the Internal Revenue Code (Except Private Foundation)	

For the calendar year 1973, or fiscal year beginning ①_____ , 1973, and ending _____ , 19 ____

Please type, print or attach label. See instruction P.	Name of organization The Nelle Plains Community Service Society	If gross receipts are normally not more than $5,000. (See general instruction A(4)) check here . . . ☐
	Address (number and street) 1400 Diamond Avenue ②	Employer identification number (See instruction P) 13-6213564
	City or town, State, and ZIP code Nelle Plains, New York 10977 ③	Date of exemption letter September 12, 1966

Enter the name and address used on your return for 1972 (if the same as above, write "Same"). If none filed, give reason.

If exemption application is pending, check this block . . ☐

Enter exemption Code paragraph

Same   501(c) (3) ④

Part I All Organizations Complete Part I If line 8 is $10,000 or less, complete only Part I. Do not complete Part II.

Receipts (Revenues)

1 Gross sales and receipts from all sources, other than shown on lines 5 and 6	⑥	50,240 ⑤
2 Cost of goods sold	1,300	
3 Cost or other basis and sales expenses of assets sold . . . . ⑦	35,000	
4 Gross Income—line 1 less sum of lines 2 and 3		36,300
5 Gross dues and assessments from members and affiliates		13,940
6 Gross contributions, gifts, grants and similar amounts received (see instructions) . . . . . ⑧		10,500
7 Total—add lines 4, 5 and 6		63,500
8 Gross receipts for filing requirements tests—add lines 1, 5 and 6 . . . ⑨	124,240	87,940

Expenses and Disbursements

9 Expenses attributable to gross income . . . . ⑩	6,200	
10 Expenses attributable to amount on line 6 . . . . ⑪	1,700	
11 Disbursements for purposes for which exempt . . . . . . ⑫	66,640	74,540
12 Excess of receipts over expenses and disbursements—line 7 less sum of lines 9, 10 and 11—Increase or (Decrease) in net worth (see instructions)		13,400

Assets and Liabilities

	Beginning of year	End of year
13 Total assets . . . . ⑬	266,500	275,000
14 Total liabilities	37,500	32,600
15 Net worth . . . . ⑭	229,000	242,400

	Yes	No
16 Have you engaged in any activities which have not previously been reported to the Internal Revenue Service? If "Yes," attach a detailed description of such activities		x
17 Have any changes not previously reported to the Internal Revenue Service been made in your governing instrument, articles of incorporation, or bylaws, or other instruments of similar import? If "Yes," attach a copy of the changes .		x
18 Is this a group return filed on behalf of affiliated organizations covered by a group exemption letter? (See instruction G.)		x
19 Have you filed a tax return on Form 990–T, "Exempt Organization Business Income Tax Return," for this year? . ⑮		x
20 Was there a substantial contraction during the year? (See instruction O.) If "Yes," attach a schedule for the disposition(s) for the year(s) showing type of asset disposed of, the date(s) disposed, the cost or other basis, the fair market value on date of disposition and the names and addresses of the recipients of the assets distributed. . .		x

21 Membership organizations enter amount allocated for political purposes . . . . ⑯

22 Clubs exempt under section 501(c)(7) enter amount of:

    (a) Initiation fees and capital contributions included in line 5, Part I . . . .

    (b) Gross receipts from general public from use of club facilities included in line 1, Part II (or line 1, Part I, if only Part I is completed) (See instructions) . . . . ⑰

23 Organizations exempt under section 501(c)(12) enter amount of:

    (a) The total amount of gross income received from members or shareholders . . . .

    (b) The total amount of gross income received from other sources. (Do not net amounts due or paid to other sources against amounts due or received from them.) . . . .

24 Enter your principal activity codes from last page of instructions	861	119	408

25 The books are in care of ▶ Nelle Plains C.S.S. _____ Located at ▶ See above address

Name and telephone number of person to be contacted during business hours ▶ Phyllis Kahn – 475-5216-6790

Under penalties of perjury, I declare that I have examined this return, including accompanying schedules and statements, and to the best of my knowledge and belief it is true, correct, and complete. Declaration of preparer (other than taxpayer) is based on all information of which he has any knowledge.

May 14, 1974 Date	_Glenn Stephens_ Signature of officer or trustee	Executive Director Title
Date	Signature of individual or firm preparing return	Preparer's address
		Emp. Ident. or Soc. Sec. No.

Fig. 24–1. The first part of Form 990, which must be completed by most nonprofit organizations.

Part I—Illustration and Comments

Figure 24–1 shows an example of Part I, filled out with typical figures of a small public charity. The circled numbers on this form refer to the comments below. Figure 24–2 shows supplementary information where required by the instructions. Note that this supplementary information is for all parts of Form 990 and not just for Part I.

1. The first fiscal year must end within 12 months of date of incorporation. The organization can choose any month as the end of its fiscal year, but once the election is made it cannot easily be changed in future years. Thus it is important during the first year to select the "year end" carefully, keeping in mind the "natural" year end for the organization. The election is made automatically when the first return is filed which must be on a "timely" basis. This means the return must be filed within four and a half months after the end of the chosen year end. The first return can cover a period as short as one month (or even a fraction of a month) or as long as twelve months. It cannot cover a period longer than twelve months, even though the first part of the period may have been a period of no activity.

2. The "employer identification number" is a number assigned by the Internal Revenue Service upon request by any organization. This number will be used on all payroll tax returns and on all communications with the IRS. It serves the same identification function that the social security number serves for an individual. The preparer of a return should always be careful to use the correct number. An employer identification number should be requested by an organization on Form SS-4 as soon as it is formed even if it has no employees. It takes the IRS a period of time to assign the number and if the organization must file a return before the number is received, it should put "applied for" in this space.

3. Request for exemption should be made as soon as the organization is incorporated and is normally made on Form 1023. If an organization has not received an exemption letter at the time of filing Form 990, it should put the words "applied for" in this space. In addition, the block in the space immediately below should be checked.

4. This refers to the section of the Internal Revenue Code under which the organization was granted exemption. This reference will be in the "exemption letter." A list of principal nonprofit exempt organizations and their Internal Revenue Code references is given on page 384.

13-6213564

THE NELLE PLAINS COMMUNITY SERVICE SOCIETY
1400 DIAMOND AVENUE
NELLE PLAINS, NEW YORK
1973 Form 990–Supplementary Schedules

Part I, Line 6

Contributions in excess of $5,000:
B. Leonard Schultz Jr.
2 Butler Road
Scarswood, New York
$25,000 cash September 11, 1973

Part II, Line 1

Gross receipts from business activities:
The organization is organized and operated
to improve the quality of life in Nelle Plains.
It has a program to further encourage and
recognize outstanding achievements and
contributions of citizens of Nelle Plains. The
awards dinner is an integral part of this
activity and therefore is not an unrelated
business income.

Part II, Line 6

Gross amount received from sale of assets:
Sale of common stock to unknown parties
through Merrill Lynch.

Description	Number of Shares	How Acquired	Date Acquired	Date Sold	Basis	Selling Price	Gain
U.S. Lock-wood, common . . .	1,000	Purchased	3/1/70	10/15/73	$35,000	$40,000	$5,000

Part II, Line 9

Contributions, gifts, grants paid (none of
recipients is a related person):
Awards for outstanding community service:
Mrs. Mary Joe Philips, 18 Birch St.,
Nelle Plains, New York $2,500
Mr. Jack Anderson, 50 Chimney Ave.,
Nelle Plains, New York 1,000
Mr. L. A. Soben, Deerwood Rd.,
Nelle Plains, New York 500
$4,000

Fig. 24–2. An example of a supplementary schedule providing information requested by the instructions for Form 990.

Part II, Line 18   Other:

	Attributable to Gross Income	Attributable to Contributions, Gifts, Etc.	For Exempt Purposes
Postage		$ 300	$ 100
Stationery & printing	$ 400	400	2,200
Professional fees	650		2,800
Operations of bookmobile			8,040
Cultural activities			14,900
Miscellaneous	150		600
Total	$1,200	$ 700	$28,640

Part II, Line 26   Investments in corporate stocks:

	Beginning of Year	End of Year
U.S. Lockwood, common	$ 35,000	—
J. J. Faraway Co., common.	58,750	$ 58,750
The Lesch Corp., common	65,000	65,000
Amer. Tel. & Tel., common	45,000	100,000
	$203,750	$223,750

Schedule A, Part IV
  Line 3(d)   Payment of compensation:
                     The payment listed in Part I of this form is the
                     only compensation paid to an officer, trustee,
                     director, or creator by the Nelle Plains Community
                     Service Society during 1973. The payment to
                     Mr. Stephens was intended as reasonable
                     compensation for his full-time services as
                     Executive Director of the organization.

Schedule A, Part IV,
  Line 5   Determination of qualifying recipients:
                     An independent board headed by the Honorable
                     George Burns, Mayor of Nelle Plains, makes the
                     selection of the individuals who will receive the
                     annual awards. These individuals are selected for
                     public recognition based upon their outstanding
                     contributions to Nelle Plains. The basis for the
                     Nelle Plains Community Service Society's tax
                     exemption is its attempt to further, encourage,
                     and recognize outstanding achievements of its
                     citizens. There are no organizations to which
                     funds are expended in furtherance of its exempt
                     function, except in the case of purely
                     administrative matters.

Fig. 24—2.   Continued.

5. "Gross receipts" means total receipts including total proceeds from the sales of securities, investments, and other assets before deducting cost of goods sold or the cost of the securities or other assets. The cost of goods sold would be shown on line 2 and the cost of securities sold would be shown on line 3.

6. "Cost of goods sold" refers to the cost of actual merchandise or goods that were sold, but not selling expenses. Selling expenses are shown on line 9. In the case of a country club, cost of goods sold would include the direct cost of food and drink sold and direct labor.

7. "The cost or other basis and sales expenses of assets sold" includes the original cost of securities or other assets. The original cost of donated securities will be the fair market value at the date received.

8. A schedule must be attached to the return listing all gifts aggregating $5,000 or more from any one person during the year. This schedule must show the name, address, date received and value of all gifts received from each such person. For "publicly supported" organizations, this information is required only if the amount of such gifts from each person is 2 per cent or more of the total contributions received during the year (in addition to being over $5,000). There are some specific rules involved, and if the organization had contributions from any one person of $5,000 or more the instructions should be carefully read and followed. In our illustration here a schedule is included in Figure 24–2, which shows that Mr. Schultz donated $25,000 during the year.

9. Gross receipts for filing requirement tests is not the same as "total income." Total income normally would not include the gross proceeds from the sale of assets, but only the profit or loss on such sale. The concept of gross receipts used in this return is a tax and not an accounting concept and it is for this reason that this figure is shown to the left of the main column of figures. Essentially this line will represent total cash received during the year as shown on the bank statement. If gross receipts are more than $10,000, Part II must be filled out.

10. All expenses associated with the "gross receipts" from other sources which were not included in lines 2 or 3 should be included on this line. Overhead related to gross receipts not included in lines 2 or 3 would also be included here.

11. All expenses associated with the soliciting of contributions should be shown on this line. A typical example would be the salary of a fund raiser.

12. Disbursements made for the exempt purpose other than for

soliciting contributions should be shown on this line, including applicable overhead expenses. It is important to remember that the Internal Revenue Service will look at this line to determine whether it appears that a substantial enough portion of contributions and dues is being expended to justify continuation of the organization's exempt status.

13. If Part II is completed, the amounts shown as total assets and total liabilities should correspond to the appropriate lines on the Balance Sheet in that Part. If the organization is not required to fill out Part II, then the "total" assets and the "total" liabilities should be determined from the organization's Balance Sheet and entered here.

14. Net worth is merely the difference between total assets and total liabilities. This has the same meaning as the term "fund balance," which is the expression used most often in this book.

The increase in net worth from the beginning to the end of the year must equal the excess of receipts over expenses and disbursements for the year (line 12).

15. If the organization had "unrelated business income" during the year it will have to file Form 990–T and should answer this question "yes." Form 990 should not be filed before Form 990–T is filed because this question would have to be answered "no" and this would only lead to further questions and correspondence. This would not normally happen because Form 990–T must be filed within two and a half months after the end of the fiscal year (March 15 for calendar year organizations).

16. Membership organizations are allowed to engage in political activity but charitable organizations are not and could lose their tax-exempt status if they did so.

17. Clubs may be challenged on their exempt status if gross receipts from the general public are more than 5 per cent of total adjusted gross receipts of the club. See page 402. Also, profit from the use of the facilities by the general public is taxable as unrelated business income even if gross receipts are less than 5 per cent. If a club has income from the general public it should obtain tax counsel.

Part II—Illustration and Comments

Part II is completed by all exempt organizations having gross receipts of more than $10,000. Figure 24–3 shows an example of Part II. Part II is fairly straightforward, and while some of the information requested may require some effort to prepare, there should be less difficulty in understanding what is requested than is the case with Part I. There are certain alternative forms of reporting the information required in Part II. For example, organizations required to submit substantially the same information to another regulatory body can, with the approval of the Internal Revenue Service, substitute a copy of that report for Part II. The instructions should be checked carefully if an organization is also submitting similar forms to other agencies.

Here are a few specific comments that may be useful. Again, the references are to the circled numbers in the illustration.

18. "Receipts from other sources" is the same item that is shown on line 1 in Part I. Be sure that the total of all the items in this section (line 8) agrees with line 1 in Part I.

19. "Gross receipts from business activities" has to be carefully considered because this is where "unrelated business income" may be "implied" if the organization is not very careful in indicating the nature of the activity. Included in this caption will be all sales of services and products, including inventory donated to the organization. Income from sales of publications, including advertising, would also be reported here.

A statement must be attached explaining how each activity is related to the exempt function and therefore why it is not an unrelated business. See Figure 24–2. The wording and description is very important and if the organization has any significant amounts of receipts that conceivably could be challenged, it is suggested that the actual wording be cleared by competent tax counsel.

20. A detailed schedule is required showing the type of asset sold, cost, to whom sold, etc. The instructions must be carefully followed to be sure that all the required information is shown. An example is shown in Figure 24–2.

21. This section showing allocation of expenses among "exempt purpose," "attributable to contributions," and "attributable to gross income" is also very important because the method and amounts of allocation among these three categories become fixed once the return has been filed, and it is very difficult to go back and subsequently change it. The risk is that the Internal Revenue Service could challenge the conclusion that certain gross receipts are related to the exempt purpose. If they were successful in this challenge, the organization would want to be

Page 2

Part II　Organizations with Gross Receipts of More Than $10,000—Complete Part II

Receipts from Other Sources (line 1, Part I)　(18)

1　Gross sales or receipts from all business activities (state nature). (Attach a statement explaining how each business activity not reported on Form 990–T contributed importantly to your exempt purpose. See instruction J.)		
Gross receipts from Awards Dinner　(19)	1,300	1,300
2　Interest		2,040
3　Dividends		6,900
4　Gross rents		
5　Gross royalties		
6　Gross amount received from sale of assets, excluding inventory items (attach schedule)　(20)		40,000
7　Other income (attach schedule—Do not include contributions, gifts, grants, etc.)		
8　Total gross sales and receipts from other sources. Enter here and on line 1, page 1		50,240

Expenses and Disbursements (lines 9, 10, and 11, Part I)　(21)	(A) Attributable to gross income	(B) Attributable to cont's, gifts, etc., rec'd.	(C) For exempt purposes
9　Contributions, gifts, grants, and similar amounts paid (attach schedule—see instructions)			(22) 4,000
10　Disbursements to or for members (attach schedule—see instructions)			
11　Compensation of officers, directors, and trustees (attach schedule—see instructions) (23)	5,000		10,000
12　Other salaries and wages		1,000	24,000
13　Interest			
14　Taxes			
15　Rent			
16　Depreciation (and depletion) (attach schedule—see instructions) (24)			
17　Direct fees paid for raising contributions, gifts, grants, etc.			
18　Other (attach schedule)	1,200	700	28,640
19　Totals. Enter here and on lines 9, 10 and 11, page 1	6,200	1,700	66,640

Balance Sheets	Beginning of Taxable Year		End of Taxable Year	
Assets	(A) Amount	(B) Total	(C) Amount	(D) Total
20　Cash: (a) Savings and interest-bearing accounts	35,000		33,000	
(b) Other	13,500	48,500	12,250	45,250
21　Accounts receivable net		14,250		6,000
22　Notes receivable net (attach schedule)				
23　Inventories				
24　Gov't obligations: (a) U.S. and instrumentalities				
(b) State, subdivisions thereof, etc.				
25　Investments in nongovernmental bonds, etc. (attach schedule)				
26　Investments in corporate stocks (attach schedule)		203,750		223,750
27　Mortgage loans (number of loans ＿＿＿)				
28　Other investments (attach schedule)				
29　Depreciable (depletable) assets (attach schedule)				
(a) Less accumulated depreciation (depletion)				
30　Land				
31　Other assets (attach schedule)				
32　Total assets (line 13, Part I)		266,500		275,000
Liabilities				
33　Accounts payable		12,500		21,250
34　Contributions, gifts, grants, etc., payable		25,000		11,350
35　(a) Bonds and notes payable (attach schedule)				
(b) Mortgages payable				*
36　Other liabilities (attach schedule)				
37　Total liabilities (line 14, Part I)		37,500		32,600
Net Worth　(25)				
38　Capital stock or principal fund balance		229,000		242,400
39　Paid-in or capital surplus				
40　Retained earnings or income fund balance				
41　　Total net worth		229,000		242,400
42　Total Liabilities and Net Worth		266,500		275,000

Foreign organizations—Enter book value $_____ and fair market value $_____ of assets held within the United States for investment.

Fig. 24–3. The second part of Form 990, which must be completed by all organizations if they have gross receipts of $10,000 or more.

certain that it had already allocated a fair proportion of expenses to this gross income in order to minimize (or, hopefully, eliminate) the resulting tax. It would be very awkward to go back and claim that a fair allocation of expenses had not been made at the time of initially filing this return.

22. A detailed schedule is required showing, among other things, to whom paid, relationship, purpose, and amount. The instructions should be carefully followed to be sure that all of the required information is shown. An example is shown in the schedule in Figure 24–2.

23. Schedule A provides a place to show the details of the information requested here. See Figure 24–4.

24. A schedule must be attached showing details of depreciation. Form 4562 can be used (this is a schedule giving the details requested) or the required information can be presented on a supplementary schedule.

25. "Net worth" has the same meaning as "fund balance," which is the term used throughout this book to represent excess of assets over liabilities of the organization. This section makes a distinction between several classifications of net worth—i.e. capital stock, principal fund, paid-in surplus, retained earnings, etc. For many, if not most, nonprofit organizations, this distinction is of no significance and the fund balance will be shown in its entirety on line 38, "capital stock or principal fund balance." Obviously, if the records show the details of net worth in this fashion they should be entered appropriately. Social clubs will probably have capital stock, and perhaps capital surplus. Foundations often keep their fund balance segregated between principal and unexpended income.

Schedule A

Schedule A is prepared by all 501(c)3 organizations that must file Form 990. This will include most exempt organizations except private foundations, clubs, business leagues, and similar noncharitable organizations. Schedule A consists of two pages, both of which must be completed (Figures 24–4 and 24–5).

Figure 24–4 shows the first page of Schedule A and has been completed for The Nelle Plains Community Service Society.

SCHEDULE A (Form 990) Department of the Treasury Internal Revenue Service	Organizations Exempt Under 501(c)(3) (Except Private Foundations Filing Form 990–PF) Supplementary Information ► Attach to Form 990.	1973

For the calendar year 1973 or other taxable year beginning ...., 1973, and ending ...., 19.........

Name	Employer identification number
The Nelle Plains Community Service Society	13-6213564

Part I   Compensation of Officers, Directors and Trustees (See instructions)

Name and address	Social security number	Title	Time devoted to position	Compensation
Glenn Stephens 14 Charlotte Drive, Waverly, New York	092-38-6879	Exec. Dir.	All	15,000
Sean Krany 1 Bridle Avenue, Nelle Plains, N. Y.	072-00-1732	Trustee	None	- 0 -
W. Jonathon Peters 22 Tall Oaks Path, Nelle Plains, N. Y.	024-46-5678	Trustee	None	- 0 -

Part II   Compensation of Five Highest Paid Employees (Other than included in Part I—see instructions)

Name and address of employees paid more than $30,000	Social security number	Title	Compensation
Not applicable			

Total number of other employees paid over $30,000 ► - 0 -

Part III   Five Highest Paid Persons for Professional Services (See instructions)

Name and address of persons paid more than $30,000	Type of service	Compensation
Not applicable		

Total number of others receiving over $30,000 for professional services ► - 0 -

Part IV   (26)

	Yes	No
1 During the taxable year, has the organization (1) attempted to influence any national, State, or local legislation, or (2) participated or intervened in any political campaign?		x
If "Yes," attach a statement giving a detailed description of such activities and a classified schedule of the expenses paid or incurred. Also, attach copies of any materials published or distributed by the organization in connection with such activities.		
2 Are you related (other than by association with a statewide or nationwide organization) through common membership, governing bodies, trustees, officers, etc., to any other exempt or nonexempt organization?		x
If "Yes," identify the organization and describe the relationship.		
3 Have you engaged in during the year, either directly or indirectly, in any of the following acts with a trustee, director, principal officer, creator, or any organization or corporation with which such person is affiliated:		
(a) Sale, exchange, or leasing of property?		x
(b) Lending of money or other extension of credit?		x
(c) Furnishing of goods, services, or facilities?		x
(d) Payment of compensation (or payment or reimbursement of expenses)? (26)	x	
(e) Transfer of any part of your income or assets?		x
If the answer to any question is "Yes," attach a detailed statement explaining the transaction(s).		
4 (a) Did the organization give notice as required by section 508(b) that it is not a private foundation? . .	x	
(b) If the organization has received a final ruling or determination letter from the Internal Revenue Service that it is not a private foundation within the meaning of section 509(a), enter date of ruling or letter . . . . ►	June 15, 1971	
(c) If the organization has not received a final ruling or determination letter, indicate, if applicable, whether the organization has received a ruling or determination letter based on an: ☐ Advance ruling ☐ Extended advance ruling. Date of ruling . . . . . . ►		
5 Attach a statement explaining how you determine that individuals or organizations receiving disbursements from you, in furtherance of your exempt programs, are qualifying recipients. (27)		
6 Do you make grants for scholarships, fellowships, student loans, etc?		x

Fig. 24–4.   Schedule A to Form 990, which must be completed by all 501(c)(3) organizations required to file Form 990.

Schedule A (Form 990) 1973   Page **2**

Part V   Reason for Non-Private Foundation Status (See instructions for definitions)   (28)

The organization is not a private foundation because it is:

1 ☐ A church, school or hospital within the meaning of section 170(b)(1)(A) (i), (ii), (iii), or (v), respectively.

2 ☐ A medical research organization operated in conjunction with a hospital as provided in section 170(b)(1)(A)(iii). Enter name
       and address of hospital..

3 ☐ An organization operated for the benefit of a college or university owned or operated by a governmental unit as provided in
       section 170(b)(1)(A)(iv). (Complete support schedule.)

(29) 4 ☒ An organization that normally receives a substantial part of its support from a governmental unit or from the general public
       as provided in section 170(b)(1)(A)(vi). (Complete support schedule.)

(30) 5 ☐ An organization that normally receives no more than ⅓ of its support from gross investment income and more than ⅓ of its support from con-
       tributions, membership fees, and gross receipts from activities related to its exempt functions—subject to certain exceptions. Refer to section 509(a)(2).
       (Complete support schedule. See instructions for method of accounting.)

6 ☐ An organization operated solely for the benefit of, and in connection with, one or more of the organizations described in blocks 1 through 5 (or for
       the benefit of one or more organizations described in section 501(c)(4), (5), or (6) and also described in 5 above), but not controlled by disquali-
       fied persons other than foundation managers. Refer to section 509(a)(3). (Attach a statement identifying and describing the organization(s) for
       whose benefit you are operated and the relationships between you and the organization(s).)

7 ☐ An organization organized and operated to test for public safety as provided in section 509(a)(4) (see instructions).

Support Schedule (complete only if block 3, 4 or 5 above, is checked)

	Calendar year (or fiscal year beginning in) ►	(a) 1972	(b) 1971	(c) 1970	(d) 1969	(e) Total
8	Gifts, grants and contributions received	48,000	42,000	35,000	28,000	153,000
9	Membership fees received	8,700	8,000	6,500	5,000	28,200
10	Gross receipts from admissions, sales of merchandise, performance of services, or furnishing of facilities in any activity which is not an unrelated business within the meaning of section 513	1,100	900	750	500	3,250
11	Gross income from interest, dividends, rents, and royalties	7,500	7,500	7,950	5,500	28,450
12	Net income from unrelated business activities					
13	Tax revenues levied for your benefit and either paid to you or expended on your behalf					
14	The value of services or facilities furnished by a Governmental unit to you without charge (do not include the value of services or facilities generally furnished to the public without charge)					
15	Other income (do not include gain (or loss) from sale of capital assets)—attach schedule					
16	Total of lines 8 through 15	65,300	58,400	50,200	39,000	212,900
17	Line 16 less line 10	64,200	57,500	49,450	38,500	209,650
18	Enter 1% of line 16	6,530	5,840	5,020	3,900	

19 Organizations described in blocks 3 or 4 above:

(a) Enter 2% of amount in column (e), line 17 . . . . ▶____4,193

(31) (b) Attach a list showing the name of and amount contributed by each person (other than a governmental unit or "publicly sup-
       ported" organization) whose total gifts for the above four-year period exceeded the amount shown in (a) above and
       enter the sum of all of the excess amounts here . . . . ▶   - 0 -

20 Organizations described in block 5 above:

(32) (a) Attach a list, with respect to amounts shown on lines 8, 9, and 10, showing the name of, and total amounts received in
       each year from, each person who is a "disqualified person," and enter the sum of such amounts for each year:
       (i) _____, (ii) _____, (iii) _____, (iv) _____

(33) (b) Attach a list showing the name and amount included in line 10 for each person (other than a "disqualified person"), but
       only if the amount for each year exceeds the greater of the amounts on line 18 for each year, or $5,000. The term "per-
       son" includes a bureau or agency of a governmental unit, and each person described in section 170(b)(1)(A)(i) through
       (vi). Enter the sum of such excess amounts for each year: (i) _____, (ii) _____,
       (iii) _____, (iv) _____

21 Organizations described in blocks 3, 4, and 5 that have received any unusual grants during any of the above taxable years,
    attach a list for each year showing the name of the contributor, the date and amount of grant, and a brief description of the
    nature of such grant. Do not include such grants in line 8 above. (See instructions.)

**Fig. 24–5.   Second page of Schedule A to Form 990, which must
be completed by all 501(c)(3) organizations required to file Form 990.**

Comments on Page 1

26. The information requested on page 1 is straightforward except for Part IV. Part IV attempts to determine whether the organization is engaging in any number of activities which, in certain circumstances, are improper. A detailed explanation of these transactions must be attached to the return. For example, most organizations compensate their officers or directors for their work. Problems can arise where the compensation is deemed excessive. Figure 24–2 contains an example of the type of information required in a separate statement.

27. See Figure 24–2 for an example of the type of statement that would be required.

Comments on Page 2

28. This section is the place where an organization states specifically why it is not a private foundation. Pages 384 to 388 discuss the various categories of publicly supported organizations (i.e. non-private foundation status).

29. This category is the one most publicly supported organizations will qualify under. See page 385 (category 1). Where an organization can qualify under this category, it should do so.

30. This category is the one resulting from the application of the "mechanical" test referred to on pages 385–386 (category 2).

31. Lines 19(a) and 19(b) are designed to determine the amount of gifts, grants, and membership fees that must be excluded for purposes of the "substantial support from the public" test. Only the excess above the amount on line 19(a) is excluded.

32. Line 20(a) is asking for the year-by-year details of gifts, grants, gross receipts, and membership fees from disqualified persons. Such amounts are excluded from the "mechanical tests" discussed on page 386, category 2(b) (1). See the footnote on page 386 for a definition of a "disqualified person."

33. Line 20(b) is asking for the year-by-year details of gross receipts from admissions, sales of services, etc., from any one person or company in excess of $5,000 or 1 per cent of total support, whichever is greater. The amounts in excess of that base amount are excluded from the mechanical test discussed on page 386, category 2(b)(2).

FORM 990–PF—RETURN OF PRIVATE FOUNDATION
EXEMPT FROM INCOME TAX

All private foundations must file Form 990–PF by the fifteenth day of the fifth month after the end of the fiscal year (May 15th for calendar-year private foundations) and there is a penalty of $10 a day for failure to file, unless it can be shown that there was a reasonable cause for not doing so.

This return consists of eight pages and to the uninitiated appears to be a difficult form to fill out. Most private foundations would be well advised to get competent tax counsel to prepare this form for them. The comments indicated below—while undoubtedly helpful—cannot substitute for the direct assistance of a tax lawyer or accountant knowledgeable in the foundation's particular circumstances.

Page 1—Illustration and Comments

Figure 24–6 shows the first page of this form. Again, the numbers on the form refer to the comments below:

1. The fair market value of assets at the end of the year differs from the net worth as shown in the Balance Sheet on page 2 of Form 990–PF (Figure 24–7) because most foundations carry their investments at cost rather than at fair market value. In this instance the unrealized appreciation amounted to $10,808,021.

2. Part I ("Analysis of Receipts and Expenditures") looks more complicated than it actually is. In this section the foundation reports its receipts and expenditures as recorded in its books. Then, through the use of a columnar arrangement, the figures are put in the appropriate columns to arrive at certain key amounts that the foundation must use to determine the amount of its excise tax and distributable income.

3. Column (A) ("Receipts and expenditures per books") is exactly what it says it is, and the foundation should record its receipts and expenditures (or income and expenses for accrual basis foundations) in this column. Record all the figures in column (A) before attempting to fill in the figures in the other three columns.

Form **990-PF**	**Return of Private Foundation Exempt from Income Tax**	19**73**
Department of the Treasury Internal Revenue Service	Under Section 501(c)(3) of the Internal Revenue Code	

For the calendar year 1973, or fiscal year beginning _____ 1973 and ending _____, 19___

Please type, print or attach label. See instruction O.	**Name of organization** The Henering Foundation	**Employer identification number** (see instruction O) 13-5326270
	Address (number and street) 60 Broad Avenue	**Date of exemption letter** December 11, 1947
	City or town, State and ZIP code New York, New York 10017 ①	**Fair market value of assets at end of year (see instruction S)** 13,708,482

Enter the name and address used on your return for 1972 (if the same as above, write "Same"). If none filed, give reason.   Same

Foreign organizations check here . . . . ▶
If exemption application is pending, check here . . ▶

Enter your principal activity codes from last page of instructions . . . . ▶ 602

The books are in care of ▶ J. Steven Zaraya   Telephone No. 212-422-6000

Located at ▶ c/o Henering Foundation, 60 Broad Avenue, New York, New York 10017

② **Part I** — **Analysis of Receipts and Expenditures (See instructions for Part I)**

	(A) Receipts and expenditures per books	(B) Computation of Net Investment Income	(C) Computation of Adjusted Net Income	(D) Disbursements for Exempt Purpose
Receipts	③	⑥	⑧	⑨
1 Gross contributions, gifts, grants, etc. (see instructions)	- 0 -			
2 Contributions from split-interest trusts (see instructions)		- 0 -		
3 Gross dues and assessments	- 0 -			
4 Interest	35,154	35,154	35,154	
5 Dividends	99,659	99,659	99,659	
6 Gross rents and royalties	- 0 -	- 0 -	- 0 -	
7 Net gain or (loss) from sale of assets not in line 11 ④	20,000			
8 Net capital gain (see instructions)		⑦ 2,274		
9 Net short-term capital gain (see instructions)			- 0 -	
10 Income modifications (see instructions)			- 0 -	
11 Gross profit from any business activities: (Gross receipts $_____ less cost of sales $_____ see instructions)	- 0 -		- 0 -	
12 Other income (attach schedule)	- 0 -		- 0 -	
13 Total—add lines 1 through 12	154,813	137,087	134,813	
14 Compensation of officers, directors and trustees (see instructions)	20,395	4,046	4,046	16,349
15 Other salaries and wages	10,211	- 0 -	- 0 -	10,211
16 Other employee benefits	- 0 -	- 0 -	- 0 -	- 0 -
17 Investment, legal and other professional services	19,138	6,363	6,363	12,775
18 Interest	- 0 -	- 0 -	- 0 -	- 0 -
19 Taxes (see instructions)	5,047	- 0 -	- 0 -	- 0 -
20 Depreciation, amortization, and depletion (see instructions)	- 0 -	- 0 -	- 0 -	
21 Rent	10,507	507	507	10,000
22 Other expenses (attach schedule)	11,340	- 0 -	- 0 -	11,340
23 Contributions, gifts, grants (see instructions) ⑤	790,059			790,059 ⑩
24 Total—add lines 14 through 23	866,697	10,916	10,916	850,734
25 Line 13 less line 24: (a) Excess of receipts over expenditures	(711,884)			
(b) Net investment income		126,171		
(c) Adjusted net income (see instructions)			123,897	

Part II — **Excise Tax On Investment Income**

1 Domestic organizations—enter 4% of line 25(b), Part I	5,047 ⑪
2 Foreign organizations—(a) enter total of lines 4, 5, and 6, col. B, Part I	- 0 -
(b) enter 4% of line 2(a)	- 0 -
3 Credits: (a) Foreign organizations—tax withheld at source	- 0 -
(b) tax paid with application for extension of time to file (Form 2758)	- 0 - - 0 -
4 Tax Due—line 1 or line 2(b) less line 3 — Pay in full with return. Make check or money order payable to Internal Revenue Service ▶ (Write Employer Identification Number on check or money order)	5,047
5 Overpayment—line 3 less line 1 or line 2	

Foreign organization—Enter book value $_____ and fair market value $_____ of investment assets held in U.S.

Under penalties of perjury, I declare that I have examined this return, including accompanying schedules and statements, and to the best of my knowledge and belief it is true, correct, and complete. If prepared by a person other than taxpayer, his declaration is based on all information of which he has any knowledge.

May 10, 1974 _____ M. _____   President
Date   Signature of officer or trustee   Title

_____ Date   Signature and Emp. Ident. or Soc. Sec. No. of preparer   Address

Fig. 24–6. The first page of Form 990–PF. This page must be completed by all private foundations.

The foundation can keep its records on either the cash or the accrual basis of accounting and the amounts shown in column (A) will be the amounts on whichever basis is used. However, the amount of contributions, gifts, and grants (line 23) included in column (D) must be the amounts actually disbursed during the year (i.e., the cash basis).

4. The net gain or loss from sale of assets will be the book amount of the capital gains or losses from sale of investments. As noted on page 391, book gain or loss may or may not be the same as taxable gain or loss. The taxable gain will be reported only in column (B), on line 8 (see comment 7 below).

5. Line 25 will be the excess of all receipts over expenditures (or vice versa) as shown by the foundation's books.

6. Column (B) looks complicated but it really is not. The amounts shown in the top section are merely those amounts which are subject to the 4 per cent excise tax on investment income. The amounts in the bottom half of this schedule are the allocated expenses which can be deducted in arriving at the amount of this taxable income. It is for this reason that there are a number of shaded areas in this column in the income section. (No figures should be put in these shaded areas.) For example, contributions, gifts, and grants are not taxable and therefore the appropriate areas in column (B) have been shaded.

The allocation of expenses should be made on the basis of the nature of the expense. See comment 21 on page 416.

The last line in this column ($126,171) is the amount of net investment income subject to the 4 per cent tax. The tax is calculated in Part II.

7. Taxable gain on sale of investments is calculated on page 5 (Figure 24–10) and the calculation on that page must be completed before a figure can be entered on line 8, in column (B).

8. Column (C) provides for the computation of "adjusted net income." As will be noted, net investment income and adjusted net income are not the same. The net capital gain of the foundation is included in the computation of net investment income, but only the net short-term capital gain is included in the adjusted net income computation. The reason a calculation of adjusted net income is made is to help determine the "distributable amount" which is computed in Part VIII on page 7.

9. Column (D) is used to report the amount of expenditures made for the exempt purpose. If the organization is on a cash basis (see

note below), the amounts reported in column (D) on lines 14 through 22 are usually the amounts reported in column (A) less the amounts reported in column (C). One exception to this is line 19, taxes. Column (A) will probably include the excise tax on investment income. This tax is not deductible for purposes of the calculations being made here.

10. The amounts reported in column (D) are those that were actually *disbursed* during the current year (i.e., on a cash basis). Therefore, if a foundation keeps its books on an accrual basis, the amounts shown in columns (A) and (D) would differ. A schedule of contributions, gifts, and grants would be attached, in a format similar to that shown in Figure 24–2.

11. This section is merely a calculation of the amount of excise tax on investment income.

Pages 2 and 3—Illustrations and Comments (Figures 24–7 and 24–8)

12. The Balance Sheet provides for showing the fund balance divided between "principal" and "income." Many foundations do not make a distinction between principal and income, in which case the full amount of the fund balance should be reported on line 19.

13. Part IV reconciles the net worth (fund balance) at the beginning of the year to the net worth at the end of the year. In most instances the amount reported on the first page as the excess of receipts over expenditures will be the only reconciling item.

14. Part V must be answered very carefully because it attempts to determine whether any of the many rules affecting private foundations have been violated (see pages 389–396). If the answer to any of the questions results in the filing of Form 4720, the foundation should consult with tax counsel because the foundation and the foundation managers may be subject to escalating taxes.

15. A substantial "contraction" has been defined as disposition of more than 25 per cent of the fair market value of the foundation's assets. Note we are talking of fair market value as distinct from book value.

16. The 1969 Tax Reform Act required foundations to put certain restrictive language in their governing instruments, or, alternatively, the state legislature could effectively amend these gov-

Form 990–PF (1973)   **Page 2**

Part III	Balance Sheets	Beginning of Taxable Year		End of Taxable Year	
	Assets	(A) Amount	(B) Total	(C) Amount	(D) Total
1	Cash: (a) Savings and interest-bearing accounts . .	39,400		227,000	
	(b) Other	4,021	43,421	5,087	232,087
2	Accounts receivable net		47,438		
3	Notes receivable net (attach schedule)				
4	Inventories				
5	Gov't obligations: (a) U.S. and instrumentalities . .	914,024		568,024	
	(b) State, subdivisions thereof, etc.		914,024		568,024
6	Investments in nongovernment bonds, etc. (attach schedule)		787,666		787,666
7	Investments in corporate stocks (attach schedule) . .		1,852,719		1,312,684
8	Mortgage loans (number of loans...........) . . .				
9	Other investments (attach schedule)				
10	Depreciable (depletable) assets (attach schedule):				
	(a) Held for investment purposes				
	(b) Less accumulated depreciation				
	(c) Held for charitable purposes				
	(d) Less accumulated depreciation				
11	Land: (a) Held for investment purposes				
	(b) Held for charitable purposes				
12	Other assets (attach schedule)				
13	Total assets		3,645,268		2,900,461
	Liabilities				
14	Accounts payable		33,691		6,647
15	Contributions, gifts, grants, etc., payable				
16	Mortgages and notes payable (attach schedule). . .				
17	Other liabilities (attach schedule) Provision for taxes.		10,926		5,047
18	Total liabilities		44,617		11,694
	Net Worth (Fund Balances) (12)				
19	Principal Fund _____		3,600,651		2,888,767
20	Income Fund _____				
21	Total Net Worth (Fund Balances)		3,600,651		2,888,767
22	Total liabilities and Net Worth (line 18 plus line 21) .		3,645,268		2,900,461

Part IV	Analysis of Changes in Net Worth (13)	
1	Total net worth at beginning of year—line 21, Column B, Part III	3,600,651
2	Enter amount from line 25(a), Part I	(711,884)
3	Other increases not included in line 2 (itemize): _____	
4	Total of lines 1, 2, and 3	2,888,767
5	Decreases not included in line 2 (itemize): _____	
6	Total net worth at end of year (line 4 less line 5)—line 21, Column D, Part III	2,888,76⁻

Fig. 24–7. The second page of Form 990–PF. This page must be completed by all private foundations.

Form 990–PF (1973)   Page **3**

Part V   Statements with Respect to Certain Activities   (14)

File Form 4720 if question J(2), K(2)(a), (b) or (c), or N(2) is answered "No" or question J(3), L(2), or M(1) or (2) is answered "Yes."

	Yes	No
A During the taxable year, have you (a) attempted to influence any national, State, or local legislation, or (b) participated or intervened in any political campaign?		x
If "Yes," attach a detailed description of such activities and copies of any materials published or distributed by the organization in connection with such activities.		
B Have you engaged in any activities which have not previously been reported to the Internal Revenue Service? .		x
If "Yes," attach a detailed description of such activities.		
C Have any changes not previously reported to the Internal Revenue Service been made in your governing instrument, articles of incorporation, or bylaws, or other instruments of similar import?		x
If "Yes," attach a copy of the changes.		
D Have you filed a tax return on Form 990–T for this year?		x
E Was there a substantial contraction during the year?		x (15)
If "Yes," attach a schedule for the disposition(s) for the year(s) showing type of asset disposed of, the date(s) disposed, the cost or other basis, the fair market value on date of disposition and the names and addresses of the recipients of the assets distributed. (See general instruction N)		
F Did you file the annual report required by section 6056 (see Form 990–AR for instructions)?	x	
G Are the requirements of section 508(e) (relating to governing instruments) satisfied?	x	(16)
(See general instruction R)		
If "Yes," have such requirements been satisfied by:		
(1) Language in the governing instrument (original or as amended), or	x	
(2) Enactment of State legislation effectively amending the governing instrument and the governing instrument contains no mandatory directions which are in conflict with such State legislation		x
H (1) Enter the names of the States required to be listed by general instruction P New York		
(2) Have you furnished a copy of Form 990–AR (or equivalent report) to the Attorney General of each State as required by general instruction Q?	x	(17)
If "No," attach explanation.		
I Are you claiming status as an operating foundation within the meaning of 4942(j)(3) for calendar year 1973 or fiscal year beginning in 1973? (see instructions for Part XII)		x (18)
If "Yes," complete part XII.		
J Self-dealing (section 4941):		
(1) Have you engaged in any of the following acts during the year either directly or indirectly, with one or more disqualified persons (see instruction B, Part V, for definition)—		
(a) Sale, exchange, or leasing of property		x
(b) Borrowing or lending of money or other extension credit		x
(c) Furnishing of goods, services, or facilities		x
(d) Payment of compensation (or payment or reimbursement of expenses) . . . . (20)	x	
(e) Transfer to, or use by or for the benefit of a disqualified person of any part of your income or assets .		x
(f) Agreement to make any payment of money, or other property, to a disqualified person (as defined in section 4946(c)) other than an agreement to make a grant to or employ such individual for any period after the termination of his government service if such individual is terminating his government service within a 90-day period		x
(2) If any of questions 1(a) through 1(f) is answered "Yes," were all of such acts in which you engaged excepted acts described in section C, Part V of the instructions?	x	(19)
(3) Have you, in a prior year, engaged in any of the acts described in (1) above that were acts that resulted in acts of self-dealing in years beginning after December 31, 1969, because they were not excepted acts described in Section C, Part V, of the instructions, and that were not corrected before the first day of your taxable year beginning in 1973?		x
K Taxes on failure to distribute income (section 4942) (not applicable for years you were an operating foundation as defined in 4942(j)(3)):		
(1) Did you at the end of taxable year 1973 have any undistributed income (line 10, Part XI) with respect to taxable years 1970, 1971, or 1972?		x
(2) If "Yes," are you applying the provisions of section 4942(a)(2) (relating to incorrect valuation of assets) with respect to such undistributed income for (a) 1970		
(b) 1971		
(c) 1972		
If "Yes," to (a), (b), or (c) see Instruction A for Part V of the instructions.		
L Taxes on excess business holdings (section 4943):		
(1) Did you hold more than two percent direct or indirect interest in any business enterprise (see instruction B, Part V "Definitions") at any time during the year?		x
(2) If "Yes," have you purchased or have disqualified persons purchased stock in a business enterprise since May 26, 1969, which resulted in excess business holdings (direct or indirect) in 1973 which are subject to tax under section 4943?		
M Taxes on investments which jeopardize charitable purpose (section 4944):		
(1) Did you invest during the year any amount in such a manner as to jeopardize the carrying out of any of your exempt purposes? . . . . (21)		x
(2) Did you invest, in a prior year (but after December 31, 1969), any amounts in such a manner as to jeopardize the carrying out of any of your exempt purposes and such investments were not removed from jeopardy before the first day of your taxable year beginning in 1973?		x

Fig. 24–8. The third page of Form 990–PF. All private foundations must complete this page. If some of the questions produce certain responses, Form 4720 must be filed.

erning instruments for all foundations within the state through legislation. Many states did so, thus eliminating the need for individual foundations to amend their governing instruments. Question G is designed to make sure that either legislation was passed or the foundation individually amended its governing instruments as appropriate.

17. All private foundations must submit a copy of both Form 990–PF and Form 990–AR to the attorney general in each state in which it is registered or otherwise doing business. Care should be taken to be sure the foundation mails both forms to the attorney general *before* filing Form 990–PF with the IRS.

18. There are certain advantages to being an "operating" foundation. See pages 396–397.

19. Questions J, K, L, M, and N are designed to determine whether the foundation is engaged in any "prohibited" transactions. See pages 395–396 for a discussion of prohibited transactions, and the footnote on page 386 for a definition of disqualified persons.

20. In most instances the foundation will have paid compensation to the foundation manager and perhaps others who fit the definition of a "disqualified person." Presumably, however, the answer to question J(2) will be "yes" and there will be no unreasonable compensation for such persons.

21. A foundation is expected to follow a "prudent man" approach to investments. However, this does not preclude a foundation from making "program-related" investments. Typically these investments involve a high element of risk and probably would not meet the "prudent man" test. The distinguishing feature of a program-related investment is that it is made to accomplish the exempt function of the organization and not for the purpose of generating income. In reality, these investments are in the nature of a grant.

Pages 4 and 5—Illustrations and Comments (Figures 24–9 and 24–10)

22. Effectively, question N(1)(d) is asking whether the foundation has made a grant to an organization other than a publicly supported organization (see pages 385–388). Where grants are made to other than publicly supported organizations the foundation is required to exercise "expenditure control" to ensure that the

Form 990–PF (1973)   Page **4**

Part V   Statement With Respect to Certain Activities (Continued)

N Taxes on taxable expenditures (section 4945).

	Yes	No
(1) During the year did you pay, or incur a liability to pay for any of the following—		
(a) To carry on propaganda, or otherwise attempt to influence legislation by attempting to affect the opinion of the general public or any segment thereof or by communicating with any member or employee of a legislative body, or by communicating with any other government official or employee who may participate in the formulation of legislation		x
(b) To influence the outcome of any specific public election, or to carry on, directly or indirectly, any voter registration drive		x
(c) As a grant to an individual for travel, study, or other similar purposes by such individual		x
(d) As a grant to an organization, other than a charitable, etc., organization described in paragraph (1), (2), or (3) of section 509(a) of the Code		x
(e) For any purpose other than religious, charitable, scientific, literary or educational purposes or for the prevention of cruelty to children or animals		x
(2) If any of questions 1(a) through 1(e) is answered "Yes," were all of such transactions excepted transactions described in section F, Part V of the instructions?		
(3) With respect to part (1)(d) of this question, if you answered "Yes," did you apply the exception in item 13 of section F, Part V of the instructions? If "Yes," attach the statement required for such exception		

(22)

Part VI   Statement With Respect to Contributors, Compensation, etc.

A. Persons who Became Substantial Contributors in 1973 (if more space is needed, attach schedule)

Name	Address
(23) Not Applicable	

B. Compensation of Officers, Directors and Trustees for 1973

Name and Address	Social security number	Title	Time devoted to position	Compensation
M. J. Kleckner 60 Broad Avenue, New York, N.Y. 10017	016-30-9268	President	All	15,395
Milton J. Spence c/o M.J. Kleckner, 60 Broad Ave.,N.Y,N.Y.	530-07-3385	Trustee	Part	1,000
Robert M. Peron c/o M.J. Kleckner, 60 Broad Ave.,N.Y,N.Y.	564-96-2346	Trustee	Part	1,000
William T. Blakely c/o M.J. Kleckner, 60 Broad Ave.,N.Y,N.Y.	133-88-1193	Trustee	Part	1,000
P. S. Kannry c/o M.J. Kleckner, 60 Broad Ave.,N.Y,N.Y.	091-61-3742	Trustee	Part	1,000
Jonathon W. Weiss c/o M.J. Kleckner, 60 Broad Ave.,N.Y,N.Y.	170-38-7981	Trustee	Part	1,000
Total . . . . ▶				

C. Compensation of Five Highest Paid Employees for 1973 (Other than included in B above—see instructions)

Name and address of employees paid more than $30,000	Social security number	Title	Compensation
No employee is paid $30,000 or more			
Total number of other employees paid over $30,000 ▶	- 0 -		

Fig. 24–9. The fourth page of Form 990–PF. All private foundations must complete this page.

Form 990-PF (1973)   Page 5

Part VI (continued)

D. Five Highest Paid Persons for Professional Services for 1973 (See instructions)

Name and address of persons paid more than $30,000	Type of service	Compensation

Total number of others receiving over $30,000 for professional services ▶   - 0 -

Part VII   Capital Gains and Losses for Tax on Investment Income   (24)

	a. Kind of property. Indicate security, real estate or other (specify)	b. Description (Examples: 100 sh. of "Z" Co., 2 story brick, etc.)	c. How acquired P—Purchase D—Donation	d. Date acquired (mo., day, yr.)	e. Date sold (mo., day, yr.)
1	Security	1,000 sh AT&T	P	11/ 1/58	12/11/73
	Security	1,200 sh Xerox	D	7/11/67	12/11/73
	Security	7,500 sh ITT	D	6/ 1/53	6/ 1/73
	Security	2,000 sh GM	P	8/ 3/71	3/27/73

(25)

f. Gross sales price	g. Depreciation allowed (or allowable) (26)	h. Cost or other basis and expense of sale	i. Gain or (loss) (f plus g less h) (27)
46,000	- 0 -	22,000	24,000
144,000	- 0 -	176,000	(32,000)
350,000	- 0 -	340,000	10,000
135,000	- 0 -	117,000	18,000

Complete only for assets showing gain in column i and owned by the foundation on 12/31/69

(28) j. F.M.V. as of 12/31/69	(29) k. Adjusted basis as of 12/31/69	l. Excess of col. j over col. k, if any	m. Enter losses from col. i, and gains (excess of col. i gain over col. l, but not less than zero)
29,726	22,000	7,726	16,274
			(32,000)
355,000	340,000	15,000	- 0 -
			18,000

2 Net capital gain (loss). If gain, also enter on line 8, Part I   2,274   (30)

3 Net short-term capital gain (loss) as defined in section 1222(5) and (6) . . . .   - 0 -

Fig. 24-10. The fifth page of Form 990-PF. This page must be completed by all private foundations.

grant is actually spent for the charitable purpose within the required time limit. Expert tax counsel should be obtained to ensure that the procedures followed by the foundation to exercise this "expenditure control" are adequate to meet the requirements.

23. See the footnote on page 386 for a definition of "substantial contributor." The only substantial contributors who need be listed in this section are those who became substantial contributors in 1973.

24. Capital gains or losses are now subject to the 4 per cent investment income excise tax. This section provides a place to record all sales during the period and to calculate taxable gains.

25. One of the major bookkeeping problems created by the Tax Reform Act of 1969 is that the foundation must determine the donor's basis on all gifts acquired after December 31, 1969, and all prior gifts where the fair market value at December 31, 1969, was less than the donor's tax basis. Gains from the sales of donated property are based on the donor's original tax basis. As was illustrated in Chapter 23, if the donor's tax basis is very low, the foundation could have a substantial gain and this gain would be subject to the 4 per cent excise tax. The amount in Part VII, column h refers to donor's tax basis for donated securities.

26. The cost basis shown in column h is the cost at which the foundation is carrying this security for purchased securities.

27. The gain or loss in column i would normally be the "book" amount of the gain which the foundation calculates based on the amounts entered in its records. Where this is the case, the total of all the figures shown in this column will be the amount reported on line 7 (column A) on page 1. The two major exceptions to this would be where the foundation carries its investments at market, and where the security sold had been donated after December 31, 1969 (in which case the donor's tax basis would be reflected in column h).

28. Private foundations are not subject to tax on the gain on securities held prior to December 31, 1969, which had accrued as of December 31, 1969. For computing gain on the sale of securities, the foundation uses the higher of its adjusted basis (column k) or the fair market value on December 31, 1969 (column j).

29. Adjusted basis at December 31, 1969, will probably be the same as cost (column h) in the case of securities and similar assets. However, in the case of depreciable assets the tax basis at that date will reflect depreciation and it is for this reason that this column is provided.

30. The net capital gain is taxable, but if, instead, there is a net loss, this net loss is not deductible from investment income to determine the amount which is taxable.

Pages 6 and 7—Illustrations and Comments (Figures 24–11 and 24–12)

31. Part IX should be filled out before Part VIII. Part VIII calculates the "distributable amount" and that calculation requires the minimum investment return calculation in Part IX. See pages 392–394 for a definition of distributable amount. Note that the minimum investment return calculation is based upon fair market value and not on book value. Also observe that the calculation provides for a *monthly* average.

32. Part X is fairly straightforward. Line 1(b) refers to program-related investments, which are discussed in comment 21 above.

33. Very few foundations will qualify under the caption "Amounts set aside for specific projects which are for charitable . . . purposes." Foundations wishing to do so should refer to tax counsel for assistance since prior approval of the IRS is required.

34. Part XI (Figure 24–12) is an extremely complex schedule which requires great patience on the part of the preparer. The purpose of this schedule is to determine whether the foundation has made the required distributions for each of the applicable years. Foundations which have distributed the required amounts will find that the amounts shown on line 10 in each of the four columns will be zero.

35. The first step in filling out this form is to record the distributable amounts in the four columns at the top of the page on line 1. Note that the 1973 amount comes directly from line 7 of Part VIII, on page 6 (Figure 24–11). The amount for the years 1970, 1971, and 1972 can most easily be obtained from the 1972 return.

36. The next step is to fill in the amount of qualifying distributions for each of the four years. Again, the 1973 amount of $850,734 will come from page 6 (Part X, line 4). The amounts for the earlier three years will come from the 1972 return.

37. The 1970 qualifying distributions should be applied first to the required distributable amount shown in the 1970 column and the balance to "corpus" in the column so headed.

38. The 1971 qualifying distributions of $435,620 should likewise be applied to the required distributable amount in the 1971

Form 990–PF (1973)   Page 6

Part VIII Computation of Distributable Amount for 1973 (See instructions—not applicable to operating foundations) (31)

1 Adjusted net income from line 25(c), Part I	123,897
2 Minimum investment return from line 6 or 7, Part IX	649,464
3 Enter the higher of line 1 or line 2	649,464

4 Enter sum of: **(a)** Tax on investment income for 1973 from Part II . . . . | 5,047

   (b) Income tax on unrelated business income for 1973 (Form 990–T) . . | – 0 – | 5,047

5 Distributable amount (line 3 less line 4)	644,417
6 Adjustments to distributable amount (see instructions)	– 0 –
7 Distributable amount as adjusted (line 5 plus or minus line 6)—also enter on line 1, Part XI	644,417

Part IX Minimum Investment Return for 1973 (Operating Foundations—See Instructions) (31)

1 Fair market value of assets not used (or held for use) directly in carrying out exempt purpose:	
(a) Monthly average of securities at fair market value	14,967,411
(b) Monthly average of cash balances	79,830
(c) Fair market value of all other assets (see instructions)	23,720
(d) Total (add lines (a), (b), and (c))	15,070,961
2 Acquisition indebtedness applicable to line 1 assets	– 0 –
3 Line 1(d) less line 2	15,070,961
4 Cash deemed held for charitable activities—enter 1½% of line 3 (for greater amount, see instructions) . .	226,064
5 Line 3 less line 4	14,844,897
6 Organizations organized after May 26, 1969, and all Operating Foundations enter 5.25% of line 5	
7 Organizations (other than operating foundations) organized before May 27, 1969, enter 4.375% of line 5	649,464

Part X Qualifying Distributions in 1973 (See instructions) (32)

1 Amounts paid (including administrative expenses) to accomplish charitable, etc., purpose:	
(a) Expenses, contributions, gifts, etc.—total from line 24, column (D), Part I	850,734
(b) Program related investments (see instructions)	– 0 –
2 Amounts paid to acquire assets used (or held for use) directly in carrying out charitable, etc., purposes . .	– 0 –
3 Amounts set aside for specific projects which are for charitable, etc., purposes	– 0 – (33)
4 Total qualifying distributions made in 1973 (add lines 1, 2, and 3)	850,734

Fig. 24–11. The sixth page of Form 990–PF. Private nonoperative foundations must complete this page. Private operating foundations have to complete only Part X. If they are using the endowment test to establish their operating status, they must also complete Part IX.

Form 990–PF (1973)

Page 7

Part XI Computation of Undistributed Income (See instructions)

	Corpus	1970	1971	1972	1973
1 Enter distributable amounts: For 1973, enter amount from line 7, Part VIII; for prior years, enter amounts from 1972 return . . . . $ 741,730		484,839	693,956	678,333 ㉟	644,417
2 1970 qualifying distributions (as shown on 1972 return) to be applied:					
(a) Amount applied to 1970, but not more than the distributable amount for 1970 . .					
(b) Remaining amount—treated as an excess distribution out of corpus . . $ 256,891	256,891				
3 1971 qualifying distributions (as shown on 1972 return) to be applied . $ 435,620					
(a) Amount applied to remaining undistributed income (if any) for 1970 .	㊱ – 0 –	484,839 ㊲			
(b) Amount treated as a distribution out of corpus (election required—see instructions) .	– 0 –				
(c) Amount applied to 1971, but not more than the distributable amount for 1971 . .			435,620 ㊳		
(d) Remaining amount (if any)—treated as an excess distribution of corpus . .					
4 Excess 1970 distributions, treated as a distribution of corpus in 1970 (line 2(b)), applied as a carryover to remaining undistributed income (if any) for 1971 . . $ 813,582	(256,891) ㊴		256,891		
5 1972 qualifying distributions (as shown on 1972 return) to be applied . $ 813,582					
(a) Amount applied to remaining undistributed income (if any) for 1971 . .			1,445 ㊵		
(b) Amount treated as a distribution out of corpus or applied to the remaining undistributed income (if any) for 1970 (election required—see instructions) . .	– 0 –	– 0 –			
(c) Amount applied to 1972, but not more than the distributable amount for 1972 . .				678,333	
(d) Remaining amount, if any, treated as an excess distribution of corpus .	133,804				
6 Excess 1970 and 1971 distributions, treated as a distribution of corpus in 1970 and 1971, applied as a carryover to remaining undistributed income (if any) for 1972 . $ 850,734	(– 0 –)		– 0 – ㊷	– 0 –	
7 1973 qualifying distributions (from Part X) to be applied . . .					
(a) Amount applied to remaining undistributed income (if any) for 1972 .					
(b) Amount treated as a distribution out of corpus or applied to the remaining undistributed income (if any) for 1970 and 1971 (election required—see instructions) . .	– 0 –				
(c) Amount applied to 1973, but not more than the distributable amount for 1973 . .					644,417
(d) Remaining amount (if any) treated as an excess distribution of corpus . .	206,317				
8 Excess 1970, 1971 and 1972 distributions, treated as a distribution of corpus in 1970, 1971 and 1972, applied as a carryover to remaining undistributed income for 1973 . .	(– 0 –)				
9 Total qualifying distributions applied to 1970, 1971, 1972, and 1973 (add amounts in each column, lines 2 through 8) * See instructions for Corpus column . .	340,121	484,839	693,956	678,333	644,417 ㊸
10 Undistributed income as of end of taxable year beginning in 1973 (line 1 less line 9) (The amount in each column other than 1973 is subject to tax and must be reported on Form 4720) . . .	– 0 –	– 0 –	– 0 –	– 0 –	– 0 –
11 Distributions required to be made by the foundation out of corpus so that restrictions will not be imposed on the charitable contributions deductions or qualifying distributions of certain donors (see instructions). Enter in "corpus" column the sum of such distributions shown in yearly columns . .					
12 Net balance of distributions from corpus available for carryover to 1974 as an excess distribution—line 9 less line 11 . .	340,121 ㊹				

Fig. 24–12. The seventh page of Form 990–PF. Private nonoperating foundations must complete this page. Private operating foundations are not subject to the minimum distribution rules and do not complete this page.

column. Note that the required distributable amount of $693,956 is greater than the qualifying distributions.

39. The excess of qualifying distributions from prior years (1970 in this instance) should then be applied to the 1971 required distributable amounts. This can be seen in the transfer from the corpus column to the 1971 column.

40. Even after transferring the excess distribution in 1970 of $256,891 there still remains $1,445 which must be distributed in 1972. Part of the qualifying distributions for 1972 of $813,582 is used to meet this requirement.

41. After using $1,445, there remains $812,137 of qualifying distributions in 1972 which can be applied to 1972, and the balance carried over. Since the required distributable amount in 1972 is $678,333, the balance of $133,804 ($813,582 − $1,445 − $678,333 = $133,804) is reported in the corpus column and can be used to meet future years' distributable amount requirements.

42. 1973 qualifying distributions of $850,734 are first applied to the required distributable amount in 1973 of $644,417 and the balance is then reported as additions to the corpus column ($206,317).

43. Line 9 is just a total line and where a foundation has made the required distributions, the amounts shown in the four columns will exactly equal the required distributable amount shown at the top of this schedule on line 1.

44. The amount shown at line 12 in the corpus column is the cumulative amount of excess distributions which can be applied to future years' required distributable amounts. In future years the application of this excess will be to the earliest year first. There is a five-year carryover, so careful planning is required.

Page 8—Private Operating Foundations

Page 8 is filled out only by private operating foundations. The Henering Foundation is not a private operating foundation and so this page is not illustrated. Pages 396–397 discuss the general requirements for being a private operating foundation and the advantages.

FORM 990-AR—ANNUAL REPORT OF PRIVATE FOUNDATIONS

In addition to preparing Form 990–PF, all private foundations having $5,000 of assets at any time during the fiscal year must also file an annual report. This annual report must contain the information specified on Form 990-AR, but there is no requirement that Form 990-AR be used as such. Accordingly, a private foundation that prepares a comprehensive printed annual report containing all of the information required in Form 990-AR can file that report in compliance with Form 990-AR requirements.

The private foundation is also required to publish a notice in a newspaper having general circulation in the county in which the principal office of the foundation is located stating that the annual report is available for six months at the foundation's office for inspection by any person. A copy of the newspaper notice must be attached to the copy of Form 990-AR (or the substitute annual report) filed with the IRS.

A copy of the annual report must be submitted to the attorney general of each state in which the private foundation has an office. This is in addition to any other reporting requirements that the attorney general may have. Chapter 25 discusses some of the reporting requirements of the various states. In addition to filing in the states in which the foundation has an office, the attorney general of any other state may request the private foundation to provide him with a copy of this annual report. Also, the Internal Revenue Service can require a private foundation to submit copies to public libraries in principal cities where the foundation is located.

The return is due on the same date as Form 990–PF—four and a half months after the end of the fiscal year (May 15 for calendar-year organizations). Since a copy of the newspaper notice must be attached to the annual report, the foundation should be very careful not to leave the actual publishing of this notice until the very last minute since it may take several days to get it published. As with Forms 990 and 990–PF, there are penalties for failure to file on time—in this instance, the foundation manager or other person responsible for filing will be personally assessed a penalty of $10 a day for every day late. Since a proper annual report has not been filed until the newspaper notice has been published, this penalty will be charged even if the annual report has been filed with the Internal Revenue Service but the newspaper notice has not be published. If the failure to file is "willful" there is an additional penalty of $1,000.

Illustrations and Comments

Figures 24–13 through 24–15 show the reporting format of Form 990–AR. (Page 1 of this form has not been reproduced since the only information it contains is the name of the foundation.) As you will see from a quick inspection, much of the information is the same as on Form 990–PF but appears in condensed form.

The following comments refer to the circled numbers in these illustrations.

1. The notice referred to here is the newspaper notice of availability of Form 990–AR for public inspection.
2. The information requested in this first section is similar to the information in Form 990–PF in condensed form, but it is not the same. Here is a comparison of the figures shown on the respective lines on these two forms:

990–AR		990–PF (Figure 24–6)
Line 1	=	Line 1 (column A)
Line 2	=	Line 13 (column C)
Line 4	=	Line 24 (column D)
Line 5	=	Line 24 (column C)

Perhaps the most important thing to note is that the 990–AR figures do not include certain income (gains) and certain expenses (taxes). Thus if you subtract the two categories of expenses shown on Form 990–AR (lines 4 and 5) from total revenues (line 3), the resulting deficit of $726,837 will not agree with the excess of receipts over expenditures on Form 990–PF (Figure 24–6).

3. A list is required of all "foundation managers." The Internal Revenue Code defines a foundation manager as "an officer, director, or trustee of a foundation." The definition goes on to include anyone having the powers and responsibilities similar to those of an officer, director, or trustee. Accordingly, if a private foundation has as its manager an employee who is not an officer, director, or trustee, he will be considered a "foundation man-

Form 990–AR (1973)   Page **2**

Annual report for calendar year 1973, or fiscal year beginning ...., 1973, and ending ...., 19........

Name of organization	Employer identification number
The Henering Foundation	13-5326270

Address of principal office

60 Broad Avenue, New York, New York 10017

If books and records are not at above address, specify where they are kept	Name of principal officer of foundation
	M. J. Kleckner

Have you attached the notice required by instruction C? . . . . **(1)** . ☒ Yes ☐ No

Revenues **(2)**

1 Amount of gifts, grants, bequests, and contributions received for the year . . . .   – 0 –

2 Gross income for the year   134,813

3   Total   134,813

Disbursements and Expenses

4 Disbursements for the year for the purposes for which exempt (including administrative expenses) .   850,734

5 Expenses attributable to gross income (item 2 above) for the year   10,916

Foundation Managers **(3)**

6 List all managers of the foundation (see section 4946(b) IRC):

Name and title	Address where manager may be contacted during normal business hours
Milton J. Spence - Trustee	c/o M.J. Kleckner, 60 Broad Avenue New York, New York 10017
Robert M. Peron - Trustee	c/o M.J. Kleckner, 60 Broad Avenue New York, New York 10017
William T. Blakely - Trustee	c/o M.J. Kleckner, 60 Broad Avenue New York, New York 10017
P. S. Kannry - Trustee	c/o M.J. Kleckner, 60 Broad Avenue New York, New York 10017
Jonathon W. Weiss - Trustee	c/o M.J. Kleckner, 60 Broad Avenue New York, New York 10017
M. J. Kleckner - President	c/o M.J. Kleckner, 60 Broad Avenue New York, New York 10017

6a List here any managers of the foundation (see section 4946(b) IRC) who have contributed 2 percent of the total contributions received by the foundation before the close of any taxable year (but only if they have contributed more than $5,000). (See section 507(d)(2).) **(4)**

None

6b List here any managers of the foundation (see section 4946(b) IRC) who own 10 percent or more of the stock of a corporation (or an equally large portion of the ownership of a partnership or other entity) of which the foundation has a 10 percent or greater interest. **(5)**

None

Fig. 24–13.   The second page of Form 990–AR.   This form is to be completed by all private foundations.

Form 990–AR (1973)   Page 3

Balance Sheet Per Books at the Beginning of the Year

Assets		Liabilities	
Cash	43,421	Accounts payable	33,691
Accounts and notes receivable . . .	47,438	Contributions, gifts, grants, etc. payable	
Inventories	- 0 -	Bonds and notes payable	
Securities		Mortgages payable	
Government obligations	914,024	Provision for	
		Other liabilities .taxes	10,926
Corporate bonds	787,666	Total liabilities	44,617
Corporate stocks	1,852,719	**Net Worth**	
Mortgage loans		Principal fund	3,600,651
Real estate			
Less: Depreciation .		Income fund	
Other assets . . .			
Less: Depreciation .		Total net worth	3,600,651
Total assets	3,645,268	Total liabilities and net worth . . .	3,645,268

Itemized Statement of Securities and All Other Assets Held at the Close of the Taxable Year

Asset	Book value	Market value
Cash	232,087	232,087
Securities:-		
Governmental obligation -		
U.S. Treasury 4-1/2 bonds due 11/1/92	568,024	537,655
Corporate bonds:		
AT&T 7-1/2% deb. due 8/1/95	387,666	392,000
GM 7% deb. due 5/1/84	400,000	343,820
	787,666	735,820
Corporate stocks:		
AT&T	410,000	874,000
Xerox	176,000	4,952,800
GM	175,500	485,120
Polaroid	551,184	5,891,000
	1,312,684	12,202,920
Total	2,900,461	13,708,482

Fig. 24–14. The third page of Form 990–AR. This form is to be completed by all private foundations.

Form 990–AR (1973)   Page **4**

Grants and Contributions Paid or Approved for Future Payment During the Year

Recipient Name and address (home or business)	If recipient is an individual, show any relationship to any foundation manager or substantial contributor	Concise statement of purpose of grant or contribution	Amount
Paid during year ⑧ Schedule attached			790,059
Approved for future payment None			

A notice has been published that this Annual Report is available for public inspection at the principal offices of the foundation, and copies of this Annual Report have been furnished to the Attorney General of each State entitled to receive reports and listed on Form 990-PF.

May 3, 1973   *M. J. Kleckner*   President
<u>Date</u>   <u>Signature of foundation manager</u>   <u>Title</u>

<u>Date</u>   <u>Signature of individual or firm preparing the return</u>   <u>Preparer's address</u>   <u>Emp. Ident. or Soc. Sec. No.</u>

Instructions

A. Annual Report.—The foundation managers (as defined in section 4946(b)) of every organization which is a private foundation, including a trust described in section 4947(a)(1) which is treated as a private foundation, having at least $5,000 of assets at any time during a taxable year shall file an annual report. A private foundation may use this form for its annual reporting requirements.

The annual report required to be filed is in addition to and not in lieu of submitting the information required on Form 990-PF under section 6033.

The report may be prepared in printed, typewritten or any other form the foundation chooses; provided that it readily and legibly discloses the information required by section 6056 and the regulations thereunder.

B. Where and When to File.—The annual report must be filed at the time and place specified for filing Form 990-PF.

C. Public Inspection of Private Foundation's Annual Reports.—The annual report required to be filed under section 6056 shall be made available by the foundation managers for inspection at the principal office of the foundation during regular business hours by any citizen on request made within 180 days after the publication of notice of its availability; or if the foundation manager chooses, he may furnish a copy free of charge to such persons requesting inspection, provided such persons do so at the time and manner prescribed in section 6104(d) and the regulations thereunder.

The notice shall be published not later than the day prescribed for filing such annual report (determined with regard to any extensions of time for filing), in a newspaper having general circulation in the county in which the principal office of the private foundation is located. The notice shall state that the annual report of the private foundation is available at its principal office for inspection during regular business hours by any citizen who requests it within 180 days after the date of such

publication, and shall state the address of the private foundation's principal office and the name of its principal manager. A private foundation may designate in addition to its principal office, or (if the foundation has no principal office or none other than the residence of a substantial contributor or foundation manager) in lieu of such office, any other location at which its annual report shall be made available.

A copy of such notice as published and a statement signed by a foundation manager stating that such notice was published, setting forth the date of publication and the publication in which it appears shall be sufficient proof of publication.

A copy of the notice must be attached to the annual report filed with the Internal Revenue Service.

A private foundation which has terminated its status as such under section 507(b)(1)(A), by distributing all its net assets to one or more public charities without retaining any right, title or interest in such assets, does not have to publish notice of availability of its annual report or furnish such report to the public for the taxable year in which it so terminates (Reg. 1.507–2(a)(6)).

D. Signature and Verification.—The report must be signed by the foundation manager.

E. List of States.—A private foundation is required to attach to its Form 990-PF a list of all States:

(a) to which the organization reports in any fashion concerning its organization, assets, or activities, and

(b) with which the organization has registered (or which it has otherwise notified in any manner) that it intends to be, or is a charitable organization or that it is, or intends to be, a holder of property devoted to a charitable purpose.

F. Furnishing of Copies to State Officers; Listing of States.—The foundation managers shall furnish a copy of the annual report (required by section 6056) to the Attorney Gen-

eral of (1) each State which they are required to list above, (2) the State in which is located the principal office of the foundation, and (3) the State in which the foundation was incorporated or organized. Such report shall be furnished at the same time it is sent to the Internal Revenue Service. In addition, the foundation managers shall provide upon request a copy of the annual report to the Attorney General or other appropriate State officer of any other State. The foundation manager shall also attach to the report a copy of the Form 990-PF (or Schedule PF (Form 1041) for a 4947(a)(1) trust) and a copy of the Form 4720 (if any) filed by the foundation with the Internal Revenue Service for the year.

G. Penalty for Failure to File Report and Notice on Time.—If a private foundation fails to file the annual report on or before the due date, or to comply with the requirements under "C" above, there will be imposed on the person (anyone under a duty to perform the act), a $10 penalty for each day during which such failure continues, not to exceed $5,000. See section 6652(d)(3). If more than one person is liable, all such persons shall be jointly and severally liable with respect to such failure. Organizations that have given notice under section 508(b) as to their status and have not received a letter from the Internal Revenue Service containing a determination as to such status—refer to Revenue Procedure 72–31, 1972–1 C.B. 759, or later revisions, for rules relating to relief from the penalty provision of Section 6652. If such failure to file the annual report or comply with "C" is willful, there shall be imposed in addition to the amount mentioned above a penalty of $1,000 with respect to each such report or notice. See section 6685.

H. Foreign Organizations.—A foreign organization which has received substantially all of its support (other than gross investment income) from sources outside the United States shall not be subject to the requirements of C and F above.

Fig. 24–15. The fourth page of Form 990—AR. This form is to be completed by all private foundations.

ager" for purposes of this definition. Note that there will almost always be more than one foundation manager since all directors or trustees are considered foundation managers.

4. This line is asking which of the foundation managers listed above are "substantial contributors." Note that to be considered a substantial contributor does not mean that the person has made a contribution in the current year; it means only that at some time, either in the present or in a past year the person has contributed 2 per cent of the total contributions that had been received by the foundation since its inception as of the date of contribution (provided the contribution was more than $5,000).

5. The purpose of this question is to disclose relationships between foundation managers and companies in which the foundation has an interest of 10 per cent or more.

6. Note that the requirement is for a Balance Sheet at the beginning of the year. The author is as puzzled as the reader may be as to why a Balance Sheet at the beginning of the year is asked for rather than at the end of the year. This is, however, exactly the requirement that Congress wrote into the law. If instead of preparing Form 990-AR the foundation elects to prepare its own printed annual report, it is suggested that the Balance Sheet at both the beginning and the end of the year be included, perhaps in a form similar to the Balance Sheet in Form 990 (Figure 24–3).

7. Here the form requires an itemized list of "securities and all other assets" held at the close of the year. All assets must be listed, including cash, accounts receivable, securities, and real estate. For most, the book value and market value will be the same. In the case of marketable securities the published market value at the end of the year should be used. The best estimate readily available of the market value of real estate should be used. There is no requirement that an organization obtain an appraisal each year.

8. This schedule is identical to the one that would be attached to Form 990–PF. An example is shown in the schedule to Form 990 (Figure 24–2).

FORM 990-T—EXEMPT ORGANIZATION BUSINESS INCOME TAX RETURN

Form 990-T must be filled out if an exempt organization has unrelated business income and the gross (not net) income was $1,000 or more. What constitutes unrelated trade or business income was discussed in Chapter 23, pages 397–399, and it was noted that *all* exempt organizations are subjec⁀ to this tax although there are transitional rules for churches. It is due 2½ months after the end of the fiscal year.

The complete Form 990-T is four pages long, and is very complicated. Page 1 must be completed by all filing organizations, but pages 2, 3, and 4 must be completed only for those having unrelated gross income of more than $5,000. Only professional accountants or tax lawyers should attempt to complete pages 2, 3 and 4.

Page 1—Illustration and Comments

Because of the complicated nature of Form 990-T, the only part of the return which is discussed is the first page. Figure 24–16 shows a completed return for an organization having less than $5,000 of gross income and a very small tax. The circled numbers refer to the comments below.

1. Notice the nature of the unrelated income—the operation of a small bingo game. While the net income from this activity will be used for exempt purposes, the activity of operating a bingo game does not directly contribute toward the exempt purposes of the church.
2. In addition to the direct expenses of the prizes, indirect expenses and overhead (such as heat, light, building costs) can also be deducted to determine taxable income.
3. There is a specific deduction of $1,000 for all exempt organizations.
4. An organization with gross income of $1,000 is still required to file Form 990-T even if taxable income after this deduction is zero.
5. The mechanics of computing the tax are complicated because there are two tax rates on ordinary income (22 per cent of first $25,000 and 48 per cent on all income over $25,000), as well as alternative taxes if there are capital gains. In addition there are certain other taxes or tax credits such as those relating to tax preferences and investment credits.
6. This section of the form is not applicable to exempt organizations of the type we have been discussing in this book. This is for trusts that are treated as though they were "individuals."

Form **990-T**	**Exempt Organization Business Income**		**19 73**
Department of the Treasury Internal Revenue Service	**Tax Return** (Under Section 511 of the Internal Revenue Code) For the calendar year 1973 or other taxable year beginning .... , 1973, and ending .... , 19		

Name of Organization	Foreign organization not having an office or place of business in the U.S. check here . . . ☐	Employer Identification Number (In case of employees' trust described in section 401(a) and exempt under section 501(a), insert the trust's identification number.)
The First Inter-Faith Church of Sprang Valley	Enter activity code from instructions for Form 990 if stated. If not stated, describe nature of unrelated trade or business activity.	
Number and street 632 Main Street		13-1211947
City or town, State, and ZIP code Sprang Valley, New York 10799	574	Date of current exemption letter and code section under which you are exempt, March 27, 1969-501(c) (3)
Name and address of trust's fiduciary		

Complete only page I if unrelated trade or business gross income is $5,000 or less.
Complete all applicable parts of the form (except lines 1 thru 5) if unrelated trade or business gross income is over $5,000.

Unrelated business taxable income computation—When unrelated trade or business gross income is $5,000 or less

1	Unrelated trade or business gross income. (State sources ...... Monthly Bingo Game ① ......)	5,000 ②
2	Less deductions	3,100
3	Unrelated business taxable income before specific deduction	1,900
4	Less specific deduction (see instruction "K(4)") . . . . ③	1,000 ④
5	Unrelated business taxable income	900

Tax Computation

Organizations Taxable as Corporations (See General Instruction B(1))

6	Unrelated business taxable income (line 5 above, or line 33, page 2) . . . . . ⑤		900
7	Surtax exemption (line 6 or $25,000, whichever is lesser). (Component members of a controlled group see page 7 of instructions and enter your surtax exemption or line 6, whichever is lesser.)		900
8	Line 6 less line 7		- 0 -
9	(a) 22% of line 6	198	
	(b) 26% of line 8		
	(c) If multiple surtax exemption is elected under section 1562, enter 6 percent of line 7 . .		198
10	Alternative tax from separate Schedule D		- 0 -
11	Income tax—(line 9 or, if applicable, line 10, whichever is lesser)		198
12	Less: (a) Foreign tax credit (attach Form 1118)		
	(b) Investment credit (attach Form 3468)		
	(c) Work incentive (WIN) credit (attach Form 4874)		- 0 -
13	Balance of income tax		198
14	(a) Tax from recomputing prior year investment credit (attach Form 4255) (b) Tax from recomputing a prior year work incentive (WIN) credit (see instructions—attach computation)		- 0 -
15	Income tax (line 13 plus line 14). Enter here and on line 23		198

Trusts Taxable at Trust Rates (See General Instruction B(2))

16	Tax on amount shown on line 5 above or line 33, page 2 (from Tax Rate Schedule on last page of instructions). .		
17	Alternative tax from separate Schedule D		
18	Income tax—(line 16 or, if applicable, line 17, whichever is lesser)		⑥
19	Less: (a) Foreign tax credit (attach Form 1116)		
	(b) Investment credit (attach Form 3468)		
	(c) Work incentive (WIN) credit (attach Form 4874)		
20	Balance of income tax		
21	(a) Tax from recomputing prior year investment credit (attach Form 4255) (b) Tax from recomputing a prior year work incentive (WIN) credit (see instructions—attach computation)		
22	Income tax (line 20 plus line 21). Enter here and on line 23		

Total Income Tax

23	Income tax (from line 15 or 22, whichever is applicable)		198
24	Minimum tax on tax preference items. Check here ☐ if Form 4626 is attached		- 0 -
25	Total tax (add lines 23 and 24)		198
26	Credits (a) Tax deposited with Form 7004 (attach copy)		
	(b) Tax deposited with Form 7005 (attach copy)		
	(c) Foreign organizations—Enter U.S. income tax paid or withheld at the source (See instructions and section 1443(a))		
	(d) Credit from regulated investment companies (attach Form 2439) . . .		
	(e) U.S. tax on special fuels, nonhighway gas and lubricating oil (attach Form 4136). . .		- 0 -
27	TAX DUE (line 25 less line 26). See instruction E for depositary method of payment . . . . ➔		198
28	OVERPAYMENT (line 26 less line 25)		

Under penalties of perjury, I declare that I have examined this return, including accompanying schedules and statements, and to the best of my knowledge and belief it is true, correct, and complete. Declaration of preparer (other than taxpayer) is based on all information of which he has any knowledge.

The Internal Revenue Service does not require a seal on this form, but if one is used, please place it here.	March 13, 1974 _Date_	_Ellen Diamond_ _Signature of officer or trustee_	Executive Director _Title_
	Date	Signature of individual or firm preparing the return Preparer's address	Emp. Ident. or Soc. Sec. No.

Fig. 24–16. The first page of Form 990–T. This form is to be completed by all exempt organizations having unrelated business income. Only page 1 is completed if the unrelated business income is $5,000 or less.

CONCLUSION

All exempt organizations except for churches and organizations with gross receipts of $5,000 or less, are involved in complying with federal tax laws and in filing tax returns with the Internal Revenue Service. For many, this is a traumatic experience because the principal forms which are used—Form 990, Form 990–PF, Form 990–AR, and Form 990–T—are written in technical language which requires expert knowledge. With few exceptions, exempt organizations are well advised to obtain competent tax advice not only at the time these returns are prepared, but also throughout the year as potential tax problems arise.

25

State Compliance Requirements

In addition to federal requirements, most states also require nonprofit organizations to register with one or more agencies of the state government. These requirements fall into one or more of three areas:

1. Registration requirements for organizations soliciting funds within the state
2. Registration of nonprofit organizations (including trusts) holding property in the state
3. Registration of organizations "doing business" in the state

These requirements vary from state to state and involve basically legal matters. If an organization is "doing business" in or intends to do business in a state it should consult with its attorney to get competent advice. The comments that follow in this chapter are intended only as an "overview" of the compliance-reporting requirements as related to the first two areas listed above. It is hoped that this overview will give the reader some indication of the financial reporting, and in some cases auditing requirements, of the various states as of the date of publication. Since the laws governing nonprofit organizations are rapidly changing, this overview is not a substitute for consultation with competent legal advisors.

SOLICITATION OF FUNDS

A number of states have laws requiring nonprofit organizations to register with a regulatory agency of the state prior to soliciting any funds within the state. This registration requirement often involves financial statements and sometimes these statements must contain an opinion of an independent accountant. Most states make no distinction between resident and nonresident organizations, and it would appear that an organization soliciting funds by mail or advertisement would have to register even though it might not have an office or employees in that state.

In addition to the initial registration, most states that have registration requirements also require an annual financial report. This financial report may also require an opinion of an independent accountant, and in some instances the state will specify the accounting principles to be followed. Obviously, where an organization must provide this type of information, particularly where the organization is not resident in that state, considerable planning is required. These annual reports are usually due between three and six months after the end of the fiscal year.

Exemption Categories

Most states do exempt certain organizations from their registration and reporting requirements. These exemptions are usually limited to one or more of the following organizations:

Category 1. Religious

Category 2. Educational, where the organization has a curriculum approved by the state or an appropriate accrediting body

Category 3. Nonprofit hospitals

Category 4. Organizations that solicit funds solely from within their already existing membership

Category 5. Organizations that solicit funds for the relief of any individual specified by name at the time of solicitation when all the contributions without any deductions, are turned over to the beneficiary for his use

Category 6. Organizations that do not actually raise or receive more than a specified amount, frequently $2,000, or do not receive contributions from more than a specified number of persons, frequently ten, *and* where no paid fund raisers are involved.

These exemptions vary from state to state. For example in New York, organizations receiving contributions of less than $10,000 are not required to register at all; if between $10,000 and $25,000 is received, a simplified form of reporting is required, but if more than $25,000 is received a much more detailed report is required which includes an auditor's report. In several states no registration or reporting is required.

REGISTRATION WITH ATTORNEY GENERAL

In addition to the registration requirements prior to soliciting funds, some states also have laws requiring all nonprofit organizations or charitable trusts to register with the attorney general or other agency if the organization or trust has assets within the state or if they are resident in the state. While these requirements are less widespread than the law requiring registration prior to soliciting funds, each organization must be careful to comply with these requirements. Since a different agency of the state is often involved, the reporting under these requirements is sometimes different from the requirements under the solicitation law.

As with the solicitation law requirements, usually an organization subject to these laws is required to both initially register and to file an annual report. The principal interest of the state is the proper administration and disposition of assets held by the organization. In some states the form of reporting follows that required by the federal government on the Form 990.

Where this is so, the problem of compliance is simplified somewhat. In several states the requirements can be met by filing copies of Form 990 plus certain additional information not required in Form 990. Some of this additional information can, however, be quite voluminous. One state, for example, requires a schedule showing all security transactions during the year.

Exemptions

Where a state has separate registration requirements for nonprofit organizations and trusts there are usually a few exemptions allowed. These generally follow the exemptions listed on page 446 for the solicitation laws.

IRS Requirement

Under the Tax Reform Act of 1969, Congress provided that every private foundation must submit to the attorney general in the state in which it has its principal office, a copy of the annual return required to be filed with the IRS. The intent of this requirement is to encourage state officials to oversee the activities of these exempt organizations by automatically providing them with financial information.

INDIVIDUAL STATE REQUIREMENTS

Summarized below are the requirements of each state with respect to both solicitation law requirements and registration of charitable organizations and trusts. As was noted earlier in this chapter, this list should not be considered all-inclusive or authoritative. The laws in many states are in the process of change as this is being written. Our purpose here is to give an overview of the requirements as of the spring of 1974. The exemption references throughout this chapter are keyed to the exemption listed on page 446.

Alabama

Solicitation: No known requirements.
Attorney General: No known requirements.

Alaska

Solicitation: No requirements.
Attorney General: No requirements.

Arizona

Solicitation: There are no state requirements for registration. However, the City of Phoenix, and perhaps other cities, has a registration law.
Attorney General: No known requirements.

Arkansas

Solicitation: All organizations must register prior to soliciting funds except for the following:
1. Categories 1, 4.
2. Category 6 with limitation of $1,000.
An annual report is required within 90 days of the end of the fiscal year on forms provided by the Secretary of State, Little Rock 72201.
Attorney General: No known requirements.

California

Solicitation: No separate requirements as such.

Attorney General: All organizations holding property or doing business in California are required to register except the following:

1. Categories 1, 2, and 3.
2. Cemeteries

Annual reports are required to be filed within four months and fifteen days after the end of the year. Forms may be obtained from the Registrar of Charitable Trusts, 714 P Street, Sacramento.

Colorado

Solicitation: No known requirements.

Attorney General: No known requirements.

Connecticut

Solicitation: All organizations soliciting funds are required to register except for the following:

1. Categories 1, 2, 3, 5.
2. Category 4 but with limitation that 80% must come from membership in both number of contributions and dollar amount.
3. Category 6 with limitation of $2,000.
4. Public libraries, volunteer fire companies, veteran organizations, and certain other specified organizations.

An annual report is required and must include an opinion of an independent public accountant if gross income is $5,000 or more. Forms may be obtained from the Department of Consumer Protection, State Office Building, Hartford 06115.

Attorney General: No known requirements.

Delaware

Solicitation: No known requirements.

Attorney General: No known requirements.

District of Columbia

Solicitation: Registration is required of all organizations receiving contributions exceeding $1,500 except for organizations that solicit solely from within their own membership. The registration is for a period of one year and an annual report is required at the time of registration. An auditor's opinion is not required. Information and forms can be obtained from Bureau of Licenses and Inspections, Department of Economic Development, 614 H Street NW, Washington, D. C.

Attorney General: No known requirements.

Florida

Solicitation: All organizations are required to register prior to soliciting funds except for the following:

1. Categories 1, 2, 3, 4, 5.

  2. Category 6 with limitation of $2,000 or 10 persons.

An annual report accompanied by an opinion of an independent public accountant is required. If contributions are less than $10,000 the format of the report is not prescribed, although it must be approved by the Secretary of State. Other organizations must file on forms provided by the Secretary of State, Charitable Solicitations Coordinator, 3399 Ponce De Leon Blvd., Coral Gables.

  Attorney General: No requirement.

Georgia

  Solicitation: All organizations are required to register prior to soliciting funds except for the following:
  1. Categories 1, 4, 5.
  2. Educational institutions that solicit solely from the student body and their families, alumni, faculty and trustees.
  3. Local community organizations that are affiliated with a statewide parent organization, which itself is registered.

An annual report is required within 90 days after the end of the year of all registered organizations which have received contributions during the prior year. The financial statements must be verified by a CPA. Further information can be obtained from the Secretary of State, 214 State Capital, Atlanta.

  Attorney General: No requirements.

Hawaii

  Solicitation: All organizations soliciting funds are required to register except for the following:
  1. Categories 1, 2, 3, 4, 5.
  2. Category 6 with limitation of $4,000 *or* ten persons or less.

The registration is for a period of one year and must be refiled each year. Financial statements are required at the time of registration and they must be audited by an independent public accountant. Information and forms can be obtained from the Director of Regulatory Agencies, 1010 Richards Street, Honolulu 96813.

  Attorney General: No requirements.

Idaho

  Solicitation: No known requirements.
  Attorney General: No known requirements.

Illinois

  Solicitation: All organizations are required to register prior to soliciting funds except the following:
  1. Categories 1, 2, 3.
  2. Category 6 with limitation of $4,000.
  3. Cemeteries and homes for the aged.

An annual report must be filed within six months of the end of the fiscal year. If more than $10,000 is received the report must include the certification of a CPA. Forms can be obtained from the Attorney General, Springfield. The form of financial statement used is a Statement of Financial Activities.

Attorney General Requirements: All organizations having assets of $4,000 or more are required to register except for the same organizations exempted from the solicitation rules listed above. Annual reports are also required within six months after the close of the year.

Indiana

Solicitation: No requirements.
Attorney General: No requirements.

Iowa

Solicitation: All organizations, except those soliciting from within the county in which located, must obtain a permit by registering annually, in December, with the Secretary of State, State Capital Building, Des Moines 50319. An annual report is required with each registration.
Attorney General: No known requirements.

Kansas

Solicitation: All organizations soliciting funds must file a copy of their charter with the Secretary of State, Topeka. An annual report must be filed by April 15.
Attorney General: No known requirements.

Kentucky

Solicitation: No requirements.
Attorney General: No requirements.

Louisiana

Solicitation: No known requirements.
Attorney General: No known requirements.

Maine

Solicitation: All organizations, except those soliciting from within the municipality in which located must, annually, obtain a license prior to soliciting from the Department of Health and Welfare, Augusta 04330.
Attorney General: No known requirements.

Maryland

Solicitation: All organizations soliciting funds are required to register except for the following:

1. Categories 1, 3.
2. Category 6 with $2,500 limitation.

An annual report is required within 90 days of the end of the fiscal year, and extensions are not normally granted. An auditor's opinion is not required. Information and forms can be obtained from the Secretary of State, Charities Organizations Registration, Annapolis.

Attorney General: No known requirements.

Massachusetts

Solicitation: All organizations soliciting funds are required to register except for the following:

1. Categories 1, 2, 3, 4, 5.
2. Category 6 with limitation of $5,000 or ten persons.
3. Fire companies, libraries.

An opinion of an independent public accountant is required in connection with registration and with the annual report. The latter is due on or before June 1st, or within 60 days after the end of the fiscal year if the organization's fiscal year ends in April or May. Forms and information can be obtained from Commonwealth of Massachusetts Division of Public Charities, Department of the Attorney General, 100 Cambridge Street, Boston.

Attorney General: See above.

Michigan

Solicitation: All organizations must register except for churches and local charities soliciting within the county in which domiciled. An annual report is also required and if contributions of $15,000 or more are received a CPA's opinion must be included.

Attorney General Requirements: All organizations receiving funds except for the following organizations must register with the Attorney General:

1. Categories 1, 2, 3.
2. Nonprofit organizations whose funds are derived from community funds or united foundation sources.

Registration is required within two months of receipt of property. An annual report is required within six months after close of fiscal year, with a certified audit although a Trustee may file a sworn statement setting forth the information in lieu of the certified audit report. Information can be obtained from the Department of Attorney General, Lansing, 48713.

Minnesota

Solicitation: All organizations soliciting funds are required to register except the following:

1. Categories 1, 2, 4, 5.
2. Category 6 with $2,000 limitation.

If contributions of $10,000 or more are received or if a professional fund raiser is used, an annual report is required within six months after the end of the year. If contributions are more than $25,000, this report must contain an audit report by a CPA. Information and forms can be obtained from the Minnesota Department of Commerce, Metro Square Building, St. Paul. Attorney General: Copy of above statements.

Mississippi

Solicitation: No known requirements.
Attorney General: No known requirements.

Missouri

Solicitation: All organizations must register with the Secretary of State. An annual registration report which is due by December 31st of the following year must be filed with the Secretary of State, State Capitol Building, Jefferson City 65101.
Attorney General: No known requirements.

Montana

Solicitation: No known requirements.
Attorney General: No known requirements.

Nebraska

Solicitation: All organizations soliciting funds must register except the following:
1. Organizations soliciting solely within their home county.
2. Religious organizations soliciting in the immediately adjoining counties where part of their membership resides.
Biannual reports are required from all registered organizations within six months after the end of the odd-numbered year. Forms can be obtained from the Secretary of State, Corporation Division, State Capitol Building, Lincoln 68509.
Attorney General: No known requirements.

Nevada

Solicitation: No known requirements.
Attorney General: No known requirements.

New Hampshire

Solicitation: No requirements.
Attorney General: All organizations must register and file annual reports except Categories 1 and 2. Information and forms can be obtained from the Office of the Attorney General, Charitable Trust Division, State House Annex, Concord 03301.

New Jersey

Solicitation: All organizations soliciting funds are required to register except the following:
1. Categories 1, 2, 5.

2. Category 6 with limitation of $10,000.

3. Any organization receiving an allocation from the Incorporated Community Chest or United Fund and not receiving contributions over $10,000 in addition to such allocation.

4. Certain enumerated types of category 4 organizations.

5. Veteran, firemen, ambulance, or rescue squad organizations which do not employ outside fund raisers.

6. Organizations for the care and treatment of invalid or crippled children.

An annual report must be filed within six months after the end of the year. If contributions received are in excess of $25,000, an opinion of an independent public accountant must accompany the report. Forms and information may be obtained from the Office of the Attorney General, Division of Consumer Affairs, 1100 Raymond Boulevard, Newark 07102.

Attorney General: See above requirements.

New Mexico

Solicitation: No known requirements.

Attorney General: No known requirements.

New York *

Solicitation: All organizations soliciting funds are required to register except the following:

1. Categories 1, 2, 5.

2. Category 6 with limitation of $10,000

3. Any organization receiving an allocation from the incorporated Community Chest or United Fund and which does not receive contributions over $10,000 in addition to such allocation.

4. Category 4 but limited to certain enumerated types of organizations.

An annual report must be filed within six months after the end of the year. If contributions received are in excess of $25,000, an opinion of an independent public accountant must accompany the report. An extension of time to file is normally granted. Forms and information may be obtained from the Bureau of Charitable and Proprietary Organizations, New York State Board of Social Welfare, Office Tower, Empire State Plaza, Albany 12223.

Attorney General: All organizations holding property for charitable purposes must register with the Attorney General unless otherwise exempted under subdivision 6 of Estates Power and Trust Law, Section 8–1.4. The registration form must be filed within six months after any property held or income therefrom is required to be applied to charitable purposes. Annual reports are due within six months after the end of the fiscal or calendar year.

---

* In late 1974, a number of changes were in process of being approved, including: a reduction from $10,000 to $5,000 in the maximum contributions an organization could have before registration was required; an increase from $25,000 to $50,000 in the amount of contributions *and revenue* which an organization could receive before which the opinion of a CPA was required; and a reduction from six months to ninety days in the filing requirement. Note that under these proposed changes the $50,000 includes not only contributions but all other types of revenue.

North Carolina

Solicitation: All organizations soliciting funds must register except the following:

1. Categories 1, 4.
2. A charitable organization which confines its solicitation and operations to the county in which located.
3. Educational institutions belonging to the North Carolina Association of Colleges and Universities.

The initial registration must be on forms provided and must include an opinion of an independent CPA. An annual report is required within 120 days after the end of the fiscal year, and must also be accompanied by an opinion of a CPA. Forms can be obtained from the Commissioner of Social Services, Raleigh. A bill is pending in the legislature which would change the current exemptions.

Attorney General: No known requirements.

North Dakota

Solicitation: All organizations soliciting funds are required to register except the following:

1. Categories 1, 5.
2. Educational institutions that are operated by the state.
3. Certain specified organizations (Boy Scouts, Girl Scouts).

An annual report is required within sixty days after the end of the year, but extension requests are usually granted. An auditor's report is not required. Forms and information can be obtained from Secretary of State, Bismarck.

Attorney General: No known requirements.

Ohio

Solicitation: Organizations soliciting funds are required to register with the Attorney General except for the following:

1. Categories 1, 2, 4, 5.
2. Organizations whose expenses are less than $500.

An auditor's opinion is required in. connection with the registration and with the annual report. The annual report is due within 90 days after the end of the year but extension requests are normally granted. Information and forms can be obtained from the Assistant Attorney General, Statehouse Annex, Columbus.

Attorney General: See solicitation requirements above.

Oklahoma

Solicitation: Registration is required by all organizations soliciting funds except for those soliciting solely from within their own membership. An auditor's opinion is required in connection with the registration and with the annual report. This opinion may be given by a public accountant as well as a CPA. Annual reports are due within three months of the end of the fiscal year but extensions are normally granted. Information and forms can be obtained from the Office of the Commissioner of Charities and Corrections, 4400 North Lincoln Boulevard, Mark Twain Building, Oklahoma City.

Attorney General: No known requirements.

Oregon

Solicitation: All organizations soliciting funds are required to register with the Attorney General except for the following:

1. Categories 1, 2, 3, 4.
2. Historical society or museums.
3. Category 6 with limitation of $250.

In addition all of the same organizations are required to register with the County Clerk of each county in which funds are solicited. The annual report to the Attorney General is due four months and fifteen days after the end of the fiscal year but extensions are normally granted. Audited financial statements are not required.

Attorney General: All organizations holding property for charitable purposes are required to register with the Attorney General, Department of Justice, 555 State Office Building, Portland 97201, except the following:

1. Categories 1, 2, 3.
2. Regulated cemetery corporation.
3. Regulated child care agency.
4. Historical society or museum.

Pennsylvania

Solicitation: All organizations soliciting funds are required to register except the following:

1. Categories 1, 2, 3, 4.
2. Category 6 with limitation of $2,000 or ten persons

Organizations exempt from this registration requirement must nevertheless submit annually, on forms to be prescribed by the Commission on Charitable Organizations, a statement setting forth the reasons for this claim for exemption. Financial statements are required in the initial registration statement, and registration must be renewed annually. An eight-page financial statement format is prescribed. These statements must be audited but the auditor does not have to be a CPA. Forms and information can be obtained from the Administrator, Solicitation of Charitable Funds Act, Department of State, Harrisburg 17120.

Attorney General: No known requirements.

Rhode Island

Solicitation: No known requirements.

Attorney General: No known requirements.

South Carolina

Solicitation: All organizations soliciting funds are required to register, except the following:

Categories 1, 2, 3, 4, 5, 6.
The registration is effective for a one-year period and must be renewed by the Secretary of State, Division of Public Charities, Columbia.

Attorney General: No known requirements.

South Dakota

Solicitation: Apparently state requirements provide for the registration of all organizations soliciting funds except those soliciting solely within their own membershp. No annual report requirements are known to the author.

Attorney General: No known requirements.

Tennessee

Solicitation: All organizations soliciting funds are required to register except the following:

1. Categories 1, 2, 5.
2. Category 6 with a $200 limitation.

The registration is effective for a one-year period and must be renewed annually with the Secretary of State, Nashville 37219. No financial reports are required.

Attorney General: No known requirements.

Texas

Solicitation: There is no requirement that organizations register although there is provision in the law that the Secretary of State may require a report every four years.

Attorney General: No known requirements.

Utah

Solicitation: There are no state requirements for registration but some counties, such as Salt Lake County, are known to have registration requirements.

Attorney General: No known requirements.

Vermont

Solicitation: No requirements.

Attorney General: No requirements.

Virginia

Solicitation: No state registration requirement. Some counties apparently have registration requirements.

Attorney General: No known requirements.

Washington

Solicitation: Every organization soliciting funds must register and file annual reports (within 90 days of end of year) with the Department of Motor Vehicles except the following:

1. Categories 1, 2, 4, where the fund raiser is an unpaid member of the organization.
2. Category 6 with a limit of $5,000 every six months.

Attorney General: Nonprofit organizations receiving property are required to register except for Categories 1, 2, 5. Nonprofit organizations exempt under federal law who have filed a copy of their declaration of tax-exempt status with the Attorney General are exempt from further registration. Annual reports are required on the fifteenth day of the sixth month after the close of the year of all registered organizations. A copy of Form 990 filed with the federal government will meet this requirement. Further information can be obtained from the Attorney General, Temple of Justice, Olympia.

West Virginia

Solicitation: There are no state requirements although several municipalities have registration requirements.

Attorney General: No known requirements.

Wisconsin

Solicitation: Every organization soliciting funds must register except the following:

1. Categories 1, 4, 5.
2. Category 2 provided solely from alumni, students, parents
3. Category 6 with limitation of $500
4. Local organization supervised by a parent organization who files a registration statement for the local.

Annual reports are required within three months after close of the year. If $10,000 or more is received the annual report requires an opinion of a CPA. Forms and instructions can be obtained from State of Wisconsin, Department of Regulations and Licensing, 110 North Henry Street, Madison.

Attorney General: No known requirements.

Wyoming

Solicitation: No known requirements.

Attorney General: No known requirements.

PART VI

SETTING UP AND KEEPING THE BOOKS

26

Cash Basis Bookkeeping

Bookkeeping is the process of recording in a systematic manner transactions that have taken place. It is that simple. There is nothing mysterious or complicated about bookkeeping. It is simply maintaining records in a manner that will facilitate summarizing them at the end of a period in the form of financial statements. For small cash basis organizations there is little need to know a great deal about accounting theory. Common sense will dictate the records that must be kept. The purpose of this chapter is to discuss bookkeeping in its simplest form—where everything is recorded on a cash basis.*

THREE STEPS IN A BOOKKEEPING SYSTEM

There are basically only three steps involved in any bookkeeping system, whether a simple cash system or a more involved accrual basis system. These are:

1. Recording each transaction in a systematic manner when it occurs. In a simple cash basis system only cash transactions are recorded. This recording could be on the check book stub or, for organizations with many transactions, it might be an entry in either the "cash disbursement record" or the "cash receipts record." In accrual basis bookkeeping, transactions not involving cash are also recorded.

* Cash basis accounting and financial statements were discussed in Chapters 3 and 10.

2. Summarizing transactions so that all "like" transactions are grouped together. This summarizing can be informally done on a simple columnar worksheet, or it can be more formally handled in a system in which transactions are posted to a formal book called the "general ledger." In either case, the objective is to bring "like" transactions together in a significant manner.

3. Preparing financial statements from the "summary" prepared in step 2. These financial statements can be a simple listing of all the major categories in the summary or it can involve some rearrangement of the figures into a more significant presentation. In either case, the financial statements are the end product of the bookkeeping system.

Illustrative Statements

Bookkeeping is truly a matter of common sense. If a little bit of thought is given, almost anyone can devise a simple bookkeeping system that will meet the needs of a small, cash basis organization. The best way to illustrate this is by showing how two organizations keep their records. The first is the Cromwell Hills Swim Club, and the second is All Saints Church. The financial statements of both organizations were illustrated in Chapter 10. The Cromwell Hills Swim Club uses the checkbook system of bookkeeping. All Saints Church uses a somewhat more formal system utilizing a cash receipts book, a cash disbursements book, and a general ledger.

CHECKBOOK SYSTEM

Most people are familiar with the first step in checkbook record keeping since almost everyone keeps his own personal checkbook. The process of recording each check and each deposit on the checkbook stub is the first step in a checkbook system of bookkeeping—the step of initially recording the transaction. The checkbook becomes the "book of original entry." Obviously, it is important to write down enough description on the stub to properly identify what the receipt or disbursement was for. In the case of disbursements, there is usually reference to a vendor's invoice or some supporting documents. It is also important to keep track of receipts by noting whose checks are included in each deposit, perhaps using the back of the check stub if there isn't room on the front. Or, alternatively, this information can be put on the copy of the deposit slip which can then be kept with the bank statement or in a separate file.

Since the checkbook becomes the source of all bookkeeping entries, it is important that all receipts be deposited intact and all disbursements be made by check. This will ensure that a record is established of all transactions. Figure 26–1 shows an example of a checkbook stub.

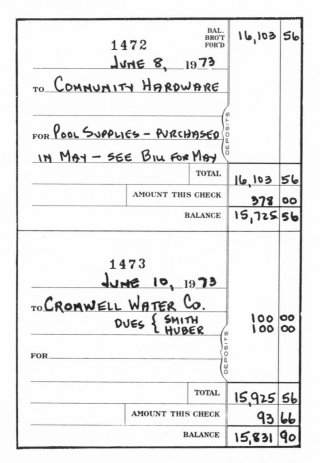

Fig. 26–1. An example of a check book stub.

Worksheet Summary

The second step of summarizing all the transactions for the period is almost as easy. Most organizations use a worksheet which has many columns, one for each major category of income or expense. Figure 26–2 shows a worksheet for the Cromwell Hills Swim Club.

It should be noted that on this worksheet each month's transactions have been summarized from the checkbook stub and entered in total. Instead, each individual transaction could have been entered on this worksheet. If this were done the worksheet could have been many pages long depending on the number of transactions. However, if an organization has many similar transactions in a period, the bookkeeper can probably run an adding machine tape of all like items and enter only the total each month from the checkbook stubs, which would be faster than copying each transaction onto the worksheet. Either approach, or even a combination, is appropriate and is a matter of preference.

Notice the reconciliation of the cash account at the bottom of this worksheet. This is the bookkeeper's proof that a mistake hasn't been made in summarizing the transactions on this worksheet. While this is shown for the entire year, in practice the worksheet would be totaled either every month or every time financial statements were prepared. At that point, the bookkeeper would want to prove the cash position in this manner. This reconciliation should not be confused with the bank reconciliation which should be prepared monthly to prove out the checkbook balance.

Payroll Register

The payroll presents a problem because the club must also keep track of the payroll taxes it has to withhold, and it must pay these amounts, plus the employer's share to the government, through the local bank. Figure 26–3 shows a typical payroll register. A payroll register in a form similar to this one can be obtained from many large stationery stores.

Since the club is following cash basis accounting, no attempt is made to record the liability for the unpaid payroll taxes between the date they were "withheld" and the date they were actually paid. In our example, employees are paid their summer wages in two equal installments on July 25 and September 5. Notice on the worksheet in Figure 26–2 that the net payroll of $5,420.00 is shown as the payroll expense in July. The payroll

Cromwell Swim Club
Worksheet Summarizing Checkbook Stubs By Month
For The Year Ended December 31, 1973

Month	Deposits — Dues	Deposits — Capital Contributions	Deposits — Loan from Bank	Interest	Expenditures — Salaries	Payroll Taxes	Mortgage Interest	Mortgage Principal	Pool Supplies	Other — Description	Other — Amount
January											
February		10 000 00									
March		40 000 00									
April	10 000 00										
May	12 000 00								2 000 00	Land / Pool Const.	25 000 00 / 32 500 00 / 30 000 00
June	3 000 00		40 000 00								
July				75 00	5 420 00		200 00			Misc.	300 00
August					1 580 00	410 00	200 00			"	400 00
September					5 420 00		200 00			"	380 00
October				50 00	1 580 00	410 00	200 00			"	200 00
November							200 00	3 800 00		Lawn Furn.	80 00 00
December							200 00				
Total	25 000 00	50 000 00	40 000 00	125 00	14 000 00	820 00	1 200 00	3 800 00	2 000 00		89 680 00

Total Deposits 115 125 00

Total Expenditures 111 500 00

Reconciliation of Cash

Balance at Beginning of Year	—0—
Total Deposits	115 125 00
Less: Expenditures	(111 500 00)
Balance at End of Year	3 625 00

Fig. 26–2.   Worksheet summarizing checkbook stubs by month.

Cromwell Hills Swim Club

PAYROLL MONTH ENDING JULY, 1973

	WAGES			EMPLOYEE DEDUCTIONS				
NAME OF EMPLOYEE	REGULAR	OVER-TIME	TOTAL WAGES	FED O.A.T.	FED. WITH. TAX	OTHER WITH.	TOTAL DEDUCT.	NET AMOUNT PAYABLE
Jones, W. (Pool Mgr.)	1000.00	—	1000.00	58.00	170.00	—	228.00	772.00
Smith, J. (Lifeguard)	750.00	—	750.00	44.00	125.00	—	169.00	581.00
Brown, J. ''	750.00	—	750.00	44.00	125.00	—	169.00	581.00
Samuels, A. ''	750.00	—	750.00	44.00	125.00	—	169.00	581.00
McNair, S. ''	750.00	—	750.00	44.00	125.00	—	169.00	581.00
Williams, A. ''	750.00	—	750.00	44.00	125.00	—	169.00	581.00
Huber, W. ''	750.00	—	750.00	44.00	125.00	—	169.00	581.00
Miller, C. ''	750.00	—	750.00	44.00	125.00	—	169.00	581.00
McDonald, W. ''	750.00	—	750.00	44.00	125.00	—	169.00	581.00
Total	7000.00	—	7000.00	410.00	1170.00	—	1580.00	5420.00

Fig. 26–3.   Payroll Register.

tax deductions of $1,580.00 are not shown since they weren't paid until August. In August when these withheld taxes are paid, the club will also have to pay employer FICA taxes of $410.00. This is also recorded when paid in August.

Unpaid Dues

The club will also need to keep track of which members have paid their dues. This can be handled by simply keeping a list of members and indicating the date "paid" after each member's name when payment is received. This common sense approach should be used with any other type of information that the club must keep.

Financial Statements

The third step in the bookkeeping system is preparing financial statements. They can be prepared directly from the worksheet summary of the checkbook stubs (Figure 26–2). Look at the Statement of Cash Receipts, Disbursements and Cash Balance . . . shown on page 130. It will be seen that this statement agrees with the totals on this worksheet. This worksheet becomes, in essence, the general ledger. This in conjunction with the checkbook and payroll register would become the "books" of the club.

Advantages and Disadvantages

The checkbook system of record keeping is very satisfactory for many organizations, but it has limitations on the number of transactions it can handle before it becomes more cumbersome than useful. This system has the disadvantage that it is not a recognized or formal system of bookkeeping and while it may work perfectly well for one treasurer, the next treasurer may find it awkward and too informal. Further, the use of worksheets to summarize the period's transactions has the disadvantage that they are just worksheets, and are likely to get lost or destroyed. So when an organization starts to have any volume of financial activity it should start to consider a more conventional and formal set of records.

CASH BASIS SYSTEM

The basic difference between the checkbook system and a more formal cash basis system is that in the latter transactions are recorded and summarized in a more formal manner. Otherwise the bookkeeping process is the same.

Basic Records

In the checkbook system we had only the checkbook stub, worksheets summarizing transactions, and a payroll register. In a more formal cash basis system we would have the following records:

Cash Disbursement Book—in which each check disbursed is recorded in almost the same manner as on a checkbook stub.

Cash Receipts Book—in which each cash receipt is recorded in almost the same manner as on a checkbook stub.

General Journal—in which noncash transactions are recorded. The principal noncash entry is the entry to close the books at the end of the year.

General Ledger—in which all transactions are summarized.

Trial Balance—which lists all accounts in the general ledger and proves that the total of the "debits" and "credits" in the general ledger is equal.*

Each of these five records is discussed and illustrated below. Before doing so, however, it is necessary to discuss briefly the concept of a "double entry" bookkeeping system and to introduce the terms "debits" and "credits."

Double Entry System

There are five major categories of accounts which a bookkeeping system keeps track of: expense accounts, income accounts, asset accounts, liability accounts, and the net worth or fund balance of the organization. For the moment only the first four will enter into our discussion. The principle of double entry bookkeeping is that every transaction affects two accounts and usually two of these four categories of accounts. For example:

An organization spends $100 to hire a secretary. The two categories affected are assets and expenses. The asset account is the cash balance (it is decreased) and the expense account is payroll expense (it is increased).

An organization receives a contribution of $50. The two accounts affected are contribution income (it is increased) and cash account (it is increased).

An organization spends $10 for stationery supplies. The two accounts affected are stationery supplies expense (it is increased) and cash (it is decreased).

An organization borrows $100 from the bank. The two accounts affected are cash (it is increased) and loans payable (it is increased).

---

* Actually the trial balance is not part of the "set of books" as such. Rather it is something prepared from the books. However, since it is important that the trial balance be prepared, it is considered part of the books for this discussion.

An organization provides Jones with $100 of service which Jones agrees to pay for at the end of next month. The two accounts affected are the income account—sales of services—(it is increased) and accounts receivable from Jones, an asset account (it is increased).

Jones pays the organization the $100 he owes. The two accounts affected are cash (it is increased) and accounts receivable (it is decreased).

Thus every transaction affects two accounts. This is why the words "double entry" bookkeeping are used. Each bookkeeping entry must affect two accounts.

Debits and Credits

The words "debit" and "credit" are bookkeeping terms to refer to the two sides of a transaction. Asset accounts and expense accounts normally have debit balances. Liability accounts and income accounts normally have credit balances. To increase an asset or expense account one would add a debit amount (i.e., the account would be "debited"); to increase an income or liability account one would add a credit amount (i.e., the account would be "credited"). Here is a summary which shows these debit and credit rules:

Category of account	To increase you would add a	To decrease you would add a	Balance is normally a
Assets (cash, accounts receivable, inventory, prepaid expenses, fixed assets)	debit	credit	debit
Liabilities (accounts payable, accrued liabilities, bank loans payable, long term debt) ...	credit	debit	credit
Income (contributions, sales, receipts)	credit	debit	credit
Expenses (salaries, supplies, cost of goods sold, taxes)	debit	credit	debit

All that needs to be remembered is that assets and expenses normally are debits and liabilities and income are credits, and that to decrease an account you would reverse the designation.

It is also important to remember that there are both debits and credits to every transaction and that in total they must be equal in amount.

Many people are confused by the rule that an asset is a debit. After all, they point out, when you have a credit balance in your account with the local department store this is certainly an asset. How does this reconcile with the rule that an asset normally has a debit balance? The answer is the perspective from which one looks at a transaction. For every borrower there is a lender. On the borrower's books the amount borrowed shows up as a liability (credit balance). When a housewife returns some merchandise and gets credit she is getting credit on the department store's books—they owe her—a liability that is a credit on "their" books. If the housewife kept her own set of books they would show that the department store owed her and this is an asset to her, and would be a debit. So when someone talks about having a credit balance with someone what he is really saying is that on the other person's books he has a credit balance.

Debits on the Left

When there are two columns, the debits are always represented on the left side, and the credits on the right side. The general ledger pages illustrated here use a three-column format—a debit column, a credit column, and a "balance" column. Here is what it looks like:

SHEET NO.				ACCOUNT NO.		
TERMS		NAME	Cash Account			
RATING		ADDRESS				
CREDIT LIMIT						

Date 19_73_		ITEMS	FOL.	✓	DEBITS	CREDITS	BALANCE
Jan	1	Balance beginning of period			100 00		100 00
	31	Receipts for month			300 00		400 00
	31	Expenditures for month				200 00	200 00

This illustrates both the position of debits and credits, and also how, following the rules above, an asset account would be increased or decreased. Notice that since cash is an asset account it would normally have a "debit" balance. Notice that the beginning balance is a debit. The increase in cash from receipts is also a debit. The decrease in cash from expenditures is a reduction of a normally debit account and therefore must be a credit. The final column is merely a running balance to aid the bookkeeper.

Some general ledgers do not have this "balance" column and are set up in a somewhat different format. Here is this same general ledger account in this other form:

SHEET NO._____							ACCOUNT NO._____			
TERMS			NAME	Cash Account						
RATING			ADDRESS							
CREDIT LIMIT										
Date 19_73	ITEMS	FOLIO	✓	DEBITS	Date 19_73	ITEMS	FOLIO	✓	CREDITS	
Jan 1	Bal. beginning			100 00	Jan 31	Expenditures			200 00	
31	Receipts			300 00	31	To balance			200 00	
	total			400 00		total			400 00	
31	Balance			200 00						

This form of general ledger is a little more difficult for the inexperienced person to work with primarily because a running balance is more difficult to obtain. For this reason, it is not recommended. However, either form is equally acceptable.

That is all you must know about the theory of double entry bookkeeping. The rest follows from these relatively straightforward rules. Don't try to figure out logically why assets and expenses are debits, or why liability and income accounts are credits. These are the rules by definition.

With the foregoing explanation about double entry bookkeeping, and debits and credits, let us now turn to the set of books that would be kept by an organization that keeps its record on a simple cash basis. The two principal books that will be substituted for the "checkbook stub" are the Cash Disbursements Book and the Cash Receipts Book. As the names indicate, one is for recording cash disbursements and one for recording cash receipts.

Cash Disbursements Book

The cash disbursements book is a book which provides a place to record all disbursements. Usually this is a wide book with ten to fifteen columns, each column of which represents one of the major categories of expense. As each check is written it is recorded in the cash disbursements book. The amount of the check is "posted" * in two places. The first is in the total column which at the end of the month will be "footed" † and then posted to the cash account in the general ledger to reduce the cash balance. The second posting will be in the column representing the category of expense which the disbursement represents. At the end of the month each of these expense category columns is footed to get the total disbursements for that particular category. These totals, in turn, are posted to the general ledger. Normally at the start of each month, a new cash disbursements page is started. Figure 26–4 shows an example of a cash disbursements book for All Saints Church.

Cash Receipts Book

The cash receipts book is very similar to the cash disbursements book and is used in the same manner. It also has a number of columns to provide for direct posting to the appropriate category of income. Figure 26–5 shows an example of a cash receipts book for All Saints Church.

Notice that there is a miscellaneous column for those items of receipts that do not fit into one of the income categories for which there are columns. At the end of the month the bookkeeper can either post all of these amounts in total to a miscellaneous category of income in the general ledger, or alternatively can analyze this column and then post to individual general

---

* The word "post" means to record or to transfer an amount from one record to another. In this instance the check is "posted" or recorded initially in the Cash Disbursements Book. At the end of the month the column totals are posted or "transferred" in total to the General Ledger.

† Footed means added together. Appendix B discusses the rules for footing and ruling.

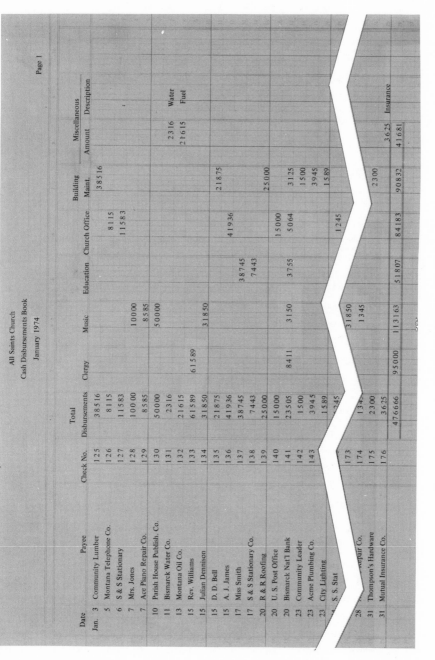

Fig. 26–4. A simple cash disbursements book.

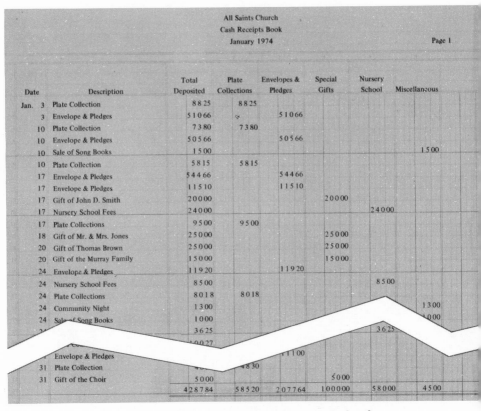

Fig. 26–5.   A simple cash receipts book.

ledger accounts based on this analysis. It should be observed that there is a similar column in the cash disbursements book for expenses that do not fall under one of the other categories.

General Journal

There are occasions where an entry must be made that does not involve cash. While this is not often necessary for cash basis organizations, there are times when adjustments must be made or when the books are "closed" at the end of the year. A General Journal is merely a separate journal (or even a separate section of the cash receipts or cash disbursements book) in which all noncash entries are made. These entries are made in traditional bookkeeping fashion showing the name of the account being "debited" and the name of the account being "credited," the amounts involved and then some explanation of the purpose of the entry. The general ledger account involved is then posted directly from this general journal entry. Here is an example of a journal entry that is being made to correct a misposting in the previous month's cash disbursements register which had already been posted to the general ledger when the mistake was discovered.

February 28
Entry #1

Debit Education expense $500.00
    Credit Music expense $500.00

> To correct error made in posting to the cash disbursement register in January. Music books purchased for the nursery school were charged to music expense instead of education expense.

Journal entries follow a prescribed format:

1. They are dated and consecutively numbered for identification purposes.
2. The name of the account being debited is entered first and is shown at the left margin. The amount is entered in the left hand column of the two columns. If there is more than one account being debited, all debit entries would be entered before entering the credits. All debit amounts on the page should line up in the same column.
3. The name of the account being credited is indented to the right of the left margin to distinguish it from a debit. The amount is likewise entered in a column to the right of the debit column.
4. A brief narrative explanation is given describing the purpose or reason for the entry.

An example of a General Journal Entry to close the books at the end of the year is illustrated on page 478. This journal entry has a number of debit and credit amounts within the same entry.

General Ledger

The general ledger is a book or ledger in which all categories of transactions are summarized by specific account. The general ledger will contain a separate page for each of the various asset, liability, income, and expense accounts. Transactions are posted to the general ledger from the cash disbursements and cash receipts books and from the general journal entries at the end of each month. The format of the general ledger account was illustrated on page 470.

The general ledger will also have an account called "fund balance" or "net worth" which will represent the cumulative net worth of the organization. The income and the expense accounts are closed out at the end of each year into this "fund balance" account. This is discussed below. New ledger sheets are started at the beginning of each year.

Trial Balance

A "trial balance" should be taken from the general ledger each month after the cash disbursements book, the cash receipts book, and individual entries from the general journal have been posted to the general ledger. A trial balance is simply a listing of every account in the general ledger along with the balance in each account. The trial balance is shown with the debit balance amounts in one column and the credit balance amounts in the other. Again, the debit column is on the left side, and the credit is on the right side. Here is an example of a trial balance.

ALL SAINTS CHURCH
TRIAL BALANCE
January 31, 1974

	Debits	Credits
Cash	$3,859.18	
Fund balance (January 1)		$4,300.00
Plate collections		585.20
Nursery school fees		580.00
Envelope and pledges		2,077.64
Special gifts		1,000.00
Other income		83.00
Clergy expense	950.00	
Music expense	1,131.63	
Education expense	518.07	
Church office expense	841.83	
Building maintenance	908.32	
Missions	—	
Other expenses	416.81	
Total	$8,625.84	$8,625.84

After the trial balance is prepared, the two columns should be footed. If everything has been posted correctly, the debit and credit columns should be equal. If it is not, it is because an entry has been misposted, or perhaps because there is an arithmetical error in arriving at the balance on an individual ledger account.

The trial balance is the bookkeeper's check to make sure that everything has been properly posted and summarized. Once it "balances"—that is, the debits and the credits in total are in agreement—the bookkeeper can then prepare financial statements directly from the trial balance.

Closing the Books at the End of the Year

One of the bookkeeping chores that can cause a great deal of confusion is how to close the books at the end of the year. It is not difficult. Here is the December 31, 1974, trial balance for All Saints Church before the books are closed.

ALL SAINTS CHURCH
PRECLOSING TRIAL BALANCE
December 31, 1974

	Debits	Credits
Cash	$ 5,307.00	
Fund balance (January 1)		$ 4,300.00
Plate collections		4,851.00
Envelope and pledges		30,516.00
Special gifts		5,038.00
Nursery school		5,800.00
Clergy expense	14,325.00	
Music expense	8,610.00	
Education expense	6,850.00	
Church office expense	5,890.00	
Building maintenance	4,205.00	
Missions	2,000.00	
Other expenses	3,318.00	
Total	$50,505.00	$50,505.00

The process of closing the books is simply the transferring of the balances in each of the income and expense accounts to the "fund balance" account. The effect is to transfer the net income into the fund balance. To make the transfer, the debit balance expense accounts must be reduced to zero by "crediting" them in the same amount. This is done for every expense account. The same process is followed with the income accounts, but since they have a credit balance in them, they are "debited." The difference between the aggregate debits and credits will be the amount of excess of income for the year and would be "credited" to the fund balance account.

While separate entries could be made to accomplish this transfer, usually a single journal entry is prepared. Using the trial balance above, the entry would look like this:

December 31, 1974
Entry 1

Debit	Plate collections	$ 4,851.00
"	Envelopes and pledges	30,516.00
"	Special gifts	5,038.00
"	Nursery school fees	5,800.00
Credit	Clergy expenses	$14,325.00
"	Music expenses	8,610.00
"	Education expenses	6,850.00
"	Church office expenses	5,890.00
"	Building maintenance	4,205.00
"	Missions	2,000.00
"	Other expenses	3,318.00
"	Fund balance (excess of income over expenses for year)	1,007.00

To close the books for the year 1974 by closing out all income and all expense accounts into the Fund Balance Account.

Each debit and credit above, once posted, would reduce the income and expense account to zero and the accounts would thus "be closed out." The fund balance account after posting the net income of $1,007.00 would then show a balance of $5,307.00, which is the net worth of the organization at December 31, 1974, on a cash basis.

Other Records

As with the checkbook system discussed earlier, a payroll register must be kept in order to keep track of employees' gross salaries, deductions, and withholdings. The same type of payroll register used with a checkbook system of bookkeeping should also be used. In addition, there are forms on which to record such items as employees' salaries and deductions, needed to facilitate preparation of the quarterly payroll tax returns and the annual W-2 statement of wages given to each employee for his tax purposes. These forms also can be obtained from stationery stores.

This chapter has not discussed some of the supporting information which the bookkeeper should maintain, giving details of disbursements and receipts. Some organizations follow the practice of making a "voucher" package for each disbursement and assigning it a consecutive number which is cross-referenced on the cash disbursement register. The voucher would contain the vendor's invoice, receiving reports, or other supporting information to show any interested person why the disbursement was made. Other organizations merely file the paid invoices by vendor name, or in check order sequence. Bank reconciliation must, of course, be prepared promptly upon receipt of the monthly bank statement. The internal controls surrounding bank reconciliations were discussed in Chapter 20.

CONCLUSIONS

Cash basis bookkeeping is basically a very simple way of keeping records since the only transactions entered into the records are those affecting cash. The principal records in such a system are the records of disbursements and receipts. These records can be informal as in the checkbook system or can be more formal as with the cash receipts and cash disbursements books. What is important is that systematic records be kept and that they be summarized into meaningful classifications. Both the checkbook system and the more formal set of cash basis records presented in this chapter meet these requirements.

27

Simplified Accrual Basis Bookkeeping

Many nonprofit organizations keep their records on a basically cash basis but record accrual entries at the end of each reporting period to convert these records to an accrual basis. These accrual entries are recorded by these organizations because they recognize that their financial statements would be distorted if unpaid bills or uncollected income at the end of the month weren't recorded. At the same time they want to keep their records as simple as possible. They do this by using what is referred to in this chapter as a simplified accrual basis system which combines much of the simplicity of cash basis bookkeeping and the advantages of accrual basis reporting.

This chapter discusses such a simplified accrual basis system of bookkeeping. This approach will be appropriate for many small- or medium-size organizations that need accrual bookkeeping with a minimum of sophistication.

BOOKS AND RECORDS

The following records constitute a "set" of books under the simplified accrual basis system discussed in this chapter:

Cash Disbursements Book. The same basic format discussed in the last chapter (Figure 26-4) is used. A separate payroll register is used to record payroll expenses and withholding amounts.

Cash Receipts Book. The format for this book is identical to the one illustrated in the last chapter (Fig. 26–5). The number of columns for the various categories of income can be expanded as appropriate.

General Journal. The same format illustrated in the last chapter is followed. In this accrual system, a number of general journal entries will be made at the end of each month.

General Ledger. The format illustrated in the last chapter is used. However, because of the greater number of general ledger accounts, the account structure is formalized through a "chart of accounts," discussed below.

Payroll Register. The format of this register differs from that illustrated in the last chapter in that this register now records directly the cash disbursement of payroll tax and withholding obligations. This will be discussed and illustrated in this chapter.

Fixed Asset and Depreciation Ledger. This is a summary of all fixed assets and related depreciation. Fixed assets and depreciation cause some bookkeeping problems; these are also discussed below.

Investments Ledger. This is a summary of all investments.

Similarity to Cash Basis

As can be seen from this summary of the records kept, most were discussed in the previous chapter on cash basis accounting. The simplified accrual system is not a much more difficult one than the cash basis system. To a large extent the simplified accrual system is the worksheet adjustment approach discussed on pages 23–24. However, in the system discussed in this chapter the adjustments are formally entered in the records.

The handling of cash receipts and disbursements is not discussed in this chapter. The reader should refer to the previous chapter to see the general format of the cash receipts book and the cash disbursements book and the mechanics of their use. In this chapter only the records and procedures not discussed in the previous chapter will be covered.

CHART OF ACCOUNTS

A chart of accounts is a formal listing of all the different accounts being used by the organization. Usually the chart of accounts has numbers assigned to each account to facilitate account identification and to more readily locate the account in the general ledger. Every account in the general ledger is listed in the chart of accounts—all assets, liabilities, income, and expenses. The chart of accounts is an index to facilitate bookkeeping.

Illustrative Example

In Chapter 11 the financial statements of Camp Squa Pan were presented to illustrate simple accrual basis financial statements. The chart of accounts for Camp Squa Pan is shown in Figure 27–1. This is a simple and straightforward chart of accounts. It uses a two-digit number, and each type of account is grouped together. Thus, all assets are shown in numbers 1–30; liabilities in numbers 31–40 and so forth.

Some numbers are skipped within each grouping; for example, account "1" is cash in bank, but there is no account "2." Instead it skips to account "3." The reason for this is to allow for future expansion of the chart of accounts as the organization expands. If Camp Squa Pan opens up a second bank account, account "1" might be for the original bank account and account "2" could then be used for the new bank account.

Notice that there are more accounts in the chart than there are accounts listed on the financial statement. This is so detail can be maintained for internal purposes. There is no reason to burden the reader of the financial statements with more details than are needed since they may detract from an overall understanding of the financial picture.

There is no "magic" way to develop a chart of accounts. The important thing is to sit down and think about the financial statement structure, the accounts which will be shown, and the detailed information that might be desired in the books. Then it is a simple matter to group like accounts together and assign numbers to them. The end product of an accounting system is the financial statements, and if the chart of accounts is properly put together it should be possible to prepare the statements directly from the general ledger without numerous reclassifications.

A chart of accounts can obviously be changed from time to time but it is difficult to make major changes in the middle of the year without creating chaos. New accounts can always be

CAMP SQUA PAN, INC.

CHART OF ACCOUNTS

Assets (1–30)

1 Cash in bank
3 Petty cash
4 U.S. Treasury bills
5 Marketable securities
7 Accounts receivable from
   campers—1971
8 Accounts receivable from
   campers—1972
9 Employee accounts receivable
10 Other accounts receivable
11 Prepaid insurance
12 Other current assets
13 Food inventory
15 Land
16 Buildings
17 Furniture and fixtures
18 Automobiles
19 Canoes
20 Other camp equipment
21 Accumulated depreciation—
   building
22 Accumulated depreciation—
   furniture and fixtures
23 Accumulated depreciation—
   automobiles
24 Accumulated depreciation—
   canoes
25 Accumulated depreciation—
   other camp equipment

Liabilities (31–40)

31 Accounts payable
32 Accrued salaries payable

33 Withholding and employer taxes
   payable
34 Accrued expenses
36 Bank loans payable
38 Camp deposits
39 Deferred compensation payable

Fund balances (41–50)

41 Original contribution
42 Retained earnings

Income (51–60)

51 Camp fees
55 Interest income
56 Other income
57 Gain or loss on sale of assets

Expenses (61–99)

61 Salaries—counselors
62 Salaries—food
63 Salaries—camp director
64 Salaries—office
65 Salaries—other
69 Payroll taxes
70 Food
75 Repair and maintenance—buildings
76 Repair and maintenance—automobiles
77 Repair and maintenance—equipment
80 Horse care and feed
90 Insurance
91 Advertising and promotion
92 Depreciation
95 Miscellaneous expenses

Fig. 27–1.   A simple chart of accounts for an accrual basis organization.

added by assigning the new account a number not previously assigned. Examples of more complex chart of accounts are shown in Chapters 28 and 29.

MONTHLY ACCRUAL ENTRIES

The basic approach to this simplified accrual basis system is to keep all records on the cash basis during the month in the manner discussed in the previous chapter but at the end of the month to make adjustments to record accrual items.* These adjustments are made through general journal entries following the format discussed in the last chapter. For most small- or medium-size organizations, there will be six to fifteen recurring journal entries each month. The recurring journal entries most commonly recorded are:

1. An entry to record unpaid bills
2. An entry to record unpaid salaries
3. An entry to record uncollected income from the sale of goods or services
4. An entry to record uncollected pledge income
5. An entry to record depreciation expense
6. An entry to record inventory and prepaid expenses

Each of these entries and the mechanics involved in determining the amount of the "accrual" are discussed below. For some organizations, only two or three of these entries will be appropriate. If the amounts involved are not material, no adjustment need be made.

Accrual for Unpaid Bills

An estimate must be made at the end of the month as to the amount of all unpaid bills. This is not difficult to do since most bills from vendors are received around the first of the month. Large expenditures of an unusual nature are usually known well in advance and bills for recurring services such as water, electricity, etc., can normally be estimated. The bookkeeper should

---

* If financial statements are prepared less frequently than monthly, then the accrual entries suggested here would be made only at the end of the period covered by the financial statements.

gather all of this information together and summarize the total of these unpaid amounts, and the expense accounts to be charged.

The accrual entry itself is straightforward. The expense accounts for the estimated or actual bills should be debited * and "accounts payable" should be credited for the total. Here is an example using the chart of accounts for Camp Squa Pan.

July 31
Entry No. 1 *

Debit No. 70 Food	$485.00	
76 Repairs—automobile	116.89	
80 Horse care and feed	259.00	
95 Miscellaneous	184.62	
17 Furniture and fixtures	250.00	
19 Canoes	485.00	
20 Other camp equipment	618.46	
Credit No. 31 Accounts payable		$2,398.97

To record the liability for unpaid bills at the end of July and to charge the appropriate expense and asset accounts.

* Journal entries can be numbered consecutively from the beginning of the year, from the beginning of the month, or, as here, by individual date. In this instance, if there were six entries dated July 31, they would be numbered from 1 to 6.

The bookkeeper will post each of these amounts directly to the general ledger from this journal entry.

Reversal of Accrual. The related problem is how to handle the actual disbursement when the bills are paid. Since the expense account has already been "charged" as a result of this accrual entry, it cannot be charged a second time when the bill is actually paid. To avoid this double charging, the accrual entry is reversed at the beginning of the following month. In this way all bills can then be paid and recorded in the usual manner on the "cash" basis. The effect of these accrual entries and the reversal in the following month is to record the accrual only for financial statement purposes.

To reverse the accrual entry shown above, the entry's debits and credits are reversed. Here is how the reversal entry would look:

* Debits and credits are discussed on page 469.

August 1
Entry No. 1

Debit No. 31 Accounts payable $2,398.97

Credit No. 70 Food $485.00
            76 Repairs 116.89
            80 Horse care and feed 259.00
            95 Miscellaneous 184.62
            17 Furniture and fixtures 250.00
            19 Canoes 485.00
            20 Other camp equipment 618.46

To reverse accrual entry No. 1 set up at July 31.

If at the end of August several of the bills from July are still unpaid, these bills should be added to the new unpaid bills and recorded as an August 31 accrual. During August when paying bills, no distinction is made between bills which were accrued at the end of July and bills which relate only to August.

Here is the general ledger page for account No. 70, Food. It shows both the accrual at the end of each month and the reversal of the accrual at the beginning of the month. Note that actual expenditures for food are posted directly from the cash disbursements book.

Food Expense—Account No. 70

			(Debit)	(Credit)	(Balance)
June	30	Cash disbursements	$ 6,151.00		$ 6,151.00
	30	Accrual of unpaid bills ..	315.00		6,466.00
	30	To record inventory of food *		$4,000.00	2,466.00
July	1	Reversal of accrual		315.00	2,151.00
	1	Reversal of food inventory	4,000.00		6,151.00
	31	Cash disbursements for July	13,163.00		19,314.00
	31	Accrual of unpaid bills ..	485.00		19,799.00
	31	To record inventory of food		5,000.00	14,799.00
August	1	Reversal of accrual		485.00	14,314.00
	1	Reversal of food inventory	5,000.00		19,314.00
	31	Cash disbursements for August	10,161.00		29,475.00
	31	Accrual of unpaid bills ..	1,156.00		30,631.00
	31	To record food inventory		1,000.00	29,631.00

* The entries to record food inventory are discussed below.

In a full accrual system, the organization would use a somewhat different approach which would not require this type of reversal of the accrual entries each month. However, that type of system is more complex. The full accrual system is discussed in Chapter 28.

Accrual for Unpaid Salaries

The easiest way to avoid having to record accruals for unpaid salaries is to pay salaries on the last day of the month. To do this, all employees would have to be paid on a monthly or semi-monthly payroll basis. This should be done, when practical, to avoid the bookkeeping problem of setting up an accrual. This is not always possible, and where it is not, an accrual entry should be set up at the end of the month for the unpaid portion of salaries.

There is usually no problem in determining the amount of the payroll accrual. By the time the bookkeeper is ready to make this accrual, the payroll covering the last week in the month will probably have been paid and the actual expense known. Unless there were unusual payroll expenses during that period, a simple proration based on the number of work days is all that is needed. For example, Camp Squa Pan pays its employees every other Monday covering the two weeks ending on that date. The last pay date in July was on the 22nd and the first one in August was on the 5th; therefore 9 days of the 14 days paid on August 5th are applicable to July. If the August 5 payroll totaled $14,000, the 9/14, or $9,000, would be applicable to July and should be recorded in an accrual entry.

The accrual entry that would be made to record this payroll would be:

July 31

Entry No. 2

Debit No. 61 Salaries—counselors	$6,000	
62 Salaries—food help	1,000	
63 Salaries—office	1,000	
64 Salaries—other	1,000	
Credit No. 32 Accrual salaries payable		$9,000

To record accrued salaries payable at July 31, 9/14 of the August 5 payroll is applicable to July

As with the accrual entry for unpaid bills, this entry should be reversed in August. The August 5th payroll should be recorded in the same manner as any other payroll.

Withholding taxes and the employer's share of payroll taxes are a special problem that can cause difficulty. They are discussed on pages 490 to 493.

Accrual for Uncollected Income

The accrual for uncollected income is made in the same manner as the accruals for unpaid bills and salaries. The bookkeeper must accumulate the appropriate information to determine the estimated amount of uncollected income. In the case of Camp Squa Pan, there are always a few campers who sign up for the first two weeks of the camp season but then stay on for additional weeks. The parents are billed for these additional amounts as soon as they decide to let their children stay for additional periods, but there is often a delay before payment is received. At the end of July, there were a total of fifteen campers who had been scheduled to leave on July 15 but had stayed through July 31, and whose fees were still unpaid. Camp fees are $100 a week, so each camper owes $228.57—and a total of $3,428.55 should be recorded as income:

July 31
Entry No. 3

Debit No. 8 Accounts receivable—campers $3,428.55
    Credit No. 51 Camp fees $3,428.55
        To record unpaid camp fees at July 31 arising from extended camp periods

This accrual should also be reversed in August, and all receipts from these campers' parents should be handled in the same manner as all other receipts. A formal accounts receivable subsidiary ledger * is not suggested. Instead an informal system should be used keeping a copy of the unpaid bill sent to the parent in a folder until paid. Once paid, the bill should be filed with the paid copies of campers' bills.

---

* An accounts receivable subsidiary ledger is discussed in Chapter 28.

Accrual for Pledges

As discussed in Chapter 9, accrual basis organizations should record all significant pledges. Pledges are not applicable to Camp Squa Pan, but if they were, the entry to record the pledge would be made in exactly the same manner as the other accruals discussed above. The accrual would likewise be reversed in the following month, and all payments received on the pledges would be treated as any other contribution.

Accrual To Record Depreciation

If depreciation is a significant expense for the organization, it should be recorded on a monthly basis. If it is not, depreciation can be recorded every six months, or even annually.

The easiest way to determine the amount of depreciation that should be recorded is to calculate the annual amount at the beginning of the year and then divide by twelve to get the amount to record each month.* This method ignores depreciation on fixed asset purchases during the year. Unless purchases or disposals are sizable, they can be ignored on a monthly basis; at the end of the year an adjustment should be made for such items. The calculation of depreciation itself is discussed on page 495.

The accrual entry that should be made monthly would be as follows:

July 31

Entry No. 4

Debit No. 92	Depreciation		$6,600
Credit No. 21	Accumulated depreciation—building		$1,200
	22	Accumulated depreciation—furniture and fixtures	600
	23	Accumulated depreciation—automobiles	3,000
	24	Accumulated depreciation—canoes	1,200
	25	Accumulated depreciation—other camp equipment	600

To record depreciation for the month of July

This entry, unlike others discussed so far in this chapter, is not reversed in the following month. Instead, depreciation continues to accumulate until such time as it is equal to the cost of

---

* In the case of Camp Squa Pan, depreciation would be recorded over the camp season of two months rather than over twelve months.

the fixed asset, or until the asset is sold. The entries to record the sale of depreciable assets are discussed later in this chapter.

Accrual for Inventory and Prepaid Expenses

Some organizations purchase inventory for resale, part of which may still be on hand at the end of the period. Other organizations prepay certain categories of .expenses, such as insurance premiums. The disbursement for these items should be treated as any other category of expense in the cash disbursement book. This means that the full amount is "expensed" at the time it is paid for. At the end of each month, it is necessary to record the amount of any remaining inventory, and the unexpired portion of insurance or similar expense. The entry that should be made would be similar to this:

July 31
Entry No. 5

Debit No. 11 Prepaid insurance	$2,800	
13 Food inventory	5,000	
Credit No. 90 Insurance expense		$2,800
70 Food expense		5,000

To record as an asset prepaid insurance premiums and food inventory at July 31

This entry should be reversed in the following period in the same manner as the other accruals discussed above.

PAYROLL TAXES

Probably the most difficult "accrual" that has to be made for an organization trying to keep its books on a simple accrual basis is the entry to record payroll taxes. In the last chapter it was recommended that payroll taxes be handled strictly on a cash basis. These taxes were recorded when they were paid and not before, and the amount recorded as salary expense on payday was the net amount of payroll after withholding deductions. At the later date when the withholding and payroll taxes were paid, this additional amount was recorded as salary expense.

This is awkward because most organizations split their payroll into two or more categories of salary expense. If payroll withholding taxes, and the employer's share of taxes have to be allocated between salary categories it is easier to do this at the time the payroll is prepared than at the end of the month in an accrual entry, or in the following month when the taxes are actually paid. In the simplified accrual system recommended in this chapter, a separate payroll disbursement register is used which is designed to record this withholding at the time the payroll is paid.

Illustrative Treatment

Figure 27–2 shows an illustration of the payroll register for Camp Squa Pan.

Notice in Figure 27–2 that the amount shown in the salary expense columns for each employee is the full gross amount of his salary. The net amount paid after deductions is shown in the net paid column. The withholding taxes are posted in total at the end of the month to the liability account in the general ledger. When such withheld taxes are paid, they are entered as a disbursement in the cash disbursements book with the offset to the withholding tax account. In the cash disbursements book in Chapter 26 (Figure 26–4), the offset (or debit) would be recorded in the miscellaneous column (account No. 33—withholding taxes payable). The total payment of withheld taxes for the month will be posted from the cash disbursement book to the general ledger as an offset to the liability account. At any month end the remaining amount in the liability account should represent the unpaid taxes.

Unlike the payroll register illustrated in the last chapter (Figure 26–3), the payroll register in Figure 27–2 is actually used to record the disbursement of the net pay to each employee. Notice that there is a space for the check number to be indicated. At the end of the month the total amount disbursed will be posted to the general ledger cash account.

Employer Taxes. There is one final problem. In addition to withholding taxes, there are some taxes which are employer taxes. An example is the employer share of FICA taxes. These amounts will be paid at the same time as the withholding taxes are paid and probably as part of the same payment. These employer tax amounts should be recorded at the end of each month in an accrual entry similar to the entry recording unpaid bills. The debit, in this illustration, would be to payroll tax ex-

Camp Squa Pan
Payroll Disbursement Register
1974

Date	Payee	Check No.	Net Pay	Salaries (61) Counselors	(62) Kitchen	(63) Camp Director	(64) Office	(65) Other	Withholding Taxes Income	FICA
July 8	John Harris	187	80 00	100 00					15 00	5 00
8	Tom Hannagan	188	80 00	100 00					15 00	5 00
8	Betty Thompson	189	80 00	100 00					15 00	5 00
8	Jim Heary	190	80 00	100 00					15 00	5 00
8	Ken Samuels	191	100 00					125 00	18 75	6 25
8	Tim Bradley	192	60 00		75 00				11 25	3 75
8	Steve Mc Nair	193	240 00			300 00			45 00	15 00
8	Bill Huber	194	100 00				125 00		18 75	6 25
8	Brian Hogan	195	96 00				120 00		18 00	6 00
8	Karl Miller	196	160 00					200 00	30 00	10 00
8	Dave Johnson	197	80 00	100 00					15 00	5 00
8	Adam Smith	198	80 00	100 00					15 00	5 00
8	Elaine Michaels	199	80 00	100 00					15 00	5 00
8	Susan Bradley	200	60 00		75 00				11 25	3 75
8	Bob McDonald	201	96 00				120 00		18 00	6 00
8	Henry Faber	202	144 00	180 00					27 00	9 00
8	Ted Morris	203	80 00	100 00					15 00	5 00
8	Byron Sullivan	204	100 00				125 00		18 75	6 25
8	Brian Collins	205	68 00		85 00				12 75	4 25
8	Al Davidson	206	144 00	180 00					27 00	9 00
8	Steve Kline	207	80 00	100 00					15 00	5 00
	Ralph Hender…		64 00						12 00	4 00
31		270	100 00						15 00	5 00
31	Ken Sheffield	271						200 00	30 00	10 00
31	Karl Miller	272	160 00	100 00					15 00	5 00
31	Jim Heary	273	80 00						18 00	6 00
31	Brian Hogan	274	96 00				120 00		18 00	6 00
			41168 59	37545 00	1480 00	600 00	3602 00	8234 00	7720 44	2571 97

Fig. 27-2. A payroll disbursement register.

pense (account No. 69) and the credit account would be to taxes payable (account No. 33). This entry should *not* be reversed at the beginning of the following period since when payment is recorded in the cash disbursements book, the "debit" entry will be directly to the taxes payable account as discussed above.

FIXED ASSET REGISTER AND DEPRECIATION SCHEDULE

Every organization, including those on a cash basis, should keep a ledger of fixed assets. As was discussed in Chapter 20, the board has a fiduciary responsibility to effectively control the organization's assets. The first step in controlling fixed assets is to know what assets the organization owns. A fixed asset ledger is merely a listing of these assets in a systematic manner. Figure 27–3 shows an example of the type of ledger that might be kept by a nonprofit organization. The first part records details on the asset itself; the second part records the calculation of depreciation.

A separate page of the fixed asset register is usually kept for each major category of asset. This categorization should follow the general ledger account description. For example, Camp Squa Pan has separate ledger accounts for buildings, furniture and fixtures, automobiles, canoes, and other camp equipment. Thus there would be a separate page for each of these categories.

Every time an asset is acquired it should be entered on this ledger. The total dollar amount shown in this ledger should agree with the general ledger account. Thus at December 31, 1973, the total of the assets listed in the automobile account will equal $13,456, the amount shown on the Balance Sheet on page 137.

In order to do this, entries must be made in the fixed asset ledger to not only record additions but also to record when an asset is sold or junked. Two entries must be made. The first is to record the date of disposal on the line in this ledger on which the original entry was recorded at the time it was acquired. This will indicate that the asset has been disposed of. The second entry is recorded in the current period to remove the original cost of the asset. To do this, the original cost is shown in the amount column, in parenthesis to indicate that it should be subtracted rather than added. In this way the amount column should

Camp Squa Pan

Fixed Asset Ledger—Automobiles

Date Acquired	Description	Tag Serial No.	Location	Cost	Depreciable Life	Date Disposed of
(1973)						
Jan. 1	Balance Forward			875600		
May 16	Ford Pick-up Truck	11761517		420000	5	
July 1	Plymouth Station Wagon	3165171 - AE		350000	5	
July 1	Trade-in Ford Purchased in 1970	G117661		(300000)		6/15/74
Dec. 31	Balance			1345600		
(1974)						
June 15	Ford Station Wagon	61875G1		421900	5	
	Trade-in Plymouth Purchased in 1973	3165171 - AE		(350000)		
Dec. 31	Balance			1417500		

Depreciation Schedule—Automobiles (5 Yrs.)

Date	Description	Total Cost	Depreciation by Year						
			1973	1974	1975	1976	1977	1978	1979
(1973)									
Jan. 1	Balance Forward	875600	175100	175100	127700	60000	20000	–	
May 16	Pick-up Truck	420000	42000	84000	84000	84000	84000	42000	
July 1	Plymouth Station Wagon	350000	35000	70000	70000	70000	70000	35000	
July 1	Sale of 1970 Ford	(300000)	(30000)	(60000)	(30000)	–	–	–	
Dec. 31	Balance	1345600	222100	269100	251700	214000	174000	77000	
(1974)									
June 15	Ford Station Wagon	421900	–	42190	84380	84380	84380	84380	42190
	Sale of 1973 Plymouth	(350000)		(70000)	(70000)	(70000)	(35000)	–	
Dec. 31	Balance	1417500	222100	241290	266080	228380	188380	126380	42190

Fig. 27–3. A fixed assets ledger and depreciation schedule.

agree with the general ledger. These two entries can be seen in Figure 27–3 where an automobile is sold.

At the time a fixed asset is acquired, the bookkeeping entry to set the asset up in the general ledger will be made automatically through the cash disbursements book. The account charged in the cash disbursements book will be the asset account, using the miscellaneous column.

The entries to record a sale of fixed assets are discussed below.

Depreciation Schedule

The second part of this fixed asset ledger shows depreciation and is used only for accrual basis organizations that capitalize and depreciate fixed assets.* This schedule is used to spread depreciation expense over the depreciable life using a columnar format. As with the fixed asset ledger, a separate page should be used for each general ledger category of assets, and often, as illustrated here it is shown on the same page as the fixed asset register.

There are many equally correct methods for calculating depreciation in the year of acquisition. If an organization wants to be accurate to the last penny, depreciation should start in the month the asset is acquired. This degree of accuracy is usually not necessary. A more practical approach that many organizations follow, is to assume that all assets are purchased half way through the year and therefore charge one half year's depreciation in the year the asset was acquired. Thus for the automobile with a 5-year life, the first year's depreciation in 1973 would be $350 ($3,500 ÷ 5 years × ½ year = $350). In 1974 depreciation would be $700.

Depreciation Spread Year by Year

All acquisitions for the year for each category should be summarized and entered on this schedule at the end of the year.†

* Depreciation is the subject of Chapter 7.

† If there have been major acquisitions during the year, such as a building, they can be entered during the year to enable the bookkeeper to start depreciating them, as part of the monthly depreciation entry. If no entry is made until the end of the year, the additional depreciation for the current year is recorded at that time.

All assets with the same depreciable life can be summarized and entered as one amount or each asset can be entered separately. The bookkeeper then calculates the amount of depreciation applicable to each future year and enters these amounts in the columns for that year. For example, if an automobile with a 5-year life is acquired on July 1, 1973, for $3,500, $350 depreciation would be shown in the column for 1973, $700 in each of the columns for 1974, 1975, 1976, and 1977 and $350 in the column for 1978. To determine the amount of total depreciation for each year the bookkeeper refers to the total depreciation in each column. In our illustration, depreciation is $2,221.00 for 1973 and $2,412.90 for 1974.

An adjustment must also be made to this schedule when the automobile is sold before it has been fully depreciated. Depreciation for future periods must be removed from the appropriate years' columns. This future depreciation is removed by subtracting it from these columns. Figure 27–3 shows the removal of depreciation on an automobile sold in 1973 and one sold in 1974.

Depreciation on Acquisitions During the Year

At the end of the year, the depreciation column for the current year is totaled. As indicated earlier, the amount of depreciation recorded in the monthly accrual entries will normally not be adjusted throughout the year as assets are purchased or sold. Instead for the sake of simplicity the same amount is used each month. This means that the amount of depreciation actually charged during the year should be compared to the current year's depreciation column in this schedule. An adjustment should be recorded for the difference.

This is less complicated than it seems. It does require that the bookkeeper systematically keep track of acquisitions and disposals. Since purchases of fixed assets are usually not voluminous this should not be too difficult.

Entries for Disposal of Assets

Many bookkeepers have difficulty in preparing the bookkeeping entry to record the sale or disposal of a fixed asset. This entry is not difficult if the objective of the entry is kept in mind:

namely, to remove the cost of the fixed asset and to remove the accumulated depreciation. Let's take a typical example of an automobile acquired in 1970 at a cost of $3,000 with a 5-year life. It was sold in July 1973 for $800.

The biggest problem is to calculate the amount of depreciation that has been taken. In 1970, the year acquired, one-half year's depreciation was taken, a full year's depreciation in 1971 and 1972, and a half a year's depreciation through June 30, 1973 (the asset is sold in July so depreciation has been charged only through June). In total that is 3 years' depreciation or $1,800 ($3,000 ÷ 5 years = $600 per year × 3 years = $1,800). Here is the entry that records this sale:

July 31
Entry No. 8

Debit No. 10 Accounts receivable	$ 800	
23 Accumulated depreciation—automobile	1,800	
57 Loss on sale	400	
Credit No. 18 Automobiles		$3,000

To record the sale of an auto acquired in 1970 for $3,000, sold in July for $800, and to remove the accumulated depreciation.

Notice that we have debited accounts receivable for $800, the sales price of the automobile. When the cash is received it will be entered in the cash receipts book and the credit will be to accounts receivable. In this way the cash receipt is recorded in the cash receipts book.

A typical variation on the above entry occurs if instead of receiving cash for the used car, this $800 is allowed as a trade-in value on a new car costing $3,500. The organization pays $2,700 and its old car and receives a new one. Here is the journal entry that would be made to record this transaction:

July 31
Entry No. 9

Debit No. 18 Automobile	$ 500	
23 Accumulated depreciation—auto	1,800	
57 Loss on sale	400	
Credit No. 31 Accounts payable		$2,700

To record purchase af new automobile costing $3,500 and trade-in of old automobile with original cost of $3,000.

Notice that the automobile asset account has been increased by $500, the difference in cost between the old and the new automobile. Instead the entry might have shown a debit of $3,500 to record the new one, and a credit of $3,000 to remove the old one. Either would be acceptable since the end result is the same. When the organization makes out its check for $2,700 it will be entered in the cash disbursement book in the same manner as any other disbursement except that the account debited will be accounts payable. This will be shown in the miscellaneous column.

With respect to the old automobile, the bookkeeper must not forget to remove the depreciation for future periods from the depreciation schedule. Notice that depreciation of $300 in 1973, $600 in 1974, and $300 in 1975 has been removed in Figure 27–3. If the auto had been sold three months later, in October instead of July, then the amount removed from the 1973 column would have been $150 instead of $300. This amount is calculated right up to the end of the month prior to sale since the monthly accrual entry has recorded depreciation to that time.

INVESTMENT LEDGER

All organizations must keep a record of the investments they own. Often this record is not formalized and when questions are raised later, the organization has difficulty in providing details. Figure 27–4 shows an example of the type of investment ledger that should be kept. The information on this schedule is pretty straightforward, except for information on the tax basis of investments received as gifts. This information is required only with respect to "private foundations" and results from the special tax rules for calculating gains for these organizations.* Other organizations can eliminate these columns.

CONCLUSION

Many organizations will find that the simplified accrual basis system presented here is a practical way to have the advantage of cash basis accounting throughout the period while still record-

* See Chapter 23 for a discussion of these requirements.

The Johanna M. Stannick Foundation
Investment Ledger

Date	Investment Description	No. of Shares/ Par Value	Cert. No.	Location of Cert.	Cost or FMV at Date Rec'd	Date Sold	Sale Proceeds	Gain or (Loss)	How Acquired	Donor's Name & Address	FMV at 12/31/69*	Donor's Tax Basis
7-14-73	IBM	100	11734	Daytona Bank	1870000				Gift	J.M. Stannick, Daytona, Fla.		2500000
7-14-73	Polaroid	300	34104	"	3300000	2-13-74	4575900	1275900	Gift	J.M. Stannick, Daytona, Fla.		1500000
7-14-73	Hercules	1775	10025	"	6072500				Gift	J.M. Stannick, Daytona, Fla.		1600000
7-14-73	Intl. Nickle	2225	21573	"	8185300				Gift	J.M. Stannick, Daytona, Fla.		1900000
	Total Dec. 31, 1973				19427800							
2-13-74	Polaroid	300	34104	Daytona Bank	(3300000)				Purchase			
2-23-74	U.S. Steel	935	G8156	"	2524100							
	Total Dec. 31, 1974				18651900							

* Required only for securities held on that date

Fig. 27—4. An investment ledger.

ing the necessary adjustments at the end of the period to convert to an accrual basis at that date. The only difficulty with this system is determining the amount of each of these accruals at the end of the period. Nevertheless this is not hard to do if it is done systematically. Most non-bookkeepers can keep books in this fashion if they carefully study and follow the examples shown in this and the previous chapter. Where problems arise that are not discussed, a common sense approach should be used.

28

Full Accrual Basis Bookkeeping

The simplified accrual system discussed in the last chapter will meet the needs of many smaller, and even some medium-size organizations. However, there are many other organizations for which this system is too cumbersome because they have a large number of transactions. For these organizations a "full" accrual system is more appropriate. This chapter discusses such a system and illustrates the principal records that must be kept.

BOOKS AND RECORDS

The following records constitute a "set" of books for an organization using a full accrual basis bookkeeping system. Listed first are the new or revised books or records discussed in this chapter:

Sales Register—this records all sales of goods and services at the time they are made (Figure 28–3).

Accounts Payable Register—this book records all purchases and other obligations at the time the bill or invoice is received from the vendor, rather than at the time paid, as in previous systems (Figure 28–6).

Accounts Receivable Subsidiary Ledger—this book records the details of all amounts that others owe to the organization (Figure 28–4).

501

Cash Receipts Book—this book changes from that discussed in the previous chapter because much of the information previously recorded in this book is now recorded in the sales register (Figure 28-5).

Cash Disbursements Book—this book changes also from that discussed in previous chapters because much of the information previously recorded in this book is now recorded in the accounts payable register (Figure 28-7).

Chart of Accounts—this chart is more complex than previously illustrated (Figure 28-1).

Next are books or records that were discussed elsewhere:

General ledger (Ch. 26)
General Journal (Ch. 26)
Trial Balance (Ch. 26)
Payroll Register (Ch. 27)
Fixed Asset Register (Ch. 27)
Investment Ledger (Ch. 27)

From this list it can be seen that there are some new "books" not previously discussed. These relate principally to books in which two types of transactions are now recorded at the time they take place rather than at the time cash is involved—the sales register in which all sales are entered and the accounts payable register in which all bills are entered at the time they are received from the vendors. The basic distinction between a full accrual system and the simplified accrual system discussed in the last chapter is that transactions are recorded at the time they occur rather than at the end of the month in accrual entries. In all other significant respects the two systems are similar.

The reader should refer to the previous two chapters for a description of previously discussed records and for an explanation of how they tie into a total bookkeeping system. These chapters are cumulative and closely interrelated.

Background for Illustrative Example

The full accrual system can best be illustrated by using a typical organization as an example, and in this chapter we will study some of the procedures followed by The Valley Country Club. The procedures discussed here are applicable to many other types of nonprofit organizations and the careful reader will be able to see how the books and procedures illustrated here can be adapted to their own organization.

The Valley Country Club's budgeting problems and financial statements were discussed in some detail on pages 299 to 309 and the reader may want to refer to the financial statements shown on those pages. This club is a typical small to medium size club. It has an 18-hole course and an olympic-size swimming pool. The only public building is the club house in which there is a restaurant, a separate bar and locker rooms. There are several small maintenance buildings.

Members may bring guests to the club but the member must pay a greens fee of $5 and a swimming fee of $2 for each guest. The members pay no fees as this is part of the annual dues. Guests are welcomed in the restaurant and bar but they must be accompanied by a member and in all cases the member is billed for the fees and charges incurred by his guest. No cash is handled and the member signs a "charge slip" for each charge incurred. No tips are allowed, since 5 per cent sales tax and 15 per cent gratuity are added to all charges. The members are billed in the first week of the month for the previous month's charges.

CHART OF ACCOUNTS

Figure 28–1 shows a chart of accounts for The Valley Country Club. This chart of accounts is considerably more complex than the chart shown in the last chapter. It is complex not only because of the greater number of accounts, but because expenses are kept by type of club activity.

Coding

Look first at the top group of accounts under the major caption, "Expenses." These are the major expense groupings. The subcodes which are immediately below this group are used with each of the major codes. For example, if salaries are to be charged to golf activities the code number would be "410." If salaries are to be charged to the bar then account "710" would be used,

THE VALLEY COUNTRY CLUB
CHART OF ACCOUNTS

Assets

10 – Cash in bank—main
11 – Cash in bank—payroll
12 – Cash in bank—savings

20 – Member's accounts receivable
21 – Employee's accounts receivable
22 – Other accounts receivable
23 – Allowance for bad debts

32 – Inventories—greens and grounds
35 – Inventories—pool supplies
36 – Inventories—restaurant
37 – Inventories—bar

40 – Prepaid expenses—insurance
41 – Prepaid expenses—taxes
42 – Prepaid expenses—other

50 – Land (original cost)
52 – Greens and grounds improvements
53 – Clubhouse
54 – Golf carts
55 – Swimming pool
56 – Restaurant equipment
57 – Bar equipment
58 – Automotive equipment
59 – Club furniture and fixtures

63 – Accumulated depreciation—clubhouse
64 – Accumulated depreciation—golf carts
65 – Accumulated depreciation—swimming pool
66 – Accumulated depreciation—restaurant and
      dining room
67 – Accumulated depreciation—bar
68 – Accumulated depreciation—automotive
      equipment
69 – Accumulated depreciation—club furniture

Liabilities

70 – Accounts payable
73 – Short-term loans payable
74 – Accrued expenses
75 – FICA and withholding taxes payable
76 – Sales taxes
77 – Real estate taxes
78 – Other taxes
79 – Wages payable
80 – Employee's tip fund

85 – Mortgages—long-term
87 – Member bonds due 1980

90 – Contributed capital

95 – Surplus

Income

110 – Initiation fees
111 – Dues—full members
112 – Dues—social members
120 – Golf fees
130 – Locker room fees
140 – Golf cart rentals
150 – Swimming fees
160 – Sales—dining room
170 – Sales—bar
180 – Other
190 – Discounts earned
191 – Interest income
192 – Cash over/short

Expenses

200 – Greens and grounds
300 – Clubhouse
400 – Golf activities
500 – Swimming pool
600 – Restaurant
700 – Bar
900 – Administrative

Subcodes

10 – Salaries
20 – Supplies
30 – Repairs and minor maintenance
40 – Other costs
60 – Depreciation

Specific Accounts

610 – Dining room salaries
611 – Kitchen salaries
620 – Food
720 – Liquor and mixes

911 – Club manager's salary
912 – Secretarial and clerical
913 – Bookkeeping
914 – Janitorial
915 – Other
940 – Interest expense
941 – Auditing and legal
942 – Postage
943 – Telephone
944 – Insurance
945 – Real estate taxes
946 – Income taxes
947 – Pension expense
948 – Electricity
949 – Water
950 – Unemployment insurance
951 – Bad debts
952 – Employer payroll taxes

Fig. 28–1. A chart of accounts for a country club.

and so forth. This type of classification allows the bookkeeper to learn quickly almost all account numbers since she has only to learn the major group codes and the major subcodes. There are also a number of specific accounts, mostly involving general and administrative-type expenses, and these are listed separately.

The income and expense accounts are three-digit codes; the asset and liability accounts are two-digit codes. In this accrual system the code numbers frequently will be used instead of account names. This is one of the advantages of having a chart of accounts. It cuts down on both the amount of writing and the space involved.

SALES REGISTER

Figure 28–2 shows an example of the charge slip used by The Valley Country Club. Notice that it is prenumbered to ensure that accountability is maintained. Charge slips are prepared for every charge to members.

Comments and Procedure

At the end of each day all of the charge slips are forwarded to the bookkeeper in numerical sequence for each activity or location. The bookkeeper should check the sequence carefully. If some of the charge slips were lost before they were recorded, the club would lose income since there would be no way to know whom to charge, or the amount.

After the bookkeeper has accounted for the sequence of all charge slips, she enters each charge slip in the sales register. Figure 28–3 shows an example of a sales register. Each charge slip has been entered individually in the sales register in order to establish a permanent record of all charges.* The distribution of the charge, sales tax and gratuity, is shown in the appropriate

---

* Some clubs do not enter these charge slips individually in the sales register. Instead the bookkeeper using an adding machine runs a recap of the charge slips for each day, by account classification. Then only the total of these charges is entered in the sales register. When this procedure is followed, the charge slips will probably be microfilmed before being sorted by member number. In this way a permanent record is created to support the summary entry in the sales register.

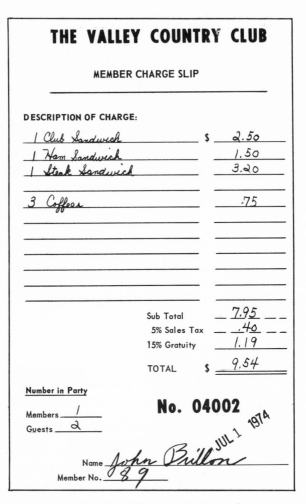

Fig. 28–2. An example of a "charge slip" used by a country club.

column.* The account numbers shown at the top of the page are the general ledger account numbers.

* While in this illustration the sales tax and gratuity amounts have been posted separately for each charge slip, some time could have been saved by entering only the total amount of the member's charge (including the sales tax and gratuity) and the income account distribution. Since both the sales tax and the gratuity amounts are a fixed percentage (5 per cent and 15 per cent) of charges, these amounts can be calculated at the end of the month by multiplying the total of all income accounts by these fixed percentages. In Figure 28–3 the aggregate of the income accounts (accounts 120–180, or $62,505.27) multiplied by these two percentages would give the amounts shown in the sales tax column ($3,125.26) and gratuity column ($9,375.80). These last two columns could then be eliminated.

The Valley Country Club
Sales Register

Date (1974)	Name	Member No.	Charge Slip No.	Total Sales	a/c 120	a/c 130	a/c 140	a/c 150	a/c 160	a/c 170	a/c 180	a/c 76	a/c 80
July 1	Jones	369	10861	9 60	5 00	1 00						40	1 20
1	Smith	700	10862	9 60	5 00	1 00	2 00					40	1 20
1	McDonald	607	10863	2 40			2 00					10	30
1	Stannick	720	8715	2 40				2 00				10	30
1	Mc Nair	605	8716	2 40				2 00				10	30
1	Riley	687	8717	2 40				2 00				10	30
1	Falvery	340	4400	4 60					3 68			23	69
1	Miller	625	4401	21 04						17 53		88	2 63
1	Brillon	89	4402	9 54						7 95		40	1 19
1	Brillon	89	22815	43 39					36 17			1 80	5 42
1	Jackson	372	22816	51 78						43 15		2 16	6 47
1	Allen	15	22817	56 15			15 00			21 80		2 34	7 01
1	Thompson	760	22818	11 52	10 00			2 00	2 60			48	1 44
1	Peterson	665	22819	15 84	5 00				13 20			66	1 98
1	Davidson	275	15001	7 20					6 00			30	90
1	Kinney	402	15002	30 00	10 00				15 00			1 25	3 75
1	Melon	615	15003	4 80				2 00				25	75
1	Ho...		15004	12 00								25	1 50
31	...nson	3?0		91		1 00							
31	Benjoya	81	5112	19 87						32 10		1 61	2 49
31	Williams	905	5113	22 80						16 55		05 83	2 85
31	Shames	701	5114	6 00								95	75
31	Jones	385	5115	6 00					5 00			25	75
31	Harris	353	5116	10 20					8 50	46 51		45	1 25
31	Johnson	390	5117	55 80							19 00	2 32	6 97
				7500 6 33	7500 1 17	1513 10	1749 71	1 60 00	36339 01	15001 27	2 41 01	31255 26	9375 80

Fig. 28–3. A sales register.

At the end of the month all columns are totaled and the totals posted to the general ledger. The total sales column figure is posted to the accounts receivable control account in the general ledger. The other columns are posted to the general ledger account indicated at the top of the column. In order to be sure that all accounts are posted, the bookkeeper puts a check mark ($\sqrt{}$) beside each column total as she is posting it.

ACCOUNTS RECEIVABLE SUBSIDIARY LEDGER

After being posted to the sales register all charge slips should be sorted down by member number and accumulated together during the month. Either at the end of the month, or throughout the month as the bookkeeper has time, an accounts receivable ledger card for each member should be posted. Figure 28–4 shows an example of the type of accounts receivable ledger which should be maintained. This accounts receivable ledger should be in duplicate, with one copy sent to the member as his monthly bill. This ledger card can be hand posted, or if the volume is sufficient, a small bookkeeping machine or one-write system * can be used to post the charge slip to both the sales register and the ledger card simultaneously.

Usually the charge slips are sent to the member with his bill. A few organizations, however, prefer to keep the charge slips as a part of the organization's permanent records and only send the member a copy of the ledger card. They will send a photo copy of the charge slip to the member if there is a question. Obviously there will be fewer questions raised if the charge slip is sent with the bill. Until the Tax Reform Act of 1969 this was largely a matter of preference. But as noted on page 403 the Club must now document certain information for tax purposes. The charge slip is the most logical place to do so, and accordingly, the Club may prefer to keep these slips permanently. One alternative is for the charge slips to be prepared in duplicate or to be microfilmed.

---

* A one-write system is a system where through specially designed forms and carbon paper more than one record is prepared simultaneously.

	THE VALLEY COUNTRY CLUB	MEMBER NAME
		BRILLON, JOHN

THE VALLEY COUNTRY CLUB

P.O. BOX 144
DAYTONA BEACH, FLORIDA 32017

STATEMENT OF MEMBER'S ACCOUNT

MEMBER NAME
BRILLON, JOHN

MEMBER ADDRESS
2641 ADAMS STREET

DAYTONA BEACH, FLA.

MEMBER NUMBER
89

DATE	DESCRIPTION	DEBIT	CREDIT	BALANCE
JUNE 30	BALANCE			345.18
JULY 1	# 4002	9.54		
1	22815	43.39		
3	4079	14.53		
3	23019	24.56		
8	11345	14.00		
8	4107	45.44		
14	4314	33.16		
14	PAYMENT		345.18	
22	# 4516	13.15		
22	23990	43.67		
31	BALANCE			241.44

Fig. 28–4. An individual accounts receivable ledger card.

There will be, of course, receipts during the month from the member paying his bill from the previous month. As discussed below, all receipts are entered in the cash receipts book and then posted to the accounts receivable ledger cards.* The individual accounts to be credited can be either posted directly from the cash receipts book or from a "credit advice" slip prepared at the time the receipt is entered in the cash receipts book. If the credit advice slip approach is followed, the slips are sorted and posted in the same manner as the charge slips. Either approach can be

---

* Some clubs will find it impractical to post receipts individually to the cash receipts book because of the large volume. One alternative is to prepare the deposit slip for the bank with the name of the member shown alongside each check listed. A duplicate copy of the deposit slip could be kept permanently, and only the total of the deposit slip entered in the cash receipts book. The copy of the deposit slip would be the posting source for the credits to each member's accounts.

used, but it is important to "control" carefully the postings to be sure they are posted to the right account.

Accounts Receivable "Control" Account

The general ledger accounts receivable account becomes the "control" account for all of the individual members' accounts. In the sales register in Figure 28–3, the total amount of all charges to the members ($75,006.33) is posted in one amount to the general ledger accounts receivable control account. The same is true with the cash receipts book; $70,001.65 would be posted (Figure 28–5). If no mistakes have been made in posting, the aggregate of the individual ledger card balances should be the same as the balance in this control account after all postings since the sources of the postings are the same. Before mailing the members' monthly bills, all individual bills should be added together to be certain that the total of these bills does agree with this general ledger control account. If there is a large volume of activity, this "balancing," as it is called, can be a major job each month. But it must be done, and the individual accounts should not be sent out until they are in agreement in total.

CASH RECEIPTS BOOK

As indicated above, the cash receipts book is the source of postings for the individual members' receivable accounts. This means that the form of cash receipts book discussed in the previous chapters must change in format. Figure 28–5 shows an example of the new format.

This is a very simple cash receipt register because The Valley Country Club makes sales only to its members, and only on a charge basis. Therefore there are seldom any receipts from sources other than the members. Since all receipts are posted to the members' accounts, the credit entry is usually to accounts receivable. There is an "other" column in this cash receipts book to provide for the occasional receipt from some other source.

Alternate Posting Procedures

As noted above, there are two ways to handle the posting to the members' accounts. The first is to post directly from the cash

The Valley Country Club
Cash Receipts

Date (1974)	Description	Member No.	Total Cash	Acct. Rec. #20	Other Credits a/c #	Amount	
uly 14	Brillon	89	34518	34518			1
14	Mc Nair	605	1621	1621			2
14	Spangle	710	2641	2641			3
14	Wander	890	1816	1816			4
14	Rengler	679	8615	8615			5
14	Mc Nair	605	861	861			6
14	Falvery	340	6000	6000			7
14	Daytona Trust		1141		191	1141	8
14	Riley	687	21450	21450			9
14	Jackson	372	15020	15020			10
14	Allen	15	13529	13529			11
14	Thompson	760	21023	21023			12
14	Williamson	905	210045	210045			13
14	McDonald	607	6500	6500			14
14	Peterson	665	8915	8915			15
14	Hannagan	349	13140	13140			16
14	Davidson	275	5595	5595			17
14	Kinne	402	11500	11500			18
14		701	21445	21445			19
1		211	1742	1742			
	Brillon	89	2510				
	Harris						
31	Mc Nally			9716			23
31	Melon	615	121516	121516			24
			7006516	7000165		6351	25
			√	√			26

√ = Posted

A/C	AMT.
191	1141 √
180	5210 √
	6351

Fig. 28–5. A Cash Receipts Book.

receipts book to an individual member's ledger card. This is probably the most common method where the volume is not too large. One alternative is to prepare an "advice slip" * at the time the cash receipts book entry is made and use this advice slip as a posting source.† Or, if a bookkeeping machine or one-write system is used, the posting to the member's account can be made simultaneously at the time the posting to the cash receipts book is made.

* An illustration of a credit advice slip is not shown. However, the format can be very simple. Some organizations even use the envelope in which payment was received as the advice slip, marking the amount of the payment on the envelope. The bookkeeper can easily work out the method that most easily fits her preference.

† See the footnote on page 509 describing the use of a duplicate deposit slip as the posting source.

ACCOUNTS PAYABLE REGISTER

An accounts payable register is a book in which all bills are formally recorded at the time they are received. In the process of recording these "payables" the expense classification to be charged is also entered, and this book becomes the primary source of charges to the various general ledger expense accounts. Figure 28–6 shows an example of the first page of an accounts payable register. The actual register could extend across a double page in order to provide enough columns for all major categories of expense. Using a double page would give about 30 columns.

Comments and Procedure

The date of actual payment is not of significance because the bill will show as an accounts payable until paid. The "date paid" and "check number" columns are provided in this register to show a record of which accounts have been paid, and which have not been paid. If there is no entry in these two spaces, the bill has not been paid and it is still an accounts payable. This is a control to keep track of the unpaid accounts payable. Each month after all general ledger postings have been made, an adding machine tape should be taken of these unpaid accounts and the total agreed with the amount in the general ledger. If the total does not agree, an error has been made and the bookkeeper should go back and check to be sure that every cash disbursement involving accounts payable has been posted as being paid in the accounts payable register.

Although it is not necessary to do so, most organizations enter all bills in this register, even those they are going to pay the day they receive them. It is easier to record an expense in this register than in the cash disbursement book since the various expense classifications are in columnar form.

At the end of the month the accounts payable register is totaled by column. The total of the accounts payable column is posted to the accounts payable liability account. This liability account will be reduced as disbursements are made, through the cash disbursement book. The various expense account columns should also be posted, and if there are any amounts in the "other" column, they should be analyzed and posted individually.

The Valley Country Club
Accounts Payable Register

Date 1974	Payee	Check No.	Date Paid	Accounts Payable (70)	-220-	-320-	-420-	-520-	-620-	-720-	Other Account	Other Amount
July 3	Allen's Lawn Needs	160	7/20	51510	51510							
3	All Pro's Invitational	162	7/21	184075			184075					
3	Aquarium Monthly	167	7/24	2500							#340	2500
3	Mc Given's Sporting Goods	169	7/26	24530		24530						
3	Best Food Inc.	170	7/26	112513					112513			
3	Jones Meat Market	173	7/26	201040					201040			
5	Ted's Frozen Foods	174	7/26	94630					94630			
5	Brown's Seed Supply	175	7/26	41200	41200							
5	Business Review	177	7/26	2000							#340	2000
5	A C Sporting Goods, Inc.	178	7/26	41200		41200						
5	Pickering Pool Supplies	179	7/26	35000				35000				
5	Morton Frozen Goods	181	7/27	85175					85175			
5	Bill's Produce Market	183	7/27	114190					114190			
6	Forrest Lawn Service	184	7/27	9510	9510							
6	Swimming Pool Goods	185	7/27	11575				11575				
6	Ludwig-Lawrence Agency	186	7/27	86150							#944	86150
6	A B C Stationery Store	187	7/27	51174							#920	51174
6	Donovin Bottled Liquors	201	7/27	201539						201539		
6	Cobb, Cole and Bond			100000							#941	100000
6	Martin & Ross Liquor Supplies	226	7/31	114050						114050		
31	Apex Dry Goods			24510		24510						
31	Photo Copy Services			100000			100000					
31	Ted's Golf Goods			9175					91710		#915	
31	Florida Golf Assoc.			3445					9175			3445
				4317956	175190	133236	559000	62030	2416144	618231		354125

Fig. 28-6. An Accounts Payable Register.

CASH DISBURSEMENTS BOOK

With all bills being entered in the accounts payable register when received, there is no longer a need to have columns for the various expense categories in the cash disbursements register. In fact, the cash disbursements book becomes a much smaller book with only a few columns. Figure 28–7 shows an example of this book.

Comments and Procedure

Notice that there are two bank account columns. Many organizations have more than one active bank account and this is how the second bank account is handled. The amount of the check disbursed is entered in the appropriate column depending on which bank the check is drawn. The offsetting debit is normally accounts payable since all bills are entered in the accounts payable register. A column for this debit to accounts payable is provided. The total of the accounts payable column is posted to the general ledger at the end of the month which serves to reduce the accounts payable amount recorded as an obligation from the accounts payable register.

There is also a column for discounts earned. If payment is made within the time specified on the vendor's invoice for cash discounts, it should be taken. Thus the amount of the check will be less than the amount of the bill, and, therefore, less than the payable set up in the accounts payable register. The discounts earned column would be the place where this discount would be shown. In this way the amount entered in the accounts payable column will be the total amount owed. The "discounts earned" column is a credit or income item. For example, note that the July 26 payment to Thompson Hardware was less a 5 per cent discount of $4.52, but the credit to accounts payable was the total amount of the bill, $90.45.

A column has been provided to record the payment of FICA and withholding taxes. The obligation to pay these withholding taxes is recorded in the payroll register (Figure 27–2), and this column, when posted to the general ledger, serves to reduce the liability.

The Valley Country Club
Cash Disbursement Book

Date 1974	Payee	Check No.	Disbursement Daytona Bank	National Bank	Accounts Payable (Dr)	Discount Earned (Cr)	Payroll Taxes (a/c 75)	Other Account	Other Amount
	Balance Forwarded from Previous Page		769502	1400375	1789492		39875		345040
July 26	Mc Given's Sporting Goods	169	24530		24530	4530			
26	Best Food Inc.	170		112513	112513				
26	Volusia Tax Board	171	348900					#945	348900
26	Thompson's Hardware	172	8593		9045	452			
26	Jones Meat Market	173		201040	201040				
26	Ted's Frozen Foods	174		94630	94630				
26	Brown's Seed Supply	175	41200		41200				
26	Johnson's Lumber Co.	176	23750		25000	1250			
26	Business Review	177	2000		2000				
26	A C Sporting Goods, Inc.	178	41200		41200				
26	Pickering Pool Supplies	179	35000		35000				
27	Daytona Bank & Trust	180	489571				489571		
27	Morton Frozen Goods	181		85175	85175				
27	Williams Printers	182	7350		7500	150			
27	Bill's Produce Market	183		114190	114190				
27	Forrest Lawn Service	184	9510		9510				
27	Swimming Pool Goods	185	11575		11575				
27	Ludwig-Lawrence Agency	186	86150		86150				
27	A BC Stationery		74		51174				
	Repair Se...								
31	Martin ... liquor Supplies	226			14050	50			
31	Thomas Lawn Goods	227	18590		18590				
			2123849	2487940	3395598	7195	529446		693940

Fig. 28–7. A Cash Disbursements Book.

As with the other books, a column is provided to record transactions not reflected in one of the specific columns. There will be relatively few entries recorded in this column. In our illustration, payment of the sales tax collections in June has been recorded in this column. The actual liability entry setting up the obligation was recorded through the sales register (Figure 28-3).

MONTHLY ACCRUAL ENTRIES

Notwithstanding the use of the various journals and registers discussed above, several entries must still be made on a monthly basis in the general journal. These entries relate principally to adjustment of accounts not involving cash.

Employer Payroll Taxes

The payroll register provides a place to record the amount of withholding and FICA taxes withheld from employees' wages. It does not provide, however, for the recording of the employer's share of such taxes. An accrual entry must be made monthly to record such amounts. The amount of FICA taxes is usually exactly the same amount withheld from employees during the period. At the time the payroll register is totaled at the end of the month, the bookkeeper should note the amount of employee taxes and then make the following entry:

July 31
Entry No. 5

Debit No. 952 Payroll tax expense $2,117.89
    Credit No. 75 FICA and withholding taxes payable $2,117.89

    To record the employer's share of payroll taxes for the month of July.

In this illustration, all of this payroll tax expense was charged to a single account. Some organizations prefer to split this expense among all payroll expense accounts. If this is done, it can either be done monthly at the time the above entry is prepared, or it can be done at the end of the year by analyzing total payroll for the year and allocating the total employer taxes charged to account No. 952.

Depreciation

An entry must still be made monthly to record depreciation expense. The procedures outlined in Chapter 27 should be followed.

Inventories

Inventories can be handled in two ways. The first way, which is probably how it would be handled with The Valley Country Club, is to charge all inventory items to expense as the bills are received, and then to adjust, at the end of the month, for any inventory still on hand. This is the method used with the simplified accrual basis system discussed in Chapter 27. The other approach is to record all inventory purchases as an asset (i.e., debit to the inventory asset account and credit to accounts payable) and then periodically to reduce the carrying value of this inventory as it is consumed. The entry for this adjustment would be a debit to expense and a credit to the inventory asset account.

Accrued Salary Payable

There is no automatic procedure to record accrued salary payable even with a full accrual system. Accordingly, an accrual entry must still be made for the portion unpaid at the end of the month. The procedures followed in this type of accrual are exactly as discussed in Chapter 27.

Prepaid Expenses

Insurance premiums, taxes and similar items should be charged to the appropriate prepaid asset account at the time they are recorded in the accounts payable register. Then, at the end of the period, the portion of this prepaid expense which has expired by virtue of passage of time or usage should be written off to expense in a journal entry. The type of entry to be made would be:

July 31
Entry No. 6

Debit No. 944 Insurance expense $100.00
    Credit No. 40 Prepaid insurance $100.00

> To record as an expense that portion of the prepaid insurance applicable to July.

This type of entry might not be made on a monthly basis if the amounts involved were not large. Often quarterly or even semi-annual entries are all that is necessary.

Reserve for Bad Debts

From time to time a reserve for bad debts will be needed. This type of entry is also handled through the general journal. The entry in the case of The Valley Country Club would be:

July 31
Entry No. 7

Debit No. 951 Bad debts $200.00
    Credit No. 23 Allowance for bad debts $200.00

> To set up an allowance for bad debts for the portion of accounts receivable that are in dispute with estate of deceased member.

An alternative approach is to record the bad debt expense only at the time specific accounts receivable are written off. If this approach were followed, then the credit at the time of write off would be to accounts receivable (account No. 20) rather than to the allowance account.

CONCLUSION

The two principal books that allow an organization to record certain transactions on an accrual basis are the sales register and the accounts payable register. Both have as their intent the recording of transactions as they occur rather than when cash is involved. As with the other records discussed in earlier chapters, they are basically common sense types of records which are designed to record transactions in a systematic manner so as to allow like transactions to be grouped together.

29

Fund Accounting Bookkeeping

There is only one important difference between fund accounting and the other accounting methods used by nonprofit organizations. In fund accounting a number of separate accounting entities are maintained which are referred to as "funds." A fund accounting system presents no special difficulty, except for the problem of keeping the transactions of these funds separated while integrating all of the funds into a total bookkeeping system. An organization using fund accounting can be on the cash basis, a simplified accrual basis, or a full accrual basis. The same type of records discussed in the three previous chapters can be used in fund accounting. This chapter will discuss only the problems related to fund accounting.

For purposes of discussion an accrual basis private school will be used as an illustration. The Roy B. Cowin School was discussed and financial statements were presented in Chapter 12 (Figures 12–6 to 12–8) and the reader may find it helpful to refer back to these statements. This school uses fund accounting and has five fund "groupings" *—general fund, board-designated en-

---

* The reader should be careful to distinguish between a fund "grouping" and an individual fund. A fund "grouping" is all òf the individual funds having similar characteristics, whereas a "fund" is an individual entity being accounted for as a separate unit. Another expression used in this chapter is "name" fund. A "name" fund is a fund that bears a name, usually of the principal donor. There may be other funds, with identical restrictions but the separate identification by "name" is maintained for any one of a number of reasons. These concepts were discussed in Chapter 4.

dowment fund, funds for specified purposes, plant funds, and endowment funds.

CHART OF ACCOUNTS

The key to a good bookkeeping system is a carefully thought out chart of accounts. This is especially true when fund accounting is used because there are a number of completely separate accounting entities each of which has its own accounts for assets, liabilities, income, expense and fund balances. Yet these separate entities must be integrated carefully into an overall chart of accounts. Each fund grouping must have an account structure similar to the other groupings, both for ease in keeping the records and for ease in preparing financial statements.

Figure 29–1 shows the chart of accounts for The Roy B. Cowin School. This chart is basically a three-digit system with the first digit designating the fund grouping. These fund groupings are shown at the left-hand top column on the chart. All asset, liability, income, and expense codes are two-digit codes and are the second and third digits in the three-digit account code. These two-digit codes are used with the fund grouping code to designate the specific fund grouping it belongs to. For example, code 107 is "general fund marketable securities" while 507 is "endowment fund marketable securities."

Expense groupings are also used in a similar manner. There are four expense groups (instruction, library, administration, and maintenance). For each of these groups there are six single-digit expense codes and they are the third digit from the left. For example, "0" is salaries. Code 60 is "instruction salaries" while code 90 is "maintenance salaries." In addition to these codes there are a few other specific codes that are not applicable to these four major expense groups and they are listed separately.

One of the features of this chart of accounts is that it facilitates the preparation of financial statements in columnar format or, if desired, in a consolidated format. All similar items are coded with the same last two digits and this can be a time saver for the bookkeeper.

THE ROY B. COWIN SCHOOL
CHART OF ACCOUNTS

Fund Grouping

100	General fund
200	Board-designated endowment
300	Funds for specified purposes
400	Plant funds
500	Endowment funds

Assets

01	Cash in bank
02	Cash in savings bank
03	Petty cash
05	U.S. treasury bills
06	Marketable bonds
07	Marketable securities
08	Investment real estate
09	Other investments
10	Tuition receivable—current year
11	Tuition receivable—prior year
12	Other receivables
13	Inventory—books
14	Inventory—other
15	Prepaid expenses
18	Land
19	Buildings
20	Accumulated depreciation—building
21	Equipment
22	Accumulated depreciation—equipment
23	Vehicles
24	Accumulated depreciation—vehicles

Liabilities

30	Accounts payable
31	Short-term loans
32	Payroll taxes
33	Salaries payable
34	Tuition paid in advance
35	Other short-term liabilities
36	Long-term debts
38	Long-term pledges deferred

Interfund Receivables (Payables)

41	General fund
42	Board-designated endowment fund

43	Funds for specified purposes
44	Plant funds
45	Endowment funds

Fund Balances

46	Unrestricted
47	Unrestricted—allocated
48	Restricted

Income

50	Tuition income
51	Other fees
55	Contributions and gifts
57	Investment income
58	Interest income
59	Realized gains or losses

Expense Groups

6—	Instruction
7—	Library
8—	Administration
9—	Maintenance

Type Expense

—0	Salaries
—1	Retirement benefits
—2	Major medical
—3	Stationery and supplies
—4	Books
—5	Other

Specific Codes

86	Insurance
87	Bad debts
88	Depreciation
89	Legal and accounting and investment fees
97	Contracted services
98	Utilities and fuel

Fig. 29–1. A chart of accounts for an independent day school that uses fund accounting.

Interfund Accounts

In fund accounting, there are frequently interfund receivables and payables. In this chart of accounts all of these interfund balances are shown in five accounts for each fund grouping. The only distinction between a receivable or a payable with a particular fund is whether it is a debit (receivable) or a credit (payable). For example, if the general fund owes the board-designated endowment fund $100, the general fund would show a credit of $100 in account 142; the board-designated endowment fund would show a debit balance in account 241. Notice the account numbers "142" and "241." The first digit designates the fund in which the account belongs ("1" = general fund, "2" = board-designated endowment fund), and the third digit designates the fund which either is owed, or owes, the $100. In the first instance, the "2" designates the board-designated endowment fund. In the other, the "1" designates the general fund.

Likewise if the endowment fund owed $50 to the general fund and $10 to the funds for specified purposes, the respective fund groupings would look like this in a columnar format:

General Fund		Funds for Specified Purpose		Endowment Fund		Total All Funds
145	$50			541	($50) credit	—
		345	$10	543	(10) credit	—

As can be seen, if all interfund receivables and payables are shown in columnar form in this fashion, the "total all funds column" will net out to zero.

"Name" Funds

No separate listing is shown for the various name funds within the funds for specified purposes or in the endowment fund. As can be seen from Figure 12–8, The Roy B. Cowin School has many such funds.

If there are only one or two name funds, probably no separate set of account numbers need be assigned. There are not usually many transactions in each such fund and it will be easier to analyze each name fund separately once or twice a year than to keep a separate set of accounts for each. But if there are many name funds, as is the case here, or if the bookkeeping is done on a bookkeeping machine where account numbers are really needed to facilitate posting, then a further account-number structure should be set up. The easiest way is to assign one more, or even two more, digits to the three-digit code to designate the specific fund involved. These would be the fourth or fifth digits reading from the left. Thus marketable securities in the Malmar endowment fund might be shown as code 507–1: the 507 being the code number for endowment fund marketable securities, and the "1" being the code number assigned to the Malmar Fund. There would be a complete balancing set of accounts maintained for this subcode "1." If more than ten such name funds were used then a second digit would be added (507–11). The same procedure would be followed with funds for specified purposes. In this way the organization can have any number of name funds all within the same chart of account structure.

BOOKS AND RECORDS

The books and records used by fund accounting organizations are basically the same records discussed in Chapters 26 to 28. A completely separate set of books is often maintained for each fund grouping rather than trying to integrate all of the fund groupings into a single set of books. With a separate set of books the general fund would have its own cash receipts book, cash disbursement book, accounts payable register, general ledger, general journal, tuition income ledger, etc. Each of the other fund groupings would also have its separate set of books, although not all of the books would be appropriate for each grouping. In the case of The Roy B. Cowin School, separate books are kept for each fund grouping, as shown on page 524.

Even where a fund grouping requires one of these books, the actual format of the book may be much simpler than the format used by the general fund. For example, the number of expense categories and volume of transactions applicable to the funds for specified purposes are relatively few, and the cash disbursement book may have only a debit and credit column with each expend-

Book	General Fund	Board-Designated Endowment	Funds for Specified Purposes	Plant Fund	Endowment Fund
General ledger ...	x	x	x	x	x
General journal ..	x	x	x	x	x
Cash disbursement .	x		x		
Cash receipts	x		x		
Accounts payable register	x				
Tuition income ledger	x				
Payroll register ...	x				
Investment ledger .	x	x			x
Fixed asset register	x				x

iture being posted individually to the general ledger. In fact, if there are only a few cash transactions during the year, the cash receipts book and cash disbursements book may not be used at all. All entries, including cash entries, would then be entered in the general journal and posted directly and individually to the general ledger accounts.

The plant fund may or may not include assets other than plant or fixed assets. If the board places donor-restricted gifts for plant additions into the fund for specified purposes then only fixed assets would be shown in the plant fund. This type of decision, of course, affects the books that must be kept. In the case of our school illustration, only fixed assets are shown in the plant fund.

Books of "Name" Funds

Each individual name fund within each fund grouping will also require separate records but these records will consist only of a set of general ledger pages for the accounts maintained for each name fund. For example, if the funds for specified purposes have two name funds, each with an opening fund balance represented by cash in a savings account and each having contributions and expenses during the year, then the general ledger accounts would be as follows:

	Name Fund No. 1	Name Fund No. 2
Savings cash	302—1	302—2
Fund balance	348—1	348—2
Contributions	355—1	355—2
Interest	358—1	358—2
Expenses	3 - - -1	3 - - -2

These general ledger accounts would be filed in account number order rather than being segregated by each of the name funds. When the bookkeeper wishes to take a trial balance of the general ledger of the entire fund grouping he will take a trial balance of the individual general ledger accounts for all of the name funds. For purposes of statement presentation these name accounts would be combined to get the figures for the fund grouping as a whole. Figure 29–2 shows an example of a combining worksheet for the endowment fund grouping. Notice how these figures tie into the financial statement in Chapter 12.

Single Set of Books

There is no reason why an organization cannot merge all of the fund groupings into one overall set of books in much the same manner discussed for the name funds above. The chart of accounts is arranged to permit this. If all accounts were combined the general ledger would be fairly sizable but then it would only be necessary to keep one general journal, one cash disbursement book, one cash receipts book, etc.

The principal advantage of a single set of books is that there is only one set of records, and this facilitates bookkeeping, particularly if the organization has enough volume to handle its bookkeeping on a bookkeeping machine or some other form of mechanized system. With almost any type of mechanization, it is simpler to have one complex general ledger system than to have many separate general ledgers.

The principal disadvantage is that it is far easier to keep all transactions relating to one fund grouping together in a separate set of records. The bookkeeper is less likely to get confused and will be able to see what is happening more easily when separate

THE ROY B. COWIN SCHOOL

PRECLOSING WORKSHEET COMBINING NAME ENDOWMENT FUNDS
June 30, 1974

Sub-Code		Accounts							
		01/02	06/07	41/45	48	55	57/58	59	61/99
-1	The Malmar Fund	$ 4,000	$ 108,655	($ 4,970)	($ 110,700)		($4,970)	$ 3,015	$ 4,970
-2	Clyde Henderson Fund		34,916		(25,601)		(1,150)	(8,165)	
-3	Evelyn I. Marnoch Fund		9,205		(10,871)		(490)	2,156	
-4	Roy B. Cowin Memorial Fund	4,496	1,850,173		(1,641,300)			(213,369)	
-5	Lillian V. Fromhagen Fund		60,076		(53,165)			(6,911)	
-6	Donna Comstock Fund		47,974		(28,160)	($ 16,153)		(3,661)	
-7	Josephine Zagajewski Fund		100,000			(100,000)			
-8	The Peter Baker Fund		20,081		(12,150)	(6,351)		(1,580)	
-9	The Alfred P. Koch Fund	7,119		(7,119)	(6,300)			(819)	7,119
	Total	$15,615	$2,231,080	($12,089)	($1,888,247)	($122,504)	($6,610)	($229,334)	$12,089

Net Assets $2,234,606

Fund balance after closing...... ($2,234,606)

Fig. 29-2. An example of a preclosing worksheet in which individual "name" endowment funds are com-

books are used for each fund grouping. Accordingly, except when records are handled on some sort of mechanized system or where the organization has an especially competent bookkeeping staff, it is probably better to stick with a separate set of records for each fund grouping.

INTERFUND TRANSACTIONS

If all transactions involved a single fund, and there were no transactions between funds or fund groupings, the bookkeeping problems of fund accounting would be relatively easy. Unfortunately, these interfund transactions often cause more difficulty than they should partly because the bookkeeper is uncertain how to record such transactions. There are a number of fairly common interfund transactions, and each of these is discussed and illustrated in the following paragraphs.

Investment Income Transfer

The transfer of investment income from one fund to another is very common. Typically, investment income earned on an endowment fund is deposited by the custodian bank in an endowment fund income cash account. Then, from time to time the bookkeeper will transfer portions of this cash to the general fund and if any of the income is restricted to a specified use, to the funds for specified purposes. Here are the journal entries that would be made if the endowment fund earned $250 of income, $200 of which is unrestricted and $50 is restricted for a specified purpose:

On endowment fund books:

Debit No. 501 (cash) $250
    Credit No. 557 (investment income) $250
        To record receipt of investment income.

Debit No. 557 (investment income) $250
    Credit No. 541 (payable to general fund) $200
    Credit No. 543 (payable to funds for specified purposes)   50
        To record transfer of investment income to general fund and funds for specified purposes.

On general fund books:

Debit No. 145 (receivable from endowment fund) $200
  Credit No. 157 (investment income) $200
      To record transfer of investment income from endowment fund.

On funds for specified purposes books:

Debit No. 345 (receivable from endowment fund) .... $ 50
  Credit No. 357 (investment income) .... $ 50
      To record transfer of investment income from the endowment fund.

In due course when the cash is actually transferred from the endowment fund, the entry on the various books would be a debit or credit to cash and a corresponding debit or credit to the inter-fund payable or receivable account.

Interfund Borrowings

Another frequent interfund transaction is the temporary borrowing of cash by one fund from another fund. Here are the entries to record the general fund borrowing $10,000 from the board-designated endowment fund.

On general fund books:

Debit No. 101 (cash) $10,000
  Credit No. 142 (payable to board-designated endowment fund) $10,000
      To record interfund loan from the board-designated endowment fund.

On board-designated endowment fund books:

Debit No. 241 (receivable from general fund) $10,000
  Credit No. 201 (cash) $10,000
      To record interfund loan to the general fund.

When this loan is paid off, the entries would be reversed.

Expenses Paid by One Fund for Another

The general fund may pay expenses which are chargeable to another fund. A common example is payment of expenses out of the general fund which are to be charged to funds for specified purposes.

In the following example the general fund paid $200 for library books, $75 of which can be charged to funds for specified purposes. Here are the appropriate entries:

On general fund books:

Debit No. 143 (receivable from funds for specified purposes) ...... $ 75
Debit No. 174 (library books) 125
    Credit No. 130 (accounts payable) $200

      To record amount of library books purchased by general fund, part of which is to be paid for by funds for specified purposes.

On funds for specified purposes books:

Debit No. 374 (library books) .... $ 75
    Credit No. 341 (payable to general fund) .... $ 75

      To record purchase of library books by the general fund, out of funds for specified purposes.

Contributions Transferred to Board-Designated Fund

All contributions not restricted by donors must be shown in the general fund. However, if the board wishes, it can always make transfers out of the general fund into the board-designated endowment fund. The contribution must be reported first as income in the general fund, so any transfer is effectively a transfer of the fund balance. Here are the entries that would be made to record a gift of $750 and the subsequent transfer to the board-designated endowment fund:

On general fund books:

Debit No. 101 (cash) $750
    Credit No. 155 (contributions) $750

      To record receipt of an unrestricted contribution from Linda Jean Baker.

Debit No. 146 (unrestricted fund balance) $750
    Credit No. 142 (payable to board-designated endowment fund) $750

      To record transfer to board-designated endowment fund of portion of general fund balance arising from gift of Linda Jean Baker.

On board-designated endowment fund books:

Debit No. 241 (receivable from general fund) $750
    Credit No. 246 (unrestricted fund balance) $750
       To record transfer from general fund of portion of general fund
       balance arising from gift of Linda Jean Baker.

Several things should be noted about this entry. First, note that in the general fund the transfer was out of the fund balance account and not out of the contributions received account. The gift of $750 must be reported as part of general fund income, and accordingly the transfer cannot come from the contribution account. Second, note that in the board-designated endowment fund the $750 receipt was shown not as a contribution but, again, as a fund balance transfer. This is the important thing to remember about transfers. They don't create income; all they do is to transfer portions of the fund balance or net worth from one fund to another. Transfers are discussed at length in Chapter 5.

Current Restricted Funds Expended Through the General Fund

A related type of transaction between funds takes place with those organizations following the accounting principle of placing all restricted contributions in a current restricted fund (the name often given to the funds for specified purposes) and then transferring to the general fund such portion of these restricted contributions as is actually expended by the general fund. This is the method recommended by a number of organizations for handling restricted contributions for current purposes.* Basically the entries to effect this transfer are quite straightforward. Assume $600 is received in the current year but only $500 is expended for the restricted purpose.

On funds for specified purposes books:

Debit No. 301 (cash) $600
    Credit No. 355 (contributions) $600
       To record receipt of $600 restricted contributions.

    * See page 184 for a discussion of this principle for voluntary health and welfare organizations, page 232 for colleges and universities, and page 263 for hospitals. In addition there is a complete discussion of the reporting practices in Chapter 9.

Debit No. 355 (contributions) $500

    Credit No. 341 (interfund payable) $500

        To record transfer to the general fund of a portion of restricted contributions for current operations that were expended during the year.

This entry appears more straightforward than it would actually be in practice because the mechanics of presentation recommended for handling current restricted contributions in this manner also provide that the initial receipt of the contribution ($600) be shown in a Statement of Fund Balances rather than in an Income Statement. Readers interested in more details on the presentation should refer to the pages indicated. In any event the entries above will accomplish the correct end objective of this transfer.

Allocation of Unrestricted Fund Balances

Allocations, or as they are often known, "appropriations," of part of the unrestricted fund balance are occasionally made by the board. While the use of allocations is not recommended because they are seldom understood by the reader, some organizations still use this bookkeeping technique to segregate portions of the fund balance for future projects. This is an acceptable practice only if the rules outlined on pages 52 to 54 are followed. When the rules are followed, the entry that would be made to effect an allocation would be:

Debit No. 146 (unrestricted fund balance) $1,000

    Credit No. 147 (unrestricted fund balance—allocated) $1,000

        To record an allocation of the unrestricted general fund balance for Project A.

Note that this entry merely transfers a portion of the unrestricted fund balance to another unrestricted fund balance. No income or expense is involved. At a future date when the expenditure is made for Project A, it will be charged to an expense account, and not to the allocated portion of the unrestricted fund balance. At that time an entry will be made reversing the entry above.

TRIAL BALANCE

One final word of caution is in order. The usual way in which posting errors are caught is through the use of a trial balance. If the debits and the credits aren't equal, the bookkeeper knows he must look for his error. The most likely posting error a book-keeper will make, when fund accounting is involved, is to enter a transaction involving two funds in only one of the two funds. The use of a trial balance, however, will not catch this type of error since the debits and credits may be equal but a complete entry omitted (both debit and credit).

Balancing Interfund Transactions

It is easy to prevent this from going undetected. What is required is a balancing of the interfund receivables and payables. If they balance out to zero, then the bookkeeper knows that both sides of all interfund transactions have been recorded. This balancing is easy to do with the chart of accounts provided in Figure 29–1 because all of the intercompany accounts are classified in one series of account numbers. Usually all that is required is running an adding machine tape of the aggregate debit and credit balances of the interfund accounts to be sure they net out to zero; if they don't, then the bookkeeper can compare, account by account, the corresponding contra account in the other fund. Thus account 142 should be the same amount as 241 except one will be a debit and the other a credit. In this way it is easy to pinpoint differences.

CONCLUSION

Fund accounting is not difficult from a bookkeeping stand-point but it requires careful organization and a good chart of accounts. It also requires care to ensure that both sides of inter-fund transactions are recorded. Other than that, fund accounting follows the same principles used by nonfund accounting organizations.

Fund accounting can be applied to either cash or accrual basis organizations. The principal problem with fund accounting is not the bookkeeping, but the problem of presentation. This is where fund accounting frequently falls down. If the suggestions and recommendations that have been made throughout this book are heeded the treasurer will be able to put together financial statements that are straightforward and clear to the unknowledgeable reader; in short, that will easily pass the "grandmother" test.

APPENDIXES

Tables of Accounting and Reporting Alternatives

TABLE A–1

Basic Accounting Alternatives for Various Organizations	Preferable*	Acceptable But Not Recommended†	Not Acceptable
Accrual basis reporting:			
Organizations with substantial amounts of unpaid bills or uncollected income	X		
Organizations that need to measure cost of services provided or which budget their activities closely	X		
Organizations that want statements prepared in accordance with generally accepted accounting principles.........	X		
Churches	X(1)		
Small social clubs	X(1)		
Country clubs, swim clubs	X		
Colleges, universities, secondary private schools..........................	X		
Hospitals..........................	X		
Voluntary health and welfare organizations .	X		
Fund-raising organizations	X		
Foundations	X(1)		
Combination cash accounting and accrual statements:			
Small organizations where books are kept by a secretary, or non-bookkeeper	X		
Organizations where competent bookkeeper is available to keep records		X	
Organizations where services provided are billed to members or others			X

*Required or generally accepted under present usage.
†Generally accepted under present usage.
(1)When there are no material amounts of unpaid bills or uncollected income the cash basis of reporting is acceptable.

TABLE A–2

Alternative Fund Accounting Practices	Preferable*	Acceptable But Not Recommended†	Not Acceptable
Use of separate board-designated funds in financial statements:			
Voluntary health and welfare organizations			X
Colleges, universities		X	
Hospitals			X
Other organizations		X	
Use of separate plant or fixed-asset fund in financial statements:			
Colleges, universities		X	
Hospitals			X
Voluntary health and welfare organizations		X	
Other organizations		X	
Unrestricted contributions added to:			
General fund	X		
Board-designated funds			X
Endowment fund			X
Restricted contributions added to:			
General fund			X
Board-designated funds			X
Endowment or restricted fund	X		
Inter-fund borrowings where:			
Borrowing fund clearly has the ability to repay the lending fund		X	
Borrowing fund has no clear way to repay the lending fund			X

* Required or generally accepted under present usage.
† Generally accepted under present usage.

TABLE A–3

Fund Transfer and Appropriation Practices	Preferable*	Acceptable But Not Recommended†	Not Acceptable
Transfers between funds:			
Transfers between funds shown in statements:			
On separate Statement of Changes in Fund Balances	X		
On a combined State of Income, Expenses and Changes in Fund Balances, after the caption "fund balance at the beginning of the year"	X		
On Statement of Income and Expenses when separate Statement of Changes In Fund Balance is also presented		X	
On Statement of Income and Expenses:			
After caption "excess of income over expenses"	X		
Before caption "excess of income over expenses"			X
Transfer from general fund to board-designated funds:			
Surplus funds not needed for day-to-day operations		X (1)	
Excess of income over expenses for the year to reduce general fund income to zero		X (1)	
Transfer from board-designated funds to general fund:			
Funds to cover the deficit for the year		X (1)	
Funds needed for current operations	X		

* Required or generally accepted under present usage.
† Generally accepted under present usage.
(1) Except for hospitals and voluntary health and welfare organizations. These organizations combine all unrestricted funds for reporting purposes.

TABLE A–3–Continued

Fund Transfer and Appropriation Practices	Preferable*	Acceptable But Not Recommended†	Not Acceptable
Appropriations:			
Use of appropriations		X	
Appropriations shown in a separate Statement of Changes in Fund Balance . .	X		
Appropriations shown in Statement of Income and Expense when a separate Statement of Changes In Fund Balance is also presented		X	
Appropriations shown in a Statement of Income and Expenses, where no separate Statement of Changes In Fund Balance is presented:			
Reported as an expense			X
Reported after the caption "excess of income over expense"		X	
Expenditures charged directly against the appropriations			X
Unexpended appropriations shown in the Balance Sheet:			
In the liability section			X
In the fund balance section	X		
The actual expenditure of amounts previously appropriated should be reported as:			
A charge directly against the appropriation			X
An expense in the current period	X		
Appropriations disclosed only in a footnote and not reported in the financial statements	X		
* Required or generally accepted under present usage. † Generally accepted under present usage.			

TABLE A–4

Fixed-Asset Accounting for Various Organizations	Preferable*	Acceptable But Not Recommended†	Not Acceptable
Immediate write-off of fixed assets:			
Churches		X	
Small social clubs without major fixed assets	X		
Country clubs, swim clubs		X	
Colleges, universities, secondary schools			X
Hospitals			X
Voluntary health and welfare organizations			X
Fund-raising organizations			X(1)
Private foundations			X(1)
Capitalize fixed assets:			
Churches	X		
Small social clubs without major fixed assets		X	
Country clubs, swim clubs	X		
Colleges, universities, secondary schools	X		
Hospitals	X		
Voluntary health and welfare organizations	X		
Fund-raising organizations	X		
Private foundations	X		
Organizations that need to know accurately the full cost of a product or service	X		
Organizations that must recover cost of assets from revenues	X		
Organizations that have unrelated business income for tax purposes	X		
Organizations that are involved in reimbursement formulas	X		
Write-off, then capitalize method:			
Voluntary health and welfare organizations			X
Organizations that raise funds for fixed assets in special fund-raising drives			X
Cash basis organizations		X	
* Required or generally accepted under present usage.			
† Generally accepted under present usage.			
(1) Unless such amounts are not material in amount, in which case they could be written off when purchased.			

TABLE A-5

Depreciation Practices for Various Organizations	Preferable*	Acceptable But Not Recommended†	Not Acceptable
Fixed assets depreciated:			
Organizations that capitalize fixed assets ..	X		
Organizations that must recover cost of assets from revenues................	X		
Organizations that need to know accurately the cost of a product or service ...	X		
Organizations that have unrelated business income for tax purposes	X		
Organizations involved in reimbursement formulas	X		
Organizations following the write-off, then capitalize method			X
Organizations that raise funds in special fund-raising drives	X		
Reporting depreciation directly in the plant fund where a separate plant fund is used:			
Where separate statements are presented for each fund................		X	
Where a columnar statement showing all funds is presented	X		
Recording depreciation in the general fund and transferring such depreciation to a separate plant fund:			
Where separate statements are presented for each fund		X	
Where a columnar statement showing all funds is presented		X	
The use of a separate plant fund when assets are depreciated in the general fund ..		X	
The use of funding techniques when a separate plant fund is used		X	
The use of replacement reserves		X	
Replacement reserves charged against:			
Statement of Income and Expense			X
Fund balance	X		

* Required or generally accepted under present usage.
† Generally accepted under present usage.

TABLE A–6

Reporting Alternatives for Investment Income, Gains and Losses, and Endowment Funds	Preferable*	Acceptable But Not Recommended†	Not Acceptable
Investment Income:			
Unrestricted investment income from unrestricted[1] funds reported in:			
General Fund Statement of Income and Expenses[2]	X		
General Fund separate Statement of Changes in Fund Balance			X
Board-Designated Fund Statement of Income and Expenses			X
Board-Designated Fund separate Statement of Changes in Fund Balance			X
Unrestricted investment income from endowment funds reported in:			
General Fund Statement of Income and Expenses	X		
General Fund separate Statement of Changes in Fund Balance			X
Endowment Fund Statement of Income, Expenses and Changes in Fund Balance			X
Endowment Fund Statement of Income, Expenses and Changes in Fund Balance and then transferred to the General Fund Statement of Income and Expenses			X
Restricted investment income from endowment funds reported directly in Funds for Specified Purposes	X		
Gains and Losses:			
Gains and Losses on unrestricted funds reported in:			
General Fund Statement of Income and Expenses	X		
General Fund separate Statement of Changes in Fund Balances			X
Board-Designated Fund Statement of Income and Expenses			X
Board-Designated Fund Statement of Changes in Fund Balance			X

*Required or generally accepted under present usage.
†Generally accepted under present usage.
(1) Including board-designated funds.
(2) Reference to a Statement of Income and Expenses within this table also refers to a combined Statement of Income, Expenses and Changes in Fund Balance.

543

TABLE A–6—Continued

Reporting Alternatives for Investment Income, Gains and Losses, and Endowment Funds	Preferable*	Acceptable But Not Recommended†	Not Acceptable
Gains and losses on endowment funds reported in:			
Endowment Fund Statement of Income, Expense and Change in Fund Balances ...	X		
Separate Statement of Changes in Fund Balance		X	
Unrestricted gains and losses on endowment funds reported in:			
General Fund Statement of Income and Expenses	X		
Endowment Fund Statement of Income, Expenses and Changes in Fund Balances . .		X	
Endowment Fund Statement of Income, Expenses and Changes in Fund Balances and then transferred to General Fund . . .		X	
Reporting unrealized gains(3)	X		
Recording unrealized losses on investments carried at cost where there is:			
Permanent impairment	X		
Temporary decline in market and no intention of selling investments		X	
Temporary decline in market but expect to sell in near future	X		
Fixed Rate of Return:			
Fixed rate of return for board-designated funds		X	
Fixed rate of return for endowment funds where capital gains are legally available:			
Transfer treated as a "transfer" *after* caption "excess of income over expenses"	X		
Transfer labeled as a transfer but included *before* caption "excess of income over expenses"			X
Transfer labeled as income or included in caption of "income"			X
Fixed rate of return percentage subject to arbitrary redetermination			X

*Required or generally accepted under present usage.
†Generally accepted under present usage.
(3) But preferable only for organizations with sizable investment funds.

TABLE A–7

Reporting Alternatives for Contributions	Preferable*	Acceptable But Not Recommended†	Not Acceptable
Unrestricted Contributions:			
Reported in General Fund Statement of Income and Expenses	X		
Reported in General Fund separate Statement of Changes in Fund Balance			X
Reported in General Fund combined Statement of Income, Expenses and Changes in Fund Balance	X		
Reported directly in a Board-designated fund			X
Restricted Contributions for Noncurrent Purposes:			
Reported in Restricted Fund Statement of Income and Expenses	X		
Reported in Restricted Fund separate Statement of Changes in Fund Balances ...		X	
Reported in Restricted Fund combined Statement of Income, Expenses and Changes in Fund Balance	X		
Reported in columnar statement showing all funds	X		
Restricted Contributions for Current Purposes:			
Reported in Restricted Fund Statement of Income, Expenses and Changes in Fund Balance, with expenditure shown in this statement only		X	
Reported in Restricted Fund Statement of Income, Expenses and Changes in Fund Balance with the expenditures shown in the general fund, and the portion expended transferred to the general fund as a "transfer"		X	
Reported in the Restricted Fund Statement of Changes in Fund Balance with the expenditure shown in the general fund, and the portion expended transferred to the general fund as income		X	

*Required or generally accepted under present usage.
†Generally accepted under present usage.

TABLE A–7—Continued

Reporting Alternatives for Contributions	Preferable*	Acceptable But Not Recommended†	Not Acceptable
Restricted Contributions for Current Purposes:			
Reported in the General Fund State-			
ment of Income, Expenses and Changes			
in Fund Balance where the amounts			
unexpended at the end of the year are			
not material in amount	X		
Reported in the Restricted Fund column			
of a columnar statement showing all			
funds side-by-side	X		
Pledges:			
Recording pledges as an asset (accrual			
basis only):			
Where material in amount	X		
Where not material in amount		X	
Recognizing pledges as income in the			
year pledge is made, when pledge is			
to be used for:			
Current year's operations	X		
Future year's general fund operations			X
Building funds	X		
Contributed Services:			
Contributed services recorded as income:			
Fund-raising services			X
Where there is no control over the			
person contributing the services			X
Where supplementary type services are			
provided that the organization would			
not normally pay someone to perform . . .			X
Services where there is no objective			
basis on which to value			X
Services normally or otherwise pro-			
vided by paid staff	X		

* Required or generally accepted under present usage.
† Generally accepted under present usage.

TABLE A–8

Alternative Financial Statement Presentations for Fund Accounting	Preferable*	Acceptable But Not Recommended†	Not Acceptable
Use of statement package consisting of:			
Statement of Income, Expenses and Changes in Fund Balances and a Balance Sheet, both in columnar format showing all funds side-by-side (Figure 12-1, 12-2)	X		
Statement of Income and Expenses, Statement of Changes in Fund Balances, and Balance Sheet, all three statements in columnar format (Figure 12-3 (top), 12-4, 12-2)	X		
Statement of General Fund Income and Expense, Statement of Changes in Fund Balances, and Balance Sheet, with the last two statements in columnar format.		X	
Statement of General Fund Income and Expense, separate Statements of Changes in Fund Balances for each fund, and separate Balance Sheet for each fund (similar to Figures 4-1, 4-2)		X	
Separate Statement of Income, Expense and Changes in Fund Balance for each fund, and separate Balance Sheet for each fund (not illustrated as such; see Figures 12-5, 4-1).		X	
Statement of Income and Expense and Balance Sheet, with changes in fund balance shown in the "fund balance" section of the Balance Sheet, both statements in columnar format (Figure 12-3)	X		
Use of Condensed or Summary Statements:			
General Fund Statement of Income and Expense (no other statement) (Figure 12-11)			X
Summary of Unrestricted Income and Expense but with detailed footnote disclosure of all activity in all other funds (Figure 12-11)		X	
Summary of Income and Expense, showing activity for all funds in one statement (Figure 12-10)	X		

* Required or generally accepted under present usage.
† Generally accepted under present usage.

Use of Rulings and Underscorings

One of the areas that causes confusion to the average reader of a financial statement is the number of rulings or underscores on a financial statement. What do they mean? When is something underscored? The rules are straightforward although somewhat complicated in application:

1. A figure is underscored when you want to indicate that you are adding all figures above the line to come to a total or subtotal which will be shown immediately below the line:

$$\begin{array}{r} 1,139 \\ 1,849 \\ \underline{590} \\ 3,578 \end{array}$$

The line here means that everything above the line adds down to the figure below the line (3,578).

2. A single row of figures is underscored where you want to indicate that this single row of figures is not going to be added into the figures immediately below the line. Notice that this occurs only when there is a single row of figures, and not several rows:

$$\begin{array}{r} \underline{1,139} \\ 1,849 \\ \underline{590} \\ 2,439 \end{array}$$

The 1,139 is not added into the figures below because there is only the single row above the line.

3. A double underscore is used to indicate that absolutely nothing more is carried below this point in this column.

```
1,849
  590
2,439
═════
   23
  161
  184
```

4. If there are several sets of underscored figures which are sub-totals, and you want to add all these subtotals together, the figure directly above the final total will be underscored and the final total will be double underscored:

```
1,139
1,849
  590
2,439
3,578
═════
```

Here is a typical example showing all the possibilities:

Cash in bank	$ 1,000
Cash in petty cash	100
	1,100
Accounts receivable—trade	133,000
Accounts receivable—other	23,000
	156,000
Total current assets	157,100
Fixed assets:	
Land	25,000
Plant	116,000
Less reserve for depreciation	(65,000)
	76,000
Total assets	$233,100

The statements should be designed to avoid subtotals as much as possible to reduce possible reader confusion. If possible the use of two columns should be used to help avoid confusion. Here is the above statement in a two column approach:

Cash in bank	$ 1,000	
Cash in petty cash	100	$ 1,100
Accounts receivable:		
Trade	133,000	
Other	23,000	156,000
Total current assets		157,100
Fixed assets:		
Land	25,000	
Plant	116,000	
Less reserve for depreciation	(65,000)	76,000
Total assets		$233,100

As with most other reporting problems, care must be taken to minimize reader confusion. If the treasurer constantly keeps this in mind, the more complicated presentations can often be presented in a straightforward fashion that will increase reader comprehension without unduly cutting back on details.

Bibliography

ALABAMA HOSPITAL ASSOCIATION. *Manual Uniform Accounting and Cost Analysis for General Hospitals.* Prepared in Cooperation with Alabama Chapter, American Association of Hospital Accountants. Montgomery, Ala.: Author, 1963, v.p.

ALLISON, J. L. *Office Management Manual for Legal Aid Societies.* Chicago: Public Administration Service, 1953, 109 p.

AMERICAN ACCOUNTING ASSOCIATION, Report of the Committee on Accounting Practices of Not-for-Profit Organizations, *The Accounting Review,* Supplement to Vol. XLVI, 1971, pp. 80–163.

AMERICAN COUNCIL ON EDUCATION. *College and University Business Administration.* Rev. Ed. Washington, D. C.: Author, 1968, 311 p.

AMERICAN COUNCIL ON EDUCATION. *Planning for Effective Resource Allocation in Universities.* Prepared by Harry Williams of the Institute for Defense Analysis. Washington, D. C. 1966, 88 p.

AMERICAN HOSPITAL ASSOCIATION. *Accounting Manual for Long-term Care Institutions.* Chicago: Author, 1968, 129 p.

AMERICAN HOSPITAL ASSOCIATION. *Bookkeeping Procedure and Business Practice for Small Hospitals.* Chicago: Author, 1956, 170 p.

AMERICAN HOSPITAL ASSOCIATION. *Budgeting Procedures for Hospitals.* Chicago: Author, 1961, 68 p.

AMERICAN HOSPITAL ASSOCIATION. *Chart of Accounts for Hospitals.* Chicago: Author, 1966, 135 p.

AMERICAN HOSPITAL ASSOCIATION. *Cost Finding and Rate Setting for Hospitals.* Chicago: Author, 1968, 103 p.

AMERICAN HOSPITAL ASSOCIATION. *Handbook on Accounting, Statistics and Business Office Procedures for Hospitals.* Chicago: Author, 1956–59. 3 sections.

AMERICAN HOSPITAL ASSOCIATION. *Internal Control and Internal Auditing for Hospitals.* Chicago: Author, 1969, 66 p.

AMERICAN HOSPITAL ASSOCIATION. *Uniform Hospital Definitions.* Chicago: Author, 1960, 50 p.

AMERICAN INSTITUTE OF ACCOUNTANTS. Committee on Auditing Procedure. *A Hospital.* New York: Author, 1956, 45 p.

AMERICAN INSTITUTE OF CERTIFIED PUBLIC ACCOUNTANTS. *Audits of Colleges and Universities.* New York: Author, 1973, 78 p.

AMERICAN INSTITUTE OF CERTIFIED PUBLIC ACCOUNTANTS. *Audits of Voluntary Health and Welfare Organizations.* New York: Author, 1967, 72 p.

AMERICAN INSTITUTE OF CERTIFIED PUBLIC ACCOUNTANTS. *Medicare Audit Guide.* New York: Author, 1969.

AMERICAN INSTITUTE OF CERTIFIED PUBLIC ACCOUNTANTS. *Audits of Voluntary Health and Welfare Organizations.* New York: Author, 1974.

AMERICAN INSTITUTE OF CERTIFIED PUBLIC ACCOUNTANTS. *Public School Costs.* New York: Author, 1963, 28 p.

AMERICAN NATIONAL RED CROSS. *Suggested Method for Keeping Chapter Financial Records.* Washington, D. C.: Author, March 1956, 27 p.

BARBOUR, H. O. *Private Club Administration.* Washington, D. C.: Club Managers Association, 1968, 630 p.

BASTABLE, C. W. "Evaluating Performance of Not-For-Profit Entities." *Journal of Accountancy,* Jan. 1973, p. 32.

BERMAN, H. J., and WEEKS, L. E. *Financial Management of Hospitals.* Ann Arbor, Mich.: Bureau of Hospital Administration, School of Public Health, University of Michigan, 1971, 386 p. (Research Series No. 6.)

BIERMAN, H., JR., and HOFSTEDT, T. R. *University Accounting: Alternative Measures of Ivy League Deficits,* n.p. April 1973, 20 p.

BRAMER, J. C., JR. *Efficient Church Business Management.* Philadelphia: Westminster Press, 1960, 150 p.

CANADIAN HOSPITAL ASSOCIATION. *Canadian Hospital Accounting Manual —Accounting and Statistical Principles and Procedures for Canadian Hospitals.* Ed. 3. Toronto: Author, 1968, 314 p.

CANADIAN INSTITUTE OF CHARTERED ACCOUNTANTS. *The Hospital Audit.* Toronto: Author, 1965, 58 p.

CARY, W. L. and BRIGHT, C. B. "The Law and the Lore of Endowment Funds—Report to the Ford Foundation." New York: Ford Foundation, 1969, 82 p.

CATHOLIC HOSPITAL ASSOCIATION OF THE UNITED STATES AND CANADA. *Guides to Hospital Administrative Planning and Control Through Accounting.* St. Louis, Mo.: Author, 1959, 57 p.

CLEVELAND HOSPITAL COUNCIL. *Manual of Hospital Procedures: Volume 1 —Hospital Accounting.* Effective January 1, 1950, Revised January 1, 1955. Cleveland: Author, v.p.

CLUB MANAGERS ASSOCIATION OF AMERICA. *Expense and Payroll Dictionary for Clubs—For Use with the Second Revised Edition (1967) of the Uniform System of Accounts for Clubs.* Washington, D. C.: Author.

CLUB MANAGERS ASSOCIATION OF AMERICA. *Uniform System of Accounts for Clubs.* Ed. 2, Rev. Washington, D. C.: Author, 1967, 140 p.

COMMUNITY FUND OF CHICAGO, INC. *Accounting and Budgeting Instructions.* Chicago: Author, June 1958, v.p.

CROWE, J. M. and MOORE, M. D. *Church Finance Record System Manual.* Nashville: Broadman Press, 1959, 48 p.

DEMAREST, ROSEMARY R. *Accounting: Information Sources.* Detroit: Gale Research Company, 1970, 420 p.

DERMER, JOSEPH. *How to Raise Funds from Foundations.* Public Service Materials Center, 104 East 40th St., New York, N. Y., 1971.

ENGLANDER, L. *Accounting Principles and Procedures of Philanthropic Institutions.* New York: New York Community Trust, 1957, 43 p.

EVANGELICAL AND REFORMED CHURCH. *Handbook for the Finance Officers of a Local Church.* Philadelphia: Author, 1961, 28 p.

FAY, C. T., JR., RHOADS, R. C., and ROSENBLATT, R. L. *Managerial Accounting for the Hospitality Service Industries*. Dubuque, Iowa: 1971, 588 p.

FOUNDATION CENTER. *The Foundation Directory*. Edition 4; New York: Columbia University Press, 1971.

FOUST, O. Q. "Churches." In National Society of Public Accountants. *Portfolio of Accounting Systems for Small and Medium-Sized Business*. Vol. 1. Englewood Cliffs, N. J.: Prentice-Hall, Inc., 1968, pp. 297–322.

GIBBS, G. *Manual for Parish Treasurers*. 3rd ed. Los Angeles: Protestant Episcopal Church in the Diocese of Los Angeles, 1971, 50 p.

GOODWILL INDUSTRIES OF AMERICA, INC. *Uniform Socio-Economic Reporting System: Manual for Financial Records*. Washington: Author, 1971. Various paging (looseleaf).

GRAY, R. N. *Managing the Church—Vol. 2, Business Methods*. Enid, Oklahoma: Phillips University Press, 1970, 212 p.

GREEN, J. L., JR. and BARBER, A. W. *A System of Cost Accounting for Physical Plant Operations in Institutions of Higher Education*. Athens, Georgia: University of Georgia Press, 1968, 103 p.

GROSS, M. J., JR. "An Accountant Looks at the 'Total Return' Approach for Endowment Funds." *CPA Journal*, Nov. 1973, pp. 977–84.

GROSS, M. J., JR. "Layman's Guide to Preparing Financial Statements for Churches." Price Waterhouse Review, Winter 1966, pp. 48–56. Also reprinted by the American Institute of CPA's.

HAY, L. E. *Budgeting and Cost Analysis for Hospital Management*. Ed. 2. Bloomington, Ind.: Pressler Publications, 1963, 304 p.

HENKE, E. O. *Accounting for Non-Profit Organizations*. Belmont, Calif.: Wadsworth Publishing Co., 1966, 145 p.

HENKE, E. O. *Accounting for Nonprofit Organizations—An Exploratory Study*. Bloomington, Ind.: Indiana University, Graduate School of Business, Bureau of Business Research, 1965, 86 p.

HENKE, E. O. "Evaluating Performance of Not-For-Profit Organizations." *Journal of Accountancy*, Jan. 1973, p. 34.

HENKE, E. O. "Performance Evaluation for Not-For-Profit Organizations." *Journal of Accountancy*, June 1972, pp. 51–55.

HOFSTRA UNIVERSITY. *The Impact of the Advent of Medicare on Hospital Costs*. Hempstead, N.Y.: Author, 1970, 230 p.

HOLCK, M., JR. *Accounting Methods for the Small Church*. Minneapolis: Augsburg Publishing House, 1961, 108 p.

HOLT, D. R., II. *Handbook of Church Finance*. New York: Macmillan Co., 1960, 201 p.

INDIANA UNIVERSITY SCHOOL OF BUSINESS AND AMERICAN ASSOCIATION OF HOSPITAL ACCOUNTANTS. *Selected Papers: Twentieth Annual Institute on Hospital Accounting and Finance*. Bloomington, Ind.: Indiana University, 1963, 151 p.

KERRIGAN, H. D. *Fund Accounting*. New York: McGraw-Hill Books, Inc., 1969, 533 p.

MACLEOD, R. K. "Program Budgeting Works in Nonprofit Institutions." *Harvard Business Review*, Sept.–Oct. 1971, pp. 46–56.

MARTIN, T. L. *Hospital Accounting Principles and Practice*. Ed. 3. Chicago: Physicians' Record Co., 1958, 296 p.

MITCHELL, HERBERT S. *Manual for School Accounting.* Danville, Ill.: Interstate, 1961, 101 p.

NATIONAL ASSOCIATION OF COLLEGE AND UNIVERSITY BUSINESS OFFICERS. *Annotated Tabulations of College and University Accounting Practices.* Washington: Author, 1964, 55 p.

NATIONAL ASSOCIATION OF COLLEGE AND· UNIVERSITY BUSINESS OFFICERS. *College and University Business Administration—Administrative Manual.* Washington, D. C., 1974. (Looseleaf.)

NATIONAL ASSOCIATION OF COLLEGE AND UNIVERSITY BUSINESS OFFICERS. *Planning, Budgeting and Accounting.* Prepared by Peat, Marwick, Mitchell & Co. Washington: Author, 1970, 149 p.

NATIONAL ASSOCIATION OF INDEPENDENT SCHOOLS. *Accounting for Independent Schools.* Boston: Author, 1969, 112 p.

NATIONAL BOARD OF YOUNG MEN'S CHRISTIAN ASSOCIATIONS. *Association Records—The Official Guide to YMCA Program Recording and Reporting.* New York: Association Press, 1964, 90 p.

NATIONAL BUDGET AND CONSULTATION COMMITTEE. *Standards for National Voluntary Health, Welfare and Recreation Agencies.* New York: Author, 1963, n.p.

NATIONAL CONFERENCE OF CATHOLIC BISHOPS. *Diocesan Accounting and Financial Reporting.* Washington: Author, 1971, 142 p.

NATIONAL HEALTH COUNCIL, NATIONAL ASSEMBLY FOR SOCIAL POLICY AND DEVELOPMENT, INC., and UNITED WAY OF AMERICA. *Standards of Accounting and Financial Reporting for Voluntary Health and Welfare Organizations.* Rev. ed. New York: Authors, 1974, 130 p.

NEW YORK (STATE) AUDIT AND CONTROL DEPARTMENT. *Uniform System of Accounts for Community Colleges.* Albany: Author, 1971, 31 p.

PEAT, MARWICK, MITCHELL & Co. *Planning, Budgeting and Accounting.* Washington, D. C.: National Association of College and University Business Offices, 1970, 149 p.

PELOUBET, MAURICE E. *The Financial Executive and The New Accounting.* New York: Ronald Press Co., 1967, 227 p.

PIERSALL, R. W. "Depreciation and the Nonprofit Organization." *New York Certified Public Accountant,* Jan. 1971, pp. 57–65.

RYAN, L. V. *An Accounting Manual for Catholic Elementary and Secondary Schools.* Washington, D. C.: National Catholic Education Association, 1969.

SCHEPS, C. and DAVIDSON, E. E. *Accounting for Colleges and Universities.* Rev. Ed. Baton Rouge: Louisiana State University Press, 1970.

SEAWELL, L. V. *Hospital Accounting and Financial Management.* Berwyn, Ill.: Physicians' Record Co., 1964, 502 p.

SEAWELL, L. V. *Introduction to Hospital Accounting.* Chicago: Hospital Financial Management Association, 1971, 200 p.

SEAWELL, L. *Principles of Hospital Accounting.* Berwyn, Ill.: Physicians' Record Co., 1960, 360 p.

SHARKEY, D. H. "Associations and Clubs." In National Society of Public Accountants. *Portfolio of Accounting Systems for Small and Medium-Sized Businesses.* Vol. 1. Englewood Cliffs, N. J.: Prentice-Hall, Inc., 1968, pp. 59–70.

SHERER, H. *Progress in Financial Reporting in Selected Universities Since 1930.* Urbana, Ill.: University of Illinois, 1950, 120 p.

SIMMONS, H. *How to Run a Club.* Harper Brothers, 1955, 380 p.

SKINNER, R. M. *Canadian University Accounting.* Toronto: The Canadian Institute of Chartered Accountants, 1969, 44 p.

SLADE, F. V. *Church Accounts—A Comprehensive Handbook Dealing with Accounts and Finance Connected with the Church.* London: Gee and Co., Ltd., 1960, 222 p.

SWANSON, J. E., ARDEN, W. and STILL, H. E., JR. *Financial Analysis of Current Operations of Colleges and Universities.* Ann Arbor, Mich.: Institute of Public Administration, University of Michigan, 1966, 443 p.

TAYLOR, P. J. and GRANVILLE, K. T. *Financial Management of Higher Education.* New York: Coopers & Lybrand, 1973, 122 p.

TAYLOR, P. J. and NELSON, B. O. *Management Accounting for Hospitals.* Philadelphia: W. B. Saunders Co., 1964, 449 p.

UNITED CEREBRAL PALSY ASSOCIATIONS, INC. *Accounting Manual—For a United Cerebral Palsy State Association.* New York: Author, 1958, 109 p.

UNITED COMMUNITY FUNDS AND COUNCILS OF AMERICA. *Accounting for Community Chests and United Funds—Principles and Methods.* Rev. 1956. New York: Author, 1956, 33 p.

UNITED WAY OF AMERICA. *UWASIS—United Way of America Services Identification System.* Alexandria, Va.: Author, 1972, 104 p.

UNITED WAY OF AMERICA. *Accounting and Financial Reporting—A Guide For United Ways and Not-For-Profit Human Service Organizations.* Alexandria, Va.: Author, 1974, 200 p. (est.)

VAN FENSTERNAKER, J. *Cash Management—Managing the Cash Flows, Bank Balances, and Short-Term Investments on Non-Profit Institutions.* Kent, Ohio: Kent State University Press, 1966, 59 p.

YOUNG MEN'S CHRISTIAN ASSOCIATION. *Association Accounting—A Guide to Financial Recording and Reporting in the YMCA.* New York: Author, 1954, 80 p.

WALKER, A. L. *Church Accounting Methods.* Englewood Cliffs, N. J.: Prentice-Hall, Inc., 1964, 171 p.

WALZ, E. *Church Business Methods: A Handbook for Pastors and Leaders of the Congregation.* St. Louis: Concordia Publishing House, 1970.

Index

557

Oklahoma, state reporting requirements, 455
Operating fund, 31
Opinion of auditor, 356–359
adverse, 360
cash basis reporting, 27–28
disclaimer, 360
unqualified, 356
Oregon, state reporting requirements, 456
Orphanage, Income Statement, 24

Part-time bookkeepers, 333
Patient revenues, hospital, 264
Payroll
preparation, service bureau, 335–337
records, 464, 492
taxes, bookkeeping for, 490–493
Pennsylvania, state reporting requirements, 456
Perpetual life, lack thereof, for nonprofit organizations, 316
Piecemeal opinion by CPA, 359
Plant fund, 34; see also Fixed assets
Plant replacement and expansion funds, 249, 261–262
Pledges, 17, 115–118
AICPA Audit Guide, 185
allowance for uncollectible portion, 116
bequests, 118
building fund, 118
colleges, 233
current year support, 117
future year's support, 116
health and welfare, 185
hospital, 259
presentation in financial statements, 117
receivable, illustrated in Balance Sheet, 21, 39, 61, 141, 146
recognition as income, 116–118
table of alternatives, 546
Pooling of investments; see Investments
Posting, defined, 472
Private elementary and secondary schools; see Independent schools
Private foundations, 389–397
adjusted net income, defined, 392
annual reports, 396, 436–441; see also Federal reporting requirements, State reporting requirements
capital losses, 390–392
defined, 385
disclosure of donor's basis on gifts on Form 990-PF, 431
distinction between principal and income, 277
distributable amount, defined, 392

distribution of income requirements, 392–394
calculation of distributable amount, illustrated, 393–394
minimum investment return for purposes of calculation, 392
excess business holdings, 395
excise tax on investment income, 390–391
financial statements, illustrated, 20–21
Form 990, 408–421
Form 990-AR, 436–441
Form 990-PF, 422–436
foundation manager, defined, 437
grants, recording of, 276
Guide most applicable, 275
investments that jeopardize exempt functions, 396
investments at market, 277
investments received as gifts, 391
minimum investment return, 392
net investment income, 390
newspaper notice of availability of annual report, 396
operating foundation, 396–397
prohibited expenditures, 396
prohibited transactions, 395–396
qualifying distributions, 392–394
requirement to publish newspaper notice of availability of annual report, 436
self-dealing, 395
special accounting problems, 276–278
tax basis of investments received as gifts, 391
taxable expenditures, 395–396
Private "operating" foundations, 396–397
Private schools; see Independent schools
Professional societies; see Associations and professional societies
Prohibited expenditures, private foundations, 396
Property, plant, and equipment; see Fixed assets, Plant fund
Provision for replacement, 249, 262
Provision for unrealized losses, 91–92, 146
Public accountants, 364
Publicly supported organizations, defined, 385–388

Qualified opinion by CPA, 359–360
Qualified distributions, 392–394
carryover, 394
defined, 392
distributable amount, defined, 392
illustrated, 393–394